THE EROTIC OCEAN

THE EROTIC OCEAN

A Handbook for Beachcombers

Jack Rudloe

Illustrations by Ingrid Niccoll

WORLD PUBLISHING

TIMES MIRROR

NEW YORK

Published by The World Publishing Company
Published simultaneously in Canada
by Nelson, Foster & Scott Ltd.
Second printing—1972
Copyright © 1971 by Jack Rudloe
All rights reserved
ISBN 0-529-01038-0
Library of Congress catalog card number: 12-145830
Printed in the United States of America
Designed by Jacques Chazaud

WORLD PUBLISHING
TIMES MIRROR

To my mother, with appreciation,
and to all the other people who helped
compile the information for this book

Contents

Foreword

The ocean has been good to me. With my nets, biological dredges, and diving gear I have made a delightful living by selling her wonderful renewable resources — the living creatures that dwell in her waters and live on her bottom. I have hauled out nets gorged with struggling fish, swum through coral reefs so breathtaking with their varieties of colors, strange-looking fish, and eerie monsters that the scenes have been etched forever in my memory. I have weathered storms at sea, lived with thundering waves pounding the beaches and howling winds during a hurricane, and taken advantage of her treasures cast upon the beach when the sea calms.

More than a decade has passed since I started Gulf Specimen Company, a small collecting enterprise. I settled in Panacea — a tiny fishing village in northwest Florida, so small that it seldom appears on maps — and began working with shrimpers, crab fishermen and gill netters. As time passed, the demand for specimens from schools, research laboratories, and hobbyists increased, and with the demand I had to learn more about the behavior and ecology of the marine animals and plants of the Gulf of Mexico and the Atlantic coast. There was, and still is, much to learn.

A collecting business is subject to tides, winds and weather. It follows the movements of jellyfish, the migrations of squid, the ripeness of sea-urchin eggs and the spawning patterns of polychaete worms. Large conchs spew out ribbons of accordionlike egg capsules, and purple sea hares ooze copious green strings containing millions of jelly-coated eggs. Female blue crabs carry thousands of developing larvae under their aprons in the form of a sponge, and commercial shrimp migrate to the deep waters of the Atlantic and the Gulf and explosively burst forth sperm and egg that unite—and the tiny planktonic larvae drift shoreward with the tides and currents, along with uncountable numbers of fish eggs, larval fish and a host of other developing creatures. The ocean is so full of life, so productive that one can only marvel at it.

In a tide pool of this erotic ocean, needly female sea urchins spew out bright red eggs into the water and the males exude white sperm from the little pores between their spines. The waters turn cloudy with gametes, and hundreds of sperm mass around a single egg, causing it to spin and gyrate. Then one penetrates and a clear fertilization membrane almost magically appears. The fertilized egg goes on spinning and then starts dividing, first into two cells, then four and now into eight and soon it hatches into a tiny ciliated larva that joints the plankton in the sea. The miracle of life, the conception of all living things, can be so easily studied from life in the sea.

At midnight in the calm bays and estuaries of north Florida, you sometimes hear male porpoises letting out exuberant whimpering calls to their mates, and under the moonlight you hear them splashing about. Then the lumbering sea turtle comes ashore, dragging her heavy shell over the white sands and depositing her eggs high up on the beach.

Throughout the marshes and mangrove swamps shorebirds lay their eggs and the young hatch and feed upon the tiny fish and fiddler crabs. The waters become milky with veliger larvae of oysters during the spawning seasons, and soon the wharf pilings and dead shells are growing anew with tiny young oysters. The waters teem with gametes of sponges, tunicates, hydroids and tiny crustacea, which unite and settle on the bottom.

The conditions must be just right for them to take hold and grow to maturity. Only a particular weed-grown rock jelly may be suitable for a terebellid worm to colonize, or only a coarse sand bottom in high saline waters is right for lancelet larvae to settle in. Grass shrimp seek the protective grasses of tidal marshes, and spiny boxfish and long-legged arrow crabs live among the sea grasses.

The ocean does not give up easily the secrets of where to find these animals. Only by traveling around and diligently searching in her rock piles and mudflats, day after day and year after year, will you learn when creatures spawn and what they eat and where they hide.

THE
EROTIC
OCEAN

1.
Rocky Shore Habitat

When the tide goes out, leaving pools among the green-algae-clustered rocks, and more rocks emerge from the sea, you stand upon the highest boulder surveying the great rocky habitat stretched out before you. The submerged becomes exposed, the tide-pool basins, hidden crevices, mussel beds, and *Laminaria* kelp are all laid bare. There are hundreds of rocks of all sizes, tide pools, rockweed washing about, the white foamy waves hissing at the base of the rocks. There is the smell of barnacles and sea urchins and live things, of pungent salt air and open sea. Gulls scream and flutter, diving down with a splash, catching the minnows that swim close to the surface. Hermit crabs drag snail shells over the rocks and into the crevices with a scraping sound. So much life everywhere is hard to conceive. The creatures of the rocks bubble and fizzle, emitting whispering sounds. Schools of small fish dart and splash for cover in the tide pool. A pistol shrimp makes a loud "pop" with its enlarged pincer, letting you know that it is hiding somewhere among the seaweed.

At first sight many of the North Atlantic rocky shore inhabitants will be conspicuous and distinguish themselves the moment you climb down to the bottom of the rocks and look into their world. Who could miss the big orange starfish, the slabs of pink sea pork or the multitudes of needly purple sea urchins and the carpets of anemones that occur in some places? It is the small creatures — amphipods, the ribbonworms, polychaete worms, periwinkle snails, nematodes, and chitons—that one must look carefully for and hunt among the rockweed and crannies. These little treasures are exposed for only a few short hours, and you must hunt and search for them before the tide returns and covers them up. After watching the creatures in their natural habitat, that hidden dark world of the tide pool, the collector knows that he can never duplicate this world in his notes, preserved collection, aquarium, or even with his camera. Perhaps not even words can illustrate it. Only the memory of how wonderful the tide pool was can remain with him.

You begin collecting at the foot of the rocks where the sea laps impatiently, waiting to pour back in. This is the last area to be uncovered and the first to be submerged with the tide, and only two or three hours are permitted to examine it. Here creatures live on rocks among the slippery algae, in rock crevices, under rocks and boring into the rocks. There is so much, so close together that it is easy to overlook some of the more odd and interesting creatures that are specially adapted to clinging to their stony perches, burrowing down into crevices and competing for space in an environment where competition reaches its highest possible peak. Virtually every inch of surface space is occupied by a plant or animal of some description.

These creatures are used to a high-stress environment and can withstand the shock of crashing waves, tons of water beating relentlessly down upon them. On some wave-swept outer beaches often as much as two tons of water per square inch thunders down, but they hold on and survive. Some seem to burrow down into stone, others are glued on with a calcareous shell, and still others cling with tubed feet.

But these outer areas of extremely high stress are apt to be relatively scanty of life, compared to the rocky shores in protected bays and sounds where the water is much less turbulent. As in most other ecological habitats, the vegetation is a key indicator to the type of habitat. Along the North Atlantic, short stubby growths of rockweed (*Fucus*) mean the rocks are frequently subject to heavy surf, but the long, slender, knotted wrack weed (*Laminaria*) that grows in a tangled mass at the base of the rocks, indicates that the bay remains moderately calm most of the time. And in still another rocky shore where the waves soar in and batter the rocks continuously, you'll find almost no vegetation except for thin, encrusting filamentous algae and perhaps a number of flattened, white barnacles.

It seems there is a general rule in all phases of ecology: the more vegetation found in any habitat, including sea grass, mangrove swamps, mudflats, and rocky shore, the more animals will be found. The rule is simple: just as animals in the terrestrial environment depend upon the jungles and forests for food and shelter, marine animals depend upon the sea grasses and algae for cover and forage. On the rocky shore the blanket of algae protects organisms from the intense heat of the summer sun, or the drying winds of winter and perhaps even the rains that occasionally occur on low tides. If the algae dies off the animals soon die also, or they leave for better territory, and the rocks become barren and desolate. Siltation from dredging, industrial pollution, sewage or herbicides pouring into the ocean can denude a rocky shore of algae. So can a population explosion of hungry sea urchins ravenously chewing away at all vegetation.

Plants are prime indicators of tidal zonation. The uppermost horizon of the rocks that is practically lifeless is darkened with dark green lichens that encrust the rock surface. This is referred to as the "black zone" and is found on rocks all over the world. Not much lives in this area; a few snails periodically crawl up on the highest part of the rocks and lap up the algae. There are some isopods, called "sea roaches," constantly scurrying about.

Below this black zone are creatures that dwell in the uppermost tidal horizon. It is a sparse, hardy fauna that can withstand long periods of exposure, intense heat, sunlight and periods of cold. I have seen barnacles growing on rocks in the Indian Ocean so hot that I was unable to walk on them barefooted, yet the barnacles could withstand it for hours until the tide returned. On the surface of these rocks among the barnacles or even high above them one is apt to find littorinid snails, isopods, and some sea-invading insects.

The mid-tide zone along the New England shores is populated by barnacles, mussels, and the leathery, dull-green seaweed *Fucus*. Limpets hide among the green forest of seaweed, along with tiny shrimplike amphipods and curly white nematode worms. This area is covered by all high tides and generally uncovered during most low tides, and the creatures there can withstand a reasonable amount of exposure.

Many forms such as sponges, bryozoans, and even tunicates that are dominant in the low-tide zone may be represented as thin, encrusting layers of tissues matted over the rocks in the mid-tide zones. Serpulid worms are common, so are oysters, and these may have a

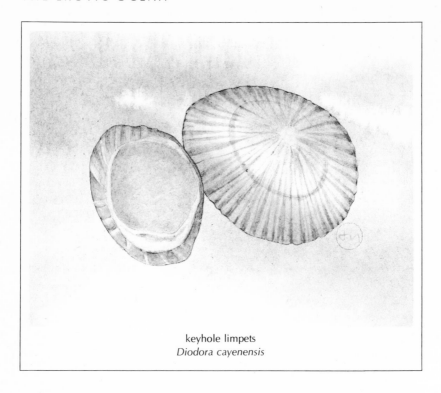

keyhole limpets
Diodora cayenensis

number of smaller nereid and terebellid worms living in their crevices and entrapped mud.

The low-tide zone is exposed only when there is a full moon. And it is these tides that the collector anxiously waits and plans for. Even though he consults tide tables and charts, he can feel the tidal rhythms in his blood, and when the sun and moon align to exert their strongest gravitational pull upon the oceans. He must arrive at the rocky shore at the right time in the morning to meet the low tides. This may involve driving all night to get to a particular jetty in time to see the rocks and all the vegetation, the grazers, and the predators exposed. They are exposed for only a few short hours, so the place to start looking and collecting is in the tidepools at the base of the rocks, one of the first places to be covered with water when the tide returns.

Tide pools and basins harbor a rich variety of sea life, numerous unattached, free-moving and fast-swimming creatures that take considerable effort to capture. Minnows dart for cover at the approach of your shadow, glassy-clear shrimp disappear into the seaweed and crabs scuttle into crevices. If you sit quietly for a few moments and just watch, you will see many animals come out of hiding. Perhaps you will see the antennae of a lobster protruding from a small cave in a boulder where you couldn't possibly reach it. Along Southern or Pacific coasts an octopus peers out of its crevice and darts across the pool to attack a crab. A mantis shrimp scurries wildly over the bottom of the pool and comes to rest under a boulder. Long slender black eels with gaping mouths shyly protrude from their lair between boulders.

Each pool is different, each has something else to offer: a purple sea hare in this one grazing on algae, a sea spider in another. Lying flat on your stomach to look into one pool you may encounter needly sea urchins with bristling, roving spines; perhaps the next pool will have a mat of red sea anemones, jade-green pistol shrimp, or perhaps you'll find one that has a big, creeping nudibranch. There may be blennies, tiny fish, or perhaps a flatworm on a bright pink cluster of tubularian hydroids.

After you have gone to one tide pool, you'll go on to the next. Tide pools are so numerous over a good rocky shore that you won't be able to explore even a mere fraction of them in those few short hours of exposure.

Although you may find starfish clinging to the sides of the rocks, you may often find twice as many starfish lining the bottom of tide pools. On the New England coast, if you look at a starfish closely, you'll find small, dancing skeleton shrimp bending up and down hanging onto its arms. In the pools the pink-and-white plumrose anemones, covered by crystal-clear water, will be flowering out in all their splendor; those that are not in tide pools but are attached to an exposed rock surface will appear as contracted blobs of jellylike protoplasm amid the seaweed. The sea slug, covered by clear water, will expand its graceful parts and move over the bottom like a ballerina, undulating her skirts.

A collector who approaches this quiet little world of the tide pool soon classifies the creatures into three separate categories. There are sessile animals such as barnacles, hydroids, and bryozoans that remain firmly fixed to the rock by chitinous or calcareous secretions. These cannot go away, they can only die off, and they will be in the same place from one tide to the next, although they can be obscured by overgrown rockweed. Loosely attached creatures such as starfish, chitons, snails and anemones slowly creep and crawl over the rock surfaces, slide in and out of the crannies and crevices of tide pools.

Unlike the sessile creatures, which you will find consistently from one tide to the next, the creepers and crawlers may have disappeared by the next time you view the rocks. They may not move three inches in a week, or they may move an inch per day. But those few inches per day over several weeks can inch them out of sight down into the rocks or even inch them to an entirely different location in the course of a year. However, if the food supply is adequate, and the water is unpolluted, free of eutrophication, the loosely attached or more sedentary forms will stay in the same general area.

The last group is free-moving, and these require a fast, gloved hand or a dip net to capture. They might be crabs and shrimp, octopus, eels and fish. They may be small flatworms that are very adept at sliding over rocks with surprising rapidity, or they may be brittlestars that snake along the bottom of a tide pool and whip out of reach when your hand approaches. Most of these rapid free-movers take advantage of deep crannies and crevices, and generally have the advantage because no one wants to reach his hand down into a cave and bring out whatever may be there, no matter how brave a collector he is. The toadfish may lurk there, the scorpionfish, or the big, waiting pincers of a crab or a lobster.

Even large creatures can be difficult to spot in a tide pool, because almost all animals there have the protection of camouflage; and perhaps on the rocky shore more than anyplace else this protection is employed. The subtle browns and grays of the rocks themselves can hide the browns and blacks of the snails and the grapsoid crabs, and the mossy reds and greens of encrusting algae blend with the reds and greens of nereid worms sliding over the surface, or hide the small snapping shrimp and other crustacea. Only the glistening shine of the fleshy blob of a sea anemone glinting in the sun lets you know that it is not part of the seaweed or rocky surface, but an animal. And only a keen eye and knowledge will help you distinguish the lacy bryozoans and the branching stems of the hydroids as not part of the seaweed.

Thaïs and Murex snails with their jagged spines can look like a piece of jagged limestone rock, and chitons pressed into a rocky crevice near some seaweed might be overlooked by even a professional collector. Eolid nudibranchs, with their frills and little fronds, are often so well matched to the rock that they are found only by accident; while you are picking up a starfish, a nudibranch may come up in your hand.

There is a good reason for all this camouflage. When the tide covers the rocks, fish predators are always on the lookout for a morsel to grab up, and when the tide exposes the marine life, gulls and terns search the rocks for sea urchins, snails, clams and fish.

Observation and the ability to recognize small, nondescript forms is your best asset on a rocky shore, so it pays to move very slowly, make your eyes seek out each little crevice, discover each little life-form.

Suddenly you may be in for a shock when something gets up and scuttles with the rapidity of a scared cockroach.

In the tropics from Miami southward, grapsid crabs live on the rocks and they have the true element of camouflage. So well concealed are they that you never suspect they are there until suddenly what seems like a piece of the boulder scuttles away. When you spot one moving about, you can sneak up on it. No sooner do you bring your hand down on it, however, than it magically disappears. Determined to capture it, you pursue it from rock to rock, crawling over boulders, jumping across ledges chasing the crab out from crevices — and almost always it eludes you.

I confess here for all to read that I am no good at catching grapsid crabs. I have been on several expeditions, to Central America and to the Indian Ocean, and I have managed to get only three specimens, while other members of our expeditions came back with dozens of specimens. In fact, there was one grapsid crab that lived at the end of the marine laboratory pier in Madagascar, and I devoted a large percentage of my nonworking time determined to sneak up on it, but I never succeeded; it was ego-shattering.

The life on the rocky shore is everchanging. From one month to the next a whole new colony of encrusting sponges may take over. Or there may be brittlestars with just the tips of their arms sticking out from the crevices. This excursion may produce nudibranchs where there were none the last time, or perhaps there is a population explosion of ghost shrimp, or the rocks can become seasonally bleak and barren of life.

Of course the only way to note these changes is to become a frequent visitor to the same rock pile or jetty. Soon the regular inhabitants become old friends, and you develop the ability to recognize even the most inconspicuous and difficult-to-see animals. A trained eye takes time to develop.

As you climb over the next ledge, then hang onto a boulder and let yourself down beside a tide pool along a North Atlantic coast, you may notice clusters of short, red, stubby hydroids (*Clava*) springing up from the seaweed and clinging to the rocks. Collecting them is easy because they grow on the seaweed, and the seaweed is plucked off the rock and isolated in a plastic bag with sea water. The problem with these hydroids is to be able to recognize them because they are almost indistinguishable from seaweed.

Only when you use a hand lens can you see their hungry little tentacles on the large round polyps constantly searching the sea for food. As with much other collecting, having found the animal in the first place, you learn to recognize it. In no time when you come upon another section of rocks you will immediately spot a patch of *Clava* on clumps of *Fucus* weed, growing off that group of blue mussels, and be able to go right up to it.

Once a year I manage to get to Woods Hole, Massachusetts, and roam the shores around Cape Cod. I have learned many secrets of the rocky shores there, and each year I learn more on my brief visits. There is a stalked jellyfish (*Halaclystus*) which lives on seaweed in Buzzards Bay, and I have learned about several areas where you can go and part the seaweed, and see the little four-lobed, stalked, red-and-green blobs washing about with the surf.

I found that rocks grown over with blue mussels in New England and the coast of New York are very productive; you have only to rip the mats of these filter-feeding bivalves off the rock's surface, almost like rolling up a rug once the initial break has been made, and you will find numbers of fat polynoid scaleworms, dozens of greenish, slow-moving isopods, perhaps small gelatinous sea anemones, numbers of tiny crabs and shrimp, and a fine network of branching white *Obelia* hydroids.

Mussels (*Mytilus edulis*) do not occur much south of Maryland, and the farther you travel down the coast through the Virginias and into the Carolinas the smaller the mussels become. In southern waters other animals such as oysters become more dominant on the rocks, or barnacles and hydroids may become more common. *Fucus* may be replaced by the algae *Ulva*, sea lettuce.

However, while the animal and plant communities vary from place to place, the techniques of gathering them will remain constant. How do you remove barnacles from rocks, or how do you break a chiton from its holdfast, or free a sea anemone without tearing it in half? If there is a shrimp hidden deep in a crevice, how do you get it out?

These require the little techniques that you learn over a period of time. There are as many of these techniques as there are collectors, and each person has his own innovation, but I shall outline some of the general rules that most ecologists, professional collectors and naturalists use.

If one general rule can be made it would be always to work against the substrate, not pull the animal from the substrate because you will invariably tear it or break it to pieces. Crabs in the crannies will sooner part with a claw, leaving it to you as the only prize. Barnacles will come off the rock if you pry them up directly, leaving their gonads attached to the surface; and their gonads are one of the essential characteristics necessary in their determination. The empty shell will not always be enough. Sea anemones will pop and ooze their mesentery when you pry them up forcibly. The same is true for echiuroids, sipunculid worms, and polychaete annelids.

There are some creatures that may be plucked off without any ill effects. In general most gastropod mollusks are jerked from their rocky perches, and all they do is draw their meaty foot into their shell and seal the entrance with their rough horny operculum. These will of course expand at a later time. Starfish, certain sea cucumbers and nearly all sea urchins adhere to the rocks with their tubed, ambulatory feet, which are like minute toilet plungers, and will sooner part with their feet than let go of their hold, so these must be torn free or you will be faced with an all-day task of breaking dozens of tubed feet loose.

Chitons, limpets and abalones all possess this amazing clinging power, and for a good reason: should they relax, one smashing wave, with the force of tons of water, would dislodge them and send them washing out to sea. Once disturbed they tend to cling even harder, and if you pull with all your might you cannot dislodge them.

But there are some good methods of removing clinging mollusks from rocks. A sharp blow to the side of them, an attack they are not accustomed to, will cause them to loosen their grasp. Once the suction is broken for an instant, their ability to cling is no longer there. If you use a putty knife and pry up under one end, the suction is broken and the animal can be lifted off with ease.

I have found sea anemones, sea cucumbers, and many other contractile invertebrates lying in a flaccid, uncontracted state on the rocks at low tide. If they are even slightly touched, they withdraw and cling to their perches and only by breaking the substrate away from these animals can they be removed. But if you use the element of surprise, sneak up on them and in a sudden snatch, jerk them from the rock, they are removed before they can respond and cling all the harder. Perhaps when the first waves start moving in and washing in and out, they contract and hold fast. It is a muscular strain for the animal to remain in a constant state of contraction and a more normal condition for it to be relaxed. But the creature that dwells in the crevice, out of touch and out of reach, is another problem. To get it out means breaking the substrate away from it.

Working against the substrate to free specimens sometimes requires a feat of engineering, particularly if the rock is hard granite. Sandstone, so prevalent in the Pacific, or compact mud and clay, can be easily broken away from under the base or around the burrow of a specimen no matter how hard it contracts. A geology hammer or botany pick is a useful tool for giving sharp, hard blows next to the holdfast until the substrate is broken and the animal comes free.

If the substrate is pliable limestone, a flat-bladed knife can be used to undermine the base of an animal. Sometimes your fingernails are enough to pry it loose. But what do you do when your specimen lives on firm, hard granite rocks? No matter how you chip and beat on the rocks, all you will produce is sparks. On shale and certain other rocky formations that shatter easily, there is considerable danger of splinters of rock flying off and getting lodged in the eye. In general, when working against so tough a perch, one would do well to seek the same specimen on a more pliable substrate. But if there is no other choice, a hammer and a cold chisel can be used.

You will develop a sixth sense in rocky-shore collecting in knowing where to look, hunting out the hiding places of the animals. Three or more boulders wedged together leaving a small opening where you can barely squeeze in may open a new realm of animals that you never knew were there. And when you crawl into that dark cave, lighted only by filtered sunlight coming down from the other rocks, you may see chunks of encrusting pink sea pork (*Amaroucium*) on the ledges, pieces of breadcrumb-sponge on the rocks. It's cool inside the cave and water drips from the roof slowly and timelessly. Massive flat sea anemones that shun the light contract and draw into fleshy blobs with the receding tide. Delicate clusters of white *Obelia* hydroids flower out from the tide pool, marble-shaped snails draw in their meaty foot when you pluck them from their perches. And down deep in the water, where it's dark and almost no light glows, a branching piece of white star coral grows upward, looking like a small torch in the dimness.

The more you can work yourself into impossible places, sometimes lying flat on your stomach, and squeezing your head into spaces, parting seaweed, the better your chances of finding the unusual, or better yet, a particularly rich area for a specific organism. You may spend the better part of a morning hunting chitons—all you get is a half-dozen for the effort of searching, turning over rocks, brushing aside algae, looking and looking and looking, almost giving up hope altogether—and then when it all looks hopeless, another chiton is found, and you go on with the hope that where there's one there's more. But in that cave, that one little inlet among all those rocks on a New Hampshire coast, above a slippery platform you find them, dozens, perhaps hundreds, chitons beyond your dreams. All of them are typically small in the North Atlantic waters, about a half inch.

At first they are so well camouflaged and inconspicuous that even the trained eye has a difficult time in finding them, particularly in that semidarkness. With your knife you pry them from the walls of the cave, from the surface of the boulders; but you leave some, and tuck this precious hiding place away in the back of your mind, so that you will be able to return to it immediately when more chitons are needed.

But if you make a trip to the Florida Keys, you will be astounded at the huge numbers of monstrous tropical chitons—three inches and larger—that line the rocks everywhere. They are as common as barnacles in the upper mid-tide horizon and can be collected on any low tide. The chitons crawl into the crevices of the limestone boulders and coralline rocks that are so common on the beaches and along the causeways. Rather than pry them off, I found that by breaking the soft rocky substratum beneath them, I could acquire a goodly number of chitons in a short time.

There are many colorful large creatures that dwell on the limestone outcrops of the tropics, many are free-moving and difficult to chase down. I have found that the plastic bag is not only good for storage and transport of sea creatures, it is an excellent collecting tool as well. Nemerteans, the ribbon worms which are apt to break into numerous fragments or violently vomit their proboscis when they are irritated, can be peacefully transferred into a plastic bag.

Scurrying amphipods, isopods, pistol shrimp and small crabs that abound under rocks are good at dodging your fingers but will run helter-skelter into an open transparent bag. And if you gently splash, or even vigorously splash, water into crevices, large nereid and terebellid worms can be washed out into your waiting bag. In general, the less you handle invertebrates the better they will survive when brought back to the laboratory for either preservation or culturing. Many autotomize—throw off limbs or break to pieces as a defense mechanism when your fingers clasp over them unless you devote infinite time and patience to collecting them. Forceps or a fine camel's-hair brush is a good tool for collecting many of the small forms that hide among seaweed or dwell in a deep crevice.

How much time you intend to spend trying to get a single ribbon worm out of a crevice with a brush or other implement without damaging it depends entirely upon your goals. To someone visiting the rocks for the first few times, there is a big rocky habitat yet to be explored and time is rapidly ticking away. In just a brief time the tide will seep in over the seaweed, the rocks will no longer be accessible, and the world of little sea creatures will be closed to the intertidal collector.

But if the weather is calm, the waters clear, a new world can be opened up by skin- or scuba-diving. The foot of a cliff or the edge of a jetty can be explored by swimming around and viewing the myriad life with mask and fins, and in this manner one sees the whole ecological pattern, not only the invertebrates on the rocks but the schools of fish that come into the rocks to feed or hide, and leave the rocks when the tide goes out. This is especially rewarding in tropical waters where teeming schools of colorful fish move in and out of rocks and coral outcrops.

To speed up time in collecting along the sheltered rocky shore, sometimes you can take a skiff out to the foot of the rocks at low tide and begin collecting. This eliminates the problems of hauling buckets and containers; you use the boat as a base of operations where you can fetch a crowbar if needed, or return a geology hammer when you are finished with it.

Always collect sparingly, whether you are gathering animals for an aquarium or a preserved reference collection; take only what you need and disturb the habitat as little as possible. The ecology of a rocky shore can be severely damaged by careless collectors; especially vulnerable are the fauna and flora that live under the rocks, away from wave shock, shifting sands, heat and bright sunlight. These are the richest areas on the rocky shore and the most abused. I have seen biology classes turn boulders over, joyfully pick up the errant polychaete flatworms, tubed worms, nemerteans, tunicates, sponges, mud shrimp and sausage worms that live in the mud beneath the rocks, and without further thought leave the rocks turned over and exposed to fatal drying heat, sunlight and the returning surf. Within a few days the rocks become barren of life, the tunicates, sponges and solitary corals die off and so do the algae. It may take weeks, months or even years for such a spot to recover fully.

You learn much in turning over rocks. Rocks that are stuck deep in the mud are generally devoid of life because most organisms require some circulation of oxygenated sea water to respire, as well as to receive nutrients. Large rocks and boulders that are lying on sand, but not embedded in substrate, are easier to turn over and tend to have a rich fauna. The communities beneath are not likely to be damaged when the rocks are returned to their normal position.

Very often boulder- and rock-strewn flats give further problems in collecting because one rock sits upon another. This makes it very difficult to collect conscientiously and maintain the habitat, because when you turn the rocks back over many of the terebellid and cirratulid tubed worms, sponges and other creatures will be crushed. Generally, encrusting algae, bryozoans, tunicates and sponges connect one rock to the next, and this bond will be broken and the animals disturbed when the rocks are lifted.

Perhaps the most important prerequisite for collecting on a rocky shore and turning over boulders is to get a low enough tide on a calm day where the sweeping surf will not disturb you or the animals on an overturned rock. I know of few experiences more frustrating than to pry up a boulder with a crowbar, or turn it by hand, and, just as you are removing a beautiful green-and-white ribbon worm, the prize of the day, have a wave come crashing in and wash the specimen and all other loosely attached creatures out into the sea.

2.
Sandy Shore Habitat

A very handsome sample of life in the sea is often washed to shore and cast up on the beaches for everyone to look at. Consequently the sport and science of beachcombing has become popular among many different types of people. Many comb the beaches in search of beach-worn seashells, which can be used for handsome decorations or have value as specimens for reference collections. Driftwood comes ashore, and on rare occasions so do various shipwrecked artifacts.

The only way to find treasures on the beach is to look, and that means meandering along the sandy shores during mid-tides, just looking. To the biological collector a wealth of specimens may be brought to shore, and when the tide is unfavorable for collecting in the intertidal zone, all one has to do is walk the beaches.

Some beaches are better than others. A sandy beach with a low gradient, gradually sloping into the ocean, lends itself to better collecting because more creatures end up on shore. A high-energy beach that drops off into deep water within a few yards from the shoreline is less likely to have a large array of specimens. Only during the most violent storms would life be washed ashore.

Beaches with powerful waves constantly dashing against the coarse sands are not as likely to have any concentration of marine life cast up. It's the shallow flat areas on high tide, coupled with rough seas from offshore winds, that bring most of the fauna to the beach.

Even if one isn't interested in gathering live marine organisms, the multitudes of shells, seaweed and other entities that have drifted about the sea or have come up from the bottom arouse your curiosity. There is a challenge in beachcombing, walking along the sands, for you never know what you will happen upon next. A piece of driftwood, perhaps a plank from some wooden craft that has drifted hundreds of miles and is grown over with goose-necked barnacles. Perhaps the paper-thin angel-wing shells are available this afternoon, or sea whips or even a few vase sponges.

You walk and look. On the beach you can be alone with the world, the peace and beauty of the landscape, or if you are with a group, you can walk ahead, investigating this piece of colored sea pork or that large lumpish jellyfish.

The sandy shore is never twice the same, and a beach that is barren and disappointing one afternoon may have rich, rewarding finds the very next morning. A shift in the wind, a change in the tide, and the world of biological treasures may be at your feet. Large fleshy jellyfish follow the currents and with the crash of a wave are stranded on the sandy shore, or sometimes they just wash up and beach with the lapping waves, and the falling tide slips out from under them. Sometimes pelagic nudibranchs come onto the beach amid piles of floating seaweed. And if you turn over clumps of sargasso weed you may find a sea horse or the sargassum fish (*Histrio histrio*). This can happen anywhere along the Atlantic and Gulf coasts where gulfweed drifts in the Gulf Stream currents.

On the South Atlantic coast strong southeasterly winds blowing for several days often drive hordes of stinging Portuguese man-of-war jellyfish on shore and strand them on the beaches. After a hurricane or a severe winter storm when the tides that have been several feet above normal recede, the beaches will be cluttered with debris from the ocean. This is the ideal time to get into one's car and drive down to a long stretch of sandy beach armed with buckets and jars.

Offshore the churning waves, sweeping currents and pounding surf uproot many sessile invertebrates, the sponges, sea squirts, the worm tubes and the clams and send them spinning and tossing to the shoreline. If you arrive immediately after the storm you may be able to pick up a tremendous diversity of shallow-water specimens that may not be available unless you go skin-diving or dredging. Creatures encountered in small numbers on the tidal flats during the lowest tides may be seen cast up on the upper beach in tremendous quantities.

Almost every year the gray sea cucumber (*Thyone briareus*) piles up on Alligator Point, Florida, beaches and we harvest them after storms, removing bucket after bucket of them for preservation as laboratory specimens or to keep alive in our tanks. Only a small percentage of the specimens are in poor condition or dead; the majority make good specimens.

Beachcombing has proved to be a superior method of collecting various animals. The holothurian *Caudina arenata* that is cast up on the New England beaches after a hurricane in huge quantities provides an example of necessary beachcombing. They live in the subtidal regions, areas never exposed by the low, low tides, yet too shallow to be taken by dredging operations.

Frequently we find displaced cockles washed up on the West Florida beaches after a tropical storm, and have on several occasions filled our buckets with them. Giant heart cockles, *Dinocardium robustum* normally live in the low, low tide zone, sometimes making shallow burrows just under the sand. Its large, pinkish brown foot hanging from between its ribbed valves, looks like a lolling tongue.

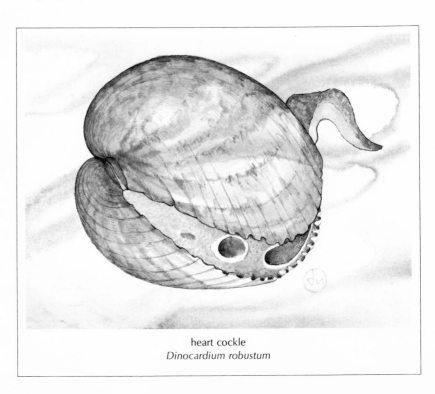

heart cockle
Dinocardium robustum

The cockle is an active animal, not like the usual run of bivalves. When cast up on the beaches it catches the eye instantly by its spasmodic, jerking movements, levering its foot into the sand and violently thrusting the shell back and forth. If the surf is too rough many of the animals will be severely damaged and torn when they are battered and dragged about in the abrasive sand. But in the more sheltered beaches they will generally arrive on shore in good shape, and if you get to the scene of this ocean disaster where all is torn loose and cast up to die, you may find and gather chunks of glistening compound ascidians, sea pork, bushy plant life and calcareous bryozoan colonies, uprooted gorgonians, living clams and perhaps a few unhappy octopuses.

Many of the large sponges such as *Halichondria* are riddled with commensals, hairy brittlestars, small pinkish sea anemones contracted and bloblike, hairy little crabs and hosts of snapping shrimp. Now and then you can find an extremely interesting sponge that may have commensal barnacles like the thorny *Acasta cyanthus* embedded in its tissues. All these creatures stand a good chance of being alive. We

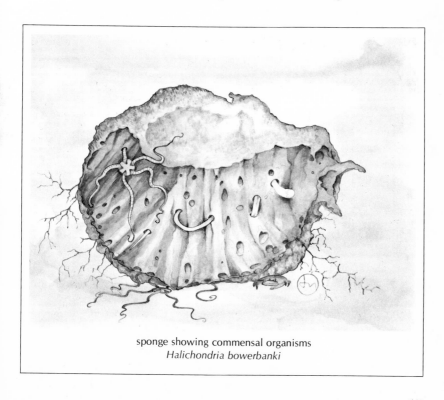

sponge showing commensal organisms
Halichondria bowerbanki

have taken many of them back and placed them in aquariums, and the survival rate has been better than 60 percent, especially on creatures that are isolated from their dying host sponge or tunicates.

But if you come to the seashore after the sun is high in the sky and the sea has receded, and the piles of seaweed are drying out and hordes of flies are buzzing around the animals, then you know that all is lost, and the smell of the dying permeates the air. Ghost crabs emerge from their holes and tear and devour at the rotting carcasses, millions of beach-hoppers come out of the seaweed and jump and bounce, foraging on the food cast up to them.

Just as the rocky shore has a tidal zonation where animals and plants colonize specific vertical areas of a rock's surface based on the rise and fall of the tides, the sandy shore also has its own form of intertidal zonation. This zonation along the sandy shore is much less pronounced and a lot harder to define, but it too has a spray-line fauna, high-tide, mid-tide, and low-tide colonizations. The farther out one walks on a sandy tide flat exposed by extremely low tides, the greater the number and variety of organisms.

The uppermost area of the beach can be a wealth of life, if one is interested in the small and obscure. In this area of dead seaweed that has been tossed about in the surf, washed ashore by an extreme high tide and left to dry out in the sun, along with bits of dried hydroids, bryozoans and fragmented worm tubes and seashells—the refuse of the sea—one finds the small crustaceans and insects that dwell in moist, damp sand and seaweed, but cannot take the continuous submersion of the ocean or they will drown. This tide zone, like the uppermost horizon of rocky shore habitat, is believed to be the merging point between land and sea creatures, and many of the semiaquatic amphipods, snails, isopods, etc., which can live for long periods of time out of water, are believed to be in the evolutionary process of changing from marine forms to terrestrial inhabitants.

Such terrestrial forms as crickets, beetles, mites, earwigs and spiders crawl about the piles of seaweed, twigs and assorted ocean debris and sea foam. The sea foam (which is precipitated protein and trace elements thrown off by the frothing surf), bits of dead fish and invertebrates provide food.

And when you turn over a clump of seaweed, millions upon millions of the beach-hoppers, *Orchestia* and *Talorchestia*, explode out like a fury of atoms in a nuclear reactor and bounce and hop wildly, pelting the collector's legs like so much pepper shot. These amphipods are essential habitat indicators. Certain species are characteristic of erosion beaches or deposition beaches, and a good ecological collection should have a representative of the spray-line fauna on a sandy beach.

Perhaps the best part about collecting the spray-line habitat is that it is accessible at any tide, high or low, and requires hardly any trouble or preparation to sample. You can be driving from Maine to Florida, come to a beach at any time, and kick over a few clumps of seaweed; then with bottle of formaldehyde in hand pick through the strands and catch the bouncing bugs.

Some of the professional zoologists that make a regular study of this area use a variety of ways to collect the small creatures in large quantities. A handful of seaweed and ocean debris is dropped into a five-gallon bucket of dilute Formalin and all the creatures frantically wriggle their way out and swim down to the bottom. The seaweed is skimmed off before it has a chance to soak up and settle to the bottom, and the specimens are isolated. However, there is still much time spent in the lab picking out the sticks, dried sea grass, blades and bits of straw and sand.

I have also seen some zoologists use plain insecticide, spraying the bugs with one of the popular insect bombs. This will immobilize and kill the creatures, but it is not a method that a thoughtful ecologist would recommend. DDT and other chlorinated hydrocarbons remain in the habitat for years and years and continue to build up in animals' fatty tissues long after they have been used and the desired specimens removed.

The isopod, *Ligia exotica,* spiders and large beach-hoppers are difficult to collect by immersion in Formalin sea-water solution, because they have generally escaped by the time you have scooped up your seaweed. I developed a technique in the Indian Ocean, and that was to use a squirt bottle filled with 99 percent alcohol, and squirt it directly on the fleeing bug.

The mid-tide region that is uncovered by all low tides tends to have a sparse fauna. Generally this zone does not have definite conspicuous representatives which distinguish it as a specific tidal horizon. There may be small numbers of clams, worms and juvenile horseshoe crabs that occur in this zone of frequent exposure, but there will be more of them farther out on the low tidal horizon.

It is only when you catch the really low tides, and walk far out on the tidal flats that you find the largest number of species and the highest density of specimens. But these low-tide areas are only occasionally exposed on the low, low tides, and the collector must sample the animal communities according to the tides.

During mid-tides when there is only a slight drop, you will devote your efforts to the creatures of the upper tidal zone that exists in the rolling surf. The outer, exposed beaches are excellent for collecting some of these rapidly burrowing creatures that have managed to survive among the shifting sands and the waves.

On days when the tide is high in the southeastern United States, the collector can take a screen down to the outer beach and sift the sand which is shoveled up and dumped on a screen. The screen is shifted back and forth in the surf; a host of interesting creatures will be exposed when the sand is washed out. Often hundreds of coquinas (Donax variabilis) are collected. In fact, so many of these polished little burrowing clams may be found on the beach that you can get enough for an excellent broth in a very few minutes of vigorous screening.

Suddenly the surf explodes with mole crabs (Emerita talpoida) and in an instant they burrow out of sight. They too are stranded on the screen mesh, and when the little oval shapes of mole crabs make their appearance, you may be able to collect many. Once in a great while you'll find another type of mole crab, Albunea, which has two long antennae and a great many sharp hooks which it all too cheerfully embeds into your fingers. But this creature is quite rare. Quite a number of large gray amphipods and thin red polychaete worms live in this upper zone of shifting sand.

The trails and burrows made by the sandy-shore-fauna are the most immediate clues to collecting them. At a glance one can spot colonies of the plumed worm (Diopatra cuprea) because their casings decorated with shell and bits of seaweed erect from the sand. Spaghettilike spewings dotting the mid-tide region tell of acorn worms that live far down in the sand. Further down the beach you may see large lumbering horseshoe crabs sliding over the ribbed sand in an attempt to get back to the sea. Hermit crabs drag their shells, making a serrated winding trail. Whelks, starfish, conchs, sand dollars are sometimes present in the panorama of the tide flat.

Where there are depressions in the sand, tide pools are formed. Some flats that have high rises here and there may be scattered with puddles, and these sandy tide pools have a little world of life of their own. They are not as rich and constant as fauna of the rocky-shore tide pools, but still, many small fish, shrimp, crabs and other little creatures stranded by the tide seek refuge in these puddles until the sea comes back to liberate them.

To collect the sandy-tide-pool creatures, you simply walk around with a bucket gathering specimens as you find them: a hermit crab here, a whelk there, one or two sea pansies and perhaps a boring sponge that has been washed ashore. A crab has died and numerous little dog whelks (*Nassarius obsoletus*) protrude their sensitive proboscises sampling the carrion smells. Then they glide out of their sandy coverings and slide over the sand and mass over the crab and soon reduce it to an empty shell. Tiny hermit crabs (*Pagurus longicarpus* and *P. bonairensis*) that dwell in the nassarius snail shells may also be found scavenging in the puddles.

Sea slugs and sea hares are often stranded in the tide pools when they ride the high tide to shore. Some of these sandy depressions hold water so continually that they have a rich vegetation of filamentous algae and even sea grass growing along the bottom. These deeper pools abound with fish. *Fundulus* or killifish minnows are most common, but young croakers, trout, spiny boxfish, filefish and a host of larval fish use the deep pools to hide, or they remain stranded there. The pools also harbor a variety of juvenile blue crabs as well as other species and dozens or even hundreds of shrimp, such as *Palaemonetes* or *Crangon.*

Life in the tide pools is easily harvested by the use of a fine-meshed dip net or minnow seine. It is much easier to gather animals out of sandy pools because they have no place to hide as they can in rocky-shore tide pools where every crevice is good security from the sweeping net.

But the sandy tide pool may be a death trap in the summertime. When the tide is out and the sun beats relentlessly down upon the six-inch to two-foot pools, the temperature soars above 95°F and the dissolved-oxygen level drops. Fish begin swimming to the surface, rapidly increasing their opercular beat, desperately opening and closing their gill-coverings. And then they begin to die. Soon the entire sandy tide pool may be littered with dead fish and shrimp. We have observed such pools in Mississippi and have found that the young blue crabs are the last to expire, but if the water is shallow the bottom will be lined with dead little crabs as well as fish.

The tide pools have a tidal zonation of their own, much like the rocky shore. The further out they occur on the tide flat, the richer and more diverse the fauna is. The sandbars that rise up and border these depressions also have a very rich fauna.

It is in these sandbars that one finds the large, conspicuous burrowing organisms, and these are spotted by their burrows, trails and signs left in the sand. When one becomes familiar with these tell-tale marks, he can determine the species or type of animal by its clues. For example, a sand dollar makes a semicircular plowed-up furrow and a sea cucumber may be noticed by its two holes poking out of the sand. Moon snails plow a wide twisting furrow, while olive snails make a short sharp slit along the hard-packed sandy surface. And burrowing sea anemones produce small holes lined with bits of shell that cling to their bodies.

Walk slowly, studying the ground so you won't miss some of the burrows or spewed-out worm casings, or that little spurt of water that signifies a clam. Clam siphons notoriously leave keyholelike slits in the sand, particularly *Mercenaria campechiensis*, the quahog, *Macrocallista nimbosa*, the sunray venus, and to a lesser degree, *Spisula solidissima*, the surf clam. Other clams like *Lucina floridana* leave a small, rounded burrow that even a professional collector might mistake for a worm's burrow. Lugworms spew out sand from their burrows, giving a clue to their presence, but these castings are different from the casting of mud shrimps, *Upogebia* and *Callianassa*.

Mollusks are the most conspicuous of all burrowers on the tidal sandy flats. *Retusa pertunuis*, the small tectibranch with its fragile bubble shell, slides along just beneath the substrate secreting globs of mucus, but its presence is known to the collector only by a fine, almost hairline continuous jagged slit in the sandy mud of the protected estuary.

The trails, signs and clues will vary from place to place depending upon the substrate, the type of sand, and the geographical range of the species. A surf clam behaves entirely different when collected in Massachusetts as compared to Florida. The northern animal makes a wide, deep burrow while the southern subspecies is usually found in the sand, recognized only by a little mound covering the shell.

Aside from annelids, mollusks and some echinoderms making the dominant burrows on the sandy shore, a few other creatures alter the substrate. The striped sole (*Trinectes maculatus*), often stranded by the receding tide, burrows down leaving a small mound of sand over it. Worm eels (*Myrophis punctatus*) frequently make neat rounded holes that could be easily mistaken for invertebrates. Sting rays and flounder that are fond of sandy shores fan holes out into the bottom, when the tide is in, and these depressions can be seen as puddles on low tide.

If the tide is extremely low during spring tides, and the sand is thoroughly dry, the burrows and trails become conspicuous. But if the tide isn't very good because an onshore wind has pushed it back on shore, then the sands are sopping wet and burrow marks quickly collapse as the sand shifts. But even on the best tides you can't expect always to find the clues on the first glance; perhaps it will take a night trip with a gasoline lantern to bring a population of animals out on the flats, or you may just have to wait until the tide starts to seep in before the action starts and animals move out of their protective substratum.

There are many little signs in the sand that are deceptions nature plays on you; water seeping back into the sand in an air pocket will look very much like a sea-cucumber hole. You may be fooled into digging after it. A sandy beach beneath a rock or cliff can be riddled with burrows, but these, it turns out, are nothing more than drops of water falling into the sand below, making a deeper and deeper hole that you're sure something is in. If you run your small finger down the hole, you can quickly discover that it terminates nowhere, or sometimes by mere observation you know that the hole is shallow and there is no purpose in following it.

Many creatures are easy to miss on the flats even by an experienced fieldworker. Collecting along the sandy shore on low tide can sometimes be a disturbing experience. You have searched a sandbar, perhaps dug up a few cockles, a clam, some anemones and tubed worms and thought that was that. While exploring the flats you may have walked miles searching for elusive animals, and upon turning around and coming back to your car, you may be surprised by the appearance of animals emerging from burrows, or newly visible burrows that you never suspected were there to start with.

When the tide starts to return, even slightly, numerous species that were previously completely burrowed begin to rise to the surface as the water soaks down into the sand. They expand into a feeding, respiring and moving position as the water covers them, and when the tide falls they contract down into the mud and their burrows are covered by sand and are completely hidden. This is their natural escape from predators, prowling raccoons and the ever-vigilant gulls.

Eggs of even the common marine animals on the sandy shore may be a bit confusing until you know them. The first step is learning to recognize that they are eggs and not yet animals. Certain annelids lay jellylike globs that are attached to a stalk that goes several inches into the sand, and these appear to the unknowing as "stalked jellyfish." *Busycon* lays a rubbery succession of capsules, each containing eggs cushioned in fluid. They undergo development, then hatch from their protective housing and emerge as small snails. However, one will not actually believe these are whelk eggs until such time that he sees a *Busycon* laying the accordionlike capsules in the sand. Mysterious strings of eggs looking very much like spaghetti generally belong to the opistobranch, *Bursatella* or *Aplysia*, or the little frilled ribbon of eggs adhering to dead shell probably came from a nudibranch. Moon snails lay their eggs in a sand collar; Ed Rickets in *Between Pacific Tides* goes into considerable detail on how he tried to trace down and see what sort of animal this sand collar was.

The beaches wash ashore cuttlebones from squid that look like some sort of fossilized fish bones. And the sand itself sometimes takes on a purple color that one may think is dye or ink from a sea hare that was stranded and washed away, but this in fact is a purple bacterium that sets in between sand grains when the beach is healthy and unpolluted.

In collecting in any habitat, particularly the sandy shore, you learn to utilize all your senses, including those of smell and sound. The acorn worm, *Balanoglossus*, has an acrid, sharp odor that is very distinct. Starfish exuding sperm and eggs have a peculiar reproductive smell, a deep rich smell. Certain sponges and alcyonarians have a sharp, pungent odor and their presence can sometimes be detected long before you actually see them.

Once in a while your sense of hearing is called to play. That weird sound may be *Loimia viridis*, the tubed worm living in its sandy tube far below the surface. It is an eerie sound, almost like someone opening the creaking door of an old inner sanctum. The worm would have escaped my attention had I not heard it.

But the usual way to get these burrowing animals is to look for the holes, trails and clues and then dig. No collector feels at home on the sandy shore unless he is adequately armed with a shovel. There is no handier tool for excavating a deeply dug-in worm, an eel or a clam. Just as the crowbar is an essential tool on the rocky shores, the shovel is the tool of the sandy flat.

Although the shovel, used properly, is the most practical way of harvesting marine animals, there is one advantage to be said for hand-digging each specimen: there is less chance of a fatal chop. The experienced eye can generally spot a burrow and know by the habit of the animal where it lies under the sand, whether the burrow is U-shaped, or like a sea cucumber, the animal itself is bent into a U. But in a tightly knit community, determining which animals belong to which tubes or burrows is a puzzle.

When your shovel stabs deep into the ground and you hear and feel a squish and pop as it cuts through a sea cucumber or tubed sea anemone, or crunches through a clam shell, nothing gives you a more sickening feeling of having senselessly destroyed life. There is one rule to remember when collecting animals in any situation and that is to work against the substrate, be it rock, shell, sand or wood, and not against the animal.

Among the more common techniques for excavating burrowing forms is washing. If there are a few inches of water covering the creature you have the advantage if you hold onto it, dig with your fingers and at the same time wash the sand from it. If you have a good-sized, fairly hardy creature, you can rapidly flap your wrist and fan away the sand under the water. This is a technique that many divers use in removing specimens from the substratum.

Washing is one of the best methods for excavating creatures in the sandy-shore habitat and it is your most certain tool in collecting. I first learned of the technique in Woods Hole when I saw collectors spade up a mound of soil, drag their shovels into a few inches of water and begin splashing the sand and mud. In rivers, torrents of liquefied mud run off the shovel and the creatures, be they acorn worm, ribbon worm, burrowing brittlestar or sipunculid, that were so secure in their firm, sandy homes, are suddenly left exposed and can be gently eased off into a waiting jar.

Of course, washing will not work very well in a clay substratum because the water simply runs off without removing much substrate. In soft mud, unless you splash very gently your animal will slip away with the water. Regardless of the substrate, however, never wash specimens off a shovel in rough surf because it takes only an instant for a large wave to undermine the sand and sweep it all away.

Marine life, in the sandy-shore habitat, possess an ability to exude copious slime and mucus and to push easily through the shifting and hard-packed sandy substratum. The ear shell (*Sinum perspectivum*), for example, expands its great meaty foot that makes up three-quarters of its body size, and with copious mucus secretions and a good bit of muscular action it can soon plow its way from the surface to several feet down. The slimy acorn worms are more elusive and depend almost entirely upon mucus secretion for mobility. By exuding it in unbelievable quantities, the sand in the burrows is soon reduced to a viscous mush which they ride up and down with the greatest of ease, at the rate of a few inches per minute. This may seem slow, but it is much faster and easier than your fingers can move through sand.

Sometimes the burrowing marine animal can give you real surprises. You see a large fleshy sea anemone with a flowering array of tentacles above the sand, or the fat hollow siphons of a clam erecting up from the mud. A spurt of water erupts, and the soft mushy flesh contracts hard and pulls down, often exuding mucus and slipping from your grasp.

The battle is engaged. This simple marine animal with its primitive invertebrate neuromuscular system is surprisingly strong and much more adept at burrowing than you are at digging. As it tunnels its way down you try to maintain your grip, never pulling too hard for fear that you'll tear it in half. By holding it, your purpose is to keep the specimen anchored, between thumb and forefinger while your other fingers dig away sand and follow after its pull.

You dig deeper, holding onto it, past your wrist, up to your elbow in the sand and mud, then finally your arm has gone down far as it can and you're stopped at your armpit. This happened to me once in Madagascar. I had sneaked up on a large green *Stoichactis* sea anemone that had spread its short stubby column of tentacles out over the sand. I pounced, and a spurt of water erupted, and with terrific force the anemone contracted down into the sand. But I had a bulldog grip on it and my hand followed after it, until I got up to my armpit. I held a vise like grip on the slimy blob, but was stuck in the sand. I could have let go and pulled myself out, but I would have lost the anemone and after all that trouble I wasn't about to do that.

I shouted to my Malagasy helpers, and seeing me lying stretched out on the sand, they thought something had happened to me. When I explained that I had an anemone down there, they laughed, and helped dig it and me out of the sand. I finally emerged triumphantly with the anemone that sits in the Smithsonian Institution today. A more effective way to collect these large burrowing anemones is to dig along side them, come up under their base and just lift them out. It is much easier and less troublesome.

I knew one zoologist on the Ivory Coast who found some siphons and dug all the way down, pulling out handful after handful of sand, snaking his fingers along and fanning out a hole, but the siphon hole never seemed to end. Finally, the tips of his fingers could feel the valves of some sort of clam, probably a Geoduct, and that was one that completely and forever got away.

There is a point in sandy-shore collecting where a shovel will do no good. You can spade up a good hole, about a foot in diameter; then you will have to go it by hand, scrabbling your finger down into the sand and mud much the way a crab burrows until you come upon your victim, seize it and pull it up. In excavating a deep, burrowing form there is a tremendous advantage in having two or more collectors wielding shovels to dig the hole out deep and wide to expose the creatures. Two collectors, digging the exit and the front of the burrows, are essential for getting up specimens of acorn worms. If the burrow of a lugworm is spotted by its spewed out casting of digested mud, two collectors digging toward each other can excavate the animal in a short while. The individual who undertakes the job by himself feels afterward that he is qualified to dig any septic-tank hole or lay any amount of pipe.

Sand at the seashore, or any place else where there is water, has a nasty way of caving in on you and filling up the hole just when you're getting somewhere. You may even see the creature's tail sticking up, you may bend down to grasp it, and then a sudden avalanche covers both beast and hole.

Sandy-shore animals are subject to great seasonal variations and movements. In the time between one spring tide and the next, the entire population of animals on the tide flats may have changed, increased or totally disappeared. The flat may be dominated by sand stars (*Luidia clathrata*) in August, will have a sand-dollar (*Mellita quinquiesperforata*) explosion in September, and a heavy concentration of surf clams in October. By November, we have noticed, a particular sand flat will be heavily peppered with burrowing sea anemone (*Bunodactis stelloides*) and substantial quantities of southern quahog clams (*Mercenaria campechiensis*). Often they are heavily concentrated during their spawning periods.

Meanwhile, not one *Luidia clathrata*, the sand star, can be found anywhere, although an occasional *Astropecten articulatus* may appear. At times great portions of the sand flats become heavily populated with the brittlestar, *Hemipholis elegans*, which may stay in the same location for a few months buried in the sand spewing out sperm and eggs.

If you are a constant visitor at low tide, you will soon regard the usual inhabitants as old friends. The blood clams (*Noeta ponderosa*), sand dollars, screw shells, moon snails and surf clams are creatures that you may see day in and day out. Some seasons they occur in greater numbers than others; in fact almost any species is prone to a sudden population explosion

The responses of animals on tidal flats and even in subtidal ranges are dependent primarily upon optimum temperatures. In winter when the sands are thoroughly chilled, it requires a minimal amount of digging to excavate a burrower. Cold slows down the metabolism of invertebrates and burrowing fishes such as soles and eels, dulls their senses and inhibits their reactions. The cerianthid sea anemone that will normally whip in its tentacles and contract into its tube at the slightest touch will hardly respond when you grab it. When it's halfway dug up, it will suddenly give a violent contraction, but that is too late. Tubed worms like *Diopatra, Polyodontes* and *Loimia* hardly move, and if the temperature is not too cold there is little chance of breaking them. However, when ice saturates the ground the southern annelids are prone to break. Even the sensitive angel-wing clam (*Cyrtopleura costata*) that can suck its siphon down 12 inches or more in just a second feebly withdraws in the frost.

Cold is a two-edged sword. Nothing can be more miserable than digging on a tidal flat with freezing cold from the North Atlantic whipping through your jacket, trying to pick animals out with numbed, frozen fingers. However, if it is the first heavy frost of the season the flats are full of specimens and the excitement of the bonanza tends to minimize the cold. After weeks of hard continuous freezes, the flats become denuded of fauna. The beaches take on a lonesome, desolate mood. Not a hermit-crab shell is seen anywhere, no crabs or worms or fish. Perhaps there are a few burrows of sea anemones still there, perhaps a numb, semifrozen clam, but all the creeping, crawling creatures that made up the community on the sandy shore have dug way down, fled to deeper water or perished.

Finally spring comes. The rays of the sun penetrate the chilled sand and sea, animals begin to come out. As the waters warm, hungry snails move in shore in search of food, worms crawl about the flats, and horseshoe crabs from deeper waters that have been hibernating deep in the mud move in. The maximum populations on the tidal flats seem to occur when the ambient water temperature reaches 70°F in the south, perhaps 60°F in the northeast. When it becomes much warmer, animals tend to move into cooler waters or contract deep into the sand and again go into a dormant state.

During the hot summers you may be standing on top of an entire colony of angel-wings and never see the first animal. But at night when it's cool, even though tepid waters lap over the sands, many of the creatures emerge to feed and mate. Sting rays move into the shallows, electric rays patrol the flats stunning small shrimp, crabs and worms with their powerful electric organs and gulping them down. The sea becomes alive.

But only in the fall of the year, the middle of September, through the first couple of frosts does the estuary drama come to life. During these months the waters and substrate are much warmer than the air, and as the ground begins to cool off many creatures appear to be more abundant. Perhaps it is that last-minute push to feed, lay eggs and move about as much as possible before the hard, cruel winter sets in.

3.
The Sea Grass Habitat

Each collecting trip is unique and has something different to offer; perhaps it's a different creature, or perhaps you'll have the opportunity to see an animal feeding or laying eggs or escaping predation, a single act that stays in your mind.

I shall never forget one collecting trip in particular that was a salient, stirring scene — one that shaped the title of this book.

It was evening in August, during a full moon, the tide seeped out of the marshes and slowly exposed the tidal grass flats on north Florida's Alligator Harbor. Even though it was daylight, a big full moon hovered in the twilight over the horizon; the creatures of the watery sand and grass flats were exposed for anyone who wanted to see.

At the edge of the marsh a great herd of fiddler crabs (*Uca pugilator*) moved slowly down the flat as the water receded. The sand was scratched up with millions of little tear marks as the fiddlers bubbled and picked diatoms and other minute organisms from between the sand grains.

When the sea grass beds emerged I trudged across them with bucket and shovel in hand. Hermit crabs (*Clibanarius vittatus*) were prevalent on the flats, both in the mud and on top of the sea grass patches, dragging their heavy, barnacle-laden snail shells along. When approached they quickly drew into their shells and bubbled up a froth. Multitudes of little hermit crabs (*Pagurus longicarpus*), wearing

Nassarius shells, scuttled energetically in the shallow sandy depressions that form tide pools. Some carried the fuzzy pink hydroid (*Hydractinia echinata*) on their shells; only a few wore the cloak anemone (*Calliactis tricolor*).

The sea grass beds were alive with juvenile fish. Hundreds, if not thousands, of fingernail-sized pigfish, croakers and killifish scattered at my approach, moving so rapidly that all I could see was a puff of sand in the water. There were tiny boxfish, no longer than a half inch moving in and out of the grass blades, and when I picked them up they rapidly gulped air and blew up like a tiny piece of bubble gum.

Grass shrimp hid in the blades, along with young commercial pink shrimp (*Penaeus duorarum*). Two chimneys of the tube of the U-shaped parchment worm (*Chaetopterus variopedatus*) erected from the midst of the flat, and in one spot I noticed the fine red tentacles of the fireworm, *Cirraformia grandis* waving up from the brown mud.

At the edge of the sea where the water gently lapped through the grass, little brownish-green sea cucumbers (*Thyonella gemmata*) were spawning. I stopped and watched them. I was enthralled. When the

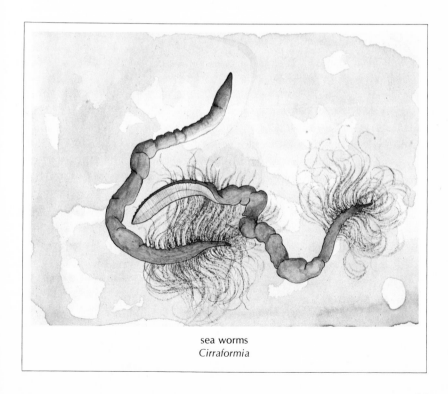

sea worms
Cirraformia

tide exposed them completely they erected their floriated crowns
conspicuously above the mud, and thrust their branched tentacles out.
Suddenly they contracted for a moment and drew their tentacles in and
then rapidly erected their floriated crowns high above the substrate,
expanded their tentacles again and leaned over. White sperm oozed
from behind the tentacles of the males and ran down over the rough,
wartlike skin and trickled down into the sea grass. The females
contracted and expanded much the same way, but thousands of tiny,
grayish-blue eggs spilled out of them and floated in the waters that
surrounded the sea cucumbers. The eggs caked up over the grass and
the spawning creatures stretched, expanded and spewed out more
eggs and sperm. As many times as I had visted these sea grass beds,
I had never been lucky enough to see this awesome spectacle of mass
reproduction of sperms and eggs, and I shall never forget that scene.

The sea grasses are home to multitudes of creatures; they provide
both food and shelter, and wherever there is grass, there is life. Schools
of speckled trout, croakers and redfish drift in and out of the green
grassy meadows that carpet the bottoms of the bays and estuaries. The
predatory fish nose down among the grass stalks gobbling up shrimp,
picking up worms and browsing for amphipods among the mats of
brownish-red algae. Blue crabs dig down into the sand, and orange
starfish creep along searching for scallops.

Sea grasses belong to the highest group of plants—the seed plants.
They possess a vigorous root system that firmly anchors the sand and
mud, they flower under water and transport their pollen in the currents
and their seeds are carried by the tide. There are five dominant species
in the Gulf of Mexico and the Caribbean. Cuban shoal weed
(*Diplanthera wrightii*), with slender flat blades, and manatee grasses
(*Cymodocea* [*Syringodium*] *filiforme*), with thin round blades, often
extend far up into the middle intertidal zones. The turtle grasses
(*Thalassia testudinum*) distinguished by their broad, flat blades are
more often encountered subtidally, growing in clear water, in coarse
shell and coralline sands. Along both the Atlantic and the Pacific
coasts another sea grass (*Zostera*) makes up dense mats of grass
meadows that bind the substratum and prevent it from being washed
away or shifted about by the currents.

Zostera, commonly called "eelgrass," does not occur in Florida
waters. However, even knowledgeable naturalists often refer to local
sea grass communities as "eelgrass" communities, and these
communities are often composed of various species of *Halophila*,

which resembles leafy terrestrial plants. This species grows from a few feet below mid-tide down to one hundred feet far out in the Gulf of Mexico. Another species, *Ruppia maritima,* often called wigeongrass, grows almost exclusively in brackish water, and was named after the fresh water widgeon ducks that feed in it.

Regardless of the species of grass that occurs on a coast, it harbors a peculiar community of marine animals that occur in a profusion second to no other habitat. Swimming along a grass flat you can easily spot shimmering blue-spotted cowfish nibbling at small crustacea at the base of the grasses. Spiny boxfish swim in and out of the grass strands in search of tiny hermit crabs, and sea horses and pipe fish cling to the stalks.

To the biological collector, the grass flats are one of the most productive areas, always worth visiting. There is always some new creature to be found there, or there is a population explosion of some desirable species. The grasses have their seasons. They begin growing profusely in the late spring, and by the middle of July they have grown so tall that it is difficult and sometimes completely impossible to see anything beneath the grass blades. I find the best time to search the grass strands is either the early spring or the late fall when the grass is shorter and more sparse and only a few inches of grass cover the flats.

When the tide goes out, spurts of water erupt from the flats; bubbling, pulsing sounds everywhere are coming from burrows and holes in the sand, among the diffuse, weaving root systems. There is a whole rich world beneath your feet. You can feel the sand and shell particles crunching under your boots, the mats of mussels, the crunchy spionid worms and the snails.

Sea grasses will grow on a variety of different substrates, and very often the type of substrate will regulate the species found. Turtle grasses grow in coarse, large-particle sands heavily mixed with shell, giving it good drainage, but sea grasses can be found growing over stinking anerobic mud, yet I have seen it also growing on limestone outcrops and on top of shell mounds. The mud harbors a rich fauna of worms among the grass roots, and the harder substratum is home to burrowing clams, snails and crustacea. Just as there are burrows on the sandy shore that point the way to the inhabitants, there are similar signs and clues in the grass, the slits that brachiopods make, the round holes of sea cucumbers and the keyhole openings of burrowing clams.

Soon all these are covered over and hidden from view by the rapidly growing grasses. To find burrows, you must wait until the tide

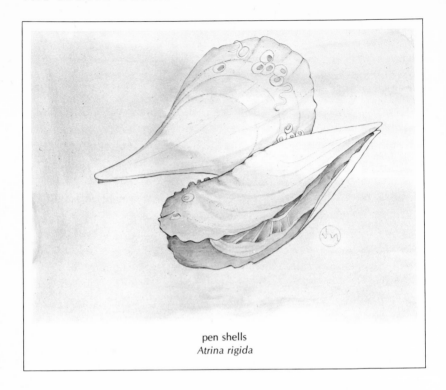

pen shells
Atrina rigida

goes out completely and the grass blades lie flat, then part the strands to uncover the sand. But this searching is slow and tedious work.

Because of the dense vegetation covering a mudflat, often the most successful method of finding creatures is to step inadvertently on them. Walking barefooted, gingerly stepping so you won't bring your foot down hard on some sharp object, your toes touch the rounded shell of a scallop, or a conch or a crunchy bunch of bryozoans or corals. I have found far more pen shells (*Atrina*) by having their pointed edge jab into my bare soles than I would have found otherwise.

Essentially there are three different groups of animals found in sea grasses. There are animals and plants that grow exclusively on the grass, using the grass blade as a holdfast itself, another group of free-swimmers or crawlers lives in the grass beds not burrowing, but hiding among the blades and stalks, and a third category of burrowing animals live among the tangle of roots.

The animals that you find living firmly attached to sea grass are seldom restricted to living on sea grass alone. The golden star tunicate

(*Botryllus schlosseri*), for example, can also be found on pilings, encrusting on other tunicates that grow on the bottom, as well as on worm tubes. If you are walking through a sea grass community, you may find the encrusting *Botryllus*. The same is true for the bryozoan *Bugula*, which are also found growing on pilings, rocks, sea walls and anything else to which they can attach. There is a small, white hydroid, *Halecium*, that seems to be restricted to living on the blades of grass. Certain encrusting bryozoans, like *Membraniopora* and *Schizoporella*, are more likely to be found on grass blades than on other areas, yet they have been found attached to rocks and shelf. The same is true of the small reddish-brown sea cucumbers (*Pentacta pygmaea*) that frequent the Gulf and can be rounded up, often by the hundreds, by the collector's swimming over sea grass and plucking them from among the vegetation. Their numerous, strong tubed feet cling to the grass, often wrapping themselves up in it.

We go to the grass flats, on a calm, clear day, and paddle along in the boat, searching. White patches of *Didemnum candidum* tunicates branch up, fat chunks of the tunicate *Distalpia bermudensis* and star-studded colonial tunicates attached to the grass are there for picking. We find the light blue soft sponges that take nickel from the sea water and concentrate it in their tissues.

But when the tide falls, the water seeps out from the grass, the blades collapse and are flattened and many of these treasures are hidden beneath piled vegetation. That is why it is best to collect these forms on a high tide in waist-deep water where you can walk. In tropical areas there are a few stinging creatures that hide out in the grass, and if you swim without protection you are liable to receive a severe sting. This may be a jellyfish, or some patch of hydroid, but your chances of seeing them in sea grass are much less than open water.

Get a long seine, about 30 feet with very small mesh, and drag it across the grass, or even use a flat scoop net with small mesh, and in a short time you'll discover one of the richest and most productive habitats.

After sweeping your net through the meadows of grass and examining the contents you will be amazed at the mass of life you have collected; dozens of small hermit crabs wearing *Nassarius* shells, flatworms, and sometimes loosely attached sea anemones. Often there will be a number of strange-looking arrow crabs (*Metoporhaphis calcarata*) with their long, spidery, needlelike legs grown over with algae. Multitudes of grass shrimp, like the needlelike green *Tozeuma carolinensis*, clear *Hippolyte* and *Palaemonetes*, flex, jump and dance on your webbing, next to a twisting, writhing pipe fish and pinfish.

The grass beds like everything else have their seasons and fluctuations of inhabitants. Seining in them one month will produce a different fauna from the next. I recall one time when a sweep of the net brought up strange, very small, green blobs with tapered tails—I had never seen them before. It was only after putting them into a jar of sea water and letting them unfold that I had discovered they were some sort of opisthobranch, and after careful examination I was able to identify it as a techtibranch of some sort. A specialist at Woods Hole tagged the name *Oxynoe* on it.

Even on your own familiar beach, especially if it's vegetated with sea grasses, there are so many creatures that you can't name them all. You learn to know a few by name, but if you can't name them at first, at least you can get to recognize them as acquaintances. There is that odd-looking furry flatworm and those familiar, elongated green shrimp, but then something like this soft-bodied orange-and-blue-spotted mollusk turns up—a total stranger—and disarms you completely. You lose that self-satisfied feeling of knowing all the animals in your community, either by name or by sight. There is a slight irritation at this point, because even after years of collecting there is always going to be something new to shatter your self-esteem, especially when you least expect it.

But you can count on seeing a number of old friends on every exposure of the familiar tidal flats. The same tunicates, the same grass sponges and the same large, hard-shelled mollusks. Almost always among the dense meadows of sea grass you will find wary scallops (*Aequipecten irradians*), and as you walk near them they snap their valves shut. Large whelks slide over the surface to stay hidden in the grass. Sea squirts like *Molgula* and *Styela* spurt jets of water, hermit crabs drag their shells around and froth at the mouth. Many of these creatures are found on sandy shores also, but there seem to be more of them among the meadows of grass because they get protection and find more food.

Blue crabs (*Callinectes sapidus*) nestle among the grass and scuttle out wildly with their pincer claws raised defensively when you happen upon them. In the summertime I have seen thousands of tiny blue crabs gathered in a single swoop of a minnow seine, few of them more than a half-inch from point to point. Everything occurs in miniature: spiny boxfish, juvenile trout, juvenile croakers, mullet and hordes of killifish, all show that the turtle grass, manatee grass and Cuban shoal weeds are the nursery grounds for many little creatures. Spider crabs (*Libinia emarginata*) with their brown, muddy color stay partly buried and blend surprisingly well. While one or two may be encountered along a sandy beach, when you walk out to the patches of grass, ten times that number are found.

Brittlestars like *Ophioderma* and *Amphipholis* sporadically carpet the sandy bottoms, but they prefer the grass as a year-round habitat. However, they will, in collecting, present certain problems when you have to disentangle their snaky arms from among the roots and stalks of the grass. If handled too roughly they break off their arms. Collecting brittlestars is only half the trouble; recognizing them amid the grasses takes keen observation. Five long, brittle mottled arms attached to a quarter-inch disk blend perfectly with the surrounding habitat that looks like ordinary roots. In order to extricate the animals you must first part the grass, strand by strand, removing each blade that is twisted inside the arms, and sometimes as fast as you uncover one arm, it writhes swiftly and wraps itself around another blade of grass. Gently, but persistently you can free the disk and out comes the specimen.

Numerous tiny snails, such as Atlantic marginella, pyrams, wentletraps and others also hide down among the blades of grass and are found if you part the grass strand by strand. But a good flat net pushed hard over the grass beds produces a multitude of small gastropods. *Bulla,* the bubble shell, may also appear in substantial numbers. In Florida and the southeastern United States one frequently finds tulip shells (*Fasciolaria hunteria*) lying partially buried in the mud beneath the sea grass.

Fasciolaria feeds primarily on small snails like *Nassarius,* and *Nassarius vibrex* predominantly inhabits sea grass communities. There is a very interesting phenomenon to watch here. When *Nassarius,* creeping along, comes across the slime trail of *Fasciolaria* it lashes about wildly, thrusting its shell out of the path with its small meaty foot, which may help it escape. But *Fasciolaria* too is active. From that beautiful polished shell, of mottled browns, grays and creams spiraling as intriguingly as the whorls of a barbershop pole emerges a long brown foot, which spreads over the hapless *Nassarius.* Other voracious predators like the crown conchs (*Melongena corona*) frequent the grass flats in search of smaller snails; and *Fasciolaria* in its turn becomes the victim.

Melongena lives primarily on oyster bars where it feeds on oysters and other whelks which are busy eating oysters. But when oysters are scarce, you can count on finding the gastropods in the sea grass where there may be an abundance of cockles, razor clams, sculptured venus clams and scallops. The grass flats are grazing grounds in more ways than one. The herbivores live there feeding on the grass and the algae that grow around the grass and the carnivores come there to feed on the herbivores, just as they do on the land.

The matted, branching roots of sea grasses lay down a firm flooring and prevent the sand from being carried away by the tides, wave shock and winds, and very little if any shift in the substrates goes on. This permits many hundreds of soft-bodied, fragile creatures to conglomerate among the root systems. But a conscientious collector must be careful if he wishes to preserve his habitat. When the sea grass is uprooted with a shovel and the sand washed away, the roots are bared and the patch of grass dies off. It is easy to destroy a habitat by extensive digging, and once a big patch of grass is gone it may never return because the substrate erodes away, forming an anerobic pit.

It is possible to do a lot of digging in a grass patch and not seriously hurt the habitat, if the digging is done carefully as follows: the grass is spaded up and the substratum among the roots is broken apart to pick out the organisms. Then you replant the grass and firmly pack it down so the incoming tide will not wash it out. Of course ducks and water fowl constantly dig up the grass while searching for worms but the grass invariably grows back.

A few holes here and there do not seem to hurt the habitat if it is not collected too routinely. But of all the ecological habitats, be it rock, sand or mud, nothing can be as readily destroyed as a sea grass habitat. To make an extensive collection, the sea grass is spaded up with a shovel, roots and all, and the sand washed away from the roots by splashing water on them. As the sand diminishes and the roots become naked, mussels, small clams, assorted polychaetes, and phoronids become obvious. Sometimes sipunculids are common, sometimes brachiopods. If the mud is put through a screen as it comes off the roots, an abundance of amphipods, isopods and other minute crustaceans are readily collected. Pea crabs, snapping shrimp, burrowing mud shrimp—the list continues to mount.

There are two general categories of animals that live in the substratum of sea grass, the ones you see and the ones that leave no visible sign or trail. The latter are encountered only when you are digging down after a specific animal and find the creature by accident.

Many worms, mud shrimp, amphipods and sand eels fit this category, but rather than randomly dig up a grass habitat in search of one of these creatures that may be found sooner or later, I find it best to go after the animals that leave signs or burrows and gather the incidentals as I come upon them.

A good example of this is collecting phoronids, the elongated, sticklike lophophorates *Phoronis architecta*, that periodically occur in great abundance on sea grass flats with hard-packed mud and shell. These creatures are not apparent because they do not leave any noticeable hole, but on the other hand the brachipod *Glottidia pyramidata* shows a distinct, penknife-like slit in the sand. And almost always, we find phoronids when digging for brachiopods.

By digging down parallel to each brachiopod slit, a chunk of grass and sod is unearthed. The roots and mud are broken apart in horizontal layers and the brachiopod's shell and pedicle foot is exposed along with the sandy tubes of *Phoronis architecta*, which stand out stiff and erect.

At the end of a morning's collecting in a brachiopod patch, a few dozen large, red cirratulid worms (*Cirraformia grandis*) are also collected as incidentals. Only occasionally can they be spotted by parting the strands of grass and looking for the fine-branching red tentacles above the mud like so many curly hairs. A ribbon worm, *Cerebratulus*, comes up in a shovelful along with numerous errant polychaete worms, small bivalves like *Chione cancellata* and, on rare and unexpected occasions, even the hemichordate *Ptychodera bahamensis*. Also exposed down in the sand may be great twisting masses of *Hemipholis elongata* (brittlestars). Of course you stand a good chance of chopping these subterranean creatures in half with your shovel, but most of these forms are capable of regeneration.

Other animals that are most prominently visible on the flats, and can be spotted from several yards away are parchment worms (*Chaetopterus variopedatus*) that erect from the grass looking like two paper-white chimneys of some little house down below. Spewed-out castings of the lugworm (*Arenicola*) are sometimes present, or the great leathery tube of *Polyodontes lupina*, the giant scaleworm, rises above the grass, often next to the tubed anemone (*Cerianthus americanus*) that makes a tube of mucus, sand and mud. The flowering tentacles of *Cerianthus* are quite an eye-catcher and the collector will dig them up almost every time. Whether it is possible to denude a grass flat of *Cerianthus americanus* or not remains to be seen; we have dug many on Bay Mouth Bar in Alligator Harbor in northwest Florida, yet the population does not appear to be damaged in any way.

In Alligator Harbor, sea cucumbers (*Thyonella gemmata* and *Thyone briareus*) dominate the sea grass community, particularly in Cuban shoal weed (*Diplanthera wrightii*) stands. They leave conspicuous burrows, spaced a few inches apart where the head and the tail come to the surface. The clear, thin-skinned *Leptosynapta crassipatina* which occurs in sand, mud and sea grass communities makes small peppershot holes similar to the elongated burrowing sea anemones, *Halaclysts*, that also live in the same communities.

Clams stray from the sand flats, thrust their siphons up and make themselves recognized by their keyhole slits. Their holes are much more distinctive among the roots of sea grasses, because they are not protruding from shifting sands where the openings can constrict and collapse from wave action and winds. Some species such as *Chione cancellata*, the sculptured venus, and the china cockle, *Trachycardium egmontianum*, are exclusively grass-flat inhabitants and seldom if ever are found on pure sandy beaches. *Atrina rigida*, the pen shell, is found only among the roots of sea grasses. The triangular shell sends a network of tough branching byssus hairs down into the mud, intertwining among the roots of the grass, much the way rock mussels like *Mytilus edulis* attach to a rocky surface or a wharf piling. In pulling an *Atrina* out of the sand you are likely to break the byssus hairs, but if the substratum is soft and pliable it can be pulled up with the byssus hairs intact.

Horse mussels (*Modiolus americanus*) send a branching intertwining network of hairs down among the sea grass roots. These often help further anchor the grass, sand and mud. And among such tangles one is likely to find spionid worms, which build sandy tubes in great twisted, tangled masses. These can be felt as you walk over the sand and crunch them under your feet. And while they are common on many sand flats, and drab and rather ugly looking, their network of twisting, sandy tubes, upon which limpets and chitons grow, affords food and shelter for dozens of other creatures, including terebellids and speonids. Flatworms like *Stylochus ellipticus* take hold; encrusting sponges like *Microciona prolifera* and tunicates grow among the spionids.

But the spionids are found in turtle grass, particularly of *Thalassia* beds. And once again, another community of animals is dependent upon the turtle grass. The importance of maintaining marine-grass communities cannot be overemphasized.

In the 1930s eelgrass (*Zostera*) disappeared from the North Atlantic coast, the victim of some parasite. Immediately afterward shellfish, such as scallops, became especially scarce. Young fish that lived among the grass feeding on the hoards of shrimp virtually disappeared, and even the lobsters that dug burrows through the grass, because food was so abundant there, dropped off in numbers. As the sheltered jungles of grass disappeared, animals found no food or protection and soon they too died off.

The plague spread to the grasses on both sides of the Atlantic. The meadows of productive vegetation turned brown and perished along the shores of the English Channel and the Scandinavian waters; only the Mediterranean and the Pacific coast were spared.

The firm network of roots was no longer there to hold the bottoms, and erosion set in. Even the wild ducks and geese suddenly found only mud along the banks of the Nova Scotia coast instead of feeding grounds, and the Canadian government had to supply grain to keep them alive.

As the grass died, the sea washed the shoals and banks away that harbored so many millions of animals. There was no home for the sea trout, the pipe fish or the sea horse, and no place for the small crabs and shrimp to hide. When the mud was swept up, the clam and scallop beds disappeared. Many populations of quahog clams and oysters were buried beneath a fine layer of silt, and even today you can dig up dead clams lying in normal positions. The young fish that took shelter in the *Zostera* patches had to move on and find shelter elsewhere. Where they could once blend perfectly with the grass and hide from predators, they were left naked, exposed, and hungry.

But the grass stopped dying, and in the last 30 years it has started regrowing, although there are still signs of destruction along the coast.

It is a normal and natural part of the food chain to have large numbers of grasses break off from the bottom of the estuaries and float about at sea. They grow to full height and flower during the summer and fall, and when waves and normal currents hit them, the leaves and stems break off and often float about in such dense masses, they look like islands or shoals emerging from the sea.

When the grasses are on the move it is practically impossible to go through them with an outboard motor without having to slow down periodically, shift the motor into reverse, spin the grass from the wheel and proceed. In Madagascar, we had an 18-h.p. motor used in collecting that would sheer a pin every time it hit a floating grass embankment. Many people curse the floating grass, but if they understood that it is an essential part of the life process, and that without it, there would be fewer fish and less marine life, they would gladly accept it.

In its floating form, we have found the grass to harbor a great many small fish that swim among the bales and under it to take refuge from the large predatory species that constantly rove the deep. Sea hares, small crabs, nudibranchs, sea horses, pipe fish, filefish, and any number of small fin fishes swim along the floating islands. But sooner or later they must get off because the grasses are doomed to hit the beach. Much of the floating vegetation piles up on shores and turns brown and dies from the dehydrating sun. Through bacterial action and abrasive sand and surging waves, the leaves are broken down into fine particles which are further broken down into detritus. This is washed out into the estuary and furnishes direct food for shrimp and many small fish. But the food chain is more complex than that.

Bacteria working on the grasses produce a number of vitamins which cause phytoplankton to bloom. They in turn produce food for zooplankton, and small fish feed upon the minute copepods, planktonic chaetognaths, and larval invertebrate and fish forms. Generally it is very simple to spot a productive area. If there are hundreds and hundreds of acres of sea grasses below the tides, and the shores are piled high with dead grass, then the area is bound to be productive. Where there is no grass there is no substantial amount of marine life.

It has been proved time and again that when the sea grasses are destroyed either through natural disasters such as an outbreak of fungus or unnatural disruptions, the density and volume of marine life drops sharply. Grasses require clear water to grow in, and when the waters become silted and turbid from channel dredging or landfill operations, light penetration is vastly reduced, and the grass cannot continue to grow.

Much of the rich and diverse populations of marine life that inhabited the coast of North Carolina have been destroyed in recent years by the continuous dredging of navigation channels. When the Army Corps of Engineers chopped a deep channel through the grass beds around the marine laboratory at Beaufort, shifting sands eroded the sand away from the roots. The channel is continuously filling up with sand and has to be "cleaned out" by frequent dredging operations which have resulted in shifting, eroding bottoms.

Perhaps someday sea grasses and marshes will be considered a most valuable natural resource, something to be cherished and preserved rather than dredged. Perhaps someday avid farming of sea grasses will take place. Look at the gains made in horticulture where resistant strains of grain grasses have been developed, where plants have been bred to grow in a variety of soils and in all different climates. Perhaps someday in the future we will see a new species of scientist called a "marine horticulturist" cultivating vast waving meadows of sea grasses that stretch for miles growing over what are now silted, unproductive bottoms, using sewage and certain industrial wastes as fertilizer in measured amounts. The St. Marks National Wildlife Refuge flooded portions of highland forests with sea water and in less than two years produced vigorous crops of widgeon grass (*Ruppia maritima*) which provided shelter for marine life and food for ducks and geese. Estuaries can be managed, but they must first be preserved.

4.
The Salt Marsh Habitat

Along the Atlantic coastline, from Nova Scotia to Central Florida
and along the Gulf of Mexico, tidal marshlands line the shores of
estuaries. This "ribbon of green" as John Teal called it in his intriguing
book, *Life and Death of a Salt Marsh*, is one of the most nutrient-
producing areas on earth. Salt marshes are only a winding strip of
green along the coastal United States; a trip in an airplane from Florida
to New York along the coastline shows that plainly. The mountains
turn to flatlands and pines, which lower down further until the green
band of marsh gold appears and then the sea begins.

The public is only beginning to realize the value of these salt
marshes as nursery grounds for commercial fish, shrimp, crabs and a
countless variety of other organisms. For years the marshes were and
unfortunately still are, considered breeding grounds for mosquitoes and
biting green-head flies. And even the novice biological collector may
find it difficult to believe that such a wealth of life lives in those vast
stretches of tall green grasses, winding creeks and mud flats.

But you have only to carry a bottle of insect repellent, wear boots
and be prepared to make a long journey through the marshes in boggy
mud, and sample the life that lives there to be convinced. A swoop of a
fine-meshed minnow seine, about ¼" to ½" mesh, will reveal the
thousands of croakers, mullet, grass shrimp and juvenile penaeid shrimp,
young crabs, killifish and in certain seasons young redfish, sand trout,

and skipjack. The autumn sees young spotted sea trout, tarpon, drum and sheepshead moving into the marshes. Threadfin herring and shad, not more than an inch long, live in the mud-bottomed marshes by the millions. When the marsh flowers and starts to turn brown, juvenile white shrimp swarm into the creeks and grow at a fantastic rate, gobbling up the tiny diatoms and minute animals that are so prevalent.

The marsh grass itself is invariably full of periwinkle snails (*Littorina irrorata*) that slide up and down on the grass stems lapping up filamentous algae. They rise to the top of the grass to escape the rising tide, and when the tide falls they return to the bottom of the stalk where you find thousands of the tiny, nondescript flat barnacle, *Cthalamus fragilis*. These little black or gray barnacles like the littorinid snails are not restricted to the marsh, but can also be found on wharf pilings, channel markers or oyster bars, or any object that thrusts up out of the water. They are, however, a dominant animal community in the tidal marsh.

Perhaps the most dominant animal in any marsh community is the fiddler crab. Hordes of fiddler crabs dwell in the hardy marsh, and there are at least three different species. The most common is *Uca pugilator* that lives in sandy marsh; *U. pugnax* and *U. minax* dwell in muddy marsh and are adapted to pick detritus particles and diatoms selectively from the soft oozing mud, while *U. pugilator* is more adapted to picking through and sorting food from sand grains. Their burrows allow water to percolate through the marsh soils, oxygenating the ground.

The marsh grass offers protection to fiddler crabs, and can make collecting them a time-consuming and particularly difficult task. To dig them from their burrows in the marsh requires prying up a tough network of tightly interwoven roots, and most collectors will prefer to wait until a more opportune time to catch the crabs.

On a warm day when the tide recedes, herds of fiddler crabs leave their burrows and parade down to the water's edge to feed and mate. As soon as the collector appears on the scene, the crabs make a dash for the marsh grass and their burrows. If they are cut off from their retreat, they will run the other way, and if a number of collectors walk around a colony, forcing them into a circle, the crabs will begin to pile up. An easy way to gather them in abundance and avoid many, many painful little pinches from the big claws of male crabs, is to dig a bucket down into the ground, walk them into a circle and make them pile up into the bucket. There is genuine military strategy in rounding up crabs. Break the assault for one moment and you can lose all your crabs before you know it.

They dash to the high beach, scuttle in and among the roots and strands of *Spartina* and *Juncus* grass, or even duck under the low lying *Salicornia* and as you run about trying to grab up handfuls of crabs, the sharp blades of grass cut your hands, penetrate pants-covered legs and hurt. So it is best if you block the crabs from retreating to the safety of their haunts. But if the grass is done away with, the crabs have no shelter, and they will die off or be eaten by predators. Raccoons and skunks visit the marsh to feast upon fiddler crabs, and they have been found in fox feces. The marsh is full of birds, including willets, egrets, clapper rails and gulls, all picking through the abundant food that lives in the marsh grass.

Other amphibious crabs such as *Uca pugnax* and *Sesarma reticulatum* are also part of the food chain, but since they do not herd they must be hunted down individually by the collector or the animal predator. As soon as they pop out of their burrow, the quick bill, claw or hand swoops down and grabs them up. But most of these crabs are expert at retreating to safety.

Down into the mud around the marsh-grass roots you usually encounter the ribbed horse mussels (*Modiolus demissus*) which push up out of the mud. In highly brackish marsh one might find the small hard-shelled clam, *Rangia cumacea,* and the best way to find them is to walk barefoot in the adjacent mud flat and feel the shells with your toes. In the upper level of the marsh, near the *Juncus* and *Salicornia* and *Iva* bushes live brackish-water earthworms, spiders, crickets and a whole variety of insects. The roots of the marsh grass protect minute crustaceans; they are generally massed with nematodes.

The marsh plants can tolerate high concentrations of salt. The elevation of the land, and the concentration of salts in the soils left by the receding tide regulate the type of vegetation and to some degree the type of fauna. In areas where the salinity of the substrate is very high because the salt has been trapped in puddles and evaporated, very little vegetation except pickleweed (*Salicornia*) exists. Since there is little vegetation the bright sunlight comes down strong on the sand, and light-loving diatoms thrive. Hordes of bacteria that live on dying marsh grass produce a vast storehouse of vitamins and nutrients, and these furnish nourishment for diatoms and phytoplankton in the rest of the estuary. The diatoms are at the base of the food chain and many life forms depend upon them.

THE SALT MARSH HABITAT

The marsh is like a gigantic puzzle. At first it is very confusing, green and winding—all grass. But if you spend a little time walking through marshes, and examining the life that dwells among the grass blades, you begin to fathom its great secrets. The marshes are the richest and most productive areas on earth. They produce far more dried plant stuff than the most productive wheatfields. But with the increase in populations along the coast, through public misunderstanding and personal greed, more and more pressure is being brought to bear on the marshlands.

Developers want to dredge them, and fill them with spoil from subtidal lands. The U.S. Army Corps of Engineers in the past has considered them nothing more than a convenient place to dump sand pumped out of ship channels, and given no thought to the wealth of life produced in the marshes.

There is need for a public education program. Much the way the forestry people talk of the value of our forests and paper resources some powerful group should publicize the values and seafood productivity of our marshlands. Many people who own marsh property haven't the faintest idea that the marshes have any value whatsoever, they don't know that they produce up to ten tons of straw and dried foodstuffs per acre per year and that this nourishes the entire estuary system and provides fertilizers for subtidal grasses. Many of these landowners are themselves avid fishermen and duck hunters and might think twice about dredging and filling their properties if the true value of the marshes were made known to them.

The productivity is not hard to understand. A vast community of plants exists in the marsh, not a high diversity, but a gigantic concentration. Along the east coast, the most important of these plants is cord grass (*Spartina alterniflora*), the broad-bladed grass that is routinely covered and uncovered by the tides. This species lives in the lowest levels of the marsh.

Along the Gulf Coast of Florida a rise in elevation will result in the growth of *Juncus roemerianus* stands. Called "needle rush," *Juncus* sticks up like millions of long sharp needles, making it painful to walk through the marshes. *Juncus* is less regularly covered by the tides than *Spartina* but both of these grasses provide nutrient value because both are perennials and die down in winter. In spring the new crop of green grass grows up and the old grass lies in great piles called "cowlicks." This decaying grass, with the help of thousands of species of fungi and bacteria, breaks down in the hot summer weather into a form of humus or nutrient soup. This decomposing material, formed into detritus, is eaten by fiddler crabs whose wastes are, in turn, utilized by other microorganisms. Diatoms are nourished by the phosphates, nitrates, carbohydrates and proteins, and the marsh becomes a seething mass of micro-organisms producing a rich earthy smell. Then the high tide comes flushing into the marsh, and summer storms take this nutrient soup and wash it out into the rest of the estuary where it is further broken down and eaten by small fish.

In an attempt to study some of the behavior of marsh animals in a closed system, we built a large concrete tank with a gravel filter and planted *Spartina alterniflora*. We secured the grass from an area that was being dredged up, and by so doing learned some remarkable things about the grass. When the dragline ripped up great chunks of the grass with roots and sod included, it deposited a number of clumps to the side which escaped being covered with fill. After two months we happened upon these sod pieces and found that even though the exposed roots were parched and dry, and the muddy soils were powdery dry, the grass came to life when buried down in our tanks and started growing vigorously culturing myriad creatures. Within a couple of weeks new green shoots were coming up which indicated to me that marshes could be transplanted. Therefore, if a developer is going to destroy a productive marsh, and has all the politicians and government officials aiding and abetting him, as is commonly the case, he should at least be made to dig the marsh up and go to the expense of planting it in an unproductive area such as a barren spoil bank.

There is a whole new line of thinking about "constructive" dredging that needs much study and experimentation. Some spoil banks may become vegetated with marsh grasses within 5 to 10 years after dredging. The type of soil has a lot to do with it, the elevation of the ground controls which plants will take over, and so on. When a channel is deepened and the spoil pumped out, it would be beneficial to all if the spoil could be bulkheaded with some biodegradable material, planted with marshes and coastal plants that would stabilize the soil and provide a habitat in a very short time for birds and fish.

Of course much would depend upon the tidal currents, the depth of the harbor, the salinity factors and a whole series of complex ecological conditions for marshes to take root and bloom. The intercoastal waterways along the Texas coast are a prime example of man-created marshes, but the creation was only an incidental effect.

The single thought of the Corps of Engineers was digging a channel, not creating a habitat.

To learn more about what happens when a marsh is dredged, we have been taking bottom samples with a bucket dredge. The dredge bites deep into the bottom of a finger-fill canal in an area that was once an expansive needlerush marsh. In every single canal when the dredge was hauled aboard, it reeked of hydrogen sulfide and was full of decaying roots, stems and leaves. So vile was this noxious bottom, that our collectors had to hold their breath while they sifted the substrate through screens. After all the mud was washed out, a great pile of decomposing roots lay twisted on the screen, and a few polychaete worms managed to survive in that stifling stink. To show the striking comparison of a healthy undredged bottom, all we have to do is go to a tidal flat next to a marsh and sample the bottom. It is rich and alive, full of amphipods, brittlestars, tiny white clams, snails, and numerous polychaetes belonging to at least three families. The productive muds are alive with filamentous algae and diatoms, all of which is missing from a dredged, silted-over, soft, oozing bottom mixed with decaying roots.

The salt marshes are one of my favorite places at the seashores. I love to drive along the roads that parallel the great green marshes of north Florida and watch the handsome snowy egrets walking along the grass flats, bobbing their long necks as they gobble up small fish. Baby clapper rails covered with fuzz scurry out onto the road while their mother hovers above your head screeching insults to divert your attention to her.

The marshes are visited each fall by ducks and geese. The marsh is full of sounds, sounds of rabbits moving through the grass, birds chirping and fish splashing. Fiddler crabs move through the grass, their bodies make a hissing sound like the rustle of leaves in a fall wind. Everywhere you look in the marsh there is life, grass shrimp raise little clouds of mud as they dart through the creeks. Blue crabs race out of the shallows toward deeper waters as your shadow passes over. Green-headed, biting flies buzz nosily overhead, and dragon flies hover above searching for mosquitoes. The grass is full of snails, the air has a good rich smell to it. Diamondback terrapins with their minstrellike faces sun themselves on the banks of the winding creeks, and needlefish patrol the surface of the waters gobbling up killifish and sailfin mollies.

While it is true that the marshes are most certainly alive, you must go into them and see for yourself or you'll never know it. I remember as a young boy, riding a train from New York to Newark, looking out of the window at the great expanses of green marshes. It didn't bother me when I saw the draglines digging it up, in fact I was sort of glad. It was a good way to keep down all those mosquitoes that came swooping into the host city at night. It was nice to know that something "useful" was being done with the marshes. I looked at New York City, so crowded and dirty, and wondered why those great, smelly "wastelands" couldn't be developed to relieve the overcrowding. I didn't know that the industrial outfalls, the garbage and the dredging made the marshes smell, and I didn't think anything lived in them.

But I found out otherwise by going into them and looking around, and gathering specimens. At first I collected as a hobby and then as a profession, and finally, after I knew the marshes, I began to appreciate them, perhaps as much as Sidney Lanier who wrote:

Ye marshes, how candid and simple and nothing-witholding and free
Ye publish yourselves to the sky and offer yourselves to the sea!

The future of marshlands and mangrove swamps along the coastal United States is far from bright and rosy. According to *Open Space Action* magazine, America's wetlands have been reduced by one-half in the past 100 years. Other estimates are 40 percent, some say only a third have been dredged and filled. Much discussion about states taking inventory of their wetlands is taking place in various legislatures, regarding the expense and who is to conduct the surveys, but in the meantime the draglines are at work in the marshes.

Florida has been ravaged by dredging operations since World War II. Many a developer has made himself rich by taking tidal lands and pumping up acreage which is sold as valuable water real estate. In fact "Dredge and Fill" was invented in Florida and spread like cancer throughout the rest of the coastal United States.

I remember seeing a Florida Development Commission newsfilm that showed a mangrove swamp and then a big dredge barge pumping up the lands. It said something like, Once a worthless mangrove swamp or marsh, this land is now the site of a glamorous housing development, shopping center and golf courses. Florida at "work, Florida's progress." And innocuous, babbling, cheerful music is played in the background, which sings of progress, beauty and truth.

By use of the hydraulic dredge whole islands can be built out in the middle of the bay where previously there was no land. In almost no time the bottom is sucked up, spewed out, and out of the muddy, turbid waters emerges a sand-and-mud lump which grows bigger and bigger the longer the dredges work. What effect this has on the plant and animal communities is of no concern to the developers. The cutterhead spins, the dredge bellows clouds of black smoke, and shallow water, productive bottoms are destroyed. Shell Point in Wakulla County, north Florida, is just one very small example. This was one of our finest collecting grounds, but since it was proximal to Tallahassee, the capital of Florida, it became the focal point for massive dredge-and-fill and land-development projects.

A marina was dredged out, and finally a mobile home park was built up. Approximately 200 acres of tidal marsh were filled, and canals chopped through bay bottoms. Shell Point was one of the standard areas that we traveled to, to harvest the sea Urchin *Lytechinus variegatus* with a scallop drag. After the dredging we went to investigate.

Even before we hit the *Thalassia* grass beds where *Lytechinus* abounded off Shell Point, we found the sandy shelly bottoms strangely denuded of life. The dead oyster and scallop shell that we dredged from this sandy bottom was usually alive with chitons, feather-duster worms and keyhole limpets, but now not a single animal appeared clinging or growing on the shells.

We approached the beaches. What had been bright green marsh had turned to scarred, raw, ugly beaches of mud and sand. Crews of men were driving bulkheads down into the sand, and draglines bit into the mud and dumped soils over the remaining *Juncus* and *Spartina* marshes. Irrigation pumps steadily drained the marshes above the draglines to make a sewage disposal plant, and muddy waters poured out of the canals into the Gulf.

At last we arrived at an area where the bottom was heavily grown over with turtle grass and dropped our scallop drag over. The motor speeded up, the lines became taut and the boat strained ahead, pulling the steel-framed net over the grassy bottom. This area always produced a wealth of grass shrimp (*Palaemon floridanus*), dwarf hermit crabs (*Pagurus bonairensis*), various tunicates such as *Didemnum candidum*, *Botryllus* and *Clavelina*. Red-beard sponge (*Microciona prolifera*) could be expected, and during the spring of the year we could also expect spiny boxfish, cowfish, a number of blennies and plenty of pipefish and

51

one or two sea horses. There should be a few dozen scallops in the catch, and of course 20 to 50 *Lytechinus variegatus*, more or less typical turtle-grass community animals.

When the scallop drag was hauled aboard and dumped out on the culling platform of our tunnelboat, we were nauseated. There were over a hundred sea urchins, all rotten, their spines falling off and their viscera oozing out of their hulls. No live scallops, but plenty of scallop shells were there, ones that had recently died. The bright orange bryozoan *Schizoporella unicornis*, that looked much like a branching fire coral, had turned brown and black, and only portions of it were alive. Even the star coral (*Astrangia astereiformis*) was bleached white and dead. The sponges were moldy, the tunicates dead and mushy, and not a single fish appeared in the catch. Much of the broad-leafed grass was already turning brown, and the matted algae were turning soft and beginning to stink.

The bay reminded my very much of our semiclosed-system aquariums and the times in the past when we had torn them down and disturbed the substrate and caused the death of many animals by the resulting siltation. According to scientific principle one cannot say positively that these animals died because of dredging. There is not enough substantial evidence on hand that their deaths were not the result of pesticides, mercury or a natural fungus or a red tide.

But never before had we pulled in a catch of corpses like that off Shell Point.

There are still no sea urchins or scallops at Shell Point, and there is not much of anything else. But who can say how long all that will last? It is not judicious to point an accusing finger at the developers and say they have destroyed the fauna, because in two years or less the fauna may come back. We can say they have destroyed forever some of our wetspace, some of our fish nursery grounds and a tiny speck of coastline compared to the vast stretches of coastline around the United States. But they are only one of many, and no matter where one goes, there is a dragline or worse still, a hydraulic dredge, waiting or working.

5.
The Mangrove Swamp Habitat

Deep within the mangrove swamps, rays of yellow sunlight filter down through the shrubby bushes, illuminating the peculiar stilt roots and waxy green leaves. The tide slowly seeps in and then seeps out again over the rotting vegetation, soft brown mud and stifling smells of eternal decay.

Mangroves are almost strictly tropical. They begin to replace salt marshes along the southeastern Atlantic coast around Daytona Beach, Florida, and extend far down into the Caribbean. Many people associate mangroves with coral reefs, but their requirements are quite different. *Rhizophora mangle*, the most common species, grows better in brackish water around the mouths of rivers and along estuaries. On some coasts they simply border the beaches, but on others they go far inland, for miles and miles, leaving the salt water and growing heavily in fresh-water areas. Much of the Everglades is grown over with dense mangrove bushes, and all along the roadsides of the Florida Keys you can see jungles of these salt-water bushes.

They propagate throughout the world by their amazing, elongated seedlings that often develop roots before they leave the parent plant. The seeds drift out to sea, and when they land on an island or shore where there is a suitable substrate they take root and in a few years new bushes grow.

In many regions of the tropics the red mangrove (*Rhizophora mangle*) is commercially important because it is stripped of its bark, which contains 20 to 30 percent tannin. A solid extract containing 50 to 60 percent tannin is prepared by pulverizing the bark into a powder. And many areas including the East Indies, East Africa and Central America export mangrove tannin to the United States. In some of the poorer tropical countries, the wood, which is hard and heavy, is used to make rafters and beams, especially since some mangrove trees grow as high as 100 feet and have aerial stilt roots that are often more than 10 feet tall.

Almost the entire coastline of Central and South America is grown over with mangroves, and shrimp swarm in among the roots and feed ravenously on the organically rich mud. Then fleets of shrimp trawlers from the United States, Honduras and Nicaragua drag their nets in the muddy estuaries and harvest millions of pounds of shrimp each year.

Just watching the boats unload their catches from Honduran waters is an experience in itself. Hour after hour I have seen an endless carpet of pink shrimp carried up on screaming, smoking conveyer belts into the processing plants where workers rapidly grade them according to size and quality. Pink shrimp, brown shrimp and white shrimp are separated into five-pound packages and carted off to the blast freezers from where they are shipped to the United States on freezer ships.

Shrimp are perhaps the most valuable product of the mangrove ecology. In the sweltering heat, the juvenile shrimp grow rapidly, far up in the protective swamps, among the tangle of roots and bushes. They achieve maturity in a few months, and grow so quickly that many industries are starting shrimp farms in Central America. Crabs are also plentiful.

Mangroves fascinate me. Whenever I travel to the tropics, I am always eager to get in and explore them. Mangroves are like marshes: you have to understand them and their value before you can appreciate them. They are a complex ecotone where two distinct habitats overlap. The mangroves harbor terrestrial animals, semiterrestrial animals and true marine animals. High above the roots, myriads of insects swarm in the leaves, and spiders crawl about the stems. At high tide, marine animals, including shrimp, crabs and fish of all sorts, move in to forage among the roots. The remaining creatures that crawl into the branches when the swamps are flooded later creep along the roots and over the mud, from one bush to the next, when the tide is out. These belong to the "twilight zone" of the semiterrestrial habitat.

Mangroves, like tidal salt marshes, are nutrient storehouses, slowly but continuously growing, shedding old leaves and growing new ones. The dead leaves pile up at the base of the roots and the anerobic bacteria act upon them, producing vitamins and releasing nutrients into the stagnating waters. The decaying vegetation then breaks down rapidly in the hot, sweltering tropical heat.

The endless network of aerial stilt roots acts as a filter and holds much of the decaying vegetation inside the swamp. This permits the organic materials to break down slowly, leaf by leaf and particle by particle, continuously and eternally increasing the productivity of the estuaries. Silt and mud and soils washing down from the mountains are trapped in the root systems, and land slowly builds up from the muck and vegetation.

Then a tropical storm comes, as they periodically do, and waves surge into the swamps and the compost of leaves. Sticks and decaying seeds are stirred up and washed out to sea. The muddy brown waters carry the nutrients fertilizing the phytoplankton and creating food for tiny zooplankton which form the basis of the food chain. Even miles away in high-salinity waters luxurious coral reefs derive much of their nourishment from the soupy sediments of the mangroves.

As ecologically important as mangrove swamps are, no one likes them. John Steinbeck and Edward Ricketts wrote about mangroves in the *Sea of Cortez:*

> We suppose it is the combination of foul odor and the impenetrable quality of the mangrove roots which gives one a feeling of dislike for these salt-water eating bushes. We sat quietly and watched the moving life in the forests of the roots, and it seemed to us that there was stealthy murder everywhere. On the surf-swept rocks it was fierce and hungry and joyous killing, committed with energy and ferocity. But here it was like stalking, quiet murder. The roots gave off clicking sounds, and the odor was disgusting. We felt that we were watching something horrible. No one likes the mangroves. Raul [one of the ship's crew] said that in La Paz [California] no one loved them at all.

My first real experience with mangrove swamps came when I was working on the International Indian Ocean Expedition in Nossi-Be, Madagascar. Systematically and completely I sampled each ecological habitat over the island. I dug creatures on mud and sand flats, I climbed over rocky cliffs and pulled anemones off boulders and captured octopuses. I dived in the coral reefs, but I left the mangrove swamps for last.

They were frightening. We traveled around them by boat and they seemed dark and mysterious. We pulled a shrimp net from the French research cruiser, *Ambariak*. The net came up gorged with shrimp, more than I had ever seen at the time. The catch was densely tangled with piles of oozing mud, leaves, stems and seeds of mangroves that bordered the shoreline. At the time I did not associate such productivity of the sea, the thousands of pounds of fish, shrimp and crabs, with the mangroves, but I know now that the area was rich because of vegetation and the brown muddy waters that were washed forever out to sea.

We had to travel far from shore and anchor at night, or untold millions of flies would descend from the swamps and stab us viciously. Being young at the time, and lacking knowledge of the tremendous importance of mangroves, had someone cut them all down I wouldn't have minded in the least.

Inside the swamps I found it unbearable, the air was stifling from rotting vegetation and no breeze, and the ground gave way underfoot. I frequently sank into the mire. Holding onto the aerial roots, I would pull myself up and move rapidly forward, keeping a wary eye out for God knows what. There were no snakes on the island, and only a few crocodiles, but then again, it doesn't take many crocodiles to eat you.

I couldn't hear myself think because of the screaming swarms of mosquitoes that revolved about my body. When I slapped at them, I killed 10 at one time. On more than one occasion I was tempted to say, "The hell with it, let some other fool go in and get eaten alive — the Smithsonian Institution will live without my mangrove swamp collections."

Had there been nothing there, I would have left shortly. But from the onset, I couldn't help but be fascinated by the strange diversity of life. Large hissing green chameleons that resembled dragons slipped awkwardly and slowly along the branches, and great red-and-black mangrove crabs scraped along the roots, rattling the bushes as they moved. Now and then the branches would rustle, and some animal or other foraging through would be disturbed and run for cover. They were always too far away for me to tell what they were.

The trees were alive with terrestrial hermit crabs, and land snails that laid little round jelly-coated eggs. Roachlike isopods slipped along the bark. Fish swam in the trapped, stagnating tide pools and muddy depressions, and we seined them out and added them to our collections. We scooped mud, and sifted out tiny crustaceans and worms that lived deep in the swamps. No one had ever taken such collections from Nossi-Be; we were the first, and it needed to be done.

We collected everything. Small green lizards crawled along the branches and we succeeded in capturing a few, and found they laid fine-shelled blue eggs on the twigs and leaves. Spiders, some brightly colored, others brown and ugly, were everywhere, spinning webs that caught in our face and hair. Occasionally small brown snakes slithered over the mud, giving me quite a start, but fortunately none was poisonous in Madagascar. However, other mangrove swamps along Africa and Central America are often full of deadly snakes.

Large shaggy oysters grew on the stilt roots along with purple-striped barnacles. The peculiar mud skipper fish (*Periothalamus*) that has popping brown eyes, no scales and a tapered tail, scuttled over the surface of the water and crawled out on the roots of the mangroves. It can live out of water for long periods of time. Large, bizzare fiddler crabs with gorgeous colors ducked into their holes among the aerial roots, which made grabbing them most difficult.

We collected drab green sea anemones clinging to the roots, brown nondescript flatworms, and lots of greenish pulmonate slugs that lived in the bushes. The air had a sweet, sickening smell from the flowering mangroves that mingled with the decaying leaves amid the roots. In places it was so thick it was hard to breathe. Nevertheless, the mangrove bushes were filled with animals. Frequent sounds of movement from birds and small mammals, breaking twigs and rattling branches, gave me an eerie and uncomfortable feeling. My ears rang with the continuous humming of mosquitoes that carpeted our arms and legs.

Aside from being an unpleasant place to collect in, mangrove swamps are perhaps the most dangerous of all collecting areas. For one thing they wind on and on, and in the dense forest of vegetation and stinking tidal mud, it is difficult to get any bearing or direction, and in a large swamp area very easy to get lost. So it is important to have a number of people on a mangrove swamp expedition.

Furthermore, certain areas have bogs of quicksand and six feet of soupy mud where a collector racing after a grapsid crab can sink out of sight and drown. Since all the bad points of this habitat are well known, it is not surprising that much of the fauna from the world's mangrove formations is still unknown.

For yet another reason mangrove swamps are an important habitat of all tropical coasts. Their development and growth is part of a gradual land-building process. If the swamps are approached in the dry winter seasons when the mosquitoes aren't too thick, then a collector can make a systematic investigation of the fauna and gather a representation of marine, terrestrial and, in certain areas, fresh-water life.

Ripping away rotten stumps of old trees, one finds burrowing shrimp (*Callianassa*) and shipworms lining the wood with tubes. Blennies and mud eels are common. But catching the fast-moving mangrove crabs is always a challenge and since they can move rapidly through vegetation, there is no way of sneaking up on one. We have found that scooping up a handful of mud and flinging it at the crab works well if you score a direct hit. The crab falls down, stunned but not damaged, and you have time to pounce on it. But many species can pinch viciously, typical of the hostile mangrove environment, so either wear gloves or use a net. And there is one crab, the coconut crab, that also frequents tropical Indo-Pacific mangroves and is capable of slashing off a finger.

The ditches and canals that run through the swamps are filled with fish. *Fundulus* minnows and small trout, catfish and many other brackish forms can be easily taken out by seining.

We have noticed in the Florida Keys that the magnificent *Condylactus* anemones in their exotic pastel greens, pinks and lavenders prefer to live around mangrove roots; and in certain areas of the Keys, particularly on remote islands, we find dozens of them clustering around the aerial stilts in a foot or less of water. Yet collectors consider them rare and seek them in the coral reefs where they sporadically occur.

But the mangrove provides protection for the anemone and, since it is visited by many larval fish seeking food and protection in the shallows, the anemones do very well eating the small fry.

Birds also make their homes in mangrove swamps, feasting upon the marine life and insects. Ospreys that also dwell in marshes build their nests in the small, low-lying mangroves. Pelicans nest in the bushes as well as egrets and herons.

Of all the peculiar creatures that live in dark, mosquito-ridden saline swamps, the giant tropical land crab (*Cardiosoma*) is one of the most eye-catching. Time and again this monstrous crab, which may span two feet from the tip of one outstretched claw to the other, has been used in fourth-rate Hollywood productions of man-eating crabs from outer space. These crabs make deep, complex burrows at the base of mangrove roots on the landmost side of the swamps and come out to munch on vegetation during the night. The local people eat them; they take them home and feed them corn to "sweeten" them, and then boil them. During their mass mating migrations, they leave their burrows and march like a herd of fiddler crabs. They swarm over banana plantations in Central America and soon devastate the area.

Land crabs live all over the Florida Keys, from Miami to Key West. They emerge at night and often get squashed on the highways by the thousands of roaring automobiles. Even though they are abundant, they are much more reticent and harder to find than specimens of *Cardisoma* found on sparsely inhabited islands in the Caribbean.

Whether their numbers can withstand the pressure of development, the millions of automobiles and the increasing population in the Florida Keys remains to be seen. The future of the Florida mangrove swamps is gloomy. At the time of this writing, draglines are ripping up subtidal limestone rocks and piling them on top of mangroves. Bulldozers plow the ancient red mangrove trees down and grind them under their tracks as new highways are being built and bridge causeways erected. Dredges are cutting navigation channels, and waters are white with siltation from crushed limestone. The seashore naturalist can't help wondering whether it will ever end.

6.
The Mudflat Habitat

Soft, oozy mud is not one of the richest places to find creatures, but it has a distinctive fauna of its own. The mudflat is home to soft-bodied, filter-feeding organisms that require little oxygen to sustain them. They sweep the water with branched tentacles, and can hold oxygen in a respiration system for long periods of time. While mudflats are sparse in general, the organisms there are singularly hardy because of their ability to go for long periods in almost oxygenless mud.

Unlike sand grains that have interstices where oxygenated water can circulate, mud tends to be anoxic. However, soft boggy mud can support life because it is generally full of diatoms and filamentous green algae that constantly produce their own oxygen. It has been shown that if a bell jar is placed over a mudflat, oxygen bubbles very soon become apparent. When bays become silted over and there is very poor tidal flush, oxygen levels in the mud may drop and the mud takes on a putrid odor, but generally it has a rich, earthy smell, indicating a healthy environment.

Polychaete worms and bivalves are the dominant members of the mudflat community, although mud shrimp, (Callianassa and Upogebia affinis) also make their burrows in the intertidal zone. Occasionally you can bring them to the surface by teasing them with a piece of grass. When a mud shrimp becomes irritated, it rises to the top, but quickly retreats down into its burrow when it realizes it has been lured out. Sometimes you can cut their retreat off with a shovel, and capture them. But digging them out is no easy matter because they appear to go down to the center of the earth.

Blue crabs roam the mudflats, looking for small worms and young fish to feed upon. The mud along the edge of the water is alive with both grass shrimp and penaeid shrimp that flee the marshes on a falling tide and dig their way into the boggy substrate to hide, or scratch the smooth surface up to rake out the tiny plant cells, diatoms. As the tide falls further they move into deeper water.

Many invertebrates require larger particles of substrate to settle in their larval stages, and they either die or move on in the soft, shifting morass. But by the same token annelids and clams in their larval stages must seek out the mud and settle to begin their growth process. Consequently mudflats are generally home to large numbers of polychaetes like *Nereis*.

On the North Atlantic coast professional worm collectors make their living gathering *Nereis virens* for the booming bait industry. They walk the mud on low tides, stepping through the soft substrate while turning over clods of mud with a heavy-duty clam rake. The clam rake exposes soft vermiform bodies without severing them the way a shovel does. Biological collectors also use clam rakes and turn up sipunculids, acorn worms, and other polychaetes. The clam rake is even good for getting nemerteans (*Cerebratulus lacteus*) without fragmenting them.

Walking on certain mudflats is virtually impossible. You can be walking on more or less firm ground, then one additional step and you are down to your waist. There are certain areas that can be dangerous: the mouth of a creek where the mud is boggy, soft and deep for six feet, and if you step into that you can go down and out of sight. Quicksand also occurs in marine habitats; if you ever feel yourself sinking, drop your buckets, lie flat in the mire and swim out slowly, until you crawl up onto drier ground like some prehistoric reptile crawling out of the mud. Mud collectors soon develop the knack of twisting the heel sideways at each step, breaking the suction in the soft mud. A boot that grips the heel well is a great help; others will be suctioned off your foot.

Most of the soft-bodied invertebrates that dwell in the mud depend on the soft ooze for protection. The acorn worms, polychaetes and nemerteans seem to be even more fragile in soft boggy mud than other places, possibly because the mud is seldom disturbed by wave action.

Mud bogs, which abound in shallow bays, river mouths, sloughs, marshes and mangrove swamps, see little current, so the mud settles, the tide seeps in and goes out. The animals are never really exposed to drying conditions, they just sink down a little deeper.

While macrofauna may be relatively scarce on mudflats compared to other habitats, the microfauna is particularly rich. Screening out the small, mud-dwelling organisms like amphipods, minute white threadlike nematodes, polychaete worms, tiny clams and snails is rewarding but often impossible because of the thick, caking mud that cannot go through a screen.

In such cases I have found it most useful to use a small gasoline-powered water pump that shoots a jet of water into the screen, washing it through the small meshes leaving the animals behind. Of course this must be done from a skiff, bringing the mud up in a bucket dredge, Peterson dredge or just a plain scooper. Numerous buckets of water sloshed into the screen cage will serve the same purpose as a pump.

Another good way to get organisms out of the mud, particularly small organisms, is to put the mud into shallow dishes and let it sit. Like other substrates including rock and coral, the animals will soon become asphixiated from lack of oxygen in the still water and crawl up on the sides of the dish or tray where they are easy to pick out. There are many creatures to find in the world of the minute, and one of these groups is the mysterious phylum Kinorhyncha which is comprised of tiny creatures measuring three or more millimeters.

Among the denizens of the mud, you find fragile, colorless brittlestars that have tiny central discs and long snakelike arms. The amphipods, isopods and mysids appear to be white or colorless, possibly because color isn't much needed in the dark, soft mud where light seldom penetrates. Since there is no real place of attachment, many species are missing from the mudflats. Skin-breathing sea urchins, sand dollars and starfish are absent. Only one or two sponges can survive in the mud, and perhaps the brackish-water hydroid *Clytia* might grow on a log that protudes from the mud, along with clusters of oysters.

However, when sand begins to mix with mud on certain portions of the flats, the sandy shore animals invade and take root. In many instances it is difficult to draw the line between sand flat, sea grass and mudflat habitats by looking at the animals because there is so much overlap. You find numerous gastropods and clams traversing both habitats, or you may find *Cerianthus* anemones growing happily in sand, soft mud, grass growing over mud and grass beds in shelly, sandy bottoms. *Leptosynapta* sea cucumbers may be abundant (10 specimens to the shovelful) in a flat of boggy, fine-particle mud, but will also be common in sandy mudflats, although they will be scarcer in hard-packed sand (one per shovelful).

There is no real established tidal zonation on a mudflat either. The further the tide recedes the more likely you are to find a greater variety of fauna, but since the animals are less dependent upon good tidal flush, good oxygen conditions and continuous submersion, you are as apt to find an abundance of creatures close to shore as far from shore. On extreme low tides you might find sipunculids in the mud, or grass-flat sponges — animals that cannot take desiccation or exposure for any length of time.

Mudflats areas are best explored from a boat, using a dredge at high tide or a coring tool. If the mud is particularly boggy a dredge will bite, become "muddied" and bogged down and be almost impossible to lift. The same dredge will pass over hard bottom with ease. While running over a bay and dropping a bucket dredge at various places, you will come up with mud on some hauls and sand or sandy mud or muddy shell on other bottoms. All that may be required to change substrates completely is two or three minutes of speeding along in a motor boat, then dropping down the dredge.

Otter trawls are useful in mudflats because the otter doors slide easily over the surface of the muddy bottom. Here you get numbers of sea pansies, sometimes lugworms, and of course shrimp, which prefer the muddy bottoms over hard-packed sand. *Squilla* (the mantis shrimp) are also denizens of the muddy bottoms and live in depths of 10 feet and more, although we have found a few burrows in the intertidal range. Menhaden are mud-lovers and feed greedily upon the diatoms and algae that live in the mud. They follow the dredge or otter boards, benefiting from the material that is stirred up on the bottom.

The advantage of having a small boat, particularly a flat-bottomed skiff that can get up into the shallows and be paddled over a foot or less of water, is tremendous compared to the amount of energy expended when trudging over a mile of boggy mud by foot, where each step becomes a chore and a torture.

Mud is interesting and we have learned to keep it and its denizens in our aquariums for study. We found that without a muddy substrate *Mya* clams autotomize their siphons; *Ensis*, the razor clams, gape their valves and after a couple of days without supporting mud will die. It seems that they require the pressure of external sand pressing against their shell to keep them closed. The adductor muscles of the shell work to force the valves closed. Unassisted they strain to hold the shell together, and eventually they weaken, relax, and the shells open and gape, leaving them exposed to predators. In a sense it's almost like a starfish holding onto an oyster, prying it apart; the oyster's muscles work to keep the valves together, however, the muscles weaken, the valves open and the starfish slides in and devours the oyster. Even if there are no predators, a clam with weak adductor muscles will die if there is no pressure of mud against the shell.

We have now developed an excellent way of keeping mudflat animals alive. A simple subgravel filter is installed in an aquarium, then a nylon stocking is cut up and fitted over the slots. Mud fresh from the bottom of the bay taken in a bucket dredge or dug on the end of a mudflat is spaded up and placed over the nylon stocking. The mud should be placed about three inches deep, although we have had it a full ten inches deep with much success.

Soon the filtering action clears the water, and life in the mud begins to adjust to its new habitat. With an absence of predators, we have succeeded in getting polychaete worms to breed, and we have had numerous mysids, copepods, nematodes and larval clams develop in the tanks. The ubiquitous polychaete, *Capitella capitata* that occurs in polluted habitats also blooms, because there are no predators to destroy it.

The mud tank can be a great place to breed live organisms to feed to sea horses and other finicky eaters that require live food. But it can also be a place of fascination. Minute creatures dance and wiggle and thrash about in the mud when you look at them under a dissecting scope. Once you've seen some marsh mud under a dissecting scope and seen how alive and rich it is, you'll never again be able to look at a dragline dredging the muck up and piling it up on the high land and smothering the marshes. It will make you sick because you'll know murder is being committed.

And when you sneak up on a school of juvenile croakers and killifish in the creekbed of a marsh nibbling at the mud, you'll know what they are eating. And when you see clapper rails meandering over a tidal mudflat, their heads bobbing up and down, you'll know what they are feeding upon. If you look at the mud with a high-powered scope you'll see thousands of diatoms, some of them reddish brown, others brilliant green, all very attractive. And amid the plant cells you might even see a struggling, kicking larval copepod, and then you'll know what a treasure is in this scoop of mud.

7.
The Oyster Reef Habitat

Oyster reefs are common along the poorly defined shoreline of the Atlantic and Gulf coasts. They grow near nourishing *Spartina* marshes, erect from sea grass and boggy mud. The greatest oyster bars are found near rivers or streams fed constantly by running fresh water. They lead a precarious existence because they cannot tolerate oceanic, high-salinity conditions, nor highly brackish water.

The oyster is at a disadvantage because it is so popular. The animals found in association with oysters are, for the most part, associating with them in the very same manner as the Walrus and the Carpenter in *Through the Looking Glass*. On the Atlantic coast if you wish to collect a number of starfish, just go to the oyster bar and you'll find them there feeding on the hapless oyster. So from the collector's standpoint, oysters are a habitat unto themselves, just the way a cluster of hydroids will become a habitat to a horde of hungry nudibranchs that nibble away at their polyps. If you want nudibranchs, you go to the hydroids. By the same token, if you want *Melongena corona*, the crown conch, you also go to the oyster bar where you'll find them feeding on both oysters and other animal predators that are eating oysters. If you find a big oyster bar, and it's legal season, you'll also find a habitat for oyster fishermen who are tearing up far more oysters than all the other predators put together for hundreds of miles around.

In searching for these natural predators, you'll find that oyster reef collecting is one of the roughest collecting areas. Walking on them is similar to walking on a great pile of broken glass and rocks. Heavy boots or strong leather shoes are an absolute must here; there's none of the freedom of barefooted beachcombing. But equally bad, if you're approaching the bar in an outboard-powered skiff, you'll find you can crack up a propeller faster that way than any other. When you hear that horrible sickening sound of the propellers against an immovable object and your motor roars, you will know you cannot go any farther.

Generally the oyster bars are covered by a fine layer of mud, frequently the oysters are overgown with a filamentous green algae of the genus *Cladophora*, and the animals that live among the oysters blend perfectly into the habitat. Unless you look carefully you're likely to overlook the crown conchs, the clams, and the mussels that dwell among the clumps of oysters.

The oysters become a holdfast for many organisms; hydroids, bryozoans, even sponges tend to encrust on them. In such a habitat one might find small sea anemones among barnacles. *Brachidontes*, the oyster mussel, spins byssus threads between the individual oysters, knitting itself into the colony. This cloister of growing colonial animals makes a home for errant polychaetes, flatworms in some places, hundreds of *Petrolisthes armatus*, anomuran crabs with flattened claws that dash to the underside of the oyster mass when you pick them up.

Numerous conditions determine what grows on an oyster reef. If an oyster reef is in high-saline conditions it is likely to be infested with crown conchs, oyster drills, flatworms and starfish. If it is seldom or never exposed, it is likely to have heavier growths of fouling organisms than a reef that goes dry on every low tide, much the same way a tidal flat has its own tidal horizons.

Oysters are commercially harvested by tonging. A pair of tongs, which you could describe as two rakes pushing together with a scissors movement, rips up oysters in from three to six feet of water and deposits them on the deck. It takes a powerful man to pull up any quantity of them. A collector going through an oyster catch on a boat can, in a short time, gather a multitude of creatures.

Turning over the clumps, you can find *Pinnotheres ostreum* crabs which are more or less commensal with oysters, the pistol shrimp, and many small nereid polychaetes. Minute *Odostomia* gastropods, which are parasitic, cling to the outer shell of the oyster. Breaking the clumps apart with a geology hammer, botany pick or crowbar, even more of the scuttling little bugs are exposed. Small fish such as blennies, gobies, clingfish and young toadfish find refuge among the oyster clusters.

Use heavy leather gloves if you can because if you work with your bare hands, getting cut and slashed is almost unavoidable. Of course few people use gloves, and at the end of the day of picking creatures out, you can feel rewarded if you have sustained only a few lacerations. The real damage comes when you pick up the oysters, or try breaking them apart by hammering them against the boat. The same oysters that can cut right through a canvas shoe if you step too heavily, can do an equally nasty job of cutting open a finger.

In a sense the oyster reef habitat is no different from other habitats as far as particular populations of animals being more or less dominant. On one particular reef in Apalachicola Bay the fishermen pull up substantial numbers of thick-shelled southern quahog clams (*Mercenaria campechiensis*), and to the collector who must have a number of them for a particular reason, they may be more easily found there than on a sand flat.

On some oyster bars clumps of oysters will be overgrown with the oyster mussel (*Brachiodontes exustus*), and these mussels can even be a pest because they double the chore of culling the commercial oyster catch, to remove the smaller, illegal-sized individuals and return them to the sea.

Oyster fishermen sample an oyster fauna that is generally not available to the collector. Using their heavy tongs they tear up the bottom at depths ranging from four to seven feet. Since the use of an oyster dredge is forbidden in most states, it is the only way to see what sort of specimens you are apt to find among an oyster colony at that depth. *Gobiesox*, the brown skillet fish that clings to shell or rock with its abdominal sucker, is quite common in the deeper oyster bars.

But you will find a handsome variety of oysters growing on intertidal bars and will have a chance to observe the interaction of the predators and commensals. The twisting deep burrows made by the stone crab (*Menippe mercenaria*) look different from the U-shaped burrow made by the toadfish. The toadfish must have water in its burrow at all times. Consequently his burrow is further down on the oyster bar.

Immediately adjacent to the oyster bar in the soupy, oozing mud I have been able to find large populations of annelids that are not encountered elsewhere. The large fat lugworm (*Arenicola cristata*) that tunnels beneath the surface spewing out mud is among them. Often as many as five or six individuals can be dug up in the immediate vicinity of the bar, five or six feet away from it, but if you move off a greater distance you'll not find any.

If you are interested in gathering a number of starfish you can go to oyster beds along the Virginia and Carolina coasts where fishermen gather them with moplike dredges and throw them on the sand to die. They also set poles in the south and let the conchs and whelks crawl up on them, remove them by the sackful and sell them to shell dealers — or leave them in the sun to perish.

One of the prime prerequisites for an oyster reef to be inhabited by predators is relatively high-salinity waters. If there is a drought and the flow of fresh waters into the estuaries is reduced, the bars are often covered with flatworms (*Stylochus zebra*). There used to be big, productive oyster bars on the Ochlockonee River until it was dammed up above Tallahassee and the bars died off.

The position of an oyster on a tidal flat is important. The dwarfed clusters called "coon oysters" grow just below the marshes. They never achieve large size because they are subject to a high-stress environment, being regularly covered and uncovered by all low tides. However, further out on the tidal flat on areas that are seldom exposed except on wind-blown tides, the oysters grow much larger.

We have experimented with growing oysters to a limited degree. The string-culture method used by the Japanese has much promise in Florida waters. Dead oyster shell is strung on wire and hung from racks, and oysters grow vigorously under the right estuarine conditions. They cannot be smothered by the bottom muds since they are suspended in the water. They have more food drifting about the currents and they are free from predators. The bushel yields on such hanging strings are tremendous.

We have also planted rocks, shell, brick, tires and almost any object in the mud to grow oysters and create habitats for specimens. When blennies are needed, or toadfish, or ribbed muscles, we simply go down to our planted mudflat and harvest them.

On an exposed oyster reef you can turn over clumps of oysters with a crowbar, pry down into oyster burrows and rip them open, and you'll find some interesting creatures. In the muddy burrows or the watery depressions beneath the oysters snapping shrimp (*Alpheus*) scuttle out of the mud, and if caught they'll make a loud "pop" with their enlarged claw.

Once in a while, when least expected, you'll turn over a clump of shell and find a large, lovely eolid nudibranch with waving fronds and tentacles. And if you're bent on finding another and turn over many, many shells, you may find a second and a third during a good day's work. Looking down among the oysters in a fouling situation, you can often find small red sea anemone like *Aiptasia*, and even feather-duster worms encrusted in their tubes, along with encrusting white serpulid worms.

If you look at the shells with a magnifing glass at the right times of the year, you may find the minute polyp of embryological stages of the stinging nettle jellyfish (*Chrysaora quinquecirrah*). It is often profitable to take several clumps of oysters, place them in a collecting bucket and let the water stagnate, driving numerous small organisms out of the oyster colonies and onto the sides of the bucket where they can be easily removed.

The Florida Department of Natural Resources watches hawklike over the oysters in the state's waters. They have stringent rules dealing with size limits, and regulations on where oysters can or cannot be harvested. Many areas are closed supposedly due to high coliform bacteria in the waters or because they are near sewage outfalls or areas where septic tanks seep into the estuary. Regrettably, they don't do much to protect the marshes that nourish the oysters.

How are marshes important to oysters? It has been demonstrated by the Bureau of Sports Fisheries in Gulf Breeze, Florida, and several other laboratories that after a tropical storm or hurricane, oyster spat production increases threefold. The reason is simple: the storm waters flood high up into the marsh, the surging waves churn up the decaying vegetation, diatoms and nutrients are flushed rapidly out into the estuaries and provide planktonic life-forms with nourishment.

While the state of Florida isn't doing very much to preserve its marshes which provide the nutrients to oysters and other marine life, it does an excellent job in promoting the use of oysters as a staple seafood item. Oysters are believed to be an aphrodisiac and the state has distributed license plates that say, "Eat Fish — Live longer. Eat Oysters — Love longer." Considering the rapidly growing populations of some of the oyster communities along East Point and Apalachicola, perhaps there is some truth to it. But to test the effectiveness properly would require a series of controlled experiments, carried out, of course, with the most judicious scientific procedure.

There is one advantage to oyster reef collecting that no other habitat offers. You can become hungry beachcombing, and if you haven't brought your lunch along, you stay hungry. But on an oyster reef all you need is your knife and you can pry open all that you can eat. But if one member of your collecting party includes a bottle of hot sauce and crackers in his bucket, gloves and an oyster knife, you'd better see if his motives aren't more gastronomic than scientific.

8.
Wharf Pilings

Although it is seldom realized, docks, wharf pilings and piers are often primary sources of marine invertebrates and certain fish. Any salt-water angler knows that if you fish with a fiddler crab off a wharf in mid-winter, you are likely to land yourself a large sheepshead.

Sheepshead (*Archosargus probatocephalus*) is one of the many fish that nose around the luxurious growths of algae, barnacles, hydroids, sponges, bryozoans and tunicates on the submerged portions of the pilings, taking their pick of xanthid crabs, young oysters, barnacles, minute snapping shrimp and probably a host of other creatures that dwell in the midst of the forests of colonial animals.

The wharf piling has a peculiar tidal zonation of its own. Naturally, when a pier extends from the dry upper beach down into the water, there will be various stages of colonization on each post as it extends further down into the sea, until you reach the very end of the pier where a great variety of subtidal creatures can grow in profusion.

But this luxurious growth, this goldmine to the collector, is a plague to the owner of the pier. First come the settling larvae of the barnacles, the growth of the hydroids and mussels or oysters, and then come the terrible shipworms. Actually shipworms are not "worms" as such, but belong to either of two phyla, Mollusks or Arthropods. Boring mollusks such as *Teredo* and *Bankia* have elongated bodies and very much resemble worms, and then there are the small buglike

71

isopods (*Limnoria rensiforms*). And if you ever turn over an untreated boat that has been in the water for six months or so and examine all the tiny pinholes in it and listen to the crunching, grinding sound of the little monsters eating away, then you know you've found a good source of *Limnoria*. This is not a comforting feeling, particularly if you own the boat, because there is a good chance that the entire bottom will have to be torn out and replaced.

Naturally a considerable industry of protective coatings and antifoulant agents has sprung up in recent years, and a great amount of study into the anatomy, physiology and behavior of boring organisms is under way by private investigators as well as the Office of Naval Research. Wooden test panels are set out in various locations and the number and variety of boring organisms and their rate of settlement is routinely checked.

Test panels are quite a saving in time and labor if you particularly want shipworms. Chopping away at logs and heavy chunks of wood is not only energy-consuming, but has a greater danger of bringing your hatchet or saw-blade squarely down on the beast you are seeking.

In proportion to the numerous creatures that will grow on wharves, the boring organisms are in the minority, as a rule. However, most of the arboreal attaching forms are found growing on rocks or sea grass so it is the wood borers that are the unique forms, and wharves, plaques and any particular wood, including eroded tree stumps, are habitats for these boring forms.

Wharf pilings are a blessing to a collector on a coast where rocks are few and far between, such as the Gulf coast. They permit access to multitudes of tunicate clusters, bryozoans, hydroids and numerous forms that would otherwise be obtainable only by dredging. There is an old dock in Panacea which I use as a source for hydroids by pulling up old steel cable that has been dumped by shrimp trawlers. During the winter these are overgrown with *Bougainvillia carolinensis*, and in the summer, *Bougainvillia* dies down only to be replaced with *Pennaria tiarella*. There is another floating dock in Alligator Harbor which becomes infested with bryozoans, and is therefore my source for *Bugula neritina*. And when there is need of this lacy, tufted mosslike creature, I have only to walk out on the dock and pick them off.

I know of no other location where the growth rate of marine organisms can be so carefully studied and measured. If you keep accurate records and watch a dock week after week, you can easily study the colonization of arboreal forms. If gorgonians happen to settle, you can watch them mature and measure them without disturbing them; the same is true for hydroids and even sea squirts. On this same floating dock I have found substantial numbers of the small sea cucumber (*Thyonella pervicax*) growing in among *Styela plicata* tunicates, and on several occasions, upon tearing the tunicates apart I have found dozens of pink flatworms (*Prostheceraeus floridanus*). These tunicates can also be counted on to produce substantial quantities of *Petrolisthes*, the flattened anomuran crab. On occasion they yield pistol shrimp and other small reddish shrimp.

On the dark underside of the dock you will find a greater abundance of bryozoans, gorgonians and encrusting tunicates like *Didemnum candidum, Botryllus* and *Distaplia bermudensis*, although there will be fewer barnacles than on the light side. All these observations are easily made because the dock is accessible; it is easy to walk out, squat down and look at the same place day after day. Consider the difficulty you'd have if you were trying to make an ecological study of a sandy shore. A particular area must be carefully staked off, poles must be driven deep into the ground. How can you be sure how much the creatures have moved from one tide to the next? If something disappears from the habitat, or grows on it, you have no idea when it came and you have no way of knowing exactly when it leaves. The same is true for studying the rocky shore; unless a rock is very well staked off and marked, you may never find it again. And these areas usually are not easy to explore; you can't just walk down to the best location when you feel like it, and study the lacy designs of bryozoans, explore the encrusted mats of tunicates with a hand lens, and even sit there with a book to key out the organisms.

If you are barnacle-collecting, you can look down and select the biggest barnacles that you may wish to use for display purposes. Barnacles usually are on the uppermost region of the piling, then come oysters or mussels. The rich fauna is subtidal, almost never exposed except for the lowest of low tides and generally is too deep for wading. Consequently scuba- or free-diving is required to collect a good representation of this habitat.

As you dive you can immediately see numerous blennies and small gobies that cluster around the clumps of oysters on the pilings, and these dart and dive into the protective colonies, and hide among the hydroids, tunicate clusters and so on. Chasing them down with a net more often than not proves fruitless because they have very good eyes and are excellent at avoiding the net. A slurp-gun has proved useful, but less expensive and sometimes even more efficient is a plastic bag.

The same plastic bag that catches flatworms and octopuses can once again be put into action. It is clear, can be molded over the piling and, gradually working your fingers around the fouling assemblages, you can chase the fish out into the opening of the plastic prison and then squeeze the edges together. And it is little trouble to get a good collection of fish in one afternoon.

Diving around the base of piers, docks and other pilings should be done cautiously, and on calm days when there is little or no wave action, because it is very easy to get caught in a current or swept head first into a post and knocked senseless. The buddy system in diving should be used here to prevent drowning.

When the water is clear and calm, few experiences can be as rewarding as diving around a well-fouled dock. Swimming slowly, almost the way a sea hare glides through the surf, you lie flat watching the creatures below. Great waving clusters of brown hydroids tinged with pink polyps float gently with the lapping waves. Compound ascidians, looking like slabs of meat in a glistening array of colors ranging from warm pinks to dull grays and greens, clump around the bottom of the piling, and multitudes of barnacles do their jack-in-the-box dance from their white shells.

Of course, if you are collecting any quantity of these animals you will want to wear gloves to prevent the nasty cuts that oysters and barnacles give. These cuts are very slow in healing, another reason why diving should be restricted to calm days. It is easy to get washed into a clump of sharp barnacles.

However, collecting fouling assemblages can often turn into a living hell, especially if the clusters of hydroids are *Pennaria tiarella*, which discharge clouds of nematocysts into the water when you start to disturb them. Or even if you brush by them as you swim past, then thousands upon thousands of potent stinging cells find their way to your face, arms, chest, and so on. A wet suit helps, but if there is any exposed skin, the little fiery welts appear, and those coming from hydroids are every bit as bad as those from the larger jellyfish; and in many instances, when temperature and salinity are just right, even worse.

Hydroids are essential animals in most zoological collections, not only because they represent the simplest order of coelenterates, but

Eolid nudibranch

because they themselves are a habitat in which numerous other creatures feed, live and hide. Whether the genus is *Pennaria*, which is painful to collect and handle, or *Obelia* or *Bougainvillia*, which is handled without painful consequence, the results are all the same if the catch is placed in buckets of sea water and allowed to stagnate slightly. After a while a host of tiny dragonlike eolid nudibranchs will come floating to the surface and suspend themselves upside down. The surface film can be removed and the nudibranchs isolated. Uncountable quantities of caprellid amphipods (skeleton shrimp) bend back and forth like tiny wires, and seemingly millions of tiny copepods, amphipods and other creatures swim around in mad profusion.

If you look closely at a freshly collected quantity in a jar of water, you are not likely to see nearly as many creatures as in the stagnated water.

You might not dream that there are lots of crawling multilegged polychaetes in the hydroids, or terebellids under a clump of tunicates;

nor that flatworms abide there, and sometimes nemerteans. You can get good pistol shrimp, and in some places even find joint-legged sea spiders (pycnogonids) among the rubble.

But even though the hydroids produce many, many creatures, they themselves are still of major interest. At certain times of the year they produce reproductive medusae and release them into the water, and on a clear day if you sit on a dock and look down, the water appears studded with the minute jewel-like jellies that are for the most part, less than one-sixteenth of an inch across. And with a fine-meshed dip net you can scoop them up, invert your net into a bucket of water, and so collect many of them. But the time for their release must be just right.

The end of the pier is a great place for watching hydroids mature over a period of time. And it is a good place to sit with a dip net and catch medusa jellyfish as they swim by, and to dip up ctenophores; but that is no longer a wharf piling habitat but the open sea and its pelagic habitat, which we shall discuss in a later chapter.

9.
The Coral Reef Habitat

Coral reefs and coral outcrops are found in tropical waters throughout the world. And the collector who takes a plane trip or cruise to the Bahamas, Florida Keys or any of the Caribbean Islands will find himself richly rewarded, especially if he is accustomed to the sparse fauna and flora of the northern latitudes.

No natural history student's education is complete until he has seen the coral reefs, the millions of colorful fish and all the other bizarre and interesting little animals that dwell on and around this living habitat of coral polyps, milliporeans and sea fans and pens. So vast is the abundance of life that you wonder where to start collecting, and the answer depends entirely on how much time you have and what specifically you want to accomplish.

Except for unpleasant coral cuts and stings that are painful and slow in healing, the coral reef is a delightful habitat. Sea-water temperatures range from 68°F to 86°F and the water is generally crystal-clear—both conditions being necessary for growth of the madreporeans, alcyonarians and gorgonians that constitute a coral community. Using simple free-diving gear consisting of a mask, fins and snorkel or elaborate Scuba apparatus, you are in a position to explore one of the most colorful gardens in the world.

In the Caribbean and the Indian Ocean, coral structures begin at the end of the intertidal zone and go down 200 feet or deeper. In such clear, exotic habitats Scuba gear permits prolonged collecting, giving the collector ample opportunity to move about in a slow unhurried fashion observing the denizens of the reef.

It becomes apparent that there are two distinct types of fauna, the sessile and the transient. Through your diving mask you will be transfixed at the beautiful lumps of brain coral, branching deer-antler corals, sea whips, sea lillies and sea feathers that spring up from the bottom. These grow with hydrozoan corals, *tibupora*, the red organ-pipe corals—some with bright green polyps others orange and yellow. Some coral structures grow to massive size, over 20 feet high and more than 10 feet in diameter.

Swimming in and out among the coral is part of the transient fauna: clown fish, soapfish, blennies, gobies, orange and green parrot fish munching away at coral polyps and algae and defecating a cloud of sand as they eat. The jewel boxes, black and iridescent blue, dart in and out of the branches of the Acroporean coral. Collecting and selling these bizarre tropical fish have become big business, and divers using a variety of nets, traps and anesthetics, work long and hard to harvest the gorgeous fish that make such handsome and expensive additions to the salt-water aquariums. Fish swim through the reefs in great schools; one can see through his diving mask the angelfish, Moorish idols, surgeonfish, an occasional trunkfish, orange filefish and wrasses. In fact, fish-watching is a fast-growing hobby and many amateurs in the Bahamas are keeping serious and extensive notes on the fish denizens of the reefs.

There is also a multitude of transient invertebrates in the coral habitat. Large hairy brittlestars crawl under the rock and coral heads, coming out only at night, but their snakelike arms often reach out from the crevices in the daytime. The dreaded long, spiny sea urchins, (*Diadema*) erect their long spines out from crevices, pointing them at the intruder in the fashion of antiaircraft guns focused on an invader. Give these animals plenty of room unless you are especially interested in securing these specimens, because they have very sharp and very painful spines that can sting like a wasp.

I have noticed that when you are determined to collect *Diadema*, they tend to withdraw deep into the rocks to get away from you. Certainly they are the most mobile of all sea urchins. Their needly spines readily penetrate thick canvas gloves that lobster fishermen use, so it is necessary to use tongs if they are to be gathered. Their spines readily break off when you are trying to extract them, and this is bad if they are needed for the aquarium or a preserved specimen. If needed for drug screening and testing (they have proved to have a high anticancer activity) then simply smash them with a hammer and remove the corpse for freezing or preserving in alcohol. The broken sea urchins will bring a number of little clown fish out of the rocks to feed on the viscera and gonads. Fish collectors often break up urchins to attract the small fish and bring them out of their hiding places deep in the rocks.

Large brown sea cucumbers are among the transient denizens lying lumpishly on the bottom, as is the fast-moving octopus that slithers out from its lair to grab at a crab. Leaf-shaped, speckled flatworms ooze out from under a rock, so colorful with their speckled oranges and blacks that the untrained eye easily spots them and wonders about them. Nudibranchs of all sizes and colors with fluted skirts and eye-catching hues are found on rocks. Starfish, slate-pencil sea urchins, lima clams, smooth coweries with tapestry-colored fleshy mantles engulfing a polished shell live on the coral. Flamingo tongues, snails and many others creep or swim about this exotic garden of color upon color in the clear blue waters.

Living on the coral itself, or on dead coral or coralline rocks, is an abundance of Alcyonarians, the soft corals with pale colors of yellows, pinks and browns, such as *Sarcophyton*, *Lobophytum* and *Sinularia* as well as treelike gorgonians. Waving sea anemones (*Stoichactis* and *Discosoma*) impressive with their overwhelming mass of flesh and abundance of short, fat tentacles, blossom out from coral structures, along with venus cup sponges, intricate lacy bryozoans and knobby black and red tunicates. Thousands of multicolored prawns, cleaning shrimp and small crabs live in the cracks and crevices of living coral. These move about only slightly, and can be called semitransient. Anemones slide over the stony faces of coral with their pedal discs moving only a few inches in a month, chitons glued to a rock may slowly but surely edge their way over to another rock. Starfish, appearing sessile, creep and inch along over a period of time, some eating coral polyps as they go.

Brilliant nemerteans with green and white candy-cane stripes live down among certain tubiporeans, and only by crushing up the organ-pipe coral to take back as a specimen are you apt to uncover this oddity. But breaking up small quantities of coral or hydrozoans, or milliporeans, is a far cry from what a collector of northern latitudes may be accustomed to when breaking up rocks in search of specimens.

Clouds of fine nematocysts are discharged into the water, and do they ever sting! A good trick is to get up current from the rocks you are crushing so the tiny stinging cells aren't flushed on top of you.

The small lumps or branches of coral are broken up and carried up to your waiting skiff. Although you can dive from the shoreline, generally the process of wading out to the deeper water means that you have to cross numbers of coral outcrops and snags and there is a chance of getting a gash on your foot. The best way to approach a coral habitat is in the manner of a fish, and that is to swim over it or tread water and hover like a surgeonfish picking shrimp out of a crevice.

Providing special care is given to a collection of coral and its small associated animals, chances are it can be kept alive in the aquarium. An important trick is to change the sea water at least five or six times after collection to wash away the discharges of nematocysts of the coral which may kill the other organisms in the bucket.

Buckets of clean sea water should be waiting in the boat when you surface, to be given to someone topside who can take care of the animals. A topside person is a great help to keep an eye out for big sharks as well as to give the specimens special care. They should be kept under canvas to shield them from the tropical sun. If fish are taken they should be either spread out in lots of buckets of shallow water, or given aeration by a battery-powered air pump, or bagged immediately with oxygen-charged sea water.

The collector, or diver in this case, works diligently breaking off coral, putting starfish and conchs into his diving bag and surfacing, unloading and going back down again. A word of caution here: since the faunal and floral communities on the sea floor in this tropical environment are so beautiful, it is easy to overcollect and gather more material than you will be able to store in an aquarium or will have the time or energy to work up as preserved specimens, and that is wasting life.

It is better to choose a few select specimens in this garden of coral and fish and take good care of them. Specialized collecting techniques are required if material is to be gathered in good shape.

Take lobster-collecting. All you ever see of a lobster is its long antennae waving suspiciously out from a lair. If you grab the antennae, the lobster will jackknife backwards and leave you holding only the antennae. However, if you grab the lobster down by the base of its antennae *near* its head, then the lobster is helpless.

Holding *Panulirus argus* by its antennae, you reach your hand in, in back of the lobster's carapace and firmly pull it out. Be sure you wear heavy canvas gloves when collecting lobsters, and be sure there is no moray eel behind the lobster. They frequently inhabit the same hole. Your canvas gloves will not protect you from the razor-sharp teeth of the big eel.

And as mentioned earlier, they will not always protect you from the sharp spines of *Diadema* sea urchins. *Diadema* makes a delightful and responsive aquarium pet, because of its active movements. A good technique of collecting *Diadema* is to create an artificial current by waving your hand vigorously before the animal, causing it to lift up off the bottom and have it float down into your waiting plastic bag. A webbed sack should not be used for this purpose because it is impossible to remove the *Diadema* without breaking its spines.

This waving technique also works well in getting flatworms, nudibranchs and tectibranchs off the bottom without handling them, which may cause damage, or without having to reach into a patch of *Diadema*, thus avoiding painful stings. One parting word on *Diadema*: always make sure you are diving with enough water between you and the spines. In an area of a strong running tide in a shallow inlet, you may find you're suddenly left stranded by the tide high and dry and, if you don't watch it, on top of a patch of *Diadema* urchins. If you do end up with a number of painful spines embedded in your skin, the best treatment I have found is to take the afflicted skin between thumb and forefinger and squeeze, thus crushing the spines up a bit.

Another of the helpful little tricks learned by hard experience is dealing with the giant *Tridacna* clams of the Indian Ocean. These tend to have commensal shrimp and occasionally small fish that dwell inside the mantle cavity. Don't risk reaching your hand in to grab the specimen even though the clam is relatively slow to respond and does not snap shut like a beartrap when you first disturb it. Find a wedge, a piece of wood, a hunk of rock or coral, and shove it into the clam's opening before sticking your hand in. And should your hand get caught, take a knife and cut through the adductor muscle on the underside.

Other real dangers of the reef are bumping into severely stinging sea anemones like *Actinodendron* that can inflict painful wounds to bare skin. Stonefish and lionfish of the Indian Ocean and Indo-Pacific are dangerous, but will not bother you unless you attack them or accidentally get stuck by their venomous spines that can cause agonizing pain and subsequent fever. In that case, it might be added, that the same treatment used on catfish and sting-ray wounds can be successfully employed: submerging the wounded area in very hot water.

Fire corals will also sting, and some people break out into a violent allergic rash. Many of the smaller sea anemones will have this effect when you brush against them, and if continuous work is being done in a coral reef, the collector should wear a wet suit and gloves.

Moray eels will bite, and large sharks often roam the coral heads in search of prey. Some of them have a staunch feeling of propriety and you are another big fish to them intruding on their domain. Give sharks the right of way. If they express an interest in you and won't leave the area, it is wise to get out in a hurry. Most shark attacks are associated with divers carrying strings of speared fish, and if you are spearfishing be on the alert. There are other large fish to be concerned about, large grouper and jewfish have attacked divers, and barracuda roam the reefs. In the Australian waters and along the tropical Pacific coast of Honduras and El Salvador, sea snakes are common and should be given a wide berth or handled with extreme care because they are deadly poisonous.

A good crowbar is an excellent tool for collecting under water because it provides plenty of leverage for prying up a coral head to get at some elusive creature beneath it, and at the same time acts as a buffer between you and some unpleasant creature like a moray eel.

While skin-diving over beds of coral and limestone rock it is impossible to see the complete wealth of life that bores, burrows and encrusts in the stony surfaces, hides down among the polyps or in encrusting algae. Even divers who have spent years in the reefs are often amazed when someone breaks up coral with a geology hammer and exposes all the myriad creatures that live inside.

To find some of the most interesting, but less conspicuous forms, break off several hunks of coral or coralline rock or soft limestone from the bottom and bring them back to the collecting base and place them in a shallow glass or enamel pan with just enough sea water to cover.

After an hour or two you may see this rock come to life and unfold a fascinating world of little creatures. Sabellid and serpulid worms, known as feather-dusters, expand a beautifully floriated crown out from tiny brown tubes bored into the rock. Closer inspection may reveal the expansion of delicate sea anemones that you never suspected were there at all, and minute crustaceans like amphipods, isopods, copepods and ostracods will swim around. Perhaps the introvert of a sipunculid will thrust out, or small fleshy holes may indicate the burrow of an echuroid sausage worm, or the presence of boring clams such as *Lithophaga, Thithodomus* and *Petricola.* Minute snails may be present, and begin crawling off the coralline rocks onto the glass. Occasionally a small chiton may be on the underside of the coral, or perhaps a limpet. If you were looking for these animals while skin-diving, even with the most careful scrutiny, chances are they would have been missed.

Even in a dish of stagnated sea water, many forms will not come out and will stay rooted in the multiple cracks, crevices and tiny crannies. It then becomes necessary to force the animals out of their hiding places.

This can be done in a variety of ways. Perhaps the safest is slowly to diffuse Epsom salts into the water over a period of two or three hours. The Epsom salts, which serve as a narcotic, cause anemones to expand their tentacles, polychaete worms to rise to the tops of their burrows, and copepods and ostracods to begin swimming about in the sea water. Then add a few drops of weak Formalin, about 3 cc-concentrate solution to a liter of water, and this will serve as an irritant to drive the animals out completely. This technique should only be used if they are going to be preserved.

It is interesting to see how many diverse and interesting rock-boring animals there are. And if you make a sampling of the beautiful coral reef fish and examine their stomach contents, you'll see many of these same animals. The vast interdependence of one creature upon the next, and their collective dependence upon a habitat, keeps coming back in all its wonderful complexities and details.

Although there is a temptation to break off a bit of coral and tear up a beautiful sea fan, one should keep in mind that reefs, especially in shallow waters near tourist areas, should be left intact so that other people may enjoy the colorful benthic communities. The coral reefs of the Florida Keys have been used by a number of collecting companies that gather beautiful tropical fish and ship them out to pet stores by the thousands across the nation.

Of all the specimens that are brought in by collectors, at least a third of them die the next day because they were improperly treated and handled in the field. In the holding tanks they are prone to disease that can wipe out the population. What with shipping difficulties with airlines and other transport, a big number die en route. Another percentage die in the pet stores, and it is estimated that only 25 percent of the fish caught make it to the hobbyist's tank.

But this collecting madness goes on. Divers use Quenaldine to stun fish, then herd them into nets or trap them out. Whether or not a reef can be stripped of its fauna remains to be seen; there are arguments both pro and con. But whether Quenaldine has a residual effect on the fish that escape should surely be looked into and investigated thoroughly. Some public aquariums claim that fish treated with Quenaldine tend to die off within two or three months after they are collected; fish, however, caught without drugs, by nets, do infinitely better.

In this era of awareness of our ecological problems, collecting in the Florida Keys and other coral reefs has become a sensitive issue among the uninformed. There are few, if any, documented accounts of collectors or hobbyists having truly stripped an area of marine life to the point where it was unable to recover and the ecological balance of the region was destroyed.

I think that it is time the issues are properly viewed. The unthinking and careless collector can somewhat damage a habitat by breaking coral, digging up wide patches of sea grass or chipping at rocks excessively with a geology hammer. But this damage is minimal and in a short time the area will recuperate, regardless of how many fish collectors and hobbyists converge upon the Keys.

But the utter destruction of the beautiful coral along the Florida Keys by continuous dredging operations, as wider roads are built, trailer parks are erected by filling in mangrove swamps and navigation channels are dug through limestone and coral beds, has caused the turquoise blue waters to become deadly white with siltation, and the sheltered tide flats have become a nightmare of stifling limestone ooze, barren of life.

Robert P. L. Straughan, a noted tropical marine fish collector, has repeatedly warned about the destruction of the coral reef in his magazine, *Salt Water Aquarist.* In the March-April, 1971, issue he wrote,

> Since my last report on the coral reefs of Florida, I made continued diving trips to the middle Keys area. What I found was *utter desolation*! Unbelievable!
> I found hundreds of thousands of *tons* of dead coral. In fact there was far more dead coral than alive, everywhere I went. In some places, the silt (apparently from dredging) was covering the entire reef and it looked like snow. Giant coral heads ten to twenty

feet high were dead, many killed completely through. Those huge boulder type corals of the outer reef with large, overhanging leafs of coral were killed without a single living polyp on the entire head from the very top to where it meets the sea floor. What a shame, what a pity! It infuriates me when I remember how the skindiver and fish collectors were made the scapegoat by a group of local scientists when they were forming Pennekamp Park. The skindiver was depicted as "Stealing" a piece of coral in our local newspaper with what looked like a trumped up photo of a diver holding a piece of coral. But now, where are all those brilliant conservationists so quick to blame the skindiver for despoilation of the reefs? I suspect they have crawled back into their books. Meanwhile, more than a *few* pieces of coral have been damaged. The whole darn reef is being killed!

The very idea of a book such as *The Erotic Ocean*, which tells people how to collect marine organisms, will infuriate a number of professors and biologists who claim they are conservationists. "Why let people go down to the shoreline and turn over rocks and gather specimens?" they ask. "Why denude the fauna and flora of our coastlines?"

I have given these questions considerable thought. Considering that all the professional collectors I know are ardent conservationists who spend much of their time and effort either fighting the power companies, the dredgers, fillers, and polluters, or giving specific knowledge out about what species are being affected and where, I have concluded that there should be many more of these interested and concerned people.

Why are these professors and paper conservationists not screaming with rage and indignation at the draglines destroying the Florida Keys? Why do we not see them at legislative hearings protesting the destruction of marshes, the installation of nuclear power plants, or the major oil spills that pollute a beach perhaps for all time? The professors we do meet at these hearings do not object to collectors. They realize that, if anything, collectors are watchdogs in preserving the habitats that produce the specimens.

I believe that the better way to get people acquainted with the destruction of their marine environment is to get them out on the tide flats and let them start collecting and observing. First you must know what animal and plant communities live in these habitats.

Public involvement in the ocean is essential, be it educational or recreational, whether it is to collect specimens and bring them home for your aquarium, or have your school, club or group of interested individuals compile a reference collection. You can get involved in the ocean in many ways, by taking underwater photographs or tagging game fish or seabirds in participation with such conservation groups as the American Littoral Society, Audubon Society, and Sierra Club or various skin diving clubs. There is strength in numbers.

10.
The Pelagic Habitat

Standing on a dock or a pier, you can gaze far out to sea, where the horizon of sky and water blend into one. The vast ocean, with its seas of minute bits of life called plankton, so thick sometimes that it seems to be a soup of living creatures, is the pelagic habitat, the world of creatures that never come to the bottom of the sea but float about in an interminable fashion, the jellyfish that float and pulsate, the millions of tiny crustaceans, the slender, darting, clear arrow worms and thousands upon thousands of other creatures.

Like many other phases of collecting and oceanography, you can go at it big, get a huge research cruiser and drift about at sea taking samples hundreds or thousands of miles from the sight of land, or you can stand on the end of your dock where just a tiny bit of the ocean comes by, and take what life you can from it.

One morning the waters around the dock will be littered with ctenophores (*Mnemiopsis macrydi*) twirling and spinning, flashing iridescence. Another day pulsating pink *Chrysaora* may be there, or the clear bell-shaped hydromedusae, *Nemopsis bachei*, are in order. But there will be hundreds of minnows, small isopods and mysids that dart about the surface and countless other creatures.

Working from a pier or dock you have one advantage that no ocean research cruiser will ever give you. You stay in a fixed locality, never varying or changing position. Because of this you can watch the drifting pelagic life that comes by and make note of the seasons.

Weather and wind have a great deal to do with the movements and migrations of jellyfish. On a clear day after there has been an offshore wind, ctenophores move into the estuaries and can be seen easily. But if there has been a northerly wind that pushes the water offshore, the marine life moves out into the depths. When the winds blow from the sea the water warms up, and ctenophores come back in. It seems that when one species of jellyfish comes, others follow and you might find small *Rhopilema verrilli* among an occasional *Beroe ovata* or the pink pulsating *Chrysaora quinquecirrha*. On the Atlantic coast the sea gooseberry (*Pleurobrachia pileus*) with its flashes of iridescence can be seen everywhere over the surface of the water as far as the eye can see, its shimmering comb plates refracting the sunlight into prismatic colors. Some come spinning up to the surface, others can be seen down deep below in the dark waters just out of reach of your long-handled dip net.

But regardless of what swimming form is around, whether it is jellyfish or swimming sea hare or pelagic nudibranch, you must get while the getting is good and take advantage of that particular moment; this is more true of the open pelagic habitat than any other because one moment the life can be there and then, with a change in the tide, a shift in the wind, totally gone. And when they move out into deeper water, they separate, drift apart and spread out into individuals now and then.

And when the pelagic forms move on, there is nothing as empty and barren as the open water. No life is visible, just the lapping waves and nothingness. There will be days, even weeks, when there is no large visible moving, floating form, and then suddenly the water is alive with everything swimming and pulsating, wriggling all at one time. So if these are the animals you want you must work, and work hard, dipping them up, placing them in buckets, sweeping the water with your net back and forth.

Collecting pelagic forms from a boat is quite another matter. If there is a pressing need for jellyfish such as *Stomolophus meleagris*, the cannonball jellyfish, and there is none to be found off the end of a pier, then a search becomes necessary. This employs the use of a power boat and two men, one to run it, the other to sit upon the bow and watch the rushing waters for scattered individuals. If the boat is making any speed at all it is almost impossible to see a moving jellyfish, or if you do see one, it is just a glimpse.

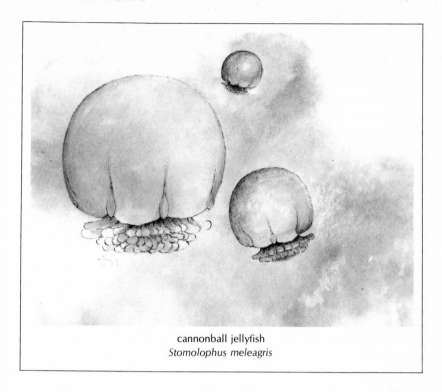

cannonball jellyfish
Stomolophus meleagris

Then stopping the boat, turning around, you rush back to the point where you saw it and it's not there. Just a few moments and it has sunk out of sight or drifted on. If you put the boat out of gear and let it drift, you might catch sight of the jellyfish as it rises to the surface, or you might see another.

Although you stand a good chance of seeing one or two *Aurelia, Rhopilema* or *Stomolophus* on any extended boat trip in South Atlantic waters you can run into huge schools of medusa forms. They travel in vast numbers pulsating on top of the water, down into the depths, sometimes as far as the eye can see. When they come inshore they can be dipped up from the pier in great numbers, but later that same school will move offshore and must then be pursued by boat.

So you find yourself whizzing over the sea sometimes so far out that land is just a pinpoint and finally disappears, and it is just you, the boat, a compass and the blue waters and whatever may be floating and swimming in them. And for great distances there is nothing, and your eyes grow tired from peering, searching.

Suddenly you're in them, just a flash of white blobs bobbing about the surface. Things begin to happen fast. You shout to the boat operator to slow down and then quickly put the dip net into action. If there are hundreds, thousands and seemingly millions of jellyfish in the water, you need never lift your dip net, just let it engulf specimen after specimen after specimen. But work within reason or you'll never be able to lift the net because it will be so gorged that the sheer weight will press the water out of many of the specimens and ruin them.

I have been discussing jellyfish at length because they are the most conspicuous creatures to be found in the open ocean, but there are many other animals that are taken in this characteristic habitat. A great many creatures get up from the bottom and swim. Horseshoe crabs can be seen swimming upside down using their gill books as paddles, polychaetes wriggle out of the depths of sand and do a swimming mating dance, but the open water is not a characteristic habitat of these forms. I use the term "pelagic habitat" in referring to the dwellers of open waters, the invertebrates and fish that are found swimming along the surface as part of their normal, everyday existence.

Marine water striders (*Halobates*) dance over the surface; *Aplysia*, which dwells on the bottom during much of its life, may be seen floating about expanding and contracting its wings, pelagic nudibranchs suspend themselves upside down from the surface film of the water. And then there are the dwellers of the floating seaweed, the brown sargasso weed that drifts about the oceans, sometimes in colonies that stretch on for miles. And this is a habitat within itself. Just scooping up a netful of this alga suspended by small round air bladders may reward you with a multitude of portunid crabs, sea slugs, filefish, pipefish, frogfish, small shrimp and other life.

A sea of plankton floats about, the minute fish larvae, the arrow worms, copepods, amphipods, forms as varied as snowflakes, both animal and plant life, and by pulling a fine-mesh plankton net through the sea an observer can get a view of what is in the sea. Perhaps if he is a student of marine life he will feel a trifle discouraged, because there is so much to learn, so many, many animals and names that no one human can be expected to learn them all, but the beauty and diversity is enough.

A preserved plankton sample is useful in demonstrating the millions of tiny animals and plants, and is necessary when sampling a body of water to determine productivity. Although there are numerous techniques for preserving phytoplankton and zooplankton, many oceanographers treat plankton by diluting it with a 7.5 percent solution of magnesium chloride for fifteen minutes. This anesthetizes all the minute contractile organisms and keeps them from shriveling up when Formalin is added. The plankton should be preserved in a minimum of 4 percent Formalin solution, which is accomplished by adding 4 parts concentrated Formalin to 96 parts of sea water containing the plankton.

Like everything else in the ocean, plankton has its seasons and peaks of abundance. Sometimes the water is so littered with plankton that your naked eye can see flashes and specks everywhere. At night the water is massed with luminescent plankton, and every time you break the surface with a net or paddle, flashes of blue light erupt mysteriously from the sea.

Night-time is the best time for collecting the pelagic inhabitants of the sea. The water is alive with all types of planktonic forms that rise from the bottom and bob, swim and float along the surface, giving the ocean the appearance of a rich soup. Although the major plankters are microscopic diatoms, protozoans, minute copepods and temporary larval stages of sessile invertebrates and fish eggs, you can often see other inhabitants like squid, with their bright green eyes, drifting along the surface in schools. A portunid crab paddles over the surface, and a twisting, writhing annelid comes twirling up.

To sample the pelagic world a collector must use nets, all types of them, ranging from fine-meshed plankton nets that have over 100 meshes per square inch to large trawls for collecting the fast-moving fish and squid. But a man skillfully wielding a dip net can do pretty well in getting the fast-moving forms in small quantities, particularly if he is working off a boat or pier with strong floodlights shining on the water.

Marine animals are generally attracted to bright lights. Often at night numbers of strange, swimming creatures swim or drift toward the lights of a pier and you can see their ghostly or glowing forms move on, the red eyes of a penaeid shrimp glowing like two small hot coals, the snaky, swimming motion of spawning worms, the torpedo forms of pelagic nudibranchs and many more. By holding a gasoline lantern off a pier — and a lantern emits an exceedingly bright glare — I have seen undulating sea hares change direction and move towards the light and into the range of my dip net.

Collecting at night can be a wonderful experience, sitting on the edge of the lighted pier by yourself with dip net and bucket, watching and waiting. For a moment there may be nothing, then suddenly the dark sea is alive with snaking, twisting forms and you dip them up and behold, they are nemertean worms (*Cerebratulus*), elongating and flattening themselves and writhing. This may happen only for a single night, when you can get several hundred, because they are spawning, and after the night of mating, they pass on; later the only way you'll be able to get them is with a shovel, one per shovelful of sand, and even then they stand an excellent chance of breaking.

The same is true of the thin-skinned sea cucumber (*Leptosynapta crassipatina*) which emerges from the sand, elongating and constricting, and then undulates its way up from the mud to join the traveling crowds of small pelagic creatures, and for a night, or several nights, these sedentary forms become pelagic. Again "pelagic" refers in this text to the open water, the moment you are upon it with dip net in hand. Should small horseshoe crabs leave the bottom and swim upside down flapping their gill books as they are prone to do on occasion, then they too enter the world of the pelagics.

In the fast-moving currents many creatures are swept along at night when they rise from the bottom. Small blue crabs (*Callinectes*) join the evening traffic, swarms of nudibranchs may appear, or pelagic anemones — and some of these are rare creatures. They may be seen once, and not again for five years, but if you are continuously collecting a coast, you'll remember them.

The pelagic life has its seasons. Just as *Bougainvillia* hydroids will profusely spring up and grow on wharf pilings during the winter months, *Nemopsis bachei*, the small hydromedusae, will come pulsating through the water like tiny, glass bells after November. In warm months needle fish come to the top, and as in other habitats theirs is an existence of eat or be eaten. The small crabs and tiny minnows that drift about are easy prey for the needle fish that slowly swims on the surface and suddenly darts out and grabs a fish in its long beak.

Ctenophores come in endless rivers, and the water suddenly appears to be filled with tulip-shaped jewels, opening and closing their petals. And when you touch them they glow with a blue ghostly light. When taken out of the water they appear colorless and transparent, except for those opaque ciliated plates which make them look like delicate, zippered seams. In the daylight the plates reflect the rich gold and fiery orange of the sunlight and the green of the sea.

But despite their form and beauty, they are gooey masses of slimy jelly. And while they are one of the lowest creatures in evolution, they are related in consistency to the highest invertebrates, the salps, which are pelagic tunicates and they too come in at night in twisting chains, and when caught in the net are also gooey masses.

And if you get a combination of ctenophores, worms, pelagic tunicates, perhaps some chance squid, marine-water striders, and so on, your buckets will be filled, and then, tired, satisfied and victorious you walk back with sloshing, filled buckets.

11.
Night Collecting

Various habitats have been reviewed in previous chapters, but primarily from the standpoint of collecting in the daytime. The creatures that live beneath rocks, or down in dark burrows sleep by day and move at night, so no matter what habitat has been explored by day, whether it is a coral reef or a muddy tide flat, the collecting may vary considerably.

Nothing exemplifies this better than a collecting expedition aboard a shrimp trawler. The powerful engines on the large boat strain ahead during the afternoon, pulling the massive nets behind. The heavy otter board, the chains and the dragging nets pull relentlessly on over the bottom, and all that is in their path is swooped up. In fact, watching such a phenomenon underwater is a bit of a terrifying experience, because you know there is no hope for the creatures in front.

When the net is dragged over the average sandy bottom in a one-hour daytime tow it may bring up only 100 pounds or less of biomass—assorted pin fish, some shrimp, sponges, etc. But as soon as the sun goes down and the same area is trawled, the catch may be 500 or 600 pounds of trash fish and shrimp when the net is lifted. And among the catch, depending on where you trawled, you will find midshipman fish, moray eels, octopuses, squid, 5 times the daytime catch of shrimp. Sea pansies are more plentiful, as are flounder, cusk eels, sharks, rays and longnose garfish. The net drags on throughout the night, and with the first rays of dawn the creatures become fewer in number. As daylight breaks and the sun comes out the biomass is substantially reduced, the nocturnal creatures hide from the light, the penaeid shrimp kick down into the sand and burrow out of sight.

The same is true for the rock piles along a New England coast, or in a coral reef, or on a mudflat. Night collecting will expose many creatures that you would not normally see, or will expose many creatures that you would otherwise have to do a great deal of searching to uncover.

To investigate the intertidal habitats you will need a bright-burning gasoline lantern, or a seal beam off a car light with a battery; even a strong flashlight will do. Scuba-diving at night is also an exciting sport, and there are new mercury lights that throw a long beam under water. Fish-watchers claim they see a great number of species in abundance that are rare in the daytime.

Crustaceans as a rule are momentarily stunned and held transfixed by a strong light; so are the numerous fish that swim directly toward a beam and often stay completely still long enough for you to get a dip net under them. The impossible grapsid crab that excels at scuttling sideways, frustratingly out of reach, can sometimes be blinded enough to let you slap a hand over him. But not always; especially when he is aware of your presence he can get away. However, you stand a much better chance of bringing back a quota at night than you do in the daytime when the crabs have a good range of vision.

Fish in the tide pools and along the edge of the littoral are also transfixed by the blinding glare and can be easily captured. I have taken many *Fundulus similis,* the killifish, in less than half-hour, dipping them up 25 at a time. Needlefish and half-beaks come out and swim to the light, and can be engulfed in the dip net. Yet in the daytime such fish are very wary and scatter at the slightest provocation. Even mullet have been known to jump into a boat that has a gasoline lantern burning.

On the flats, sea cucumbers that stay buried among the roots of the sea grass will poke their tentacles out and sweep the waters for plankton. When grabbing them behind the tentacles with thumb and forefinger you can hold them in place and keep them from contracting down into their burrows, and quickly scoop them out. On flat intertidal rocks sea cucumbers will appear and erect their tentacles, yet in the daytime they may be down in the crevices so deep that only a blasting cap could root them out. The same is true of the big chitons that shun sunlight but inch out, a millimeter at a time. Sea anemones that may be seen at day are twice as conspicuous and expanded in the darkness. Nudibranchs glide out from their small crannies, and the cave-dwelling octopus slithers out into the night traffic to search for crabs. The elusive moray eel that may expose only its head, if that much, in daylight, oozes its long speckled body out of its lair and searches for octopus or small fish to eat. Everything is on the prowl at night, feeding, striking, foraging and spawning. Splashes are heard along the calm shallows as a shark moves into a school of anchovies, or a grouper strikes at a mullet.

Shrimp with glowing red eyes swim slowly around in tide pools, jackknifing out of the water and splashing when they are disturbed. They too are attracted by the glaring gasoline lantern and are held transfixed long enough for you to get your dip net under one and snatch it. Your light may reveal mantis shrimp (*Squilla empusa*) that live deep within the burrows at the foot of the rock or make tunnels under the rock or burrow into the limestone.

Of course, night-lighting on rock piles or anywhere else has its

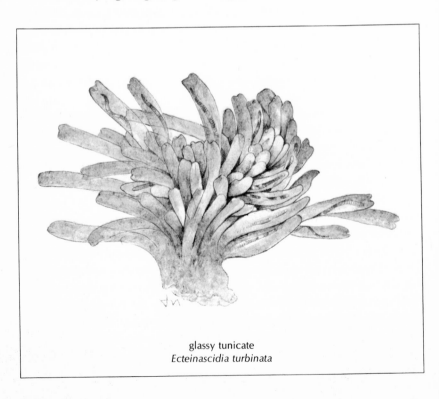

glassy tunicate
Ecteinascidia turbinata

disadvantages. No matter how careful you are, and no matter how bright your light is, it will not take the place of bright daylight, and you are bound to be missing a great many diurnal small animals that dwell in crevices or encrusting colonial animals. And then again there is the danger of a bad slip and falling, but perhaps one of the eeriest feelings is to wander down along some strange coast at night, with nothing but darkness and you all alone, and the sea and its creatures. You wonder if you'll find your way back to your car or boat. On a quiet night with just a bit of heat lightning in the distance and the silhouettes of oak trees, the big moths and bugs that fly at your light, the humming of mosquitoes in your ears and, in the tropics, perhaps a bat winging its way towards you.

I would suggest night-lighting trips only after you have become thoroughly acquainted with the terrain. It would not do to drive to some unknown coastline and start looking over the beaches by lantern-light. The chances of getting lost are excellent, even for a good navigator far out on a tide flat with only a gasoline lantern, the stars above and Stygian darkness all around. There may also be unexpected dangers, areas of extremely boggy mud. If you are well acquainted with the location during the day, and have collected a series of fauna, you will be much more adept at moving around at night, and will appreciate the differences between the diurnal and nocturnal faunas.

Just before dawn a change occurs and the animals begin to settle down and sleep. As the sun rises, the sea cucumbers withdraw their feeding tentacles and draw down into the mud. Sea anemones suck into their burrows and worms go back into the sand. The toadfish return to their holes among the oyster bars and the snapping shrimp scuttle down into their crannies. The brittlestars that carpeted the bottom slither and creep back down into the debris, to hide under the mats of algae and wait for darkness to come again.

Along the outer beaches the ghost crabs, feeling the first rays of dawn, move up toward their burrows, and disappear with the sunrise. And the speckled leopard crabs (*Arenaeus cribrarius*) that crawl up to the water's edge along the sandy beach and dig in with each wave and hold on through the sweeping sands go back into the sea and dig down into the sand and out of sight. The sharks that have been swimming inshore leave for deeper water with the falling tides. And the collector, lugging buckets or perhaps dragging a wire basket in a floating inner tube behind him walks up on the beach. The sea hisses, and the waves come washing in as the wind shifts. It is time to go home with his catch.

12.
Pollution in the Marine Environment

There is much that you can do individually to combat pollution in our lakes, rivers, streams and estuaries. The environment must be surveyed and its animal and plant communities assessed *before* a major pollution disaster sets in, because you never know what may happen to your favorite stretch of tide flat or marshland.

A reference collection of marine life combined with a fauna and flora checklist becomes an important tool in determining what effects subsequent pollution or dredge-and-fill activities have upon an area. To build up such a collection requires sampling all ecological habitats whether they are mangrove swamps, marshlands, coral reefs, rocky shores or mudflats. Every possible technique of collecting should be utilized, including trawling, dredging, sifting mud, turning over rocks and washing seaweed for minor crustaceans. All this knowledge becomes doubly important if something nasty happens such as an oil spill or the installation of a nuclear power plant that will discharge heated effluent into the estuary and kill or alter the environment.

Your specimens obtained from all this collecting should be well preserved, readily identifiable and well documented with as much ecological data as possible. Even if an area is heavily polluted, with sewer outfalls belching foamy, fetid effluents and paper mills dumping sulfide wastes in the same area, a thorough biological survey of existing organisms is essential.

It is essential because there is a temptation on the part of industry and various chambers of commerce to say that a bay or estuary is already dead from past pollution, and therefore nothing will be lost if the area is dredged and filled or that new pollution added will make no difference since the damage is already done.

The collector can use his technical knowledge and his specimen-gathering techniques to show that the estuary may still be alive. The organisms may be saturated with pesticides or full of trace metals and phenols, but they are still alive and should not be destroyed.

Simply because the waters smell bad, or they have fish kills from time to time, is no reason to say an area is "dead." Bob Boyle, in his book *The Hudson River*, goes to great lengths to show that the Hudson is still very much alive and full of life, although many claim it is polluted beyond repair. Many rivers and bays that have become sewage dumps are full of parasite-ridden fish. If the collector can hold his breath and walk among the noxious fumes of industrial outfalls in the New Jersey marshes and the bay of Delaware, he will be surprised at the number of fish, crabs and shrimp that live in the ditches. Snails still crawl about in the filth. These areas are sick, but they are not dead. The time it will take to reach tolerance levels, however, remains to be seen.

I have seen great expanses of tidal marshes in Massachusetts at Lynn, full of tidal creeks rich with rock crabs, alive with killifish and grass shrimp. Across the river, the huge city dump of Boston stretches out for miles in all its unsightliness and stench. Gulls are perched on the littered shorelines near the bridge. They wait for more fresh garbage to pick, garbage from restaurants and the kitchens of everyone's homes. But across the river where the marsh is still green, even though the soils smell putrid, there is still life and lots of it in the ditches. How much life there was in those ditches before the dumps were put up, I don't know, but the stinking marshes of Lynn still have life. Perhaps for another year, perhaps for five, ten or twenty. But can we afford to wait and see?

Nonetheless, the attitude prevails that the marshes are dead, that this area cannot support life, and therefore the adjacent green marshes that reek of hydrogen sulfide should be filled in and "made useful." To me these fungus-ridden little fish in the stinking ditches, with the slimy green-algae-covered crabs and the snails still crawling in fetid wastes are a hopeful sign that the environment can be made healthy again. But time is running out.

A number of companies already possess the technology to help clean up the environment. There are ways of irradiating sewage outfalls to prevent bacteria blooms, and sonic-vibration methods of removing soot and smoke from air-pollution sources. You must assume the attitude that it is not too late, and that much still can be done if only we become informed and involved.

In this age of interest in ecology, and with interest in federal and state programs to clean up and restore the environment, much thought should be given to preserving the unpolluted and undisturbed areas while they are still here. There are still large portions of American coastline that are relatively untouched, unpolluted, and are highly productive biologically. It is true that these areas have fish that may contain high levels of persistent pesticides in their tissues, and poisonous trace metals may be more widespread and prevalent in fish and oysters than state boards of health and water pollution control administrations care to admit, but nonetheless there are vast areas of productive sea bottoms, tidal marshes and shallow bays that are full of fish.

It costs a great deal of money to stop the numerous chemical companies from discharging toxic effluents into Chesapeake Bay, more than it takes to set aside a little fishing community like Panacea on the west coast of Florida, buy up the land and set it aside for the public's recreation and a source of protein for present and future generations.

But no area is an island by itself, it is linked with other bays and estuaries by the sea, by currents and the migrations of marine life from one bay to the next. And while there are bits of American coastline that are still untouched and unpolluted, only a few hundred miles away or less there is a paper mill pouring sulfates and possibly mercury into the water, or a nuclear power plant discharging heated effluents, or a harbor whose bottom is being ripped up and the bottom life destroyed by the strangling silt that remains suspended in the water.

Another form of pollution that has been plaguing the lands, the forests, the streams and the mountaintops is litter, and now it is plaguing the sea. On the surface of the waters around Florida are thousands and thousands of pieces of Styrofoam that float about the ocean for an eternity, slowly if ever breaking down. The Styrofoam comes from picnic baskets, from fishermen's corks and from packing materials. It drifts about the seas, it breaks into little pellets which also drift about until they get waterlogged and then sink. And every day, especially during the summer when bathers come to the shore, more and more Styrofoam litters the beaches and the sea.

100

The bottom of the sea in many areas looks like the city dump—strewn with rusting beer cans and sanitary napkins, cluttered with soft-drink bottles, and bedecked with newspapers and plastic bags. To a Scuba diver the wonders of a coral reef in parts of the Keys can turn into the unpleasant experience of swimming through a submerged city dump. And often along sea grass beds there is so much garbage that the vegetation is flattened.

The bottom of the estuaries, bays and open oceanic waters in northwest Florida is still relatively clean. And when a trawl net swoops down and samples the bottom only occasionally do you find a Coca-Cola bottle, a rusty beer can or a pile of slimy newspaper among the catch. There are still vast areas of the coastline where you find none of this, but litter is purely a function of population and time. And when the coast becomes developed there will be much garbage on the bay bottoms where presently there is none.

It may not seem like much to throw one beer can overboard, but when you consider that the can sinks and then someone throws in another, and another, soon the bottom is not pristine and pure anymore. I shall never forget trawling in Boston Harbor. Working with Jim Clark, a young graduate student at Harvard, who frequently went out on fishing trawlers in the Boston Harbor because he knew the fishermen well, we left on a 45-foot vessel. When we were past the airport, and saw the jets taking off and landing, we dropped the otter trawl. When it came up it was packed with tin cans, broken glass, decaying wood, rusty nails and an abominable black slimy bottom. But in the catch were hundreds of flounder, small lobsters, starfish, sea urchins and untold numbers of green rock crabs. It has always truly amazed me that marine life could live in such a disgusting mess, but they managed to. The fishermen used very thick, heavy gloves to cull the catch and rake the trash fish and the garbage overboard. I spotted a rather weird amphipod and could not pick it up with gloves on, and in my enthusiasm I took off one glove, picked up the animal—and cut my fingers on a razor blade. A bad infection set in; even though I treated the wound, it took weeks to heal.

The waters around New York City abound with filth. Almost daily barge loads of sewage sludge are hauled out into the Hudson bight and dumped at sea. I can look at Los Angeles and San Francisco and Galveston Bay for pollution, but I can also look in my own Florida's Panhandle and find it in entrenched ugliness.

St. Joe Bay in northwest Florida is a classical example of pollution

101

in the marine environment; it is an area of tremendously high productivity that seemingly is being slowly and steadily killed by discharges of wood pulp and sulfide wastes from the St. Joe Paper Company.

This is most certainly a tragedy and a crime against ecology because St. Joe Bay is one of the most beautiful scenic areas in north Florida as well as a vast storehouse of marine life. Great expansive flats of Cuban shoal weed and turtle grass stretch out as far as the eye can see. And even today, if you are there in the evening, on low tide, you can see children wading in the grass flats, carrying buckets and sacks laden with scallops. At the head of the bay there is so much life in the shallows you can't help but be amazed. Needle fish patrol the surface gobbling up sheepshead killifish that dart out from the marshes. Starfish creep over the bottom, and brightly polished olive snails emerge from the sand to feed upon carrion. And in the white sandy patches between the strands of turtle grasses are small horseshoe crabs, the ones we collect for aquarium specimens because they are only two inches across their carapace.

For the past 10 years I have waded along the tide flats of St. Joe picking up sea hares, collecting hermit crabs grown over with pink sea anemones, and digging up lugworms. Whenever we needed the speckled sea cucumber (*Theelothuria princeps*) or the giant single-celled alga (*Acetabularia crenulata*), we headed to St. Joe Bay which is 80 miles away from our laboratory in Panacea.

When I first started collecting specimens for a living, I worked aboard a shrimp trawler that regularly fished in St. Joe Bay. We always caught a load of shrimp and almost always I was rewarded with tiny octopuses, midshipmen, moray eels and a whole variety of sponges and other creatures. St. Joe Bay was very good to me.

There was only one thing I didn't like about it, and that was the St. Joe Paper Company. Off in the distance up at the mouth of the bay, a number of great smoke stacks belonging to the paper company disrupted the scenic beauty of this beautiful marshy bay. Stifling white smoke that reeked of sulfides and made your eyes burn, belched out into the atmosphere, and when I drove into St. Joe, my nostrils burned with a sickening sulfur smell which I tried to ignore.

Then it happened. On July 17, 1969, the huge accumulation of bark, fiber, craft and other wastes, which the paper company had generated over the last few years, broke loose and avalanched into the bay. It was destined to happen. Over the past five years they had been accumulating huge amounts of bark and pulp that was stripped off the trees and deposited in huge, unsightly piles. Their equipment simply couldn't handle it all, and over 3000 tons of bark wastes were swept out into the Gulf and carried downshore by currents and littered approximately fifty miles of beaches in Bay, Gulf, Walton and Okalossa counties. A month later a second avalanche of wastes belched into St. Joe Bay, but this time it only polluted 15 miles of adjacent beaches.

Floating mats of decomposing, putrid wood chips piled up on the gleaming white tourist beaches of Panama City. Motel owners, sports fishermen and concerned citizens in these areas demanded to know where it was coming from. Who was dumping it? Why?

The story of the spill raged through the headlines, flashed on television and radio. Bathing was impossible in that vomitlike mixture of fetid pulp, so many tourists simply packed up and went home. No one had the slightest desire to swim in the abrasive, sulfurous-smelling pulp or even spread their blankets on a bark-littered beach.

The paper company had no comment, but a noted oceanographer from Florida State University appeared on television and offered obscure reasons for the pollution phenomena. His opinion was that the pulp had somehow blown in from offshore, possibly hundreds of miles out in the Gulf of Mexico. To prove his theory, he dug down through the pulp and picked up a handful of *Sargassum* weed, the type that drifts about the ocean suspended on the surface by flotation bladders filled with air, and talked about the seaweed: since this was a pelagic species that drifts about the oceans, then in all likelihood the bark had drifted in shore with *Sargassum*.

The interviewer, who later told me that he could hardly believe his ears, asked the professor if he didn't think there was a chance that it came from the paper mill which loomed in the background. The noted professor shook his head and said that the bark may have been dumped by barges towing it far out at sea, or that it could have possibly erupted from the sea floor. Perhaps it was a submerged, fossilized forest or peat bog that belched forth through some strange, volcanic upheaval and currents carried it landward. The noted professor finally admitted that ultimately he wasn't sure where it came from—there could be a number of sources.

The television station had obviously interviewed the wrong man. There were a number of biologists with high integrity at Florida State University who would have willingly given a forthright answer, because they spend long, hard hours working on pollution problems. Because this professor was the head of the marine laboratory and chairman of the department of oceanography, he was chosen for the interview.

However, the owner of the St. Joe Paper Company had sold the university land on which to build their new oceanographic laboratory complex at Turkey Point in Franklin County, Florida, and donated additional land for their use. In fact, the new facility was named the Edward F. Ball Marine Laboratory in honor of the owner of the paper company in appreciation for his generosity.

Nobody believed that the pulp came from an upheaval of the ocean floor. There were too many angry people, and the Florida Air and Water Pollution Control Board investigated and indicted the St. Joe Paper Company for polluting the bays and beaches with 3000 tons of bark and wood chips. From aerial photographs they learned that the paper company had actually built up a land mass of pulp in the intercoastal waterway.

The state of Florida is in the process of filing suit for the insignificant sum of $50,000 for damage caused by the dumping of bark, craft, and wood fiber. The paper company plans to clean up its waters by 1973, but this will involve dredging its beaches and sale of submerged state lands.

St. Joe Bay's problems may be only beginning. In the early 1960s approximately 600 acres of submerged lands, located at the head of the bay, the most productive part where shrimp and scallops grow in luxurious sea-grass meadows, were sold to two private interests for the small sum of $10 per acre, with the provision that the submerged lands had to be dredged and developed within six months. This was not done, fortunately, so the final sale price for the bay bottoms went to $100 per acre. No conservationist or state biologist was asked to make a survey; the sale went on without anyone's knowledge. One rightfully might ask, "How could this happen?"

North Florida is an underdeveloped and depressed area. Many towns and cities along the 200-mile stretch of beach welcome industry with open arms, no matter how dirty or how bad their pollution records. A few years ago, when visitors complained about the stench in the air, people would often say, "That stink is *money*. The paper company gives us jobs."

In the early 1950s the Florida legislature voted to make the Fenholloway River near Perry in north Florida a "public sewer" to be used by industry for dumping wastes. In a few short years they converted a beautiful, wild river where fishermen once landed tons of mullet, speckled trout and redfish, into a stinking airless body of water that gushed yellow pulp slime out into the Gulf. Numerous people have witnessed the fall migrations of mullet hit the paper mill's yellow effluent, turn around and run out to sea to escape it.

The north Florida environment has very few friends willing to spend the time, money and effort to save it, but it has a great many enemies. Escambia Bay in Pensacola is noted for its constantly recurring fish kills due to poor circulation from uncontrolled dredging and filling, and industrial pollution and sewage which is continuously dumped into the waters.

I know full well that as I walk over my favorite salt marsh or fishing area, someone is probably looking at an aerial photograph of the same area, planning to dredge and fill it, or make it into a parking lot, shopping center or housing development. I have come to hate those little red land-survey flags that suddenly appear in the marshes or on beautiful wooded forests; they are as characteristic of destruction as the chancre sore is of syphilis.

I soon realized that I had to get involved. I could not close my eyes to the evil and just go on collecting specimens and selling them to universities. If I did not take action, it was obvious that nothing would stop the destruction of north Florida estuaries from dredgers. Only a few local people would really care how polluted the waters became so I began a campaign to educate the public with a barrage of local television programs, lectures, public field trips, radio interviews, and I saturated the press with news releases.

Our surveys have not stopped. We have sampled mud bottoms from finger-filled canals, sifted the hauls and compared them with life in productive, healthy bottoms. The mud from dredged areas reeked of hydrogen sulfide and supported almost no life. I worked with scientists at the Sandy Hook Marine Laboratory in New Jersey and at the Woods Hole Oceanographic Institution and learned sampling techniques and methods of testing water quality. My desk was heaped with literature on thermal pollution, sewer outfalls, pesticides and mercury instead of institutional purchase orders.

Since St. Joe Bay was a prime collecting area, I decided to start taking an inventory of what benthic life still remained. Leon Crum, my chief collector, had worked the head of St. Joe Bay periodically during the year that followed the spill and usually came back with handsome catches of horseshoe crabs and sea urchins, but quantitative commercial collecting is much different from taking qualitative samples. So we drove to St. Joe one morning with our bottles, jars, preservatives and dip nets and I brought my camera.

The beaches around Port St. Joe were still unpleasantly littered with bark and wood chips. Much of it had been washed out to sea. Nonetheless, when we dug down into the eelgrass for specimens and sifted the substrate through screens, there was the ever-present milky-yellow wood fibers mixed deep in the sand and mud. Although a few hardy polychaete worms managed to live among the decomposing fiber, the substrate did not produce the rich assortment of brittlestars, ostracods, amphipods and other minute crustaceans that were found in other areas only 10 miles away. No matter where we went in St. Joe Bay we found wood fibers, so I finally decided to risk trespassing and explore the tidal flats behind the paper company at the mouth of the bay.

We drove over a bridge, which afforded a wide view of the industrial complex. On the left side of the road was the paper company with its acres of pine logs piled up like mountains, great digesting tanks, storage vats, huge ugly buildings, belching smokestacks and grinding, noisy machinery that never shut down. On the right side of the road was Glidden Chemical Co., polluting the air with its smokestacks. We wondered about their effluents, too.

We parked our vehicle on the shoulder of the highway and hiked toward the beach. The beach was not visible from the road, because our vision was blocked by a huge spoil bank that had been dredged up and deposited between the highway and the shoreline. Before we could get to the spoil bank we had to cross a swamp, a dying swamp. It was foul smelling, full of twisted tangles of blackened bushes, thorny vines which tore at our skin and clothing. We waded through boggy wood pulp and slimy mud. The water in the swamp was sullen and livid, and full of rotting reeds. The area had a tortured look about it. A putrid-smelling canal filled with greenish-white pulp juice oozed along over blackened, dead soils, winding its way down to the bay.

We were glad when we reached the base of the spoil bank, anything to get out of that slimed, fouled cesspool. It was a long, hard climb to ascend the mountain of white sand, but at last we reached the summit and saw the beach. I had expected pollution, but nothing in my imagination equaled what I really saw before me.

Almost a full mile of what was once a beach with marsh and

white sand was now a garbage dump, piled as high as my chest with decomposing, brown wood pulp. Some of it was still wet, but other sections were covered with dried pulp caked into massive lumps. The stench was overpowering, I gasped and urged Leon forward. He was reluctant and was afraid that we might sink into that stinking morass out of sight forever, but I coaxed him on. As we stepped over the pulp, our feet sank with a revolting suction sound. A noisesome smell went up, and the rotting ooze squished beneath us.

At one disgusting moment when I was backing up to take a picture of the disaster, it happened. I sank down through the muck right up to my chest, and was stuck. At that particular moment I lost all heart, I stank in my own nostrils and told Leon not to bother to excavate me, just shoot me on the spot. I wanted to die.

With frantic kicking and Leon's help, I pulled out and we continued. Why did I go on with this agony? There were two questions I wanted answered. What effects was this glop having on marine life? And was that paper plant still discharging it? We continued stepping over the pulp working our way slowly down toward the edge of the beach. I learned that the best way to walk in it was to press a collecting bucket down into the pulp and use it for leverage to get from place to place.

Just a mile down the tortured, polluted beach, the huge factory bellowed white smoke into the atmosphere. The machinery rumbled with a low din and I wondered if company employees were watching us. I envisioned security guards peering at us through binoculars and any minute I expected to hear the wail of sirens. But this worry was unfounded at the time because St. Joe Paper Company was so entrenched in the community they couldn't care less who saw their pollution.

At last we reached the edge of the sea where coffee-colored pulp fiber suspended in the sea water lapped up against the shore. It seemed the entire ocean was one fine emulsion of fibrous, rotting brown material, but 10 feet out on the tide flat we found firm ground and proceeded up the shore toward the looming smokestacks.

What effect did this pollution have on marine life? Everywhere we looked on the beach we found dead horseshoe crabs. We counted over 300 corpses in less than a half mile; they ranged in different stages of decomposition from dried animals that had been dead for months to freshly bloated corpses. *Limulus polyphemus* comes to the beaches to lay its eggs in the spring, and what it had met with was this suffocating mass of rotted wood pulp. Over two months had passed since the major mating migration season was over and we were probably seeing only a minute fraction of the animals that had been destroyed. I have often counted 1500 crabs on a mile stretch of beach during the mating season.

We found one large female that was feebly alive, and when we pulled her from the fiber we found her gills to be clogged with nauseating pulp. We washed her off in the coffee-colored, emulsified water and added her to our collecting bucket. Later, back at our laboratory, she died even after being placed in clean, running sea water.

As we walked along the water's edge down toward the mill, there was not a ripple of life anywhere. Not a darting minnow or a scurrying blue crab. We dug down through the pulp and shoveled up a sand sample. It stank terribly and Leon immediately predicted there wouldn't be a speck of life in it. He was right. After sifting it, we found not a single nematode or worm of any sort. Later on, under microscopic examination, we couldn't even find a protozoan. It was depressing to see how totally dead the waters were behind the St. Joe Paper Company. Finally we reached the canal, and there we saw it, great piles of floating, gummy wood pulp were being discharged at sea: they drifted down the company's canal, out into the bay and were washing back on the beaches and piling up on the old wood pulp. By discharging it slowly over a long period of time, they minimized the chances of the wastes drifting down to adjacent communities.

After shooting several rolls of film we started back toward our truck. Instead of walking through the pulp, we sensibly followed the shoreline, traveling west until we came to a bridge where the pulp decreased and finally some brownish-yellow sand appeared. When the pulp was less than an inch thick, and some sand bottom showed, we managed to catch a couple of silverside minnows with our net. Further down we spotted some small blue crabs and when we finally got out of the pulp entirely and took a seine sample, pulling our fine-meshed net over the sands, we caught several thousand grass shrimp (Palaemonetes pugio), each measuring less than a half inch.

The shrimp were forced back from the pulp because the oxygen demand of decomposing wood is staggering. It consumes far more oxygen than any amount of fish, and has the same effects of eutrophication, which is ultimate oxygen consumption. Consequently, when the fish and shrimp can get even a few feet away from the suffocating, pulpy mess, they can get an adequate oxygen supply and survive. Furthermore, they may have even been feasting upon the bacteria that was working on the wood pulp.

What long-range effects those brown, coffee-stained polluted waters have upon aquatic life remains to be studied. There may be pollution at work that we can neither see, taste nor smell. Pollution biologist Robert Livingston of Florida State University tested the waters of St. Joe and found high concentrations of methyl mercury. Mercury is used as a fungicide in making paper and is discharged into the bays and estuaries along with the pulp wastes. Later we sampled fish from Shell Point, almost 100 miles away from St. Joe and sent frozen specimens to a laboratory in Wisconsin, which tested them for mercury. They were shown to have approximately 0.04 parts per million of methyl mercury in their tissues. The Federal Food and Drug Administration condemns fish for marketing that have a mercury level of 0.05 parts per million. How long the fish will be "safe" to eat, and how long the fish will live, is known only to God.

We drove to a fish company to wash the filth and stench from ourselves and talked to some of the shrimpers. In between unloading shrimp from rusty, squeaking conveyer belts they told us about St. Joe, and to a man, from the fish company owner to the shrimpers, they were angry about it. "Hell," said one unshaven, rough-looking shrimper, "if they keep dumping that crap into the bay, in five years it will be completely dead. They started dumping about two years ago, and now there are places that you can't make a five-minute tow with your nets without getting it so full of pulp that you can't lift it."

Another fisherman added, as he shoveled ice on a box of shrimp, "If that stuff gets in your net, why it takes a full night to wash it out and shake it down. Last year a bunch of beach seine fishermen struck a school of fish and got so much wood pulp that their net was completely grounded. They lost the school and spent the whole day cleaning the nets out."

"The clam dredges come up full of pulp," another man told us, "and since they've started dumping, shrimping has fallen off to almost nothing. Three or four years ago you could tow all over the bay and catch four to five hundred pounds a night; now a man's lucky if he gets a hundred pounds."

But they all agreed that the bay was far from dead yet.

As we collect on the marshy islands at the head of St. Joe Bay, and suddenly happen upon a huge number of gastropod mollusks

109

lying dead and broken in the sand, sogging in the mud by the thousands, we cannot help wondering if the ocean isn't giving up and dying off slowly.

We should not jump to conclusions, looking at those ugly smokestacks across the bay bellowing putrid sulfur-smelling smoke into the sky. Perhaps the conchs died of a mysterious virus, a natural temperature or salinity change, or perhaps it was pollution but not paper-mill pollution or a sudden influx of pesticides that may have wiped out the entire population?

As I look at the dead conchs all up and down the beach, mixed with the empty shells of horseshoe crabs and spider crabs, now worn and battered by the waves I wish I had been there when the conchs died. Water samples could have been taken to determine the pH (acidity or alkalinity) or the dissolved-oxygen level, or samples of the conchs and the water could have been shipped to a testing laboratory to check for trace metals or pesticides. The turbidity of the water could have been measured, and if there was pollution from the mill, it could have been reported and publicized.

The paper companies are installing filtering devices, and I suppose that we will have to live with the pollution for the next four years. Many scientists, including Jacques Cousteau, say the ocean is dying, and some claim it is already too late. But I am an optimist and feel the damaged waters may someday recover if mankind takes action now, and stops merely talking about taking such action.

The disastrous oil spill near Woods Hole that occurred in September, 1969, gives me some faint hope that the environment will be able to recover if and when pollution is cleaned up.

When the barge *Florida* belonging to the Northeast Petroleum Company went aground off West Falmouth, Massachusetts, approximately 170,000 gallons of No. 2 fuel oil spilled into the water. In the days that followed the shorelines were littered with almost continuous windrows of dead fish and dying marine invertebrates. "It was clearly evident that we were viewing a massive and immediate kill of at least the larger and more obvious organisms belonging to the entire spectrum of animal life found in the area," wrote Dr. Howard Sanders of the Woods Hole Oceanographic Institution, who with his colleagues investigated the spill.

If such an oil spill had to happen anywhere, it is probably best that it happened at Woods Hole where there were dedicated scientists who took the time off from their regular duties and research programs to make an ecological survey. Furthermore, the fauna of Woods Hole is perhaps better known than that of any other location in the United States.

Dr. Sanders, Max Blumer, George Hampson of the Woods Hole Oceanographic Institution and Paul Shave, a commercial biological collector, worked frantically to inventory the dying organisms. They learned that certain forms such as amphipods were highly susceptible to the oil while nematodes were relatively resistant. The presence of oil and benthic mortality was detected down to 42 feet and after the initial mortality which killed off thousands of large and small animals, the oil remained in the habitats and continued to kill. As the oil was liberated from the muddy bottoms, secondary mortality was still occurring.

For many months the waters and substrate in Wild Harbor were completely dead. Marshes turned black and died off, but life started slowly creeping back in. As many as 2000 small drab polychaetes (Capitella capitata) that live in a small tube, appeared in each shovelful of sand. Capitella capitata is a worldwide pollution indicator. A great many blue mussels which lived on the rocks and banks were killed off, but a few survived, although with shrunken and emasculated gonads.

George Hampson told me how Mya, the soft-shelled clam, made gyrating pits and craters in the mud. They made the tide flat look like the surface of the moon and before they died, they were seen with their siphons extended, lying limp or gyrating in the sand. This is most unusual behavior for them. Normally when you are clamming, you have to throw a rock on a bed or dig rapidly to make Mya reveal itself by its frightened spurt of water. And then it promptly digs down and out of sight. They extend their siphons at night only, and can then be captured with a blinding gasoline lantern. Razor clams also failed to retract into the mud, and they too died. The death list went on and on — quahog clams, lugworms, eels, crabs, killifish, and mud shrimp. The sands were stained yellow and the air reeked of oil. Bushels of snails were dead and rotten ooze poured out of their shells.

George Hampson and Howard Sanders had some recommendations about what to do when there is an oil spill. Immediately after a disaster, a biologist or concerned citizen should rush to the scene and begin gathering dead animals and preserving them. All the soft-bodied animals such as worms, sea anemones, sponges, and ascidians will decompose and wash out to sea in a day or two, and if you wait too long there will be no evidence. Before you know it, the beach will show little sign that it was once full of dead animals and the entire area will simply be denuded of life.

However, even if you arrive late on the scene, you can get a good "before" picture by carefully looking for the remains of dead animals. By sifting sand you can often find the remains of dead amphipods that have a hard shell which does not deteriorate. Snail shells with their operculum intact are evidence of a kill, and even the horny proboscis of clam worms can tell of the numbers of worms that were killed.

It may take several days before the multitudes of dead bottom invertebrates and fish begin washing inshore. The beach should then be rigorously patrolled. Take five-gallon cans, jars, or buckets of 15 percent Formalin and drop the animals in as you find them. If they are rotten, save them anyway, although during an oil spill the animals do not decompose readily. However, if there is a thermal discharge from a nuclear power plant or death caused by anoxia, decomposition sets in very rapidly.

It is most important that you take pictures of dead animals to supplement your preserved collections. These pictures can be later used as conclusive evidence on the effects of the pollution. It is also important to take pictures of the physical shoreline because after an oil spill erosion characteristically sets in. As the tubed worms and other tiny creatures that bind sand grains together with mucus and excretions are killed off, the sand begins to shift and piles up on the sand flats.

After the Wild Harbor spill, the oil company sent in "clean-up" crews which immediately began raking up the oily sand and gathering dead animals for disposal. A similar "clean-up" crew was sent in to dispose of tons of fish killed by Con Edison's power plant in the Hudson River. They hauled them off by the truckload and buried them hastily with bulldozers.

It is imperative that you get in ahead of these "clean-up" crews because while they are ridding the beaches of dead animals in the name of public health, they are very conveniently removing evidence of their destruction. Then during subsequent pollution hearings spokesmen and attorneys will claim that their pollution did little or no damage to fish and wildlife.

Unlike the spills at Santa Barbara and Puerto Rico, the Wild Harbor spill did not have a dramatic effect on bird life. A few terns and clapper rails were soaked with oil, but it was not like other oil spills where birds died by the thousands.

And when I visited Wild Harbor in Falmouth, Massachusetts,

almost a year later, I saw numbers of birds walking around portions of the marsh that had not been too heavily polluted. Wild Harbor is a beautiful area; one has only to stand on the road and view this magnificent marsh area and adjoining little pond and quaint, colonial-style New England houses to realize the damage that was done and the heartbreak of the residents.

Many people from Falmouth went clamming at Wild Harbor, but they will probably never be allowed to clam there again. Dead clam shells were everywhere, and even though thousands of juvenile *Mya* clams had recolonized the area, they would probably never be fit to eat because it has been shown by Max Blumer that hydrocarbons from the spill concentrate in their tissues and never leave once they are accumulated. In fact, the hydrocarbons are passed on and magnified in predatory organisms higher in the food chain.

Perhaps in five to ten years the rest of Wild Harbor will return to normal. It still doesn't have the large polychaete worms, or many of the crabs and larger fish, but the tide flats are showing some hopeful signs of recovery. Working with the scientists of the Woods Hole Oceanographic Institution, we seined small grass shrimp (*Crangon*) and a number of killifish from the oil-soaked mudflats. Large patches of the once expansive green marsh were black and dead, but a few green shoots were popping up through the oily sands.

With the falling tide, a shimmering iridescent oil slick appeared at the border of the polluted marsh and lapped in and out with the ebb and flow of the water. It was painful to look at the destruction, and every step through the mud brought out a fresh gush of oil. But there were fiddler crabs living in the dead marsh, digging burrows through the oil-saturated substrate. The sand siftings still contained thousands of *Capitella capitata*, but their numbers were diminishing as the fish and shrimp were gobbling them up.

I found some colonies of pink sea anemones and sponges growing on the bridge over Wild Harbor, which had not been badly polluted. There was still life in Wild Harbor and signs that the area may recover. But we can ask ourselves: How long, until the next time? The only way to discourage polluters is to get involved.

Whenever an oil spill, a pollution discharge from an outfall, or a fish kill occurs, there are series of steps you can take to report it to the proper authority and get some action.

1. Report your findings to the regional office of your state Air and Water Pollution Control Board.

2. Report the disaster to your state Department of Natural Resources (salt water or fresh water division, depending upon the location of the pollution).

3. Notify your local Audubon Society, Sierra Club or other conservation organizations. Team up with other conservationists in the area, invite them to look at the damaged area, and write letters.

4. Notify the newspapers, give them all the facts, especially information on the species that were killed, how many, and so on. The only action that will fight a pollution problem is publicity, and public support, and radio and television and newspapers are the best way to obtain this. Give the public the facts, tell them that salt marshes are valuable, and how important the tiny, marine fauna are and how they can be so easily destroyed.

It is going to take a willingness on the part of industries and municipalities to clean up our waters, not full-page ads in popular news magazines. Effluents will have to be monitored and their effects frequently tested. At long last our society is beginning to wake up to our environmental problems. A decade ago there would have been little concern raised over an oil spill or a build-up of poisonous trace metals in the waters. But now there are pollution control boards, and people who were once laughed at as "butterfly-chasers" and "birdwatchers" are finally being listened to. But it is not a moment too soon.

13.
Setting Up
a Salt-Water Aquarium

Frequently, throughout the following chapters, mention will be made of the behavior and abilities of certain species, and how well they survive in an aquarium. It is therefore useful to know basically how to set up and maintain a salt-water tank. The subject deserves a book by itself, because there are many little details that will have to be overlooked and will be discovered by the aquarist through trial and error. But enough of a general outline will be given here so one can get a tank, set it up and start keeping specimens alive.

For years in biology courses specimens were observed only as lifeless, rubbery entities in harsh-smelling formaldehyde, or were faded in alcohol. Then with the development of temperature-controlled life-support systems that could contain both cold- and warm-water specimens, teachers, researchers and hobbyists turned their interest toward keeping some of these bizarre, wonderful creatures alive and healthy in captivity. Only by observing them day after day, seeing how they capture their food, prey upon each other and by becoming involved in the problems of maintaining them do you realize the complexities and interactions of creatures in the sea. There is the thrill of watching a sea slug lay a network of finely etched eggs over the glass, your disgust and anger when the lightening whelk devours your prize lion's paw scallop, but a valuable lesson is learned in community grouping. And when the spider crab molts by pulling its long, snaky legs out of its old discarded shell, and emerges soft-shelled, but twice its former size, you have seen a drama unfold.

In the past salt-water aquariums have suffered a bad reputation. It was and still is reputed by fresh-water aquarium stock-dealers that salt-water specimens are very hard to maintain in captivity, that water fouls up easily and the tank must be kept scrupulously clean. It was believed that the amount of effort put into a marine tank was more than double that of a fresh-water tank, but all this is not true.

True, fish arrived at the few dealers that handled them in such poor condition that it was a wonder that any species survived at all. But with the establishment of superior collecting enterprises throughout the world, the care exercised in packing and the selection of healthy, undamaged disease-free specimens, an aquarist can get selections of magnificent coral-reef fish and invertebrates from Asia, India and South America. There are still mortalities in shipping fish and there is still much to be learned.

Strangely enough, getting estuarine species is much more of a problem, since most pet stores do not handle them. This necessitates the collecting of these animals yourself. And with proper care in the field, and in shipping or transporting specimens, you can bring animals from the sea back to your own tanks to study and enjoy.

There is much to be learned about the maintenance of salt-water systems, and you find more authorities full of conflicting information than you can comfortably digest. There are numerous books (a few of the better ones are cited in the bibliography), but most are full of colorful pictures of beautiful coral-reef fish, and have very little information on how to maintain them, how to stabilize the pH and salinity of the water.

A general outline of setting up and maintaining a salt-water aquarium is furnished here. It is more concerned with estuarine species than with oceanic animals, but the techniques of filtering and maintaining the tanks are applicable to most aquarium situations.

Selecting an Aquarium

Naturally the larger the volume of water, the better the survival rate. A minimum of 10 gallons is recommended for a small assortment of invertebrates and perhaps one fish. The rule of thumb is 10 gallons of water for each pound of biomass, or two gallons of water for each inch of fish. Some aquarists have figured water volume to be proportional to the dollar value of the specimens, the more expensive the specimens the more gallons required.

Marine aquariums need not be expensive. They can be made of glass or Plexiglas or even commonly available metal-framed tanks. They simply have to be able to hold water. Many of our holding tanks are constructed with 3/4'' exterior plywood with a subgravel filter and have a 250-gallon capacity. These can be cheaply and easily built. Inexpensive plastic-lined swimming pools can be filled with sea water, filtered, and will hold sharks, sea turtles and even porpoises. Each aquarist's needs will be different, and each will require a different system to satisfy him.

Filters

Always use under-gravel or "biological" filters that recirculate the water by air lift and cover the entire bottom of the aquarium. These are the most superior of all filters for a salt-water aquarium because they break down organic waste materials (fish excreta, uneaten food and decaying plant material) by bacterial action. Aeration through an air-lift tube at the base of a subgravel filter supplies oxygen to the aquarium and also pumps water up from beneath the gravel substrate, creating a very slow, gradual suction which circulates water down through the gravel bed. The oxygenated water passing through the gravel bed prevents an anerobic condition from forming while bacteria decompose the waste matter. If the gravel starts to turn black or smell, the water is not circulating properly and your filter may be dirty and need cleaning.

Spread calcareous gravel or limestone pebbles about three inches thick evenly over the bottom filter. The particles must be large enough not to clog up the fine slits in the filter or water circulation will be retarded and lethal levels of hydrogen sulfide will build up. If burrowing fish and invertebrates are to be maintained, coarse gravel should be topped with a coarse grade of beach sand or as a poor second, extensively washed, crushed oyster shell (pullet feed) which is available at most feed stores.

Avoid siliceous gravel commonly sold at aquarium stores as this does nothing to buffer the water and may add to the build-up of toxic materials. The slow dissolution of calcium carbonate from shell,

117

coquina sand or limestone will help stabilize the pH (acidity or alkalinity) under normal, uncrowded conditions.

Auxiliary power filters with glass wool and activated charcoal will give added filtration and eliminate dissolved carbon dioxide and unsightly, discolored, yellow water. Power filters should circulate the volume in the aquarium three to five times per hour and can be effectively used in conjunction with subgravel filters, particularly if there is a heavy load of specimens placed in the tank.

Activated charcoal will lose its effectiveness in a few weeks, so it is best to change it from time to time, or it can be removed and heated in a frying pan and it will once again become activated. Some aquarists have experimented with activated charcoal, planting it directly into the subgravel filter, and have had excellent success with their fish and sparkling clear water, although the black particles do make the tank look a bit unsightly, almost like a sea bottom covered with tar. It is recommended that glass wool used in outside filters should be washed occasionally, but never discarded because of the valuable microbes which build up in it and help break down fecal matter in the tank.

Setting Up the Aquarium

When filling the aquarium, place a dish over the filter material and pour the water directly on the dish to avoid stirring up the bottom. From the day the aquarium is set up to the day it is dismantled, the less the bottom substrate is disturbed, the better the survival of the animals. No matter how extensively gravel or shell is washed, the water will be clouded with a fine calcium carbonate silt for a few hours until it settles down into the filter and becomes part of the substratum. An outside power filter will help clean up the water and restore clarity in a shorter time.

Within a few weeks enough marine algae and organic deposits will build up to accommodate detritus feeders such as brittlestars, sea urchins, sea cucumbers, snapping shrimp and multitudes of annelids. Pieces of coral and "living rock" (limestone riddled with boring organisms) greatly assist in curing an aquarium. The more algae there are growing in an aquarium, the better the invertebrates and fish appear to survive. The algae constantly release oxygen into the water at night and absorb carbon dioxide, although the cycle is reversed during the daytime. If an adequate air filter is used, the algae's oxygen consumption should not have any detrimental effect. Algae also absorb nitrates from the system, and nitrates and nitrites are the biggest killers. A healthy cured tank may not be crystal-clear because it has green algae growing over the grass and matted up in the gravel, but many invertebrates, including sea anemones, sea cucumbers, sea squirts, crabs and shrimp have been kept for years in such systems.

We have had amphipods reproduce in subsand filters and furnish food for larger animals. Starfish crawl up the glass and small snails forage about feeding on the algae. The simple 20-gallon aquarium can become a balanced system if basic rules of stabilizing the salinity and avoiding overfeeding are observed. Your tank can be a trouble-free, self-sustaining unit or a mess of water pollution that will make Lake Erie look like a crystal-clear spring.

Water Quality and Control

The aquarium should be filled with natural or synthetic sea water. If using synthetic salts, use well-advertised brands that have national reputations. Instant Ocean and Rila Marine Mix have proved effective with many creatures. Beware of off-beat brand names that are often circulated among pet stores, they may be instant death to a variety of delicate marine invertebrates. Fish are generally tough and some species can almost live in a solution of table salts. When mixing synthetic sea salts always use glass or nontoxic plastic containers, never mix salts in metal containers.

Many professional salt-water aquarists insist on natural sea water, and claim it is best for maintaining invertebrates and fish. The water can be recycled for years through filter systems, adding distilled water as the aquarium water evaporates. Sea water is bulky to handle and presents problems in transportation.However, if the ocean is nearby it is certainly cheaper than buying synthetic salts. Be sure to collect your sea water away from shore where there is less chance of domestic pollution. Store natural sea water in the dark or keep it in light-proof containers, as it seems to improve with age. In a small aquarium, at least 25 percent of the water should be changed every 30 to 60 days to eliminate nitrate and nitrite build-ups. Special algae filters have

119

been developed by some aquarists to eliminate the nitrate problem and some systems have been highly successful.

The design is basically simple. Water is either steadily or sporadically (depending upon the size of the tanks) pumped from the aquariums into an algae reservoir. The reservoir is generally a large concrete or wooden tank placed outdoors in bright sunlight or kept indoors under bright floodlights to proliferate the algae growth, which absorbs nitrates from the sea water. Then by either pumping action or gravity flow, the water is circulated back into the aquarium where the specimens are held. Fish maintained in water that is treated in this fashion are healthier, have fewer diseases and survive longer. Invertebrates thrive and the water remains crystal-clear.

Marsh tanks might also be explored for solving the nitrate build-up. Our most successful aquarium is a large concrete tank with cord grass and needlerush marsh planted in one end. It has never had a single pollution problem in three years of continuous operation and has never yet had to be cleaned.

Temperature

Optimum temperatures for estuarine species that range in geographic distribution from the Carolinas to Texas is 68°F to 70°F. These shallow-water estuarine species can generally tolerate temperature ranges from 60°F to 85°F. However, when water temperatures rise or fall to extremes many motile invertebrates and practically all fish seek deeper waters where bottom temperatures are more stable. During these periods of hot or cold weather many invertebrates either burrow down into the substratum or regress into a dormant stage. The ones that cannot take the rises and falls generally die off.

Tropical species from the West Indies, Florida Keys or other tropical regions including the Red Sea, Indian Ocean and Indo-Pacific are best maintained in the 75°F to 85°F range. Many experts believe that tropical species are very close to their threshold of temperature tolerance, and much variation can cause them to go into heat or cold shock—hence thermal pollution problems.

North Atlantic and Pacific species must have cold water or refrigerated systems to keep them alive. Temperature in these tanks should be kept between 45°F and 65°F. It is interesting to note that many species have a very wide distribution and range from chilly New England waters down to warm temperate seas. However, for best results one should keep the specimens at temperatures that are ambient to the waters in which they were collected. Some aquarists have had luck adjusting species from cold waters to tanks kept at room temperature over a long period of time. The technique here is to use a great deal of sea water and have very little crowding. However, there are Arctic species that range as far south as Cape Cod, and these are highly sensitive to warm water.

The estuarine species of the middle Atlantic and Gulf states require the least concern for the casual aquarist and collector. One can go away and leave the specimens in an unheated room and absolute disaster will not result if the water temperature drops down to 45°F. They might find their fish lying sluggishly on the bottom of the tank, some might even have died, but the majority of the invertebrates would be alive. If tropical animals are subjected to extreme cold, then absolute disaster will result.

Salinity

The optimum salinity level for a standard marine aquarium is 30 parts per 1000 (30°/$_{oo}$) or a hydrometer reading of 1.025. This level is critical for many tropical species and oceanic, nonestuarine species that will perish in brackish water. However estuarine species, which live in areas where large rivers pour into the sea, are subject to wide variations in salinity.

Many of the species described in this book can withstand salinities ranging from 10 to 35 parts per 1000, or one-third to full-strength sea water. It is our experience that estuarine species do best at salinity ranges around 24 to 27 parts per 1000 or a hydrometer reading of 1.020 to 1.025 at 65°F. However, many an aquarist has successfully mixed estuarine and oceanic species in the same tank, keeping the hydrometer readings at 1.025.

Maintaining the proper salinity in a salt water aquarium is not difficult, but very important. If adding natural sea water, simply fill the tank until the desired water level is achieved at the top of the tank and make a crayon mark on the glass even with the water level. When using synthetic sea water, make the crayon mark when the hydrometer reads approximately 1.025. When the aquarium water evaporates, simply add distilled water or dechlorinated tap water until the water level rises to the crayon mark. *Never add additional sea water;* this increases the salinity.

This is perhaps the most important step in the survival of your animals. The average aquarium with an air-powered subgravel filter bubbling cheerfully away will lose a substantial volume of water into the atmosphere, particularly on a warm day. The water evaporates but the synthetic or natural salts remain behind in the tank and concentrate, which can kill all your animals. A glass cover will retard evaporation, but some aquarium experts believe that nitrates will build up in the system as a result.

A simple diluter, which can be easily installed in your salt-water aquarium, will automatically replace fresh water into your evaporating tank. First the proper specific gravity is established, and a mark made on the glass even with the water level; then a large flask (2000 cc or more) is filled with distilled water, placed in a ring stand and inverted over the aquarium. A glass tube inserted through the flask's stopper permits a slow, steady seepage of distilled water into the aquarium as the water level drops from evaporation. This system works something like a float-switch on a toilet tank, maintaining the water level in the aquarium and at the same time a stable salinity balance.

pH Levels

Under optimum conditions the pH should range from 8.0 to 8.3 in a marine aquarium. Most species can tolerate lower ranges down to 7.0 for short periods of time, especially estuarine species. However, the pH level should at all times be closely watched. A simple pH test kit with a range from 7.6 to 8.6 is an essential part of an aquarium kit. A natural growth of algae will help absorb nitrates and assist in pH control.

Low pH levels are an indication that something is wrong. Generally the water turns cloudy and has a slightly putrid smell, indicating something is dead, or there is hidden, uneaten food decomposing. Dissolved oxygen levels drop rapidly during bacteria blooms and resulting oxygen starvation will cause fish to rise to the surface and increase their opercular beat. Bloated, contracted anemones are a good indication of pH changes. Remove dead animals and/or uneaten food at once and put on an extra filter until the water clears. If this fails, change the water.

Feeding

Use chopped bits of clam, shrimp, squid, or fish to feed most aquarium animals. Crush food into a fine watery paste and pipette over coral polyps and anemone tentacles. Brine shrimp (*Artemia salina*) available at most pet stores, is excellent for feeding small fish and sea horses. If fish is not available chopped beef may be used to feed carnivores and lettuce or spinach can be fed to herbivorous species. Many species will eagerly eat tiny pieces of bread or grains of cereal.

Do not contaminate the aquarium by overfeeding or put in more food than the specimens will consume immediately. Most fish can go two weeks and longer without eating anything, and in all cases *underfeeding is safer than overfeeding.* Do not put food in the aquarium more than three times per week. Keep cleaning shrimp (*Hippolsymata wurdmanii*), small crabs and snails to help clean up excess food. But remember that these organisms are only a help, not a cure.

Once a tank is cured, plankton and diatoms living on other animals, on rocks and in the sand will bloom and will serve as food for a variety of larger organisms. This is called a "balanced system" and can possibly make additional feeding unnecessary.

Algae Control

Avoid eutrophication, use a scraper to clean tank walls every week or two. Herbivorous gastropods and tectibranch mollusks can act as natural cleaners but they cannot prevent massive algae blooms. Keep tanks away from direct sunlight, and excessive algae blooms will be substantially reduced. Some algae are excellent, but you don't want the water to look like pea soup.

Community Grouping

There are no set rules except that you should try to separate carnivores from herbivores and filter-feeders. Conchs and starfish will devour clams, fish will eat worms and shrimp will eat amphioxus. Large crabs are destructive to everything and should be kept isolated. Rocks, coral and gorgonians provide natural cover for smaller animals such as flatworms, minute crabs and brittlestars and keep them from being eaten by fish. Octopuses require an empty snail shell or a bottle to hide in. Keep a log on which species are compatible, which survive. This will aid with future selection.

Maintaining and managing a salt-water aquarium is a new and growing science; there is much to learn about relationships among animals and what requirements are necessary for keeping many invertebrates alive for extended periods of time. For example, anyone who learns how to keep jellyfish in captivity for six months has accomplished something. Many luxurious species of tropical corals and gorgonians simply will not live in captivity for more than a few weeks, no matter what system is tried. Getting salt-water fish to reproduce in captivity remains a problem; however, numerous invertebrates can be readily propagated in a simple tank. The rock anemone (*Aiptasia pallida*) is a notable example: within a few weeks after they are placed in the tank, hordes of little anemones will cover the rocks.

Some biologists have succeeded in raising second-generation sea urchins, and some have had starfish reproduce by the hundreds in their tanks. We have cultured chicken liver sponges (*Chondrilla nucula*), lugworms and snails in captivity. We have had no less than one million sand-burrowing amphipods raised in a large subgravel filter, but admittedly all this has been without help or supervision. We inadvertently did something right.

Unpacking and Acclimating Specimens

Basically, specimens are added to one's aquarium in two ways: you either collect the animals, bring them back and acclimate them to an aquarium, or you purchase them from a marine specimen supplier. The procedures for acclimating them are the same.

Unpack specimens in dark or subdued light. Intense light may cause some fish and cephalopods to go into shock. Float the bags in the aquarium to bring the water temperature up or down to ambient or room temperature. After an hour or two, open the bags and check the water temperature. If there is more than a 2°F difference between the two bodies of water, let the bags remain floating.

Acclimate the new animals to the tank by slowly increasing the volume of water in the bags by trickling in sea water from the receiving aquarium. If the water in the bags is not fouled by excretion from the specimens, add about a third of it to the aquarium. Always watch the reaction of the specimens during transfer; if they act nervous or contract, stop the operation until they have time to adjust.

Some species will adjust immediately to the new environment, others take several hours or even half a day. This period is the most critical part of their survival. It is quite discouraging to bring a big collection of animals back from the field and see them die as soon as they are placed in the aquarium because they were not properly acclimated. And if you have purchased your specimens, remember that most guarantees of specimen shippers cover only live arrival and do not extend to the survival of the animals in your aquarium, so do everything slowly and carefully.

The following chapters will deal with marine animals in their phylogenetic arrangement, beginning with sponges and working up through the evolutionary scale to fishes. Some techniques and notes on the longevity and culturing methods are included, along with general information on how to preserve specimens for museum and teaching purposes. There is much to be learned on both fronts, and live specimens for the aquarium collector and pickled specimens for the museum collector are not at separate ends of a rope in a tug-of-war. To classify many specimens they must be first preserved. An aquarium is a joy to observe, but it is a temporary thing, always changing like the ocean as new animals are brought in and old ones die off. A good aquarium collection needs to be balanced with an ever growing and expanding reference collection of preserved animals from specific areas. If a new jellyfish or sea slug drifts into the area, it may be kept alive briefly and observed and studied before it dies, but it should be placed in formaldehyde and documented with ecological data as positive proof of its existence. This is a very important step in determining the zoogeographic range of the species.

Many of the creatures discussed in the following chapters range from Nova Scotia to Texas. A few bizarre tropical forms occur in the northern Gulf of Mexico, having strayed up from the West Indies and the lower Caribbean, but the majority of the species occur in substantial numbers along the Carolina and Georgia coastline. Although there are some general notes and descriptions, the sections dealing with the different phyla are not intended as any sort of field guide or laboratory key. They are just descriptions of creatures I have collected on the tide flats which have caught my fancy. Some marine animals are treated more extensively than others, generally because they are more abundant or there is more to say about them. An aggressive, pinching blue crab that scuttles across the deck of a shrimp trawler with its claws raised, ready to grab onto anyone that approaches, demands more description than some obscure species of encrusting sponge that sits eternally on the bottom pumping water through its canal system.

There are many common Atlantic and Gulf forms that were not even mentioned simply because there is no room. To attempt to list even a small portion of the thousands of species of marine invertebrates in the Gulf is well beyond the scope of this book.

The reader is referred to a number of excellent references that will guide him to marine life. Minor's *Field Guide to Seashore Life* is perhaps the best illustrated, but the names are a bit out of date. Abbott's *American Seashells* is an excellent guide to the hundreds of marine mollusks that might be encountered, and Breeder's *Fishes of the Western Atlantic* gives helpful descriptions. Perhaps the best reference to North Atlantic invertebrates is *Keys to the Marine Invertebrates of the Woods Hole Region* compiled by Ralph I. Smith. However, the student should not overlook some of the splendid books on Pacific coast animals, notably Rickett's and Calvin's *Between Pacific Tides*. While the species are generally not the same, the same genera of animals found along the shores of the Pacific Ocean also exist on the Atlantic.

Unfortunately, there are many creatures along our coasts that do not appear in any common keys. They appear in scientific literature tucked away in dusty museum libraries and they are known to only a few specialists. With the ever increasing interest in our environment, it is important that everyone learn the names of our coastal creatures so we can take a valid inventory of our natural resources.

14.
Phylum Porifera
The Sponges

In almost any marine habitat, along any beach or rock pile, or in a dredge haul, at least one species of sponge will be encountered. There are approximately 5000 known species of sponges, and they range in distribution from the edge of the sea to the depths of the ocean.

Until 100 years ago, sponges were considered to be some sort of sea vegetable because of their lumpish, sessile nature, always being found growing on the bottom, attached to a rock or clinging to a blade of grass. To the early naturalist, it was inconceivable that such organisms growing in such a lumpish fashion, not visibly eating or responding to touch, could be anything but a vegetable. But in reality they are an animal, and a very simple one at that.

Structurally they are unique among the members of the animal kingdom because their anatomical organization is based on an arrangement of cells, not tissues. A sponge has no mouth, internal organs or nervous system. To derive nourishment from the sea, sponges pass currents of water through their bodies removing nutrients and plankton. The water enters through one or more pores called ostia, is pumped through an internal canal system by choanocytes or collar cells which are very similar to certain flagellate protozoans. The collar cells filter out the food particles, and their beating flagellated tails push the water on through the sponge where it is expelled through excurrent openings called oscula.

dried sponge assortment

The number of oscula, their size and shape often help determine the species, although sponges are generally classified by their spicules and fibers, calcareous or siliceous structures that give sponges their rigid form. There are three main classes of sponges, based upon the nature of their spicule skeleton arrangement. The class Hexactinellida, or glass sponges, have six-rayed siliceous spicules and are found in depths ranging from 300 feet to three miles. Sponges of the class Calcarea, or calcareous sponges, are small, marine forms less than six inches in height and usually dull in color. They are most likely to be encountered in shallow water along the North Atlantic coast and are the only sponges with calcium-carbonate spicules.

The largest group of marine sponges belongs to the class Demospongia (noncalcarea) and usually have a fibrous skeletal material composed of a scleroprotein called spongin. Some species of Demospongia have siliceous spicules and a few have no skeleton at all. While the structural characteristics are important in determining the groups and species, the diver swimming along the bottom of a bay or rocky reef will notice only the striking differences in forms, colors, and sizes of the sponges in the community. Only after he has collected a bag full, prepared them for microscopic examination in the laboratory, measured the spicules and counted their rays, will he be able to return to the depths and make tentative identifications.

Diving over a bottom rich in sponge life is like diving in a magnificent garden. In clear water on limestone rocks and coral bottom, in depths ranging from six to 60 feet, you will see, through your diving mask, an unimaginable diversity of form and color. Everybody is familiar with the natural bath sponge which is harvested commercially, or the synthetic one which is replacing it, but few people outside of marine biology are aware of the wild, mad forms of sponge growth that take place. Sponges mimic almost anything. There are sponges that resemble great brown masses of tangled seaweed belonging to the genus *Haliclona*, or others like *Cliona* can look like numbers of yellow corncobs erecting from the sandy floor. Bright orange finger sponges (*Axinella polycarpa*), aptly named, reach from limestone rock like devil's fingers and look rather threatening. And the huge basket sponge (*Ircinia fasciculata*) can look like the

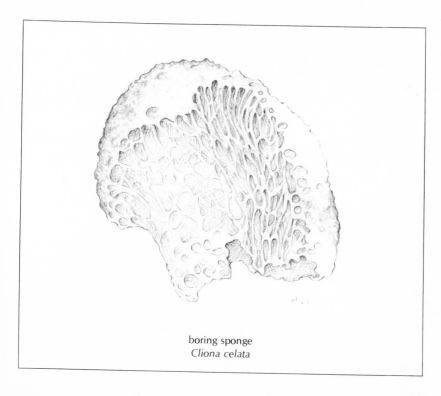

boring sponge
Cliona celata

cannibal's proverbial cooking pot, big enough to cook a pig.

And nature abandoned all restraints when she created the loggerhead sponge *Spheciospongia vesparia* that spreads out like a huge, brown boulder that has tumbled into the sea. And one form of compacted sponge resembles small white rocks and acts like fragments of glass when you handle it. There is always a temptation to squeeze a sponge when you pick it up, but with some species you had better not attempt it; they have the consistency of hard coral or, like the glass sponge, leave your hand filled with splinters that are not easily removed.

Sponges are splendid ecological indicators. There are grass-flat sponges (*Leucosolenia canariensis*) and encrusting yellow sponges (*Lissodendoryx isodictyalis*) that dwell on wharf pilings and encrust shells. Some purple, red and yellow sponges live only on limestone outcrops. Others live on rocky shores of northern coasts, some live on mud bottoms, and others prefer sand or gravel bottoms. There are brackish-water sponges as well as the high-salinity sponges, intertidal species, shallow-water varieties and species restricted to the great depths.

Their colors range the spectrum of the rainbow, from pale creamy white to royal purples, deep greens, orange and absolute scarlets and there are a few species, in the genus *Dysidea* that are lavender in color but some can be absolutely blue, a very rare color in nature. But these sponges concentrate nickel in their cells. Color is often a primary characteristic in identifying sponges, and it is important to keep good color notes, although by far the best method of keeping color notes is to take a color photograph. Color pictures of sponges do not have to be elaborate underwater shots; merely take a freshly collected sponge, put it on a sand background or any other background and take a picture of it. Assign the sponge and the picture a number to keep a cross-reference collection going. Keeping notes on the texture of a living sponge is often just as important as the color. Some feel coarse, others are slimy and leathery, and some are brittle as tufts of bryozoan mats. *Halichondria* is an extremely soft sponge that gives under the slightest pressure of your fingers, while *Tethya crypta* is a dense, firmly packed sponge, and *Geodia* can be as hard as a rock.

Even such aids as peculiar shape, size, texture and color are not always reliable keys and should be considered tentatively. For precise identification, the sizes, arrangement and shapes of the spicules must be examined under a dissecting scope. This is necessary because sponges growing on the seaward shore can look entirely different from the same species growing in a protected harbor. Depth, current and light will often affect coloration, size and shape. For this reason, sponge experts are reluctant and slow to provide ecologists with names for their collections. It takes only an instant to collect a sponge, but it may take hours, days or weeks to classify it.

A few sponges may be tentatively identified by their odor. If you happen to be aboard a shrimp trawler some night in the Gulf of Mexico, and waves are showering over the deck and the boat is rocking from side to side, and you are the least bit prone to seasickness, it will take only one garlic sponge to finish you off. The large, brownish, vase-shaped *Ircinia fasciculata* emits such a revolting stench, even when it is alive and healthy, that it will make even the iron-stomached seamen feel queasy. It is one species I have learned to identify in a shrimp trawl catch long before I even dig through the pile of fish and find it.

The identification of sponges is important in making a general survey of the marine fauna and flora of an area. They are found in all the habitats, encrusting on rocks or pilings, erecting from sea-grass bottoms or growing in massive clumps on sandy bottoms. Although they can be collected by hand, a dredge can be a most effective means. Along many portions of Florida's submerged lands a five-minute tow with a scallop drag can produce several hundred pieces of boring sponge (*Cliona celata*), which can weigh over 100 pounds.

Cliona celata in its larval form settles on dead and living shells, bores tiny holes and within a few months grows to a massive yellow glob. Soon it erects from the bottom like a corncob. When they are cast up on the beach, bright yellow *Cliona* turns brown but can be most attractive when dried. Periodically another attractive sponge, *Microciona prolifera*, the red beard sponge which grows on dead shell and rock, is cast up on the beach after a storm, but it too loses its color.

Although we often find basket sponges (*Ircinia*) and garlic sponges, and even huge loggerheads full of shrimp, thrown upon the shore, their occurrence is sporadic and nothing dependable. However, one small and very unusual sponge, *Xestospongia halichondrioides*, can almost always be found on north Florida beaches.

Xestospongia halichondrioides, the hermit crab sponge, is one of my favorite sponges because it is the only sponge that travels. It is a smooth, colorful species that grows exclusively on snail shells that may be inhabited by several species of hermit crabs and occasionally it occurs on living snails, especially *Cantharus*. To the collector the sponge has many advantages: it is small, compact and so vividly orange or green in color that it makes a handsome addition to any salt-water aquarium, but it also fits easily into a small bottle for preservation.

Xestospongia halichondrioides is a puzzler. Its association with hermit crabs and snails was first described by Dr. Harry Wells, a well-known invertebrate zoologist who was working on marine life in Alligator Harbor. However, we repeatedly sent samples to Yale and learned that the basic identification of *Xestospongia* may be completely misleading; it may not even be that genus, let alone that species, but at present a name like "hermit crab sponge" is better than none.

hermit crab sponge
Xestospongia halichondrioides

While specialists are arguing about the taxonomy of this species, we are puzzled about the relationship of the sponge to the crab. It hasn't been thoroughly studied and seems to be devoid of rhyme or reason. One often wonders how the crab manages to move about with such a massive sponge on its back, and from the observations we have made of sponges and crabs, it seems that the crab doesn't move about very much at all.

Paguristes hummi is a peculiar, fuzzy, little hermit crab described by Marvin Wass from Alligator Harbor and named after the oceanographer and algae specialist, Harold Humm. The relationship of this crab and the sponges makes some sense, since *Paguristes hummi* is a filter-feeder and strains plankton and detritus from the water. *Paguristes* has been called "the sponge hermit crab" because it has only been found inside these small orange or green lumpy sponges. However, a number of other hermit crabs are also found overgrown with *Xestospongia*, including *Pagurus impressus, P. bonairensis, P. longicarpus* and *P. policaris*, which would find the sponge a burden because they must forage around the bottom for food.

All the hermit crab sponges can be instantly recognized by a small round opening on the bottom, or flattened, side of the sponge where the crabs can duck their head, thorax and forelegs in and out. On very small sponge lumps, I have seen the crab bravely carrying the encrusting colony on its back, moving slowly over the bottom.

It seems that the sponge absorbs much of the gastropod shell; we have cut sponges open and found the shell worn very thin or completely missing. Quite often just the sponge lump is found with no crab or snail in it, or when you cut a sponge that may be eight inches across you'll find a quarter-inch snail shell completely engulfed and overgrown. Since there was no snail or crab inside to push out an opening, the sponge mass grew into a large flattened colony without an opening.

Dr. Wells described "false shells" from these sponges, which we have also observed along the beaches of Alligator Point. When the sponge dies it decomposes in layers and the sponge mass takes on the exact shape of the snail shell that is inside, only on a much larger scale.

It has often amazed me that a creature as abundant as the hermit crab sponge, with its vivid, striking colors, does not have more scientific attention given to it. But this is simply a matter of locality. Had the sponge occurred abundantly along the coast of Massachusetts near Woods Hole instead of northwest Florida, its morphology would have been completely described, the relationship between the crab and the sponge carefully studied, and its value as an experimental animal for embryology, physiology and biochemistry thoroughly exploited.

However, there is hope for this species. Since we have started distributing them, the research and teaching community has greatly increased the demand for them. Years ago, after a few dozen were taken aboard our shrimp trawler, we culled the rest overboard, but this is no longer the case. We keep them all. Furthermore, we have noted areas where they are more abundant. At certain times of the year they manage to collect at the bottom of deep channels where they can be dredged in large numbers. This makes me think the crab has something to do with it, dragging the sponge away from the shallows to deeper, warmer waters.

After a hurricane or some strong offshore winds, hundreds, even thousands, of *Xestospongia halichondrioides* are cast up on shore, and the art and science of beachcombing is employed to harvest them.

Sometimes the sponge is damaged this way, and when brought back to the aquarium soon turns milky white as its tissues begin to decompose. The majority survive and are fit for specimens. *Xestospongia* is one of the finest sponges for the aquarium because it leads a rugged existence moving about the bottom, dragged by the crab and pushed by currents. It survives for months in a simple salt-water aquarium, and when all the other sponges have died and rotted away *Xestospongia* is still moving healthily about the aquarium. We have had many colonies outlive the crab within.

Preservation of Sponges

Preservation of sponges is a relatively simple affair, since they do not have muscles to contract or a nervous system which must first be insensitized. Unfortunately, all those beautiful colors, the orange reds, vivid yellows and greens, fade into dull brown colors and in a short time this once-beautiful creature is reduced to a horrid-looking black mass which clouds and discolors alcohol and leaches out all its organic substances into the solution. Some species which have a naturally strong odor when freshly collected will develop an even stronger, lasting fetid odor when preserved, even if they have been soaking in alcohol for years.

The classic method of preserving sponges has been to plunge them into 90 percent ethyl alcohol and later transfer them to a 70 percent ethyl alcohol solution. If you are going to undertake a project of building a representative collection of sponges from a particular area, be sure to have plenty of alcohol available. A 55-gallon drum would not be too much for most collections. The juices within the sponge wreak havoc upon alcohol, and certain species can turn the solution to a black soupy mess even after several complete changes of fresh alcohol have been made. Furthermore, water is often drawn from the sponge into the alcohol solution, lowering the concentration to the point where preservation is no longer effective and bacteria move in and soon reduce the collection to a gummy, smelly, useless muddle.

Dr. Willard D. Hartman, a renowned sponge specialist at Yale University, once wrote me a letter suggesting that sponges be initially fixed in neutralized Formalin (1 lb. of hexamethylenetetramine added to one gallon of commercial Formalin, or 37 percent formaldehyde). This stock solution is used for making up a final solution of 10 percent Formalin. After two or three days, or even a week, the material should be transferred to 80 percent alcohol. This method of fixation preserves the tissues for histological examination.

If they are not preserved in buffered Formalin, the sponges will soon be reduced to a gummy mass due to the action of the formic acid on the sponge spicules.

It is not practical to preserve a large sponge in any solution because many species can fill a 5-gallon can by itself, and some could easily fill a 50-gallon drum. With big colonies such as these, it is adequate to cut off a small piece and preserve it. A piece 2 by 4 inches is ideal, because it can later be used for slide preparations. However, at least a description of the sponge, its size, shape and color, is essential to cross reference with the preserved sample.

If time and space permit, the sponge may be dried in its entirety for a general collection and cross-referenced with a piece of well-preserved sponge colony which is kept in a 3- or 4-ounce jar. Dried sponges can be quite beautiful and can make a handsome addition to a reference collection, but nothing can smell worse than an improperly cured sponge.

Curing can be accomplished by soaking the sponge in neutralized

Formalin for a couple of days or immersing it in alcohol. Formalin tends to render the sponge colony brittle, and invariably the tissues soak up the preservative and that tangy Formalin odor will usually remain. Alcohol is best, but it is expensive. However, even that problem can be solved if you do not discard your used alcohol. After preserving crabs, sponges, sea cucumbers, and other animals as well as sample sponges, throw all the used and discolored alcohol that is left over from changing solutions into a container. Then add about one-third percent alcohol to the discard solution and immerse sponges, sea whips, crabs, starfish, sea urchins or anything else that you wish to dry. After one or two day's soaking, remove them and place them on wire racks. For decorative effects, dried sponges may be dipped in dye or paint to restore their natural color.

Spicule mounts can be made from dry sponges as well as from alcohol specimens. Basically the spicules are teased off the sponge colony and mounted on slides. However, if permanent slides are to be made, hand sections a few microns thick should be sliced from well-preserved specimens and mounted so the flagellate chambers and the cell structure can be studied. An elaborate procedure of mounting spicules under cover slips, running them through stains and washes is usually followed. Such procedure can be found in Wagstaffe and Fielder's *Preservation of Natural History Specimens* or in M. W. deLaubenfel's paper, "A Discussion of the Sponge Fauna of the Dry Tortugas."

15.
Phylum Coelenterata
Hydroids, Jellyfish, Corals, and Others

The phylum Coelenterata is a large and difficult invertebrate group for the biological collector to deal with. The phylum is highly diverse, including hydroids, jellyfish and anthozoans (which are comprised of corals, sea fans and sea anemones). All of these organisms have one thing in common, a centrally located mouth surrounded by one or more whorls of stinging tentacles. Only in the Coelenterata (with a few exceptions) does one find those little stinging organs called nematocysts which are located in specialized cells called cnidoblasts. These contain the long, coiled threads of toxic protein, which rapidly uncoil and stab into an unsuspecting victim, giving it a severe and often immobilizing sting.

Most nematocysts are too small to penetrate human skin, and in most instances all you receive is a sticky feeling after handling the tentacles of large sea anemones or colonies of hydroids, but some jellyfish, man-of-war and hydroid colonies can deliver a most severe and shocking sting. There are cuboidal jellyfish in Australian waters that have killed people, and cubomedusae that invade the southeastern Atlantic coast from time to time and drive tourists out of the water to the beaches. Sun scald jellyfish and stinging nettles have closed down bathing areas, and in Florida the man-of-war is the biggest pest.

However, despite their unpleasant stinging problem, they are a wonder of color, form and beauty, and many collectors, including myself, are intrigued with the phylum Coelenterata.

Class Hydrozoa

If you're diving around an old wharf, a sunken boat or the base of some pilings, chances are you'll encounter one or more species of Hydrozoa, which is a class of coelenterates containing approximately 2100 species. You may not notice them because most species are not flamboyant enough to attract attention; often they are drab in color, and at first glance appear as seaweed. Some look like brown algae and tufted bryozoans that also grow on wharf pilings, boat bottoms or rocks. Even the colorful, showy hydroids like *Tubularia* with their large heads bristling with colorful tentacles appear as drab-colored stems of seaweed at first glance.

When a cluster is pulled from its holdfast, placed in a petri dish and examined under a dissecting scope, its intricate beauty comes into its own. The hydroid colony has a stem with variable numbers of little polyps growing on it, each polyp has tentacles studded with knobby nematocysts. And upon viewing them, you become lost in this small, complex and alive world. Hungry polyps, some looking like snapdragons, others like daisies, expand their knobby, translucent tentacles, flexing and slowly waving them and, suddenly and quite unexpectedly, snatch at a bit of planktonic life, stinging it, drawing it in with one violent contraction, digesting it and expanding out again. There are many polyps in a colony, hundreds of them, some doing nothing, others in motion; it's all quite confusing and difficult to follow with the eye, but all very intriguing.

The life history of the hydrozoan deserves special mention. From the profusely branched stems of many of the commonly encountered forms spring small medusa buds. These are sexual organs, delicate little jellyfish that swell and grow until they are large and ripe. At just the right time of year, when the water temperature is right for that particular species, and the tide changes, the medusa buds, called

cluster of *Bougainvillia carolinensis*

gonophores, break off and float freely about the bays and estuaries, and even drift out to the open ocean.

The little bell-shaped medusa is much more highly organized than the polyp, having a well-developed digestive and nervous system and sense organs (ocelli and statocysts) that are in a sense like eyes and ears. The medusae are separately sexed and while floating freely about the waters in teeming multitudes, they discharge their sperm and ova which unite. The egg divides and grows to a blastula stage which develops sometime later into a free-swimming planula larva. The planula larvae soon settle on a desirable surface such as an old tire, an unpainted boat bottom or a wharf piling and start a new colony of hydroids growing.

139

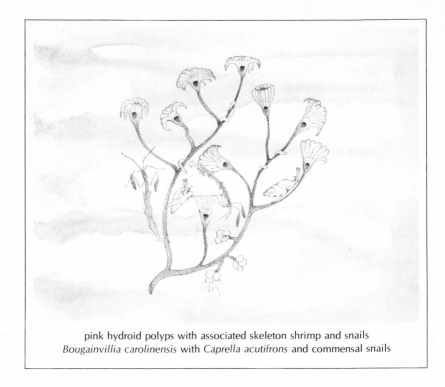

pink hydroid polyps with associated skeleton shrimp and snails
Bougainvillia carolinensis with *Caprella acutifrons* and commensal snails

Hydromedusae are generally studied by biological oceanographers who frequently capture them in plankton hauls. The taxonomy of hydromedusae is in a state of mass confusion even in parts of the world where there has been a considerable amount of study on them. The benthic specialist has developed a system of classification based upon a sessile, hydroid colony, counting and describing tentacles, medusae buds, stems, color and all the other intricate features that he sees when he examines a colony closely. The plankton specialist describes the structure of the free-swimming medusae, and, in some instances, has given the hydroid polyp stage and the medusa stage entirely different generic and specific names.

Fortunately, not all of the hydrozoans propagate in this confusing manner; many are asexual and use budding to reproduce, or produce gametes that settle on the same substrate and begin to grow, making their life history easy. Most of the large, conspicuous hydromedusa stages originally break off from obscure, small polypoid stages that may appear as bits of white fuzz growing on turtle grass or at the base of a piling. When the gonophores break loose they grow rapidly

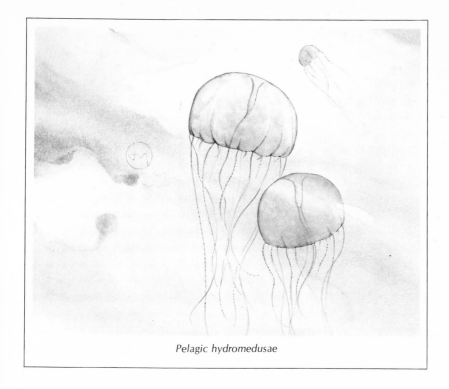

Pelagic hydromedusae

and sometimes become much bigger than the parent colony.

A collector can help clear up this state of taxonomic confusion by getting hydroids just before the medusa buds break free. Although this is seldom easy, sometimes you could be happening along a piling and take a sample of the hydroid and notice immediately that it is in the process of spawning medusae. The green sea glimmers with the iridescence of small hydromedusae breaking off. A fine-meshed dip net or plankton net swooped through the waters will get a number of the already freed forms and they can be kept alive if they are gently deposited in a fresh bucket of sea water.

Although the dock owner will generally regard hydroids as a pest because they add to the undesirable growth of fouling organisms, if he likes to fish he should regard them as an asset. Hydroids are a great place for teeming multitudes of small organisms to hide in. The average clump of hydroids will have little dragonlike nudibranchs crawling on it, larval snails, bristle worms, and skeleton shrimp in their never-ceasing rhythm bending and flexing up and down. The hydroids soon attract mud crabs, and grass shrimp (*Palaemonetes, Palaemon* and *Hippolsymata*) which dig into the holdfasts of the hydroid colonies to find food. Porcelain crabs (*Petrolisthes*) filter-feed around the hydroid, and numbers of juvenile blue crabs or adult xanthid crabs no wider than a half inch across their carapace come there also. Blennies and gobies live among the colonies feasting upon all the little associated creatures.

A single cluster piece no more than three inches square might yield 50 flexing and bobbing skeleton shrimp (*Caprella acutifrons*), tiny snails, mussels, larval clams and several dragonlike eolid nudibranchs, no telling how many copepods and amphipods and small nereid worms that crawl about the stems. Perhaps there will be a flatworm or two and probably a number of attached or encrusting matted bryozoans, tunicates or even sponges. In fact I know of no other small area where there are so many, many creatures representing the animal kingdom.

All these little animals provide food for fish. I have noticed that relatively new wharf pilings that are not as heavily colonized with hydroids generally have far fewer fish hanging around them. The old,

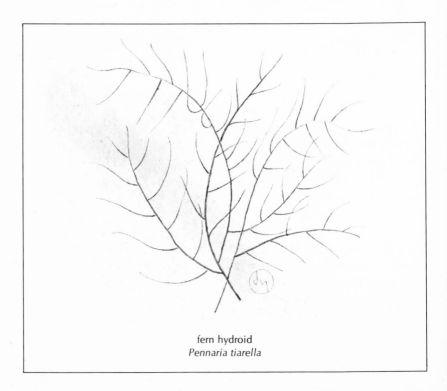

fern hydroid
Pennaria tiarella

overgrown docks produce the best channel bass, sheepshead and drum.

A note on the methods of collecting hydroids should be provided. When the colony is removed from a piling, pull gently at its holdfast instead of jerking it off because the polyps may be damaged in the process, especially if your grip on the bottom slips and your fingers crush the living portion of the organism. A knife is useful for scraping the pilings, or a regular scraping tool does well. If the hydroids are growing on oysters or barnacles they can be easily taken off by breaking the living substrate away from the dead one.

Keep your hydroid collection in containers with plenty of sea water, and above all keep them cool. They are constantly releasing nematocysts into the sea water when confined and this causes them to deteriorate faster. I have found that hydroids deteriorate more rapidly than almost any other creature. Keep buckets covered, and change water often, especially in summer months.

With the exception of one or two species, most hydroids quickly die back when they are removed from their natural habitat and placed in the aquarium. I met one zoologist who successfully grew many fouling species by carefully pipetting clam juice over the hydroid colony every day. He had his tank rigged up with rapidly circulating water from two powerful outside filters, and took special pains to see that his colony thrived.

It never hurts to try hydroids in a salt-water aquarium. Long after the colony dies back the amphipods and other organisms continue to live, and they remain as perpetual food for sea horses, pipefish and other hard-to-feed salt-water fish.

Hydractinia echinata
Hermit Crab Hydroid

Hydractinia echinata is a must for every aquarium. It is another one of those interesting commensal relationships where one animal lives upon another without doing any apparent harm, as opposed to the relationship of direct parasitism, where the parasite partakes of the host's body fluids and damages the host over a period of time.

But not so with *Hydractinia*, the bright pink fuzzy hydroid that encrusts snail shells occupied by hermit crabs. When you look into a tide pool or walk a sandy beach and see little snail shells move about with crabs inside of them, you can instantly spot *Hydractinia* covered specimens. They are pink, rather mossy or fuzzy and quite attractive. In the colder months the pink fuzz blossoms out and looks even luxurious.

While *Hydractinia* is another Maine-to-Texas form, it is much more robust and developed on specimens in the northern region. Specimens I have gathered at Cape Cod, for example, covered a much larger area, often completely engulfing the shell of a large hermit crab, as opposed to sparse populations of hydroid fuzz on crabs in Florida.

The hydroid colony itself grows luxuriously on the crabs kept in aquariums, and investigators using both open- and closed-system aquariums have claimed excellent results with the hydroid.

This hydroid is a perfect example of polymorphism, where a single colony on a crab can have a number of branched, elongated and knobby-type tentacles. And the polyps can be seen to feed actively.

Although *Hydractinia echinata* is principally found on hermit crabs, it has, in a few rare instances, settled on stones or pilings in small patches where there is a fast-moving current and plenty of clean water. The colony thrives best where there is constant movement, and a busy hermit crab scouring over the bottom devouring a bit of rotten fish, or eating a worm, gives it plenty of water movement; also, the polyps probably partake of minute particles of food thrown up from the hermit crab's dinner. Although there is no definite proof, one can conjecture that the stinging nematocysts of *Hydractinia* make a hungry fish think twice before devouring a coated crab. So in a sense a mutualism develops.

True mutualism can be defined as a biological relationship where one organism grows upon another to the mutual benefit of both. The term "symbiosis" usually is applied to lower plants and the classical example is given between the algal and fungoid elements in lichens. But in all actuality the effort to differentiate symbiosis from commensalism and parasitism proves most baffling. Perhaps "mutualism" is a better word in the case of the hydroid *Hydractinia echinata* and the hermit crab.

Commensalism can be defined as two different species living together in a constant association. Only one derives benefit from this relationship. The small white flatworm *Bdelloura candida* is an example; its host, the horseshoe crab, provides shelter, transportation and food from the tiny scraps of food kicked up by the crab.

Commensalism tends to evolve toward parasitism where one organism lives upon the blood and body fluid of the host's body, causing the host a certain amount of harm. This is clearly illustrated in tapeworms and flukes, but the line of parasitism and commensalism becomes obscured in many other organisms.

The "commensal" barnacle *Octolasmis mulleri* is a prime example. It lives on the gills of brachyuran crabs and some lobsters, taking food from the water currents that circulate through the host's gills. However, they can become so numerous on the surface of the crab's gills, and so crowded in the gill chamber that it is questionable whether the crab is able to respire properly. Generally when we find shrunken, sick crabs that are overgrown with barnacles and algae, an autopsy reveals their gills are choked with *Octolasmis* barnacles, indicating the barnacles are commensal to the point of parasitism.

The association between *Hydractinia echinata* and other hermit crabs is probably a loose form of symbiosis or mutualism. We have not found hermit crabs covered with *Hydractinia* in the stomachs of fish. The real test will come when a crab covered with *Hydractinia echinata* is placed in an aquarium with a flame-streak box crab (*Calappa flammea*) that preys upon hermit crabs.

Biologists have tried to test this association with hermit crabs covered with cloak anemones (*Calliactis tricolor*) and found the box crab didn't hesitate to rip the hermit crab apart. So where do these relationships really stand? Perhaps in nature and not in the aquarium these associations work.

Most hydroids do very poorly in a marine aquarium and die after a few days. *Hydractinia echinata*, however, is an exception because they live for months. Another hermit crab hydroid, *Podocoryne carnea*, looks very much like *Hydractinia*, only they produce free-swimming medusae which are a delight to watch under a dissecting scope. Fortunately *Podocoryne* can also be successfully maintained in the laboratory.

Physalia
Portuguese Man-of-war

Far out in the great blue Atlantic, uncountable millions of Portuguese man-of-war (*Physalia*) follow the Gulf Stream as it flows north. If there have been three days or more of prevailing easterly

145

winds, during the winter the strange floating jellyfish with their sail-like pink and bluish floats inflated largely with nitrogen gases, and their extremely long purple tentacles, often measuring 40 to 50 feet, come drifting into shore, bobbing above the waves until the seas cast them high on the beach.

Then no beachcomber could miss them. Every few feet of beach is occupied with one of these eye-catching blue floats, and there is a temptation to bend down and pick one up. Don't, unless you have rubber gloves, because they carry one of the most severe stings of any creature in the sea.

In Daytona Beach, Fort Lauderdale and other east Florida coast cities, the Coast Guard gives daily predictions of the number of *Physalia* expected to hit the beaches. When a heavy invasion of man-of-war comes ashore, the beaches are closed to bathing entirely.

Few creatures on earth are so beautiful, yet so devastating. The novice might be thrilled with them at first, bend down to examine their long streamers of purple tentacles, look at their little round swimming bells and their blue sail, never suspecting that this creature of beauty can deliver a most painful and immobilizing sting. The exact nature of the poisons is unknown, but some physiologists believe that three toxins are involved, one producing paralysis of the nervous system, another inhibiting respiration and the third resulting in extreme prostration and death if a very large dose is received.

On occasion swimmers become entangled with *Physalia* tentacles and wind up in the hospital to be treated for shock. Drowning after being stung is the greatest danger, although there was one death directly related to the *Physalia physalia* poison at Daytona Beach, Florida.

Unfortunately there is no really good treatment for man-of-war stings. Warren Zeiler, a curator of the Miami Seaquarium, was kind enough to let me print here the treatment instructions that he keeps posted on his laboratory wall.

Ocean water should be poured over the injured parts; it is important that you do *not* use fresh water. Do not rub the area with sand, but remove the tentacles immediately, preferably with a glove. Alcohol should be poured over the wounded area, and flour, baking soda or shaving cream applied to the irritated area which appears, in a few moments, as a large red blotch or welt. The absorbative materials should be scraped away with a sharp knife or instrument and the wound washed again with sea water. A corticosteroid-analgesic balm is then administered to the surface, preferably by aerosol and, if condition warrants, the victim should be rushed to the hospital.

This general technique works well for stings from jellyfish of all kinds. In many instances *Physalia* receives blame for stinging attacks on bathers, when in fact it is not *Physalia physalia*, but the dreaded cubomedusa, *Chiropsalmus quadrigatus*, or sea wasp, that is responsible. Sea wasps move swiftly into the shallows, expanding and contracting their completely transparent bells and are never seen by the swimmer.

Physalia can always be seen. Unlike some other species of siphonophores that can deflate and sink out of sight to avoid a storm at sea, *Physalia physalia* is incapable of regulating its gases and stays constantly afloat. It can be seen in the roughest surf, riding on top of the waves with its blue float moving ahead of the wind.

The Portuguese man-of-war belongs to the order Siphonophora, which is a suborder of the class Hydrozoa. Although it is commonly considered as one of the jellyfish, it is more closely related to the tubularian hydroids than to a true scyphozoan jellyfish. Siphonophores are a very complex group of polymorphic organisms all living together on the same animal. Like a conglomerate corporation they are made up of independent organisms: pneumatophores or floats, nectophores or swimming bells that propel the colony, hydrophalla, leaflike protective zooids, gonophores or reproductive polyps and dactylozooids and tentaculae, which are tentacles armed with numerous powerful stinging cells.

The Portuguese man-of-war has only one real natural enemy, and that is the sea turtle. I have seen hordes of them at sea, and in the midst of them two or three giant loggerhead sea turtles (*Caretta caretta caretta*) eagerly munching away on the tentacles. The turtles are not immune to the severe stings; their eyes become puffed and swollen and red. They seem to go into a feeding frenzy and madly stuff themselves, and in the midst of devouring *Physalia*, they lose their coordination. They look terrible.

Watching this scene, you cannot help but wonder if sea turtles are getting drunk on eating man-of-war. There couldn't be much nutrient value because they are almost all water. Perhaps the nematocysts work on their nervous system the way alcohol or narcotics work on ours, but when the man-of-war are in, the turtles are after them. After they have been gorging themselves, they are much less responsive, and will not duck under the water at the approach of a boat, the way turtles normally do.

There is also a small banded man-of-war fish (*Nomeus gronowi*) that feeds around the base of the tentacles devouring *Physalia's* leftovers and droppings, and even nibbling on the stinging tentacles. The fish, however, is not immune to the stings and when the fish is swooped up in a dip net with *Physalia*, it will be stung to death promptly.

Class Scyphozoa

True scyphozoan jellyfish are a familiar sight along the seashore, and they can usually be seen pulsating along the shallows, contracting and expanding their umbrellas. Along the southeast Atlantic and Gulf of Mexico coasts a number of species are common. In the summer months millions of pale white *Stomolophus meleagris* rapidly move through the blue water, stinging everything in their path. We have actually seen them drive off a school of sharks and make porpoises leave the bay.

Large rubbery *Rhopilema verrilli* are visitors to north Florida shores during the late Fall, and they are seen commonly throughout the winter cast up on the beaches. Occasionally the saucer-shaped moon jellyfish (*Aurelia aurita*) travels into the estuaries of the Apalachee Bay, but it is a very unpredictable form, and gives only a slight sting when handled, and never causes any trouble.

This is quite the opposite of the more sporadic cubomedusae *Chiropsalmus quadrumanus*, the American version of Australia's sea wasp. Daytona Beach suffered an outbreak of these crystal-clear, bell-shaped devils that moved quickly, quietly and unnoticed through the shallows where bathers were enjoying the surf. Suddenly cries of pain were heard and people fled the water. They never saw what hit them. Some people were so severely hit they had to be hospitalized.

Chrysaora quinquecirrha
Stinging Nettle Jellyfish

Chrysaora (Dactylometra) quinquecirrha is one of the commoner jellyfish of the Atlantic and Gulf coasts, often appearing in such vast numbers that they make swimming impossible and have closed down many recreational beaches of the Chesapeake Bay region. But to the observer and student of nature, they are one of the most interesting and colorful creatures to watch, both in form and in movement. The umbrella is pale white, ribbed with reddish markings that much resemble the spokes of a wheel, and when you see them from a boat they resemble numerous little red wheels pulsating along the surface. Fine reddish tentacles also trail down from the umbrella and these promise a painful death to all creatures that pass under it.

The minnow that swims by and is touched by the tentacles stiffens and dies from the venomous sting. For the diver who is swimming bare-backed through a colony, flashes of scalding fire sweep over his back leaving red, fiery welts. Enough *Chrysaora* can hospitalize a diver and in an extreme case cause his death by drowning.

The jellyfish move on, sometimes as many as 10 per cubic yard of surface water. They are a fearsome force, devouring all that meets their path. But they are more often than not accompanied by small silver fish that swim about their tentacles with apparent immunity. However, you soon find out that they too are not at all immune to the nematocysts when you scoop up the *Chrysaora* and the associated fish in the net. As soon as the fish are engulfed in the stinging slime of their "host" they stiffen and die almost instantly. Even if they are placed in a bucket with the jellyfish, the discharged cnidoblasts and the gooey slime soon wipe the fish out entirely.

A study should be made of the potency of jellyfish nematocysts under controlled temperature, salinity and pH conditions of the water to find out why they are more potent during certain times of the year than at other times. Often during the winter you can scoop up handfuls of *Chrysaora* without any apparent sensation and then there are other times, especially during the summer, when a single strand of tentacles will cause an extremely painful sting. Investigators who routinely study *Chrysaora* in Chesapeake Bay have told me they have experienced differences in *Chrysaora*'s stinging abilities.

A general rule should be followed with *Chrysaora* and all other

149

medusa jellyfish. If they must be handled bare-handed, then pick them up by the medusa bell. Although a dip net is one of the better ways of collecting them, specimens that are to be kept alive for study are best collected by dipping them up in a bucket of water.

During the winter and late spring they wash ashore and become stranded on the beach. If they have not yet hit the shoreline (which is generally instant death for them) you can walk along the shallows of an inlet and pick up excellent, live pulsating specimens. This is another form of beachcombing and one of the easiest methods of collecting. Many of the shoreward-blown specimens I have found were filled with freshly devoured green nereid polychaetes.

In recent years *Chrysaora quinquecirrha* has become a terrific problem in the Chesapeake Bay region and has caused the tourist industry to lose money. During the summer months swimming is impossible. Consequently motels, restaurants, curio shops and the communities that depend upon the summer influx of bathers are in trouble. Biologists have been tackling the problem of sea-nettle migrations to see if there isn't a way to increase the predators on jellyfish. A small eolid nudibranch is fond of feasting upon the sessile larval stages of *Chrysaora quinquecirrha*.

It has been discovered that they have beneficial effects because it is believed that they balance the ctenophore, or sea walnut, populations which feed extensively on oyster larvae. Juvenile harvestfish, *Peprilus paru* have been observed swimming around the tentacles along Chesapeake Bay and in Florida waters, using them as protection as well.

Nevertheless, the tourist industry would like them abolished, and has unsuccessfully tried to keep them from invading swimming beaches by setting nets, but the major portions of the tentacles and medusa bodies manage to sweep by and get to the swimmers. Chemicals have been tried as control measures, but there is no chemical known that will destroy only jellyfish and not other forms of marine life. The solution to their control would be the development of some inexpensive chemical effective only on the sea nettle and not harmful to anything else.

Some biologists have unofficially expressed the theory that the drastic increase in sewage pouring into the estuaries has provided nourishment to maturing jellyfish. Others suspect that natural predators may have declined because of pollution. If so, we should not be too surprised if stinging nettles reach epidemic proportions in time to come.

150

Class Anthozoa

Now we come to the anthozoans, the largest and by far the most important class of coelenterates. There are approximately 6000 species of anthozoans classified in several orders and subclasses, including hard and soft corals, sea whips, fans, antipatharians, sea pens, zooantharians and sea anemones. Many of the subclasses are poorly represented in the coastal waters of the United States and many groups are found only in the Indian Ocean; so for simplicity's sake, and the sake of the beachcomber, I am going to break them down into coral-types and anemones.

Anthozoans are not simply organisms; they comprise an entire habitat in many parts of the world. In the tropics great coral reefs are made up of millions of living polyps and furnish a home and food to thousands of colorful fishes. Coral heads are grown over with sea anemones, soft corals, sea fans and antipatharians. Sea urchins feed on the polyps and the lime structures are riddled with boring clams and feather-duster worms. A whole ecological community is built up around the anthozoans, and at the head of the food chain is man in his pirogue or outrigger canoe with a hook and line or a bamboo trap, catching parrot fish or sharks to eat.

There is nothing to compare with the outrageous colors of soft corals, the organpipe coral's green polyps and red sea whips, the staghorn corals, brain corals and massive yellow anemones, some measuring 3 feet across. You should go to the tropical waters, put on a diving mask and see this splendor for yourself.

Anthozoans are poorly represented in semitropical and temperate zones, are fewer in numbers, and comprise only a small part of the total biomass. In the northern Gulf of Mexico there are a few species of sea whips, some soft corals, and a few corals. Sea anemones are common on certain sand flats, and small species are often found encrusting rocks and wharf pilings. But to find them you have to look for them, not like the tropics where they glare at you from every direction.

The further you go out into the Gulf, the more anthozoans you will encounter, especially the corals such as *Cladophora, Oculina* and *Solenaster*. However, these corals appear as small outcroppings, and in only a very few places do they make up much of the bottom community.

There is one exception, the sea pansy (*Renilla mulleri*), which is related to the sea pen. Sea pansies occur in shallow water, and sometimes are so abundant that they literally cover the bottom and will gorge a shrimp net. They are a warm-water form that does not venture far above the Georgia coast. Other species of *Renilla* are abundant on the mudflats of southern California. *Renilla mulleri* is an interesting and unique alcyonarian, and deserving of special attention.

Renilla mulleri
The Sea Pansy

The sea pansy (*Renilla mulleri*) is a delight to watch when it is alive in an aquarium. The colony expands, puffs out and blossoms with hundreds of white polyps, each covered with eight feathery pinnate tentacles. Sea pansies are aggressive feeders and you can watch the polyps go wild in the aquarium as they stretch out to grab at this bit of food or that.

If there is just a trace of mud on the bottom of a large, flat pan with a few sea pansies, you can see from their winding serrated tracks how they inch themselves along the bottom. This accounts for their sudden appearance in a harbor or shallow bay; just when you think you've pinpointed them, and go back with a dredge or trawl a week later, they've all left.

At certain times of the year sea pansies come inshore, and quite a few can be picked up along the mud and sand flats at a dead low tide. They can withstand a few hours of damp exposure, but it takes a keen eye to spot one down in the sand.

Renilla mulleri ranges from a few scattered individuals to such dense populations that the entire bag of a shrimp trawl can be filled with them. At night they resemble a bag of blue fire as the net is hauled aboard. Each animal has dozens of little pinpoints, particularly around the margin of the colony, glowing brightly. This feature alone has made them popular because they lend themselves to study in the laboratory. The parchment worm, ctenophore jellyfish and midshipman fish in the Atlantic waters are also luminescent, but only the sea pansy can be so easily handled. The midshipman survives well in the aquarium, but it is a rare fish and hard to collect, but the sea pansy can be taken in almost any dredge haul and will survive for months in a simple aquarium providing it is kept in a large volume of water and given sand and mud to bury in.

The sea pansy's luminescent qualities have been extensively studied by investigators at the University of Georgia, working at Sapalo Island. They discovered that *Renilla rensiformis*, a small form found on the Atlantic coast, has a much higher concentration of luciferin, an enzyme responsible for bioluminescence, than its Gulf cousin, *Renilla mulleri.*

Why a sea pansy lights up when stimulated remains open for speculation in any case. Only nudibranchs eat them, so it would not be much of a protective device, nor would it be a mating device. Biologists have long pondered why some marine animals have luminescent powers. Why does a parchment worm in its long tube, nine-tenths of it hidden down in the mud, glow in the dark? For whose eyes does it glow? And one wonders why the sea pansy lights up, and even further, why the Atlantic species have more "fuel" than the Gulf species.

Leptogorgia virgulata
Sea Whip

The colorful sea whips (*Leptogorgia virgulata*) that spring up from rocky bottoms, looking like plastic-coated wire, can be found all along the southeastern United States coast. Their colors range from dark purple to red, orange, yellow and white—and so striking are the diversities of hue that one might think they are different species, but this is not so.

They grow rapidly in Alligator Harbor; rocks and pilings that have been put down in the summer may have a small crop of *Leptogorgia* growing around their bases by the following spring. And I have seen bottoms plucked of all gorgonians and the next year the bottom will once again be covered.

They frequently encrust cockle shells, which is particularly desirable for aquarium use, and wash to the beach after a high tide. If you have to rip a gorgonian from its holdfast, it becomes unmanageable in a small aquarium and has to be wedged into a corner to stand erect. So it is best to collect them attached to a piece of rock or shell.

It's easy to tell whether you have living animals or not; just place them in water for a few hours and row upon row of fuzzy white polyps will appear out of the horny skeleton. These polyps are not as sensitive

153

as *Renilla* polyps and will not respond as quickly to probing. Also, transmission of stimuli is limited. It is possible to sever a stem with a sharp scissors and not cause the polyps to retract.

Gorgonians require a considerable amount of feeding or the colony begins to degenerate. This is readily detectable by the colorful horny skeleton falling off, leaving a black wiry cortex, once again bringing up the analogy of the plastic-coated wire.

Small specimens do moderately well in an aquarium if clam or fish juice is pipetted over the polyps. They can be taken by breaking off the rock to which they are attached, and will make a nice perch for sea horses.

There is a small barnacle, *Balanus galeatus*, that lives within the colony, and it appears as a small nodule. The barnacle may be an internal parasite of some sort, since its feeding legs are never seen to extend outside of the colony, although further testing may prove otherwise.

Leptogorgia has a surprisingly wide range. It is found in the shallows along the semitropical United States and can be commonly dredged off Cape Hatteras and the Virginia coast. A few reports indicate it has been collected off New York and New Jersey coasts, although these are rare instances.

What is most peculiar about this animal is that it is totally absent in tropical waters off the West Indies and the Florida Keys, indicating that it cannot tolerate really warm water. In the summertime in Alligator Harbor, around August, many colonies die off.

There are a few other gorgonians that are taken off north Florida, but only rarely in shallow water. *Lophogorgia hebes*, purple in color, looks more like the dried-out sea fan one sees in souvenir shops and restaurants. The polyps are dark in color and are not as large as *Leptogorgia* but it appears to survive a much longer period of time in captivity.

Astrangia astereiformis
Northern Star Coral

The Northern Coral *Astrangia* is another famous genus popularized by biological supply houses throughout the United States because it is one of the few corals that grow abundantly at Woods

Hole. For almost 100 years boats have dredged pink-and-white clusters of it up from the Falmouth Channel, where *Astrangia danae* grows into flat, rocklike, short-branched clusters.

Astrangia, whether the species be *danae* or *astereiformis* or *solitaria* or some other, has a fascination of its own. Each corallum, the limestone cup, sprouts a large polyp with fingerlike, knobby tentacles that expand in the sea water, reaching out for food. There is something so colorful about these colonies, so beautiful that they catch the eye. They are called star coral, because they seem to shine up from the muddy bottom with a glowing luster.

Probe with your fingers and they will instantly contract, drawing down into the limestone cup and out of sight. The once radiant colony will suddenly turn into nothing more than a piece of colorful rock. With *Astrangia* you can demonstrate that coral is indeed a living animal and not a rock as one might suppose because you can see all these little animals react.

If you probe only one polyp, you will see it contract, then its neighbor respond as the stimulus travels over the surface of the colony; but it soon fades, and only a portion of the colony will be affected.

If you take clam juice or even a bit of hamburger and place it above the colony, you can watch the hungry polyps expand and slowly sweep the water with their tentacles — a fascinating feeding demonstration.

Most corals are hardy animals in an aquarium, but *Astrangia astereiformis* is remarkably so. We have kept specimens for five months in a shallow pan of sea water, changing it every two weeks and giving it very little attention. If they are fed they will survive for an indefinite period of time. Although in an aquarium, filtered sea water and continued feeding are highly recommended. For most classroom purposes it is enough to set clumps of *Astrangia* out in pans of shallow sea water, less than three inches deep but enough to cover the colony and let the polyps expand, and the specimens will survive for at least two weeks.

Their oxygen requirement is not great, and as in the case of certain sea anemones, enough oxygen is retained in the sea water if the depth is no greater than three inches, the natural, surface-tension saturation level. Considering the great difficulty encountered when preserving corals with their polyps expanded, it may prove far more practical for all institutions to study them alive.

Phyllangia americana
Rosebud Coral

For studying large, feeding polyps, *Phyllangia* surpasses *Astrangia* and almost any other coral for that matter. Although some corals have much larger polyps, never will you find more well-defined tentacles or obvious nematocysts in such a hardy coral.

Phyllangia americana is closely related to the celebrated *Astrangia* but is less well known because it is a semitropical coral. Like *Astrangia* it is a more or less encrusting variety found growing out in four- to six-inch colonies on limestone outcrops or on shells dredged up from 60 feet or so out in the Gulf of Mexico.

The fishermen refer to them as "rosebud" coral because each polyp is well defined and looks like a small pinkish-red flower. The tentacles are whitish to green, and sooner or later because of its beauty it will catch someone's eye.

I have hunted *Phyllangia* for years, and have found it growing only in one location in Alligator Harbor, under the pier of Wilson's Beach. Why this area is so heavily populated with this coral remains

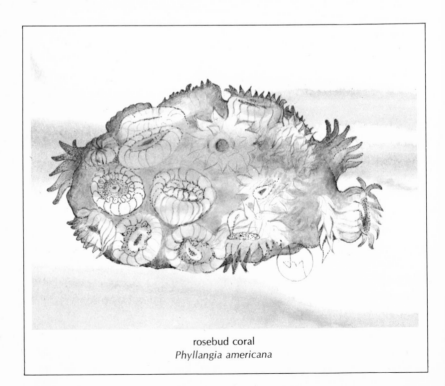

rosebud coral
Phyllangia americana

something of a mystery but the next place it is discovered is offshore in deep water. Perhaps they require filtered sunlight or even darkness associated with greater depths because all one has to do is swim a few yards out from the pier, dive over very similar rocky outcrops grown over with loggerhead and boring sponges and not uncover a single specimen.

Their striking colors make it easy to spot the coral as you swim over it, much the same way *Astrangia* can be spotted as it erects from a silty bottom.

Apparently the growth rate of *Phyllangia* is stable and steady. Before we used an epibenthic dredge to haul up shells from considerable depths, we collected *Phyllangia* only under Wilson's pier. Years ago, before learning the extreme limit of its range to this unique spot, I heavily collected it for preserved orders and virtually stripped out the bottom. The following year new patches of it began returning, and today, more than six years later, it is as abundunt as it ever was.

Phyllangia has remained one of the hardiest animals to be placed in an aquarium. Anthozoans in general are extremely tough, and although public aquariums do not generally attempt to keep corals, many specimens are fairly rugged. Extremely tropical corals, like brain corals (*Diplora clivosa*) or rose coral (*Manicina areolata*), will die down if the water temperature drops to 60°F or less, but such corals as *Astrangia*, *Phyllangia*, *Siderastrea*, *Cladophora* and *Oculina* that range up to North Carolina waters and even more northerly are likely to survive for a long period of time in icy waters.

The colonies should be fed regularly, about once a week, just like the fish or anything else in the tank. A good method of feeding them is to take an eyedropper of clam or shrimp juice and gently squirt it above the polyps. They will rise out of their corallite, expand greatly and sweep the water for food. This prevents excess food from gathering in the tank to decompose and cause a septic condition which may kill your other specimens.

Siderastrea radians
False Brain Coral

This is a southern, brown, lumpy coral that appears to like harbor conditions and can tolerate lots of silt and low temperatures, and even a great variation in salinity. Local fishermen call it "brain coral," which it certainly is not. Although I have never seen *Siderastrea radians* exposed by low tides, I have stood on a rocky outcrop at St. Teresa Beach in north Florida on an extremely low tide pushed out by northerly winds and broken it from its substrate in just six inches of chilly water where the temperature must have been below 40°F.

Almost anywhere along the southern coast where there are rocky outcrops, *Siderastrea* is likely to be encountered, ranging in quantity from a few scattered colonies to fairly dense masses. We have encountered it offshore past #26 Bell Buoy but never in the dense quantities that it has occurred in off St. Teresa Beach.

Siderastrea seems to require substantial light to grow to any size because under Wilson's Pier I never find any. But all I have to do is swim off a few yards from the edge of the pier where there is sufficient light, and I can see the brown lumps scattered all over the bottom, some colonies rising like little hills up to a foot high.

This coral is a general habitat for numerous other creatures. The base of the colony, which is dead coral and limestone rock, from which the living colony has grown up, is usually riddled with boring organisms. Feather-duster worms (*Sabella melanostigma*), peanut worms (*Dendrostomum alutaceum*), boring mussels, (*Lithophaga bisulcata*) and dozens of other creatures can be isolated.

But with the exception of the commensal barnacle *Creusia*, all these other forms can be found in adjacent limestone rock, and only the mussel actually bores deep into the living coral colonies. *Creusia*, which was first described by Darwin in a related coral, appears as a nodule with a hole in it.

Siderastrea is a good coral to keep in an aquarium although its survival time will be limited. The polyps are small, densely packed into a colony, and appear as a sort of slimy brownish fuzz covering a rock. An examination of the polyps under a dissecting scope reveals them to have short, knobby tentacles with greenish pigment in each colony.

If part of the coral is gently stroked, all the polyps will retract. Transmission of impulse within the colony is feeble and it can be seen that only the disturbed area retracts, looking just as if a finger had been rubbed across a dusty window.

Bunodactis stelloides
The Gray Warty Anemone

On certain, very specific sandflats of Alligator Point on dead low tide, you can walk along at certain times of the year and see perfectly round deep pits in the sand, ringed with bits of shell. These signs point to *Bunodactis stelloides*, a rather drab-looking gray sea anemone with hundreds of short, stubby tentacles.

When you thrust your shovel down next to the burrow and pry out a scoop of sand, the anemone comes out looking like a long stalk of greenish-gray celery, but after a few seconds of rapid contraction, spurting water out of its mouth and other little openings it soon reduces itself to a tight little ball that resembles more a boiled onion covered with warts. Many are attached to clam and cockle shells beneath the sand.

Bunodactis stelloides has distinguished itself as an experimental animal in recent years. Unlike the well-known Atlantic anemone *Metridium senile*, if you touch a *Bunodactis* it will draw its tentacles

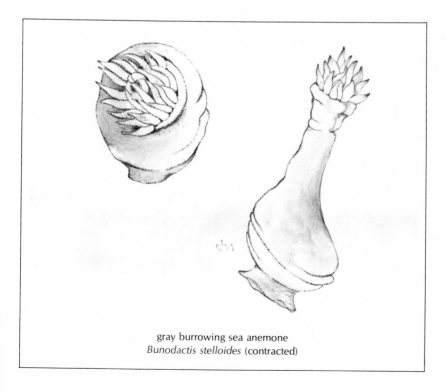

gray burrowing sea anemone
Bunodactis stelloides (contracted)

159

in and contract, but it will also expand its tentacles within a very short time. *Metridium* remains contracted and may not recover for five or six hours or longer. Often it remains contracted and dies, although some aquarists have maintained *Metridium* for years in a simple, refrigerated closed-system aquarium.

Bunodactis stelloides appears to be limited to the southeastern United States, requiring firm sandy substrate to burrow in. Its range extends from North Carolina to Texas, and in some areas the little gray blobs of young *Bunodactis* are found attached to rocks.

Although they are found inshore in protected harbors, the majority of the population lives on outer, high-energy coast lines. They feed frequently on mole crabs (*Emerita talpoida*) that rapidly wriggle down into the sand, and sometimes wriggle down to the waiting stinging tentacles of *Bunodactis*.

In the aquarium *Bunodactis* may be fed bits of clam or chopped shrimp. As far as survival goes they cannot be surpassed by any other sea creature; one laboratory has kept animals I shipped to them six years ago just in trays of sea water, feeding them now and then and keeping the salinity stable. While they are not spectacular in color, they do add an interesting biological note to an aquarium.

Calliactis tricolor
Cloak Anemone
_____

Calliactis tricolor, the cloak anemone, is one of the most celebrated of all marine animals. It lives on shells occupied by hermit crabs in warm waters all over the world, and there is no more fascinating, yet amusing sight than a large hermit walking across the floor of an aquarium on its pointed legs, almost tiptoe style, with reddish-pink-and-brown striped cloak anemones blossoming out, contracting down, drawing in their tentacles and expanding out as the crab walks on.

There is believed to be a definite symbiotic relationship here. The crab carries the anemone from place to place so it can get food, and in return that multitude of flowery pinkish-white stinging tentacles offers protection to the crab from some large, hungry fish.

One begins to question how symbiotic a relationship this is when some food is dropped into the aquarium and the cloak anemone stretches up over the crab and snatches the food before its host has a

cloak anemone
Calliactis tricolor (expanded)

chance at the morsel. On the other hand, if the anemone doesn't act quickly the crab will pounce on the meat and stuff itself, and the anemone will get only a taste instead of a meal.

Because of these amusing antics they have distinguished themselves as a must for the household aquarium. Unfortuntely their range is limited to the southeast, occasionally one is found along the North Carolina coast, but their range is generally considered to be Florida waters.

Calliactis tricolor also appears to have seasònal peaks and declines. The hermit crabs can be found inshore but without anemones during the winter months, but spring brings more and more anemones on hermit crabs. They are found on all species of hermit crabs, but especially favor the big, red, hairy hermit *Petrochirus diogenes*, where

161

cloak anemone
Calliactis tricolor (contracted)

one animal will have as many as 20 anemones on it. When there is a shortage of crabs, I have seen *Pagurus pollicaris* in a two-inch moon-snail shell carrying as many as four anemones; the shell was completely covered by the pedal discs.

They probably prefer *Petrochirus* because this hermit is found in high-salinity conditions, entering the shallow harbors only when salinity and temperature conditions are stable. Also, this crab seldom enters the intertidal zone and is not left out on the beach for long periods of time.

Rarely have I found *Calliactis tricolor* on *Melongena* or *Polinicies* shells occupied by *Clibanarius vittatus*, the hardy striped hermit that can withstand long periods of exposure. They are almost always found crawling on top of sandbars or even climbing high into tree roots on high tide. The cloak anemone cannot withstand the exposure, desiccates quickly and will die in air, and therefore seems able to choose its host.

In the aquarium I have seen them avoid *Clibanarius* and stick with the hermit crabs that prefer a subtidal existence. When no other hermit is available the anemone may allow itself to be transferred to the shell of *Clibanarius*. However, I have seen many anemones simply cling to the glass and slide gradually up above these hermit crabs and have nothing more to do with them.

Watching hermit crabs transfer anemones is an enthralling experience. You would almost think that the cloak anemones are some sort of prestige symbol, and the hermits simply can't get enough of them. One hermit comes up on another, taps on its shell with its chela and begins to squeeze the anemone off, pressing at its pedal disc. The sea anemone readily lets go and with the help of the hermit crab reattaches on the new shell. The old hermit crab sits by and politely lets this happen, because later on he will go to another hermit crab and steal its anemone.

It seems a shame to preserve these lovely creatures, and it really isn't necessary because the species is well known. Nonetheless, to add them to an alcohol collection along with data and distribution records, it is a good idea to preserve the anemone in an expanded condition with the hermit crab extended from the shell.

Place them in a solution of magnesium sulfate for a few hours which will kill the hermit crab. Remove it from the shell, and start working with the anemone. This is necessary because the hermit continually moves around and causes the anemone to contract and expand with each bounce. Allow the anemone on the empty shell to expand and try poisoning with very dilute Formalin or, after 24 hours, kill by rapid fixation with hot Formalin.

Cerianthus Americanus
"Sloppy Guts" Anemone

If you walk along a sea grass flat at low tide when just an inch or two of water is beneath your feet, you are likely, sooner or later, to encounter *Cerianthus americanus*. Its long maroon to dull-brown tentacles erect from the mud, so striking that it would take a dullard to overlook it entirely. But when you go closer, and step a little too heavily, suddenly there will be a spurt of water and the beautiful tentacles pop down into the sand, so quickly that you begin to doubt you ever saw it in the first place.

All that will be left is an inch of flaccid, grayish, fleshlike tubing sticking up like a chimney opening. *Cerianthus* lives in this long tube,

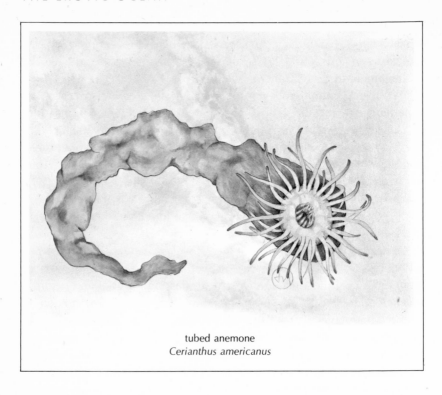

tubed anemone
Cerianthus americanus

often more than 18 inches long reaching far down into the mud. The tube is created by the anemone's ability to secrete copious amounts of mucus, which mixes with sand and mud, and by sliding up and down it builds into a rather mushy tube that takes little effort to tear apart.

What is most surprising is that after you go to the effort to spade up *Cerianthus* and bring it safely out of the sand without tearing it, the animal itself, when removed from the tube, measures less than six inches. The tentacles are retracted and the animal doesn't look very pleasant.

Cerianthus, the tubed sea anemone, is perhaps one of the most sensitive of all coelenterates. It rides up and down its tube like an elevator, and usually remains on the surface feeding but at the slightest disturbance it will rocket to the bottom. When you walk away or wait 15 minutes off to the side without moving, the anemone will inch its way to the top and poke its inquisitive tentacles out. When the coast is clear it comes out even further and in no time expands its beautiful array of maroon-colored or lavender tentacles.

No matter how careful or how quick you are in trying to grab one and pinch its tube off before it can retreat, the *Cerianthus* will rocket its way down in an instant. But it is contained in its tube nonetheless, and may therefore be captured with persistent digging. If you dig long enough and patiently enough you will come to the end of its tube, but if the tube is in a solid pack of shell and sand, then it will be most difficult to excavate. Sometimes, if the substrate is soft and boggy, you can get a good grip on the tube and by applying a firm pressure pull the tube and the anemone up intact without breaking the surface of the substratum with a shovel. But this is rare, and in the majority of cases the tube will break in half.

There is one good technique to try with Cerianthus in cold weather when the temperature is about 30°F and the creature's metabolism is greatly slowed. With a quick shovel chop you can sever its tube below the anemone and block its descent before it can respond to stimuli, which saves much digging.

Cerianthus americanus is a magnificent addition to the aquarium and survives for years, if fed properly with ground shrimp. The slimy, sandy muddy tube is not a thing of beauty, so you might try removing it from its tube by either slitting the tube longitudinally or cutting the end and squeezing the animal down and out. I have removed them from their tubes and placed them in an aquarium. In just a few hours they were well on their way to making new tubes secreting mucus and incorporating the bottom gravel, which is not unsightly.

Cerianthids tend to be filter-feeders, although they will snatch a fish or piece of hamburger with little hesitation. They withdraw into their tubes and come out when ready for another quick meal. *Cerianthus americanus* has achieved much fame in the classroom and laboratory. They are brilliantly phosphorescent when exposed to ultraviolet light, and their hydraulic thrust is something of an aquarium novelty.

Preservation

Despite the worldwide distribution and abundance of coelenterates along the coasts of the world, they generally have poor representation in most museum collections, since many workers prefer not to bother with them. This is especially true of the fragile, soft-bodied hydromedusae, the big watery jellyfish and the fleshy sea anemones and soft corals which are generally slimy and hard to handle and even harder to identify.

On the other hand, stony corals, milleporinas, tubiporeans, hydrocorals and the wiry horny gorgonians appear more frequently in museum collections, since they can be easily dried for study. And because they are easy to prepare, a good deal is known about the species and their distribution throughout the world.

The soft-bodied contractile forms require a considerable amount of care and workmanship. The specimens should be well expanded and thoroughly preserved. Unfortunately many of the original descriptions were made from shriveled up, contracted specimens often improperly fixed or partially mascerated because the specimens were hastily prepared and placed in the wrong preservative to start with. There is a serious need for collectors to replace these old, worn-out museum specimens with fresh, well-preserved and documented animals.

To understand why the Coelenterata are more difficult to preserve than most other invertebrates, you should know something about their anatomy and physiology. Considering the phylum as a whole, the muscles of most coelenterates are capable of tremendous contraction, drawing up to 5 percent of their normal size. The sea anemones, corals, jellyfish and other members of this group lack a central nervous system and also lack polarization of the nervous impulses. The impulses seem to transmit with equal speed in all directions, resulting in extreme autonomy or independence of parts. So in narcotizing a contractile coelenterate, you are not dealing with a central nervous system but with a whole network of isolated systems.

If you remove a few tentacles of a sea anemone or slice off its pedal disc and maintain this dissociated part in an aquarium, you'll find it will behave and respond in much the same way as the intact animal. Lacking polarization, which is characteristic of a central nervous system, reflexes are poor and transmission through the tiny nerve fibers is extremely slow, 7 cm/sec in the sea pansy *Renilla*, 12 to 15 in the plumed anemone *Metridium* and 24 cm/sec in the jellyfish *Pelagia*, compared with 12,500 cm/sec in man. Yet the nervous system can conduct without decrement and without fatigue. If you cut a jellyfish like *Pelagia* or *Stomolophus* into a dozen concentric strips, the dissociated parts will continue to pulsate for a day or longer in an aquarium with clean running sea water.

The combination of a most primitive nervous and muscular system capable of tremendous contraction, makes the coelenterate one of the most troublesome groups to anesthetize. Anemones, corals and hydroids often preserve out with only half their tentacles expanded, the other half withdrawn. Only a few polyps on a contractile alcyonarian may succumb to anesthetic, while others will violently contract upon contact with the fixative.

Preserving coelenterates in a well-expanded, natural position can be a very tricky business at best. Just when the preparer thinks his animal has fully succumbed to the anesthetic and he is pleased that his animal does not respond to probing he will be horrified to see the animal draw in its polyps and contract its entire body as he pours in the killing fluid.

Little is really known about the mechanisms of anesthetics on the neuromuscular system of invertebrates, or for that matter, vertebrates. The problem of how a nerve is deadened and why is just being approached by biochemists and electron microscopists examining the nerve structures of higher animals, and I will not attempt to put forth any of the theories here, but if more were known about the mechanisms and effects of anesthetics on the invertebrate nerve plexus, then perhaps a simple method could be worked out for anesthetizing the very simple coelenterates. Novacain, even cocaine and opium fail to have any good effect. A number of anesthetics and techniques can be used, and many of them have good results.

Some of the best-preserved coelenterates I have ever seen were done by Milton "Sam" Gray, who was the renowned collector of the Marine Biological Laboratory in Woods Hole. A year or two before he died, we met at the Gray Museum, and I held up a bottle of his preserved *Astrangia* coral, and asked him how he managed to preserve it in such an exquisite manner, with all its little polyps stretched out, with its wartlike studded tentacles as erect as they were in the seawater tables, branching out to sting a bit of plankton that floated by. I had just started out in the collecting profession, and Sam was the wizard, the old sage of the trade. I was a little dismayed at his answer.

"I'm not about to tell you," he said, "it's one of those secrets. But I will pass one thing along to you, you work at your specimen, stay with it all night, keep adding anesthetics or whatever you're going to do with it, watch its every move and reaction, and learn how to preserve it. Lock yourself in a room, stay away from everyone and don't tell anyone your secret when you master it. Keep them guessing."

But this has never been my philosophy. Perhaps it is in my nature that when I find out something I have to tell everyone about it — keeping secrets has not been one of my virtues. Once or twice, when I have really invested time and effort into preserving corals, I have produced specimens as beautifully expanded as Sam Gray's. I have produced ctenophores that have not been frayed and broken, and I have developed some pretty good techniques for preserving flatworms and mollusks.

Class Hydrozoa. Hydroids are generally classified by the shape of their polyps, perisac, arrangement and morphology of their stems and sexual buds. While these characteristics can be studied from specimens immersed in Formalin or alcohol or even from dried materials, it is generally desirable to preserve the colonies with their polyps well expanded and tentacles stretched out in a natural feeding position.

Upon returning to the laboratory, place the hydroid colonies in deep trays of fresh sea water and add magnesium sulfate, magnesium chloride or menthol crystals. A frequently used technique is to add weak alcohol or immerse the hydroids in a 10 percent alcoholized sea-water mixture.

Since they possess a weak neuromuscular system, hydroids will generally become anesthetized in less than a half hour if the solution is kept at room temperature. When they no longer respond to probing, flood in a concentrated solution of alcohol or Formalin. They may be stored in 5 percent buffered sea-water Formalin or 70 percent ethyl alcohol.

Hydromedusae, the free-swimming bell-shaped sexual buds of the parent colonies, require a much different method of preservation and handling. Place them in an 8 percent magnesium chloride solution or a solution of menthol crystals and watch until they become immobile. They tend to deteriorate almost immediately upon death, so they must be promptly fixed with Formalin.

Hydromedusae should be stored in a 5 percent sea-water Formalin solution, preferably neutralized Formalin, and kept in dark, amber-glass bottles to prevent crystallization of the formic acid, which tends to destroy specimens in clear-glass bottles.

Class Scyphozoa. Most museum and reference collections are starved of jellyfish. The only reason they are so seldom collected is because they are so difficult and slimy to handle. Rubber gloves should be used at all times when working with scyphozoans to avoid getting stung.

Jellyfish are generally easy to preserve. Although some contraction will set in when they are immersed in fixative, most collectors do not bother with prior anesthetization. Specimens should be dropped directly into 10 percent sea-water Formalin solution. The consistency of the jellyfish is an important factor: some species are very fragile and watery (up to 99 percent water), while others are very firm and have higher concentrations of mineral salts that make them quite solid. The watery ones are apt to tear during preservation unless they are gently handled.

Some specialists recommend that the fragile forms be initially placed in a 5 percent Formalin solution and two days later transferred to a fresh 10 percent solution so they will not become brittle. The proper concentration of preservative may take some experimenting, and you should test the consistency of the tissues periodically by feeling them to see if they are hardening properly.

Most important, do not crowd or compress jellyfish in any way. Specimens with long, trailing tentacles such as *Chrysaora* and *Cyanea* are best supported with a circular wire or glass rod placed under the tentacles during the hardening process. I have seen some specimens with a piece of monofilament line inserted through the bell which is suspended in solution by a cork.

When preserving species that have no color of their own, a little Bouin's fluid or cupric acetate should be added to the solution to give it color and contrast.

Siphonophores such as *Velella, Chrondrophora* and *Physalia,* the Portuguese man-of-war, present a problem in getting their air sacks down into the bottle. It can be like forcing a balloon underwater. However, I have seen *Physalia* in museum collections floating above the Formalin and there doesn't seem to be any harm done to the specimens.

All jellyfish should remain in a 10 percent buffered Formalin solution. Many manuals recommend that they be transferred to alcohol, but specialists who frequently work with specimens that have withstood the test of time in dusty museum collections find that alcohol causes shrinkage and distortion, even with specimens run through a tedious alcohol series.

Class Anthozoa. Sea anemones are by far one of the most difficult groups to preserve because of their ability to contract rapidly from a beautiful flowerlike form with waving tentacles into a blob that resembles a boiled onion. Contracted distorted specimens that have been dropped in Formalin can, with great difficulty, be identified by anemone experts, but the task is arduous and requires that the animals be sectioned.

To preserve them with tentacles fully expanded requires that they be slowly anesthetized. Before adding an anesthetic to a dish of anemones allow them to expand fully. Magnesium chloride added slowly to the dish is most effective, and so are chlorotone and menthol crystals if administered in small amounts.

After the anesthetic is added, the specimens should not be disturbed, because once an anemone closes during anesthetization it will usually not open again. Like many contractile invertebrates, the time it takes to render anemones insensitive varies with both the species and the individual. For this reason it pays to isolate them in separate dishes during preservation.

The responses of the anemone should be checked at frequent intervals, since an anemone becomes insensitive just before it dies. Certain small species may become insensitive in an hour, while

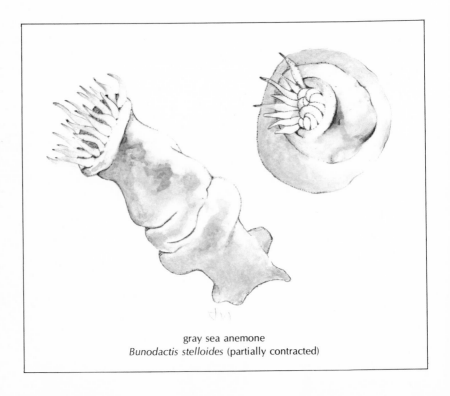

gray sea anemone
Bunodactis stelloides (partially contracted)

others require five or six hours, and a few will still respond to stimuli after 12 hours and longer. At the time of death decomposition sets in almost immediately and a rotten anemone is of little use.

To fix an anesthetized anemone, inject it through the mouth with full-strength Formalin. Keep a steady stream over several seconds to keep it inflated during its last feeble death contractions. Add enough Formalin to the solution of water in the dish to increase the concentration to 15 percent and allow the anemone to harden for a day before transferring it to 10 percent Formalin for storage.

Alcyonarians, the soft corals, sea pansies, sea pens, antipatharians sea whips and fans all have numerous small, white, feathery polyps living in a horny, chitinous skeleton. Almost all these forms have minute spicules very similar to sponge spicules, and the ultimate identification is based upon the size, shape and arrangement of these spicules. Specialists merely tease off a few spicules and examine them under the dissecting scope and put a name on the colony. The spicules are mounted on microscope slides and treated like sponge spicules.

However, most of these specialists who routinely classify these animals make notes on their size, living shape and color, and then unceremoniously drop them into alcohol or buffered Formalin until the tissues are hardened. Then they are removed from solution, dried in the shade and packed in newspapers. Some specialists will cross-reference them with specimens that have been preserved in alcohol or 10 percent buffered Formalin.

Preserving alcyonarians with their polyps expanded can be most time consuming and quite often unsuccessful, even with numerous anesthetics, including a 7.5 percent isotonic solution of magnesium chloride, good fixation and sufficient attention. *Alcyonium carneum*, an attractive pink soft coral that is occasionally dredged off Woods Hole, more often than not ends up looking more like a compact red sponge than a flowery living soft coral blossoming with thousands of feathery polyps. Superior results are achieved by adding a few drops of Formalin.

Sea pansies, *Renilla mulleri* and gorgonians such as *Leptogorgia virgulata* and *Lophogorgia hebes* easily succumb to magnesium sulfate or magnesium chloride after a few hours. When the polyps hang limp the colonies should be fixed in buffered Formalin and transferred to 70 percent alcohol for storage.

Madreporarians, the stony corals, must be cleaned of their polyps

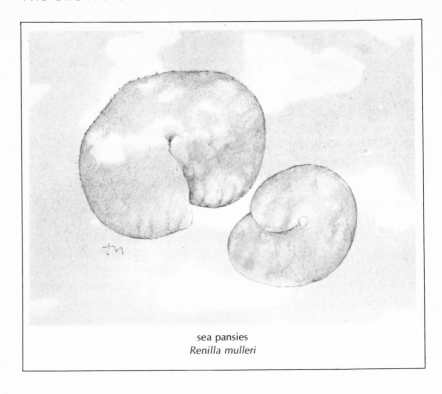

sea pansies
Renilla mulleri

and soft parts for identifications. Classification is by the structure of their hard calcareous exoskeleton, and to prepare them for study, all you have to do is let them soak in fresh water until all the polyps rot out. A little bleach can be added to kill the odor.

A pressure hose is applied to wash all the rotten soft parts out until clean skeletal cups remain. Then place the coral on a wire meshed drying rack until completely dry and wrap them carefully in newspapers for storage. But corals should be viewed in their living state if they are to be appreciated. The magnificent polyps erecting with their warty tentacles are attractive.

Preserving them with their polyps expanded is more of an art than a science. The anesthetics are slowly added, the reactions of the polyps carefully observed. Like many of the soft corals, the stony corals can try one's patience. *Astrangia danae*, the Atlantic star coral which is dredged up and preserved routinely for classroom study, is a prime example of frustration. After dripping in a saturated solution of magnesium sulfate, or a few drops of propylene phenexetol, the polyps will become expanded and hang limp. A great amount of fixative is

sea whips
Leptogorgia virgulata

necessary to penetrate down into the coralla, hardening the polyps. And even with all this work and tedious man-hours invested, the chances are great that last-minute contraction will result when the fixative is flooded in.

It is common for half the polyps to be extended, some partially retracted and the rest completely withdrawn. I once sent some *Astrangia* to the United States National Museum for identification. I had spent all night anesthetizing it, had siphoned off the water, and even boiled concentrated Formalin in a beaker, and amid choking and gasping, flooded the noxious solution in on the stupefied colony.

My efforts were a complete success. The polyps gave only the tiniest contraction, and the large, knobby tentacles were fixed fully

173

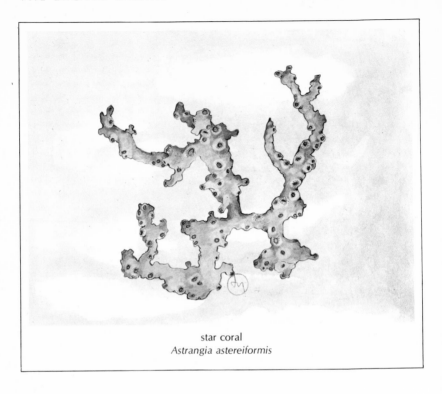

star coral
Astrangia astereiformis

distended. The specialist at the USNM who received the specimen wrote back and told me that he was glad to get the specimen but if I wanted the coral identified down to species, he would have to boil away my beautifully expanded polyps and examine the coralla to make positive identification. He suggested that I send him another cleaned and dried piece.

Coral that has been anesthetized and fixed for study, is best preserved in a 10 percent buffered Formalin solution or 70 percent ethyl alcohol, after running it through two weaker solution changes.

16.
Phylum Ctenophora
The Comb Jellyfish

Ctenophores are one of the most beautiful, frail creatures to be found anywhere in the ocean. Some are shaped like little glass balls, others like tulips, almost perfectly clear except for their ciliated comb plates that look like zippers. In the daylight the zippers catch glints of sunlight and glow with a radiating iridescence, and at night they are luminescent and glow with a brilliant neon blue when handled.

For this reason, the sea walnut and other ctenophores have been popular in invertebrate zoology and evolution courses and as curiosities. They have a more developed nervous system than coelenterates and lack nematocysts. But so fragile is this form that if even slightly handled it breaks to pieces and only shreds of jellyfish arrive in the laboratory.

The way to avoid this situation is to avoid handling them at all. *Mnemiopsis, Beroe* (the thimble jellyfish) and *Pleurobrachia* (the sea gooseberry) should be dipped up with a flat, small-meshed nylon net that supports the animal, but does not jostle or let it spin. The creature is lifted from the sea for just a second before it is placed in a bucket of water. While walking back from a pier or unloading from a boat, the bucket should not be sloshed about, but handled like eggs, gently.

If sea walnuts (*Mnemiopsis macrydi*) are particularly abundant and cover the surface of a calm sea, your best results are obtained if you dip them directly into a bucket.

175

sea walnut
Mnemiopsis macrydi

We have shipped ctenophores throughout the United States and have had varied results. In many cases they get to their destination alive and unbroken, but there are instances where only shredded, semidecomposed animals have arrived. In all cases of success, small animals, no longer than a half-inch, were used. They appear to have more consistency and less surface area to be broken, they require less room in a container, so smaller plastic bags charged with oxygen can be used. They can also be packed with enough cushioning material, like foam rubber and newspaper, to survive.

We have kept young specimens alive for two weeks in closed-system aquariums, giving them plenty of sea water, about five gallons per animal. It is almost essential that no other specimens be maintained in the same tank because they can readily shred the little *Mnemiopsis* specimens.

It is best to classify comb jellyfish before preserving them, since all the drawings and original descriptions have been made from living animals. The sizes, shapes, lobes and often color are all characteristics, and all of them are distorted through tremendous shrinkage and lost in the preservation process. The presence or absence of tentacles, arrangements of the ciliated comb plates are features that may be preserved if a little care is taken. Fortunately identification of ctenophores is not too difficult, because even though they occur in vast swarms—often tons of them are sucked up into ships pumps— there are only some 80 species to be found worldwide.

Most biologists, making an ecological study of a particular area, work with living specimens and dissect them while they are alive, using a good key such as Mayer's *Medusae of the World*. Most of the keys were compiled from zoologists looking at ctenophores aboard ship, drawing pictures as they undulated in a dish of sea water.

Preservation

There is no animal as difficult to preserve as the ctenophore. The form is so fragile, the consistency so thin, that preserving a natural-looking specimen that is a reasonable facsimile of the living animal is almost impossible. Comb jellies are 99 percent water, and unless treated with much care, will either undergo tremendous shrinkage or dissolve into a formless, mascerated mass of jelly with all their structure lost.

Smaller ctenophores, like *Pleurobrachia pileus* of the North Atlantic coast, can be preserved without difficulty or any special fixative: they are solid to start with and end up as little firm balls that you can almost bounce when they are placed in fixative. It is the big watery forms like *Mnemiopsis* and *Beroe* that are most difficult to prepare, and many museum collections completely lack representatives of these species.

After much trial and error we developed a technique of fixing most large watery ctenophores. They can be placed in a variety of fixatives providing the fixative is chilled down to 30°F or below. We have actually packed 10 percent Formalin mixed with a 5 percent solution of nitric acid with ice cubes and then gently dropped in sea walnuts and produced fine, well-hardened specimens that did not undergo shrinkage. The same solution at room temperature, however, caused the animals to shrink radically.

After the ctenophores have turned white or opaque they should be removed from this fixative and washed thoroughly in fresh water.

Chromic-acetic acid fixative, made up with 4 parts chromic acid, 1 part glacial acetic acid and 400 parts sea water, has been used extensively in preserving sea gooseberries on the Atlantic coast. We have found it is effective, with small *Mnemiopsis*, to add a handful of crushed ice to the solution. *Beroe ovata* tends to become brittle, and often preserves best in a simple 10 percent Formalin solution if the fixative is chilled.

This species is best supported with glass rods to keep the oral cavity from contracting during preservation. The blunt end of a test tube can be inserted and twirled around, thus inflating and distending the thimble jellyfish at the same time.

All acid fixatives, whether they are nitric acid or acetic acid, must be gently washed out of the tissues or discoloration and eventual deterioration will result. Specimens should be left in the hardening solution from 10 minutes to 4 hours, depending upon the volume of the animal and its general consistency. When the comb plates become well outlined and opaque, it is time to transfer them. Never pick them up directly; always dip ctenophores up with a spoon that includes cushioning fluid. This will keep them from shredding during transfer.

Selecting the final preservative is often the major problem in preparing ctenophores. Formalin will disintegrate many of the large watery species after a few weeks, so many experts recommend using ethyl alcohol, gradually increasing the concentrations over a long period of time. Start with a 15 percent solution and gradually build up the solution by doubling the concentration every 24 hours. However, if signs of shrinkage occur, stop increasing the alcohol concentration.

We have had some success using a buffered 7 percent Formalin solution made up of 50 percent sea water and 50 percent fresh water which appears isotonic to the animals. This solution minimizes shrinkage and has worked well on some *Mneniopsis* and *Beroe*. Only a very few ctenophore specimens can stand the test of time. Generally only those that are kept in dark-colored bottles do not disintegrate in preservative. Make sure the bottle is brimful of preservative because an air bubble can be absolutely destructive to the fragile jellyfish when the bottle is picked up and examined.

17.
Phylum Plathyhelminthes
Parasitic Flukes and
Tapeworms and Flatworms

The phylum Plathyhelminthes is made up of three classes:
Turbellaria (free-living flatworms), Trematoda (parasitic flukes) and
Cestoda (tapeworms, also parasitic). It is beyond the scope of this
book to discuss the taxa of the latter two groups because they are
encountered only when dissecting the tissues of a fish, reptile or sea
mammal, or while teasing apart the organs of certain invertebrates.
Almost any shark that you cut open is bound to be loaded with
tapeworms; sea trout are likely to have trematodes embedded in the
muscles and groupers appear to be eaten up with a variety of worms. If
you start doing much dissecting and looking, the abundance of
parasitic worms is enough to turn one into a vegetarian.

The species of trematodes and tapeworms all generally look alike;
some are bigger than others. A specialist might be able to distinguish
family differences at a glance, but even the expert can't tell if the
tapeworms dissected from a sting ray are *Acanthobothrium dujardini*
or some species of *Echeneibothrium* until he puts one under a
dissecting scope, examines its scolex (head), counts the number of
hooks on the scolex, and looks at the segments. Histological sections
of fixed specimens may be necessary to examine the gonads.
Trematodes must also be fixed and sectioned to make a proper
identification.

Not a great deal is known about the life cycles of many marine trematodes and cestodes. During part of their life cycles some species cyst up in invertebrates such as shrimp, clams and oysters. These are eaten by larger predatory fish and the parasite is passed on. Tracing a parasite's life cycle is like detective work: bits and pieces of information are gradually put together until an overall picture of the worm's development is drawn. Did the shark pick up its parasite by eating croakers or redfish? These are checked to see if the same parasite exists.

Parasitologists are delighted with an animal that has a more or less consistent incidence of parasitism. When you can go to any particular species of fish, split it open and produce a particular species of digenic trematode or a tapeworm, and do it 99 times out of 100 before the astonished eyes of a group of biology students, then there is an all-around good feeling of accomplishment and knowledge of your subject.

The little mud snails (*Cerithidea scalariformis*) are a good example. Simply crack them open in a dish of sea water and soon the water teams with small, white, barely visible tapeworm larvae. If you fillet a spotted sea trout (*Cynoscion nebulosus*) and find a number of milky white, elongated worms boring into the muscle in a most disgusting fashion, these are probably the digenic trematode *Choricotyle cynoscioni*. Almost every trout is heavily infected in the north Florida waters.

A less predictable parasite is the trematode *Phrorschis acanthus*, which lives its larval stages in the gastropod mollusk *Thaïs*, commonly found eating oysters or crawling over rocky shores. When the *Thaïs* shell is crushed, the tissue cut into, you will find that one out of four specimens contains small nodules of the trematode *Phrorschis acanthus*. It will stretch out to four or five times its contracted length in sea water, reaching several inches long.

In its adult stage this fluke is parasitic in the cloaca of sea gulls and terns—an unlikely alternate host since these birds aren't great *Thaïs* eaters. Trematodes and tapeworm larvae are often found in the tissues of marine invertebrates. *Prochristianella penaei*, a cestode, is known from commercial pink-and-white shrimp, but the definite host is unknown. To find them, the gut must be mascerated and examined under a dissecting scope.

The beachcomber naturalist may be revolted at the thought of dissecting a fish or invertebrate exclusively for parasites. However, when examining specimens, you should always keep an eye open for consistent increase of heavy infection. A major increase in trematodes, tapeworms and arthropod parasites such as copepods and isopods may be caused by increases in domestic and industrial pollution. When the water quality declines, fish tend to become weakened and more susceptible to all forms of parasitism and disease.

Class Turbellaria

Unlike the other two classes of Plathyhelminthes, turbellarians are free-living and do not possess the habit of sucking blood and body fluid from another animal to make their living. These little flatworms are represented by many orders; most of them are extremely small and live in the mud or in rocks and can barely be seen by the unaided eye. Most collectors are not concerned with them; however, in almost any mud sample a number of them can be observed by letting the substrate stagnate in a bucket until the worms are starved of oxygen and crawl out onto the sides of the container. Batches of seaweed, tunicates, sponges and hydroids all produce large and small flatworms in this manner—it is a very common trick.

The colorful polyclad flatworms that glide and ooze over rocks, slipping into crevices and hiding in seaweed are more abundant on some coasts than others. Many large, conspicuous forms are commonly collected on the rock piles of the Pacific coast. Along some coastlines almost every overturned boulder will yield a specimen. In the tropics polyclad flatworms are even more abundant than in temperate zones, but at least one or more species of the order Polycladida can be found along the North Atlantic coasts; but they are usually few and far between.

A New Englander visiting the tropics for the first time will find the large, gorgeously colored flatworms startling. You'll find they can move quite rapidly, which is equally startling. As the polyclad flatworm glides and slips over the surface of the underside of the rock, you will need absolute patience and caution in collecting it. Picking them off a rock is often almost impossible because they are so easily broken and tatter and disintegrate at your touch. These forms should not be handled at all.

On occasion the small ones will ooze along and crawl up onto the point of a flat-bladed knife, but more often than not they will turn aside and slip down into some minute crevice. A flat-bladed knife is useless on a very rough surface. Prodding it with a knife-blade may draw it out, but you will be lucky if you get a perfect, untattered specimen no matter what technique you use. Steinbeck and Ricketts, in the Gulf of California, used a fine camel's-hair brush, gently lifting the flatworm onto the hair and rinsing it into a vial of sea water. I reiterate that small animals, particularly flatworms, should be kept in strict isolation, because they are almost never found again if mixed with other creatures in a collecting bucket.

One method that has had considerable success is to mold the opening of a plastic bag over the rock in front of the worm, lightly splashing it from behind with sea water, ultimately forcing it to go into the bag. Unless you firmly press the plastic down into the rock the polyclad flatworm will slip right under it and escape. It may also go as far as the margin of the plastic, nose suspiciously about it, then back away.

If your finger is nudged behind the worm, it may be forced to go into the bag. Then that triumphant feeling returns that makes collecting worthwhile when the worm has finally entered your bag and you lift it up, splash in a little sea water and watch delightedly, nay gleefully, as it swims around like a butterfly in its plastic prison or crawls forlornly up the plastic sides.

Bdelloura candida
Horseshoe Crab Flatworm

The first flatworm you will add to your reference collection of Atlantic coast marine animals will be, in all liklihood, the horseshoe crab flatworm (*Bdelloura candida*). They are available to one and all along the Atlantic and Gulf coasts, but not on the Pacific because horseshoe crabs do not occur there.

All you do is go down to the beach in some bay or estuary and find a horsehoe crab (*Limulus polyphemus*). Some detail is given to its habits in another chapter; here we note that it usually comes to

shore in rough weather on a high tide, or on occasion is found
burrowed up on low tide during the summer months.

Pick up this harmless creature by its long, daggerlike telson and
turn it over. This armored-tank-like creature with its scrabbling frantic,
running legs; long, sharp tail; and flexing, bending abdomen may look
formidable and capable of defending itself, but in actuality it is
perfectly harmless. The tail is merely a levering device so it can right
itself when thrown on the beach at high tide.

Look among the legs on a heavily infected specimen and you will
see little yellowish-white blobs speckled throughout its underside,
many on the legs, shell and gill hooks. These are the triclad flatworm,
Bdelloura candida.

The older the crab is, the darker the shell and the more slipper
limpets it has growing on its back, the more feathery white hydroids
you sometimes find on its legs, the better its chances of being infected
with *Bdelloura.*

The life history of *Bdelloura* is a bit of a mystery. They are not

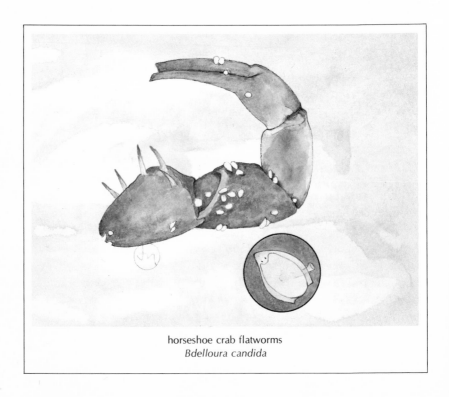

horseshoe crab flatworms
Bdelloura candida

known to be actual parasites of the crab, but commensals. They are never found in association with anything but the horseshoe crab and because they are so common they have become an essential part of the laboratory demonstrations of both a flatworm and a commensal relationship. When they are isolated from the crab they will not feed and shrink over a few weeks.

Apparently when the crab sheds its shell, it sheds the *Bdelloura* also. I have found that when *Limulus* comes into shore after lying dormant and hibernating during the spring it has a much heavier infection of *Bdelloura* than later on in the summer.

Collecting *Bdelloura* from scrabbling legs of *Limulus* is a challenge. Holding the crab down on its back, pressed against a table firmly, with one hand, your other hand pulls the little mushy triclad flatworms off with a forceps and shakes them off in a dish of sea water. They like to cling tenaciously to the forceps or your fingers.

This method of getting them off individually is good for collecting small quantities—or large quantities if you have the time. We have found an excellent way to "wipe" them off, using a very dry piece of paper towel held in a pair of forceps, dragging it over the crab. The towel absorbs the slimy juices of the worm and the worm comes off clinging to the piece of paper towel.

A technique that seems to work well for getting larger quantities off is to give the crab a quick soaking in a 5 percent ethyl alcohol solution for 10 minutes and to shake it vigorously in the same solution until the stupefied worms fall off. This does not have any detrimental effect on either the crabs or the worms if the alcohol solution is then replaced with good, clean, fresh-running sea water.

Living *Bdelloura* flatworms are used in classical experiments demonstrating chemotactic responses. The worms are placed in a vial that opens out into a Y-shaped tube. At the end of one terminal is some horseshoe-crab juice, at the other is nothing or some other kind of food. Invariably the worms work their way up to the horseshoe-crab juice or even water that a horseshoe crab has been soaked in.

Bdelloura candida is one of the toughest, hardiest creatures in the sea and may be kept alive for months in nothing but slightly aerated sea water. If it is not fed it will shrink to tiny fragments over a period of time, however; it is best kept alive by keeping the host horseshoe crab alive.

Prostheceraeus floridanus
Sea Squirt Flatworm

In Alligator Harbor and a few other restricted areas of north Florida we have a beautiful pinkish-orange flatworm called *Prostheceraeus floridanus*. Since it is only found living on sea squirts (*Molgula occidentalis* and *Styela plicata*) we have dubbed it "the sea squirt flatworm." Over the years I have observed them to be highly sporadic, appearing in large numbers during the winter months and virtually absent from tunicates during the hot summer. However, at times during July and August we have found three or four specimens amid masses of sea squirts.

Prostheceraeus floridanus is a rather handsome polyclad flatworm, not only because of its color but because it can be quite large, some specimens measuring a full inch, although the average length is a half-inch. They live down among the crevices of sea squirts, crawling along the outside of the tunic-skins, but the majority of the flatworms are found on the ventral side of a sea squirt colony.

To find them you have to rip the sea squirts apart, breaking the large clusters of 10 or 20 *Molgula* or *Styela* into smaller units, keeping your face averted because these sea squirts really do squirt out in all directions like 20 water pistols. The bright orange blobs are the flatworms and they stand out quite distinctly. Every cluster of *Molgula* or *Styela* may have three or four flatworms, and sometimes as many as eight or 10. But when the temperature goes to extremes, a 25-gallon container of sea squirts torn apart and processed will produce only five or six *Prostheceraeus floridanus*.

Sometimes we have found *Stylochus zebra* and *Stylochus ellipticus* living on sea squirt colonies, but this is not a predictable relationship. The only place we have found *Prostheceraeus floridanus* is on *Molgula* and *Styela* and we can therefore call it a commensal relationship. The flatworms obviously derive food from the tunicates, but the tunicates do not appear to benefit from this relationship.

A number of researchers and teachers throughout the country who have maintained *Prostheceraeus floridanus* in salt-water aquariums have told me their specimens laid eggs and they were able to watch the development and hatching of these eggs. This has started several research programs with this pretty orange flatworm, which have given us the opportunity to learn more about it.

In maintaining them, it is best to keep a cluster of *Molgula occidentalis* or *Styela plicata* sea squirts in the tank so the flatworms can feed upon them. The greatest numbers of flatworms occur on sea squirts that are beginning to degenerate; certain individual animals in the colony have died and they are slightly rotten. If a large volume (20 gallons) of water is maintained in the aquarium, one or two dying animals will not cause contamination but will provide a steady source of flatworm food.

Stylochus ellipticus
"Oyster Leech"

Stylochus ellipticus and Stylochus zebra are often referred to as "oyster leeches" because both species can and do concentrate in very large numbers on oyster bars, and have been accused of having a detrimental effect on the population. However, they are as sporadic in nature as jellyfish. Sometimes every sponge, hydroid cluster and sea squirt will be crawling with them. No matter where you look the great flattened gray-and-brown *Stylochus*, which measures an inch long on the average, is there; but when you want them there isn't one to be found. While the commercial oysterman may be unhappy when he finds his oysters crawling with flatworms, the collector and the zoology student will be delighted with them.

At best *Stylochus zebra* and *S. ellipticus* are only minor predators on oyster bars and cannot be placed in the same category as starfish or oyster drills, although from time to time there has been some concern about their ultimate effects on the oyster population in the Tampa Bay, Florida, area where the flatworms sporadically plaster the oysters.

We have found a fairly dependable way to collect *Stylochus zebra*, the pretty whitish flatworm with an attractive branching network of gonads. They like to live in snail shells occupied by hermit crabs, and the more barnacles, algae, or bryozoans growing on the crab, the better your chances of finding flatworms. Collectors in Woods Hole, Massachusetts, routinely gather them in this manner.

All you do is collect a bucket of hermit crabs and allow them to sit in stagnated sea water overnight. In the morning the sides of the bucket will have one or two zebra-striped flatworms crawling on them.

A somewhat predictable way to gather the other less attractive species, *Stylochus ellipticus*, is to scrape a bucket of barnacles off a wharf piling and let the water stagnate. To speed up the process a handful of magnesium sulfate, common Epsom salts, can be dumped into the bucket and this will aid in driving the flatworms out of the barnacles to the sides of the container.

For awhile we thought we had a culture system going on our floating dock because we were getting *Stylochus ellipticus* from clumps of barnacles raked off the adjacent pilings. However, a couple of months after we started harvesting them, not a single flatworm was to be found anywhere on the dock, so they have remained true to form — unpredictable.

Preservation

Flatworms. Here we come to a step in the study of flatworms that is a challenge and a difficulty. There are many techniques that may be used in preparing them, but all the beauty and color of a flatworm will be lost, its original shape will not be preserved in the slightest and it will not look anything like a real live flatworm no matter what you do to it. Generally a preserved flatworm ends up looking like a piece of stiffened paper all bleached out in the preserving fluid.

Since the flatworm undergoes such contraction it is imperative that the collector furnish as much diagnostic information as possible. Take notes on the color, then measure the length of the extended specimen and describe its shape when moving. An outline sketch showing color pattern and tentacles (if present) is highly desirable. Note whether the dorsal surface is smooth or papillate, i.e., covered with little furry projections. The form and relative development of the tentacles are important characteristics in the family Cotylea.

Flatworms are classified by the arrangement and structure of their highly branching gonads and by their eye arrangement. This cannot be determined accurately in living or preserved specimens, so they must be sectioned and the internal organs examined. Only a few specialists are going to take the time and trouble to make histological sections. However, the biological collector can provide valuable specimens if he fixes them properly in the first place.

Libby Hyman pioneered the taxonomy of free-living flatworms, in addition to authoring three monumental volumes on the invertebrates which have become the basic tool for classifying the various phyla, subphyla, orders, classes, subclasses and even families. Before her death I visited her at the American Museum of Natural History in New York and she suggested preparing the animals as follows: when they are moving and extended in a minimum amount of sea water, suddenly pour in a killing solution of sea water saturated with mercuric chloride. Be sure the solution is saturated by having crystals in the bottom of the bottle. The animal will probably curl up and contract violently, but this is not important. To prevent breakage it is imperative that you do not attempt to straighten the animal or handle it in any way.

After 30 minutes pour off the fixative and rinse the animal thoroughly in tap or distilled water. Soak it in four or five changes of tap water for 15 minutes each time. Place the flatworm in 35 percent alcohol for 15 minutes, then 50 percent and 70 percent at 15-minute intervals. To assure that all mercuric chloride has been removed—and this is very important—add a few drops of tincture of iodine. If the iodine disappears or turns pale this shows mercuric chloride is still present. Continue to add drops of iodine until the iodine color no longer weakens. Then wash out the excess iodine in rinses of 70 percent alcohol and send the animals to specialists with notes.

All this procedure is necessary for providing a specimen from which a specialist can make an accurate identification. However, a tentative identification can be made from living specimens and something of their structure learned if they are slightly flattened by a coverslip. By judiciously controlling the amount of water on the slide or smearing the coverslip with vaseline, the specimens can be made to stay compressed without their annoying habit of slipping out. Classification down to family, if not genus, can be accomplished with aid of a taxonomic key to the flatworms.

Tapeworms and Flukes. Tapeworms may be killed by extending the live worm on blotter paper saturated with Bouin's solution or FAAG. For taxonomic purposes be sure the scolex, or head, is intact or it will be rendered useless as a specimen. The large tapeworms are best handled by picking each specimen up by its larger anterior end and allowing it to hang down until its own weight causes it to stretch. Then immerse the tapeworm in killing fluid. Contraction may result unless this operation is performed carefully.

A good technique has been developed by parasitologists to prevent contraction. The anterior portion of the worm is held with a pair of forceps and is then twirled about a dish of preservative. The centrifugal force of this spinning worm keeps its elongated body forced out and extended while the killing fixative does its work.

If you don't get tired of twirling the worm in this poison before it fully expires, the tapeworm will die in a fully expanded state, having done its best to give a last-minute contortion. This technique also works well with ribbon worms, bristle worms and even very long earthworms. All you need is a wide tray with plenty of room to spin your worm.

The procedure for preparing trematodes is somewhat different. The fish, reptile or mammal is opened and the organs removed. These are opened and the rugae and folds of the digestive track are scraped and examined for the presence of small imbedded worms. The parasites are removed, placed on slides and artificially flattened. Trematodes can be somewhat anesthetized by using distilled water which causes them to relax, sometimes to the point where artificial flattening becomes unnecessary. Then they are fixed in Bouin's.

There is one technique that can make all the unpleasant field dissection somewhat unnecessary. In the August 15, 1965, issue of *Turtox News* (Vol. 43, No. 8) Eagle and McCauley described a technique of preserving trematodes in deep sea fish: "The fish are injected through the mouth and anus with distilled water using a large 50 cc veterinary-type syringe. About 100 cc of distilled water are sufficient to saturate the body cavity and digestive tract of a fish weighing approximately 400 grams. The fish are placed aside for about one hour and are then injected with AFA. To compensate for the distilled water already present, a concentrated solution, composed of 10 parts Formalin, 50 parts ethanol, and 2 parts glacial acetic acid (AFA) without the distilled water is used. The fish are stored in 10 percent Formalin and taken back to the shore laboratory where a detailed microscopic autopsy is carried out."

Using this technique on various fish, a collector can make the most of an unusual specimen he hauls in from shallow or deep water. The fish can be preserved for trematodes in the field without actually looking for the parasites. The tapeworms will preserve out in an identifiable state also. But whether the parasites are preserved inside the fish or are removed and individually prepared, it is essential that the worms be prepared immediately after the death of the host because many of them deteriorate very rapidly.

Some flukes are external parasites of fish and may be found attached to their bodies, especially in the mouth cavity, fins and gills. These must be individually treated with distilled water and separately preserved.

18.
Phylum Nemertea
Ribbon Worms

Cerebratulus lacteus
Ribbon Worms

On almost any decent-sized mudflat along the Atlantic and Gulf coasts you will encounter ribbon worms if you hunt long enough. If you are digging for clams or anything else on the flat, sooner or later a shovelful of sandy mud will reveal an elongated, unsegmented and flattened slimy pink worm that has tremendous contracting abilities. This is probably the nemertean *Cerebratulus lacteus*. It can stretch itself out to two or three times its length, often over three feet, and then quite rapidly draw up to a stocky 12 inches.

If you proceed in irritating it, trying to pull it free from the sand, for instance, the worm will suddenly shoot out its long, white proboscis, which measures about one-third the length of its body. So suddenly does this occur, and with such a shocking motion, that it accomplishes its goal on the novice; he withdraws his hand in horror.

If you persist in chasing and capturing this creature, like some flatworms, it has the ability to autotomize or fall to pieces. Or, if it does not, it becomes so excited it abruptly vomits its proboscis, which it normally uses to spear food.

Cerebratulus lacteus seldom leaves a distinct burrow or other sign that quickly tells the digger of its presence. Some flats along the New England area are so riddled with them that a single shovelful will reveal a dozen or more. But it is not so in the Gulf. I have encountered them among the roots of sea grass, I have seen them on sandflats and occasionally in boggy mud.

On rare occasions these nemerteans are prone to little swimming excursions and may be netted off piers. On one occasion, I remember collecting a large, handsome specimen by hearing its strange sounds. One January morning I was digging on a tidal flat in Alligator Harbor and I heard a distinct hissing and saw bubbles emerging from a tiny hole in the hard-packed sand. Quickly I dug down and to my surprise an 18-inch *Cerebratulus lacteus* was revealed. It was the very last creature that I would have expected to find, and I certainly wouldn't have found it unless I paid attention to the strange noise.

Large conspicuous nemerteans are abundant on the Pacific coasts, and they also abound on tropical rocky shores. The same technique employed for getting large flatworms off rocks can be used on nemerteans, chasing them out of crevices with splashing water and washing them into a plastic bag. Both polyclads and nemerteans shun bright daylight and live under rocks among encrusting coralline algae.

Regardless of what size the nemertean is, breaking it or letting it vomit its proboscis should be avoided, whether the specimen is to be preserved or brought into the laboratory to be studied alive. The laboratory nemertean (*Cerebratulus*) is often collected in bulk along the New England coast by commercial collectors. There they have large fat animals that often measure three feet long, where the same species in the south is eight or nine inches at most, and quite fragile and thin.

Those large, fat forms can be removed from their burrows by a coiling technique. Once the ground is broken with a shovel and the animal is on its way, it can be coiled around a stick, and if a gradual coiling pressure is exerted against it, it will not break. The collectors who gather them plunge them into sea water that has been previously chilled by adding ice sealed in plastic bags. When they hit the chilled water they contract quickly and do not break. Once they are in a calmed arrested state, they can be brought back to the laboratory and worked with at leisure. However, the cooler the temperature, the easier they are to handle.

Like so many other marine invertebrates, the larger, conspicuous forms are very well known and are available in all the keys. But for someone who wishes to make a contribution to science by looking for the rare and unusual, the smaller nemerteans are the creatures to look for, the tiny ones that would be overlooked unless one went to special effort to collect and prepare them.

These small forms live in coral, in rock and in limestone. They are found on sargasso weed, they live in *Fucus* weed on the rocks, and in sand and mud. And since there is a need for collecting these small forms, I shall outline one of the techniques that can be used for finding them.

When gathering coral-reef forms, take lumps of coral and set them in trays of sea water covering the coral chunks. Let this sit for an hour or two, and the large, conspicuous nemerteans will come out, along with many small flatworms, polychaete worms, brittlestars and various minute crustaceans such as amphipods, copepods, ostracods, etc.

Preservation

Most of the nemertean worms cannot be identified by sight in the field, even by experts. Like the flatworms, identifications must be based upon histological sectioning and arrangement of such internal anatomical features as the muscle layers in the body walls.

As with polyclads, the serious worker will want to make sketches from the live animal, noting its colors and color-patterns. Some are very beautiful, striking green with candy-cane white stripes, or blushing crimson. All this will be lost when they are placed in fixatives and leached in alcohol. On drawings be sure to sketch in the eyes, cephalic slits and furrows. The length and the width should be measured, but considering that they can shrink down to 25 percent or less of their original size, they should be observed for some time and their normal length, the one they stay at the longest time, recorded. It is important to list their shrinkage and expansion sizes too.

For some nemerteans, like the family Hoplonemertinidae, knowing the size and shape of the stylets on the proboscis is useful in the final identification of the animal. A squeezing preparation must be made by putting a slide coverslip on the smaller specimens that average one to five mm. Flatten it without disintegrating the specimen, but flatten it until it completely throws out its proboscis, which is measured and preserved in the same vial as the specimen.

If the proboscis is vomited during the preservation—and this will happen on a large number of animals—be sure to keep it in the same vial as the original animal. This is very important; if vomited and mixed with other species, identifications can be misleading.

Nemerteans must be anesthetized before they are preserved, otherwise they twist and contort. An aqueous solution of 1 percent chloral hydrate or menthol is added to the sea water. Smaller forms will become stupefied faster than larger, bulky forms, which require a good six to 12 hours to succumb. I have found that chilling the sea water to the freezing point, then adding chilled alcohol, is excellent for anesthetizing ribbon worms, and propylene phenoxetol has been successful in some instances.

As soon as the animals are not moving they are ready for fast fixation in Bouin's fluid or FAAG tapeworm fixative. Unless the nemertean is thoroughly stupefied and on the verge of succumbing completely to anesthetic, it will undergo some violent reactions as the harsh Bouin's fluid penetrates deep into its tissues, fixing its nerves and muscles. And this will spell disaster. The preparer may become discouraged when he sees his nemerteans fragmented, after all his effort and gentle care. They had seemed almost lifeless, no movement was perceptible even with gentle probing, but when the harsh fixative was flooded in, he helplessly watched them break into pieces.

I have learned that it is important to keep the animal as straight as possible during the preservation process. It may be stretched out by pulling on the head and tail with forceps, so that it cannot knot up. Spinning them in fixatives, using the same method described in the tapeworm section, can produce fine, stretched-out nemerteans.

Soon it dies stretched out and elongated and may end up in only a slight arc. You can't help but get the feeling that you are thwarting an animal from wanting to die in a natural squirmy heap and your persistence beats down its energy and willpower until it gives up.

This slightly unpleasant feeling is soon overcome in the months ahead when you have a well-preserved, straightened specimen sitting in alcohol, however. It is perfectly permissible if the animal is slightly curled, because serial sections are made from the head, caudal lengths of the body and posterior part.

After 24 to 48 hours in Bouin's the specimens should be transferred to 70 percent ethyl alcohol and that solution changed once to get rid of all the Picric acid. Bouin's fluid seems to give the best general results for fixation, although some specialists swear by Zenker's fluid and Formalin.

19.
Phylum Annelida
Bristleworms, Leeches and Earthworms

Class Polychaeta

Bristleworms are found in every single ecological habitat and have special adaptations for living in each situation, in dredge hauls from the depths of the ocean or burrowing in the sand just below the high-tide range. They are in tubes encrusting on rocks, commensal on hydroids, sliding through the canals of sponges, boring into coral heads. They are found in the most stinking anerobic mud, and they are encountered swimming freely in the ocean.

If you do any collecting at all, even a one-time, casual visit to the seashore, you are apt to meet bristleworms. They range in size from ones that are a few millimeters and are parasitic on the gills of lobsters to monster nereids ranging up to five feet. Their morphological adaptations permit them to live under mud, to filter-feed on plankton or to attack other small marine creatures savagely with grinding pincer jaws.

In color, beauty and form they have few equals. Giant blackish-brown lugworms have bright red gill tufts lining their bodies, white parchment worms glow in the dark and there are worms with a fantastic array of waving tentacles. The list goes on and on and would require a book in itself to give a fair description.

But the smaller worms are equally diverse and numerous, and certainly important in scientific value. Numerous specialists have studied polychaetes throughout the world because they are so interesting a group and because they are a good, standard ecological-habitat indicator.

There are small worms that you are not likely to see unless you really look for them. Generally they will be less than one inch, living in the canals of sponges or in the convolutions of corals. Sifting just one shovelful of sand may bring up a few hundred individuals. Generally these smaller forms are not likely to be damaged in collecting but must be preserved and isolated shortly after collection.

A large number of polychaetes in a sand sample does not necessarily indicate that the sand is healthy. One polychaete, *Capitella capitata*, appearing in large numbers is a sure-fire indicator of a polluted environment. A good example of the appearance of this worm occurred at Woods Hole in 1969 when a gigantic oil spill plagued Wild Harbor, Falmouth, Massachusetts. Biologists from the Woods Hole Oceanographic Institution were on hand to make observations, and found that within a few weeks all life died off. A few months later, and still no life existed, except for a sudden influx of these small reddish, nondescript worms that looked more like earthworms than true bristleworms. They are a worldwide species, found around every sewer outfall or badly polluted sea bottom.

The variety and density of polychaetes and other infauna in bottom samples will often tell of the productivity of a substrate. For example, a healthy sand sample from the Atlantic coast estuaries may contain numerous nereids, terebellids, perhaps some *Glycera* blood worms, eunicids, spionids and the tiny but beautiful syllids. Identifying these worms down to family is a major undertaking, since keys to local species are difficult to come by. Even if you are not interested in trying to identify any of these worms, it is an experience to observe them. Simply sifting bottom samples through screens, even window screens at the edge of the beach, will produce a handsome tangle of polychaetes in a nonpolluted area.

Only by getting your feet wet and muddy can you learn how much life is in the substrate. I remember one hearing before the Florida cabinet where a developer requested a permit to dredge up several thousand cubic feet of submerged bottom to be used in a landfill project. He claimed the bottom was "spongy," full of oozing mud, had no sea grass beds and did not support any life. A permit was granted for no other reason except that sea grass beds were absent.

I have taken a scoop shovel, dug up a sample of a similar bottom and sifted it through a screen and later spent hours peering at the siftings through a dissecting scope, examining the dozens of little, pink polychaete worms, tiny clams, amphipods, synaptid sea cucumbers and tiny brittlestars. However, the most impressive of all those little bottom-dwelling creatures were the polychaete worms. They were magnificent, some swimming along energetically waving their needly bristles, others in sand tubes with clear body walls sliding over the bottom of the dish. On some worms I could see their entire digestive system and a mass of tiny red blood cells moving through their primitive circulatory system. Some of the tiny nereids had savage little beaks, some had feathery tentacles, and still others had recessed parapodia and looked like little fat earthworms. Almost all of them had brilliant iridescent colors under the light of the dissecting scope.

After watching all this, I well understood why schools of tiny fish would hover over the shallow mudflats. They were picking away at all that life in the muddy bottoms. Had the Florida cabinet looked through a dissecting scope at the little polychaetes and other infauna of the developer's proposed dredge area, I wonder if they would have granted the permit so quickly.

Polychaete annelids are not only important as food for fish and water fowl, and an important part of the food chain; they are an important animal in the study of zoology and evolution.

Evolutionists have long regarded the polychaete worm as one of the most significant animals in the kingdom because they represent the greatest structural difference to be found in a single phylum. However, they have a condition in common called metamerism, which is the division of the body into similar segmented parts which are arranged in a linear series along the antero-posterior axis. It occurs not only externally in an organism but under ideal conditions internally as well. And in the annelids all body organs, blood vessels, nerves, gonads, etc., are repeated in each segment. Few polychaetes attain such an "ideal" condition, but *Nereis* does.

That is why *Nereis* is the most well-known of all marine annelids, and is used by the thousands in schools and laboratories throughout the world, to teach the principles of metamerism. But to the average New England fisherman, *Nereis,* the clam worm, is even better known to bait a hook with and catch almost any fish desirable.

It has turned into one of Maine's leading sea-product industries, and dozens of worm industries and no telling how many hundreds of clam-worm diggers have appeared in the last few years. Bushelfuls of long, slimy pink worms packed in sea moss are shipped out all over

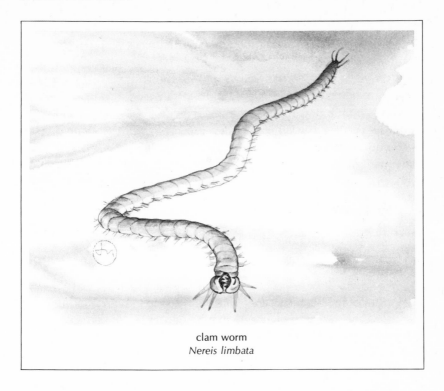

clam worm
Nereis limbata

the nation, and sports fishermen up and down the Atlantic and Pacific coasts bait their lines with *Nereis diversicolor.*

But like so many other New England forms, when they reach the Gulf, they begin to shrink. *Nereis diversicolor* doesn't make it to the South at all; it's strictly a cold-water form and its range ends somewhere between Virginia and North Carolina. But there is another nereid that also dwells along the low-water mark of New England, *Nereis limbata.* This form is geographically widespread and abundant everywhere, although it is small and not exploited for the bait industry.

Since the genus *Nereis* has all the characteristics of the "ideal" polychaete, *Nereis limbata* has been studied in the laboratory because it can withstand ambient room temperatures which colder New England forms cannot.

We find them in mud, in dredge hauls of grass and shell and particularly on sea squirt clumps taken in Alligator Harbor. Like anything else they have a seasonal variation, and at times tearing apart sea squirts yields only a few specimens; at other times several hundred can be produced. One advantage to *Nereis limbata* is it measures

199

under four inches and can be easily placed in a petri dish and examined under a dissecting scope. They are active, and wriggle excitedly.

Nereis limbata has the well-developed mouth parts that make them formidable to small organisms. They can even manage to get a good pinch on a finger, but nothing like their large New England relative that has a powerful, well-developed proboscis that can pinch deep into your thumb, which then spouts blood. It takes a good fisherman to hook one just right and not get pinched. If you plan to work extensively with *Nereis* then heavy leather gloves are necessary.

Lysarete brasiliensis
Crab Trap Worm

The biologist has set standards for the ideal organism that demonstrates metamerism, and the systematist has gone so far as to determine the "ideal" polychaete that has a number of perfectly metameric characteristics. The angler and sports fisherman also have high standards for the annelids, and out of the thousands of species of annelids, only a few meet the requirements.

Such a worm must be fat enough to bait a hook, tasty enough to draw fish, long enough to be cut into numerous pieces and hardy enough to survive for 15 minutes on a hook. *Lysarete brasiliensis* meets all the requirements and then some.

According to a taxonomist's guide, it is not a well-known species. The first I ever heard of it was when some crab fishermen bringing in their catch handed me a rusty can filled to the brim with highly iridescent, pink worms that exuded more slime than any other creature I had ever seen. The length of the worm was equally fantastic, over two feet.

A polychaete worm of so many interesting characteristics is indeed worthy of study, so we began determining its abundance, distribution, locality and culturing methods.

Only on very rare occasions were they found intertidally, and then they were smaller, less magnificent specimens than the ones pulled up from deep water in the crab traps. Their distribution also seemed limited; few specimens were taken west of the Ochlocknee River. Only in the vicinity of St. Marks National Wildlife Refuge were any appreciable numbers taken, and all of them in crab traps.

To keep count of the numbers collected, as well as to build up our stock of specimens, we paid a bounty to the fishermen. Hardly a day went by that they didn't have a rusty tin can filled to the top with worms. Starting in January we were getting a few specimens, averaging five and six each day; by March the catches were increasing to 25 each day, but in April they began to drop off. It is possible that small fish devour the worm as quickly as it enters the trap when the weather warms up and the fish come inshore.

During the colder months when the sea-water temperature averages less than 65°F no small fish are to be found, but in April there is a considerable change. By June and July not a single *Lysarete brasiliensis* is to be found anywhere.

To date they are too scarce to consider marketable for fish bait, but who is to say that extensive exploratory dredging in their habitat would not yield additional specimens? They are definitely carnivores and hang around crab traps to partake of the bait; in many instances the crabbers have found them wound around the mullet and alewife stuffed into the bait cages.

From a scientific standpoint, *Lysarete* may have numerous uses. I know of no worm that exhibits such striking iridescence. They have survived in our sand beds and crawled under a filter and thrived for months when there were no predators to disturb them. But of all the marine animals I have ever seen, nothing can compete with *Lysarete* for its huge amounts of copious, clear mucus. If you place it in a pint of water, within a few hours half the volume of the solution will be filled with slime. The shining pink worm seems to have an untapped reservoir, and produces a tremendous volume of slime within a very short time.

And it is no wonder that they seek out the rotting bait in crab traps. Their chemoreception is acute; if a piece of shrimp is dropped into a sand tank, a great commotion arises in the sand, and in seconds *Lysarete brasiliensis* thrusts its long, pink head out and makes its way to the food. It does a thorough job of gobbling down every last bit of shrimp, providing other sand-dwellers don't get it first.

Chaetopterus variopedatus
Parchment Worm

While walking on the sea grass flats at the edge of the sea, you may see two hollow, white-tipped tubes sticking up from the mud, much the way two chimneys stick up from a house. The two tubes are

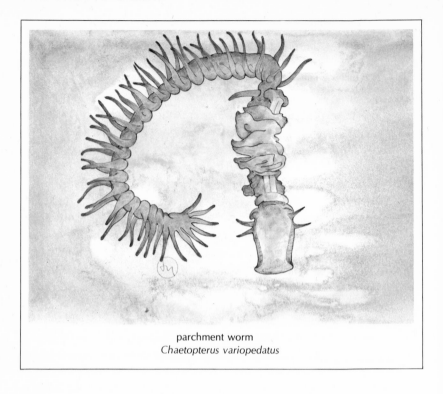

parchment worm
Chaetopterus variopedatus

spaced anywhere from eight inches to a foot apart, and at first you may think you've got two separate burrowing animals, but this is not so; this is the parchment worm (*Chaetopterus variopedatus*).

Of all the peculiar annelids in the sea, *Chaetopterus* is one of the most notable. It lives in a long, whitish U-shaped tube made of dry, parchmentlike material which it secretes and mixes with sand. The two tubes sticking up are actually the terminal portions of each tube. The ends of its tubes are distinctive from all other tubes because they are not sealed, they are completely open, and the tube ends arise from the mud or sand 8 to 14 inches apart depending upon the length of the worm. Some of them have a third tube or false terminal coming up, which adds to the confusion. You can always dig up a *Chaetopterus* by locating *both* ends.

To the chagrin of the collector often only one end of the tube is immediately visible, particularly if you are digging in dense sea grasses at low tide, and it takes quite some time to squat down, study the ground and find the other opening. Digging a shovel parallel to the two tubes and giving a steady pry, you will probably unearth a large portion of the worm. Then, if you grab both ends of the paper white casings, fold them together and clamp them with one hand, you can excavate the tube, intact with worm, using the other hand to scoop the sand away. Unless you keep the ends clamped, it is very easy to squeeze the worm out, and once *Chaetopterus* is removed from its tube, its life is greatly shortened.

Chaetopterus, because of its peculiar characteristics of bioluminescence and its very large, clear eggs, has distinguished itself as an experimental animal, and is much in demand by research laboratories. Upon removal from its tube, you will note that it has multitudes of greatly modified gills that it uses to beat and pass oxygenated water through its tube, something that is much needed in the anerobic mud.

The parchment tube can be replaced by a glass one so the animal can be seen filter-feeding and can be observed for a few days. If you place it in a pitch-dark room and stimulate it by touch, the slimy, strangely formed worm will glow with a magnificent blue light. And it has been pondered by evolutionists why this worm, which lives hidden away from all other creatures securely in its tube, has this power of luminescence.

Chaetopterus variopedatus has never distinguished itself as a long liver. Apparently, once it is dislodged from its sandy substrate, even though it is kept intact within the tube, its days are numbered. We have kept some in our tanks for several weeks at a time, gently squeezing the tube every few days to feel if that soft, squirmy animal is inside. But sooner or later the tube is empty, or a slimy, dead ooze comes out. Recently, however, we have improved our techniques by digging the tubes down into the sand tanks, propping the ends up so they stick out of the sand, and the worms survive better. A small percentage of the parchment worms can regenerate their tubes in a good sandy aquarium with good filtration, providing the bacteria count is low. The parchment worm seldom occurs in the intertidal zone along the Massachusetts coast, but since it is such a popular species, divers go down anywhere from 30 to 60 feet, recognize the chimney tubes erecting from the sand and scoop the substrate away to bring up the animal. They have to be careful, not get impatient and try to yank the tubes out, or they will tear the tubes, breaking the specimen and rendering it valueless.

When *Chaetopterus* gets into its southern ranges along the North Carolina and Georgia coasts, it is frequently found in the intertidal

203

zone; and in Florida, it is a very common sight to one who searches the seashore at low, low tides.

Diopatra cuprea
Plumed Worm

You can easily recognize *Diopatra cuprea*, the plumed worm. It has a leathery tube, and its adhesive qualities attract bits of shell and seaweed. Three to four inches of tube is flaunted above the sand, decorated with sea shells and hydroids. Along coasts where rock, shell or wood holdfasts are few and far between, *Diopatra* tubes become home to a strange admixture of fouling organisms.

Since plumed worms are scattered over the entire tidal zonation of a tide flat, they take on a curious tidal zonation of their own. *Diopatra* found on the upper reaches of the beach may have only bits of stringy brown seaweed and shell growing on it. These foreign objects adhere to the top of the tube in its initial construction because it is made of copius oozing mucus, strengthed with sand and mud. As the tube hardens, the shell and seaweed are engulfed and held in the fabric. Generally the mid-tide has tubes grown over with bryozoans or even barnacles, or serpulid worms. On the lower tidal level of the flat which is seldom uncovered by the tides, you are apt to find hydroid clusters, encrusting sponges, small sea anemones and on occasion some encrusting tunicates like *Botryllus schlosseri*. These encrusting organisms are frequently inhabited by hairy brittlestars, minute crustacea and numerous small errant polychaetes.

The worm and the tube come up in one shovelful. You'll notice immediately that only the portion of the tube that erects above the sand has the decorations, the rest of the tube is uniform and of a stringy, leathery construction, brownish black in color, although some are white.

Upon digging *Diopatra* up, you can determine whether you have a good tube or an empty one by lightly squeezing it, and if you feel a meaty lump that squirms a bit, you have a good worm. In many cases the worm has vacated the tube, and when you dig it up, all you get is the tube. After you have dug up enough of them, you'll be able to tell an empty tube; it pulls up easily because it's rotten. The animal is not home to secrete a constant supply of mucus to keep the tube lined, sand- and shell-draped and reinforced. But in open, outer beaches where *Diopatra* builds a very thick, well-constructed tube, you may have to pull it apart to see if a worm lives inside. By looking down the mouth of the tube, often, but not always you will see the worm's heavily tentacled head.

In the aquarium, *Diopatra* will often leave its tube and crawl out and construct new tubes in your tanks. However, if the tubes are originally planted in an upright position in the gravel and sand, the worm remains in its tube.

If you have to remove it from its protective housing, you can almost depend upon it to autotomize, especially around its posterior end. If the tube is carefully cut open with very sharp scissors, the worm can be persuaded to come out intact. Also, be a bit careful in handling *Diopatra* because it has a well-developed set of mouth parts and is capable of delivering a nasty bite. The worm itself is an attractive specimen; aside from its tentacled head and bushy rows of parapodia, its body has a shimmering iridescence which shows up brilliantly in sunlight or under ultraviolet rays.

Diopatra can be expected to occur anywhere along the Atlantic and Gulf coasts. Only the biggest specimens have distinguished themselves as fish bait, but it is a well-known species in the laboratory. In all their range, from Maine to Texas, they are one of the more abundant and conspicuous polychaetes.

Loimia viridis
Green Tubed Worm

Loimia viridis is a six-inch, pallid green terebellid annelid that lives in an elongated, U-shaped tube built of mucus and sand grains. In a rough sort of way its tubes resemble *Chaetopterus*, but the resemblence stops there. *Loimia* is a remarkable, sound-producing worm that lives deep in the sand; when they appear on a sand flat, they are often so dense that you can see as many as four individuals to a square foot.

However, you may never notice them. When I encountered my first *Loimia viridis* I didn't give it any particular attention, but I remember squatting on a flat digging up *Bunodactis* anemones when I heard a bubbling, creaking sound that seemed to come from all around me. Naturally I wanted to know what was making all the noise so I put my shovel down and listened. But I could not locate the source, the grass flats seemed endless, worm tubes thrust up here and there, hermit crabs bubbled and frothed at the mouth and a scallop snapped its valves shut, but where did this noise come from? My Airedale that had been working alongside me, digging up clams, walked over and sniffed a hole in the sand. And there it was, a tube sticking up, making the loudest racket of any marine invertebrate I ever heard.

Digging up *Loimia* was another matter entirely. With most of the tube worms, *Chaetopterus, Owenia, Diopatra, Polyodontes,* etc., one generally pries the ground up and pulls the worm free once its suction and support are broken. But *Loimia's* tube is so fragile and deep that it is a major feat to bring one up intact.

The tube is U-shaped, as mentioned earlier, but the ends are very long, often more than a foot, and constructed of very fine material, so fine that you can crush it between your fingers with very little effort. Only if you're lucky enough to find a specimen with a smaller tube can you bring the whole thing up intact, and even then the tube breaks immediately.

The worm itself is a typical terebellid, with a wild array of branchiae extending out from its head. Among all the tubed worms they survive the longest when removed from their protection. We have kept one individual for a month in a mudflat tank, and after a while it grew a conglomerate of sand grains and mud particles around it, although only the length of the worm and not in a U-shape, probably because our tank didn't provide enough substratum.

Polyodontes lupina
Giant Scaleworm

Although *Polyodontes lupina* is one of the most impressive of all worms, it is almost impossible to find listed anywhere in the literature. The only information on such a sinuous, slimy monster coated with dragonlike scales lies hidden in the scientific papers of polychaete specialists.

Its distribution is uncertain, but probably tropical because no record lists it as occurring in New England. John Steinbeck in *The Sea of Cortez* discusses having found a long scaleworm that lived in a *Cerianthus*-like tube, and indeed, when I first came upon *Polyodontes* I assumed that it was a long, slimy tubed sea anemone until I brought it back to the laboratory, and to my astonishment, an exceedingly ugly worm came writhing out.

When you think of a scaleworm like *Polynoe* or *Lepidonotus* you probably visualize a small, stubby creature no longer than an inch, but when a brown, dragon monster measuring eight inches or longer comes writhing out of the equally unattractive muddy brown, forked tube, naturally you are in for a shock.

As it writhes from side to side its scales flex and ripple down its body. Actually the scales are quite beautiful, having speckled whitish spots, and on some *Polyodontes* the scales are blue-tipped.

We have found *Polyodontes* to be thoroughly restricted in their habitats and localities. In west Florida they gather abundantly on offshore sand mounds and are found only at the edge of the tidal flat, on the lowest of low tides. Since the tube is so extremely tough and leathery, once the ground is broken by a shovel, they can be pulled right out of the ground with little chance of breaking the tube. The bottom of the tube is forked, and on some occasions, probably during time of mating, we have found two worms to the tube.

I have not been able to determine their seasonal variations in the Apalachee Bay region of northwest Florida. At times everywhere you go on the reef's edge you will pick up worms, in September of 1967 we picked up quite a multitude. But in September of 1968 not a single specimen was to be found on the reef, just empty tubes. These empty tubes are quite deceptive because they survive well, and only after you've dug them up do you find they are full of sand.

Unlike *Chaetopterus*, the giant scaleworm does not mind leaving its tube and establishing another. We know nothing of its feeding habits, but it can be assumed to be some sort of filter-feeder.

Polyodontes has a true parasitic snail, *Cochliolepas parasitica*, that dwells under the scales of the worm itself. After you get over the shock of seeing such a monstrous scaleworm, you will then notice the small reddish, flat vitrennelid snails clinging to the worm under its scales. This snail is found nowhere else except on the worm, and what specimens have been reported of the snail have formerly been few and far between.

The specimens of *Cochliolepas parasitica* that we collected were the first to be added to the Harvard mollusk collection, and the specimens I preserved in a relaxed condition were the first good specimens to be donated to the Academy of Natural Sciences of Philadelphia. The worm is rare in almost every other collection as well.

An amateur collector, digging along the flats, turning over rocks, and wondering at the creatures he finds can make a significant contribution.

Lepidonotus sublevis
Scaleworm

The little fat scaleworms (*Lepidonotus sublevis*) are inconspicuous and relatively uncommon in the south. But in the north, it is almost impossible to rip up a small clump of mussels, hunt through the byssus hairs and not find a half-dozen. The inventive angler has learned to poke a small hook through this worm, drop it off the end of the jetty and come up with handsome striped bass and other fish.

The worms are almost never larger than one inch. They are fat, rounded, and their back has scales on it, much the same way fish have scales on their bodies. It is a tough, almost indestructible annelid that lives in almost any aquarium where it can be given shelter, although it definitely does not qualify under the section of beautiful, descriptive and colorful marine animals. If you get a good look at it under a magnifying glass it appears as a small abomination, which might, if considered, make it run high in the poll of what animal the Loch Ness monster might resemble.

In the south, along the Florida beaches, we have encountered it living commensally in shells with hermit crabs that are grown over with bryozoans and algae. Once in a while a Busycon egg case is riddled with them, and I recall one instance when 87 specimens were removed from the egg case. Whether they were eating the eggs or just finding shelter is not known.

Owenia fusiformis
"Stickworm"

Of all the little burrowing, tube-dwelling polychaetes, *Owenia fusiformis'* tube-building has been studied most extensively. The thin, green worm with bamboolike segments is quite an architect and can put together one of the toughest and well-formed tubes of any of the annelid phylum.

There is good reason. *Owenia* does not abandon its tube like most polychaetes, but carries it about and uses it to burrow to great

208

advantage. Although the tube is rigid it has great flexibility, which is attained by using flat sand grains incorporated into a mucus-secreted membranous lining, arranging them so that only one edge is attached, the rest overlaps adjacent sand grains. It gives the outside of the tube the appearance of roofing shingles.

It takes a good bit of energy to pull the tube apart since it is so well cemented together, but when you succeed you will see a peculiar green worm with small, degenerate parapodia that have little function except to enable it to move up and down the tube. Errant polychaetes that move and forage for food have well-developed parapodia, but the tube-dwelling filter-feeders are another matter, especially one like *Owenia* that carries its tube around. *Pectinaria*, the cone-shaped worm, is much the same way.

Naturally, *Owenia* survives well in aquariums; almost any of the truly anerobic sand-dwellers do. They can be removed from their tubes and placed in a sand tank and the process of tube-building can be viewed in a matter of two days. The exterior of the tube varies greatly depending on what sort of substrate the worm has to make its construction with.

For example, *Owenia* living on the sheltered bay side of Alligator Harbor and St. Teresa Reef are heavily grown with tiny bits of shell and even some seaweed mixed together, giving them the appearance of Spanish architecture. The *Owenia fusiformis* from the outer open Gulf shores which have a finer suspension of sand, have much less shell and a much less rough appearance.

The remarkable feature about collecting *Owenia* is that you may never know they are present until you shovel up sand anticipating some other organism and find as many as six individuals in your shovel scoop. They can lie completely buried, or at times with just the very tip of their tubes protruding. When they are in season the entire flat is dominated by them, yet a few weeks later not six individuals will be collected in a full day's digging.

Sabella melanostigma
Feather-duster Worm

When the dredge hauls up a number of limestone rocks and shells, and the catch is placed in a vat of sea water and left undisturbed for a few hours, you are certain to see the maroon crowns of feather-duster worms (*Sabella melanostigma*) expand out.

I know of no other annelid that can respond so quickly. *Sabella's* tentacles are highly modified and light sensitive so that even a shadow passing over causes them to retract quickly, and the worm darts into its tube so that you may question that you ever saw it. The *Sabella* of the North Atlantic and Gulf coasts are quite small and insignificant compared to the luxurious tropical flowering feather-duster worms that can be seen by divers from quite a distance. But as soon as the diver's shadow passes over or he makes the slightest vibration, the worm is gone.

So the problem arises, regardless of the size of species of *Sabella:* How do you catch it? In coral reef situations when the worm is embedded in a giant wall of coral and rock there may not be an answer short of blasting the rock away; it becomes one of those creatures that is denied to you.

But in small chunks of limestone rock and pieces of coral the feather-duster worm is accessible. A sharp blow with your hammer and the rock splits. Gently pulling it apart you see the tube, and free it from the hard substratum. Too hard a pull and the worm will break in half, but with just the right tension the worm will be pulled out of its burrow and exposed.

You do this only if the worm is needed for a preserved museum specimen or for some biochemical analysis. If the worm is desired as a living specimen then it is to be kept in its original substrate and placed in an aquarium where it will expand its beautiful feathery tentacles when conditions are right. I have noticed that *Sabella melanostigma* may go several days without coming out, then on other days with filtered sunlight, it will remain out.

A mixture of clam juice or shrimp juice and water is adequate food, and with proper care, sabellids can be an added joy to the aquarium for months.

Class Hirudinea

While leeches are commonplace in fresh water, they are extremely rare in the sea, and unless you really search, chances are you'll never see any. The place to look is on fish, particularly flattened fishes such

Horseshoe crabs *(Limulus polyphemus)*
converge upon the beach in copulating pairs
during the spring. The male rides piggyback
on the female and fertilizes the masses of
jellylike eggs that she deposits in the sand.
(photo by Gulf Specimen Company, Inc.)

Collectors digging for brachiopods and annelids on an exposed sea grass flat in Alligator Harbor, Florida. *(photo by Gulf Specimen Company, Inc.)*

Seining in a tidal marsh in Skipper Bay, Panacea, Florida, off the St. Marks National Wildlife Refuge to demonstrate the vast amount of juvenile fish, shrimp and crabs that depend upon these wetlands for food and cover. *(photo by Gulf Specimen Company, Inc.)*

t left:
n otter trawl gorged with fish, shrimp nd crabs is being hauled aboard Gulf pecimen Company's collecting vessel, enaeus: A typical catch of a healthy, roductive estuary. (photo by ulf Specimen Company, Inc.)

During the summer months the mud flats come alive with herds of fiddler crabs, *Uca pugilator,* all moving and feeding at the same time. They pick through the sand for detritus particles left by the outgoing tide.
(photo by Gulf Specimen Company, Inc.)

The ear shell *(Sinum perspectivum)* emerges from the sand beneath Cuban shoal grass. (photo by Gulf Specimen Company, Inc.)

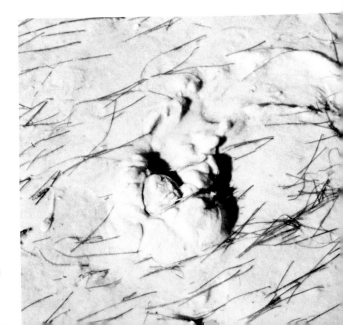

Red-footed sea cucumber *(Pentacta pygmaea)*
is commonly found in grass dredge hauls.
These have especially large modified tubed
feet which they use in fastening themselves
to blades of grass and to sea shells.
(photo by Ralph Buchsbaum)

Left-handed whelk (*Busycon contrarium*) lays a series of necklacelike egg capsules made out of a horny material. These capsules are often found by beachcombers, who wonder about the kind of an animal they have found. *(photo by Gulf Specimen Company, Inc.)*

At right:
Dwarf octopus *(Octopus joubini)* is a small species seldom measuring more than an inch. It lives in empty sea shells or in rock crevices, feeding upon tiny crabs.
(photo by Ralph Buchsbaum)

Mantis shrimp *(Squilla empusa)* is a denizen of muddy bottoms, living in burrows at low tide. It has protruding green eye stalks, jagged cutting uropods and sharp, slashing claws that make the collector wary of capturing one.   *(photo by Ralph Buchsbaum)*

Purple sea urchin (*Arbacia punctulata*) bristles its long sharp spines as it clings to rock piles. It ranges from Maine to Texas and has become a classical animal in embryology. Biologists seek it for its large, easily extracted eggs, which are excellent for studying cell division.   *(photo by Ralph Buchsbaum)*

Red cleaning shrimp (*Hippolsymata wurdmanii*) is an attractive red striped shrimp found along the Carolina and Florida coasts living in sea squirts and sponges. In captivity they will clean your fingernails, actively searching for something to eat.   *(photo by Ralph Buchsbaum)*

At right:
Tubed anemone (*Cerianthus americanus*) erects beautiful purple tentacles from a rather ugly tube constructed of mucus, sand and mud. Tubed anemones are common at low tide along mud and grass flats. *(photo by Ralph Buchsbaum)*

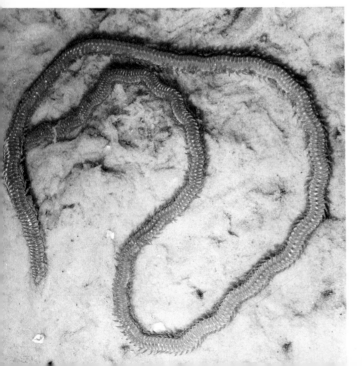

Above:
"Staghorn" bryozoan
(*Schizoporella unicornis*)
grows in little orange
clusters along sea grass
flats in Florida. Their
calcareous little
compartments house tiny
ciliated zooids and the
colonies are often
mistaken for coral.
(photo by Ralph Buchsbaum)

Crab trap worm (*Lysarete
brasiliensis*) is one of the
largest, most beautiful
iridescent polychaetes to
be found in the Gulf of
Mexico. They secrete
much mucus, which aids
in their burrowing. They
also enter crab traps and
were given this common
name for lack of a better
one. *(photo by Ralph
Buchsbaum)*

Angel-wing clam Cyrto-
pleura costata) lives deep
in the mud and sand,
thrusting its long pink
siphon to the surface to
draw in water containing
plankton and detritus.
*(photo by Ralph
Buchsbaum)*

Below:
Giant eastern murex
(Murex fulvescens) is a
ravenous predator of
clams and other large
gastropods. They can drill
through a hard shell with
their radula, leave a neat
round little hole in the
shell of their victim and
then slide on to the next
one. *(photo by Ralph
Buchsbaum)*

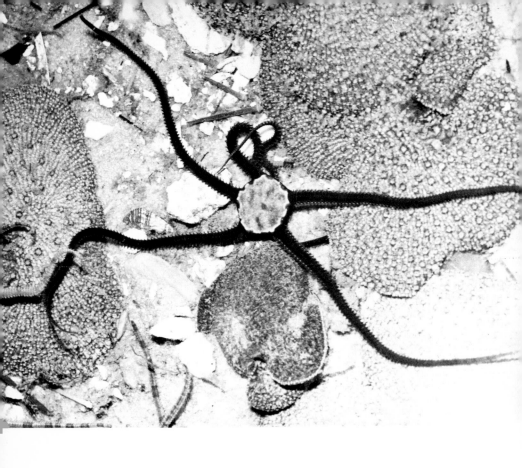

Above:
War-legs brittlestar
*(Ophioderma
brevispinum)* snakes
along the muddy bottom
with its long, lashing
arms; they converge
upon carrion in massive
groups. Anglers often pull
their lines up and find a
writhing mass of
brittlestars on their bait.
(photo by Ralph Buchsbaum)

Common bay scallop
(Aequipecten irradians) is
the most active and
responsive of all bivalves.
Light-sensitive blue eye
spots fringe their mantle.
When a hand or predator
approaches, they rapidly
snap their valves shut and
often swim away.
(photo by Ralph Buchsbaum)

Striking a gill net in tidal marsh for mullet and trout. This is part of Alligator Harbor in Franklin County, Florida, an area that may soon be gutted by the U.S. Army Corps of Engineer's Intercoastal Waterway.
(*photo by Gulf Specimen Company, Inc.*)

A heavily polluted beach one mile west of the St. Joe Paper
Company in Gulf County, Florida. Wood chips, pulp and bark
are dumped into the estuary and pile up on the beaches,
smothering all the life beneath it.
(photo by Gulf Specimen Company, Inc.)

Collector Leon Crum
investigates an oil spill at
Shell Point Beach in
Wakulla County, Florida.
The oil which was
dumped from a disabled
barge has seeped into the
tidal marshes and taken
its toll of birds and sand-
dwelling invertebrates.
*(photo by Gulf Specimen
Company, Inc.)*

Fish kill in Pensacola Bay, Escambia County,
Florida, thought to be the result of pollution
from industrial and domestic sources
combined with restricted water flow and low
oxygen conditions created by thoughtless
causeway dredging. *(photo by Mike Turrisi,
Carrabelle High School)*

Sea gulls and terns follow shrimp boats,
gobbling up the trash fish as fast as it is culled
off the deck. Nothing in the sea is wasted.
(photo by Gulf Specimen Company, Inc.)

as rays and flounders, and there, on occasion, you will find some belonging to the family Ichthyobdellidae.

Periodically we have looked for marine leeches, and have learned to examine the abdomens of large butterfly rays (*Gymnura micura*) caught in the shrimp nets. We are likely to find small pink-colored *Branchellion ravenelli*, leeches with red leaflike gills and a large, round flattened sucking mouth. Sometimes as many as 50 leeches occur on a single ray.

There are other tiny leeches that are often found on toadfish. *Keys to the Marine Invertebrates of the Woods Hole Region* refers to several species found on summer flounder and skate, and one species, *Icthyobdella funduli*, found on the long-nosed killifish, *Fundulus heteroclitus*. We have never, however, taken any leeches on *Fundulus heteroclitus* in the Gulf of Mexico.

Leeches should be preserved after they have been anesthetized with magnesium chloride, chloral hydrate or propylene phenoxetol. We achieved some good well-expanded specimens by freezing them once. Formalin or Bouin's solution transferred to alcohol is adequate for preserving them.

Class Oligochaeta

Although it is not commonly known, earthworms or oligochaetes occur in the sea. In fact they are very common along the high intertidal zone and along the upper reaches of tidal marshes. We have made large collections of oligochaetes from rocks placed on the high beach, gathering them easily because they were partly exposed and only partly buried.

Earthworms are identified by their internal anatomy, and specialists working with the group (and these are few and far between) must section the worms and examine their intestine and crop before positive identification can be made.

The worms are killed in alcohol, straightened on blotter paper and finally preserved in 10 percent Formalin. A good collection of oligochaetes is important for anyone building up a reference collection of the high-beach infauna.

Preservation

Preserving polychaete annelids is a matter of experimentation, often of discovering the best method for each order, class and family because they are so diversified in structure as well as habitat and temperament. The techniques vary according to the specialist working with the worms, how expert they are in judging twisted-up worms and whether they want a well-expanded specimen with no major contortions.

Tiny nereids found in between sand grains and seen only in a dish of substrate under a dissecting scope will generally preserve out in good condition if formaldehyde is poured on top of them. And large polychaetes like *Lysarete* or *Arenicola*, a foot or two in length, require special handling. So no generalization can be given about the handling techniques.

Although identification can be made from contorted, shriveled-up and knotted specimens that have been dropped into Formalin, it is generally desirable to have a well-expanded specimen. The time and the anesthetic required to render a polychaete insensitive will vary considerably. Many will become completely immobilized after they have soaked in an 8 percent magnesium chloride solution for four or five hours, others may sit in solutions saturated with magnesium sulfate or chloral hydrate overnight and still respond to touch, and will contract when preservative is added.

We have learned to produce well-expanded, well-preserved specimens in the shortest possible time by treating them as follows: the specimens are anesthetized partially in magnesium sulfate for an hour. Alcohol is dripped in and the animals closely watched to see that the solution is not too strong to cause death contractions. When they are fairly immobile a 2 percent solution of Formalin is dripped in until they die. The proboscis of nereid worms will generally expand, and tube-dwellers will readily crawl out. The worms are then straightened by removing them from the weak killing solution and placing them, ventral side down, on blotter paper and straightening them, *not* stretching them. After a few seconds rigor mortis will set in and the worm will remain straight. They should then be placed in a tray of 10 percent Formalin to harden.

Worms may be left in Formalin indefinitely or transferred to alcohol. Color notes are essential in some species and should definitely be taken from living specimens, since polychaetes rapidly fade in preservative.

20.
Phyla Sipuncula and Echiuroidea
Peanut Worms and Sausage Worms

Sipunculids

Sipunculids represent one of the minor phyla that lie betwixt and between. They are the peanut worms, devoid of segments, having an anterior snout which thrusts in and out like the finger of a rubber glove, and when completely expanded mushrooms into tentacles.

However, aside from their fascinating biological interest and their peculiar behavior exhibited while thrusting their introvert wildly in and out, sipunculids have attracted attention from fishermen who are ever on the lookout for bait. They are muscular and nicely fit a hook, and in areas where large burrowing forms occur, they are popularly sought.

In Madagascar I found sipunculids much in demand as bait and learned an effective trick from the Sakalava tribe for removing the deep burrowing species. They insert a very long flexible wire all the way down the hole until they feel the animal squirming. The holes are deceptive as they appear to go straight down for a foot or more, but they then level out horizontally before another, poorly defined opening occurs. The Sakalava, who use them to bait mangrove snappers, instantly dig down to the exact location of the worm with their hands—much the way a terrier digs for a rat—and yanks it out. Sometimes a veritable tug of war ensues. Then they carry the long pinkish-white worms by the dozen, hung strung out over their extended arm.

The most common of all the sipunculids in the Gulf is *Dendrostomum alutaceum*, which has earned the name of peanut worm, because when fully contracted, it looks exactly like a peanut. But unless you are particularly in search of *Dendrostomum* chances are you'd pass your entire lifetime along the coast and never know it existed.

Only if you take a chunk of lime rock dredged or dived up from six feet or deeper and give it a sharp blow will the firm, round bodies be exposed. *Dendrostomum* burrows into rock and coral; how it does it is not known—perhaps by thrusting its introvert hard against the surface, perhaps by some chemical action. But we have found them deep inside the hardest of hard rock where even the boring date mussels (*Lipthophaga bisculata*) do not penetrate.

Sipunculids have considerable biological importance. Therefore, we have come to give them considerable attention in recent years and have instituted numerous searches for *Dendrostomum*. Surprisingly, they do not occur in just any subtidal piece of rock. They have occurred in lumps of coral, *Siderastrea radians*, and for a while we suspected that they were more abundant there than any other place. Quite a few lumps of coral were sacrificed before we found that they

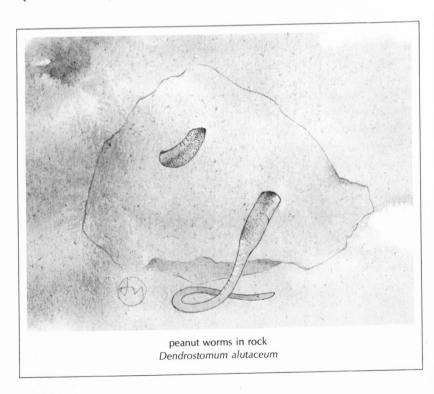

peanut worms in rock
Dendrostomum alutaceum

would also select a chunk of lime rock and heavily colonize it.

For example, one piece of rock weighing five pounds or so might yield a dozen animals, while the next five pieces taken from the same general locality would not yield three specimens. At the end of an afternoon when you are collecting a number of animals, you will be splattered with rock fragments and worn out, looking like a 49'er panning for gold. Breaking the rock must be done very carefully. If you bring your hammer down too hard you are liable to crush your sipunculid, as well as other animals.

Dendrostomum alutaceum is one of the hardiest animals I have ever collected. They will survive in a bottle of sea water for months, possibly years, without any deterioration or much shrinkage even when removed from their rocky burrow. If given organic material (detritus) they will eat in captivity, utilizing their tentacles.

Preservation of Sipunculids

Sipunculids are identified by their muscle bands, the shape and size of their introvert and by their various internal organs. Although a specimen preserved in Formalin or alcohol will not be without value, specialists prefer to have well-expanded specimens with the introvert protruding.

They are, for the most part, remarkably resistant to anesthetics. Continuous soaking in Epsom salts may cause them to become hyperextended or to bloat.

A technique widely used by sipunculid specialists is to rinse live specimens in tap water to remove the salt, then place them in *distilled* water. After a few hours most of them will die expanded, even to the tentacles, but some resistant specimens will remain stubbornly contracted and die that way.

Steinbeck and Ricketts in *The Sea of Cortez* suggest that you first anesthetize sipunculids by sprinkling powdered menthol crystals on the sea water in a scrupulously clean glass dish. "These worms are so delicate that metal or metal salts will cause them to draw in their heads immediately. The more refractory forms, after a few hours' treatment with menthol, are killed by letting fresh water gradually replace the sea water. This must be done over a period of several hours."

Magnesium chloride made up in an 8 percent isotonic solution might be tried. I have had good results on *Dendrostomum* using propylene phenoxetol and achieved good distention of the tentacles.

But regardless of the narcotizing technique used on the peanut worms it is important that they be well straightened before placing in a bottle. Specialists recommend a 50 percent alcohol solution with enough Formalin to equal 2 percent, adding just a tiny amount of corrosive sublimate to give good hardening of the intestine. They may be preserved in a 10 percent to 12 percent Formalin sea-water solution if they are allowed to harden in pans for 24 hours before transferring to a storage bottle. Distorted, bent sipunculids are practically valueless.

The entire phylum of Sipuncula was given the common name "peanut worms" by a specialist who was looking at contracted specimens. And certainly species of the genus of *Dendrostomum* when contracted in Formalin do look like peanuts. However, had the specimen originally been expanded with its bushy introvert protruding, or had the specialist been examining one of the elongated *Golfingia* the entire genus might have been given another common name. But in the meantime, "peanut worms" will have to do.

Another rather unwholesome-looking species, *Siphonomecus multicinctus*, appears sporadically on north Florida's sandflats. Some specimens measure a full two feet in length, are as thick as your thumb and have a dark skin color and a fleshy texture to match. On rare occasions they appear in shrimp trawl catches, and for quite a long time we considered them to be a very rare and unobtainable species.

However, we found that clam boats working off Port St. Joe often bring them up by the dozens. In fact, we were once able to purchase a bushel basket of these worms and that was a memorable sight, and would make anyone who sings the despairing worm song of rejection "Nobody loves me, everybody hates me . . ." bite his tongue.

Echiuroids

Thalassema mellita
Sand Dollar Sausage Worm

Echiuroids are a small group of unsegmented worms commonly called "sausage worms," characterized by their grooved introvert. They are found burrowing in the mud, living in shell and even in rocks throughout temperate and tropical regions. Several species are well known in biology classes, especially the California "fat innkeeper" (*Urechis caupo*), which has a number of animals living in its burrows as permanent guests, including a scaleworm, pea crab and transient goby. Another genus, *Bonellia*, is unusual because the males are parasites, living on or within the females.

When I had first started seriously collecting for a living, I had an order from Duke University for *Thalassema mellita*, the echiuroid that lives along the southeastern United States. According to the Florida State University annotated check lists they were supposed to live in dead sand dollar tests. The worms enter the test when they are very small and become too large to leave. For weeks I searched over miles of tidal flats, picking up every dead sand dollar test that I found. All the sand dollars on the beach were *Mellita quinquiesperforata*, and it seemed logical that I would find echiuroids there because they were named *Thalassema mellita*, probably after the genus of sand dollar, *Mellita*.

But this was not the case. Day after day I slogged along the hot flats looking for them. *Mellita quinquiesperforata* tests along the Carolina coast are supposed to be riddled with them, but not along the west Florida coast, or so it seemed. Finally the order was canceled. Not until 1968, when we purchased our trawler *Penaeus*, did we find them. When the heavy steel dredge was hauled aboard after being pulled over sand bottom in 60 feet of water, it was loaded with dead *Clypeaster subdepressus* and *Encope michelini* sand dollars grown over with bryozoans and serpulid worms. Eagerly I broke them apart by tapping them gently with a hammer.

In almost every dead sand dollar was a large fat echiuroid (*Thalassema mellita*), measuring an inch to three inches in length. They were handsomely purple or red and had a bright frilly white proboscis with a groove. The mystery was solved. Since then we have routinely

217

gathered them, and kept them in the aquarium still inside the dead sand dollars where they have thrived. I shall always remember how delighted I was to see those worms.

Preservation of Echiuroids

In general echiuroids should be preserved in the same manner as sipunculids. Most of my preservation techniques have been based upon the highly retractile *Bonellia* found under rocks in Madagascar, but they appeared to succumb to an overnight bath in a saturated solution of magnesium sulfate. They are best fixed in Formalin, after the introvert hangs limp, and injected to preserve the digestive and reproductive systems by which they are identified.

21.
Lophophorate Phyla
Moss Animals, Phoronids and Lamp Shells

Zoology is far from a cut-and-dried science. All one has to do is get a large number of invertebrate zoologists together in a conference and bring up the taxonomy of where various minor groups of invertebrates belong in the animal kingdom and on the evolutionary scale, and the discussion can get quite lively because there are such divergent opinions.

There are many different schools of thought, and each has evolved a separate terminology. Whether one should call a bryozoan an ectoproct or a coelenterate or a cnidarian appears to be left up to the individual worker. Dr. Libby Hyman consolidated many of the invertebrate phyla in her six-volume work, *The Invertebrates*, which is a must for everyone who studies marine life.

Dr. Hyman lumped three related minor phyla (Ectoprocta, Phoronida and Brachiopoda) together because of their food-catching organ called a lophophore. Roy Waldo Minor in his handbook of Atlantic seashore life lumped the ectoprocts (bryozoans) into the phylum Proscopygia, and considered them as a separate group, and he considered the brachiopods as a subphylum. However, bryozoans, phoronids and brachiopods are now considered as separate phyla by most zoologists and we shall lump them into the lophophorate coelomates, and that is the way it shall stand in this book.

It so happens that in north Florida's Alligator Harbor, all three lophophorate phyla are well represented, and all happen to live abundantly together on the same grass flats. When the intercoastal waterway is cut through Alligator Harbor, all three lophophorate groups will probably be covered with mud and destroyed; no one except biology students will know they are gone.

You can feel the calcareous bryozoans crunch under your feet, or see the keyhole slit of brachiopods, and see the stiff gray tubes of phoronids in each shovelful of earth overturned on the grass flats. They provide wonder and curiosity to those who look for them, and shouldn't that be worth something?

Phylum Bryozoa

Bryozoans are commonly called "moss animals," probably because they look so much like plants. A bryozoan either resembles a tuft of seaweed or an encrusting alga. However, when you observe them under a dissecting scope and see all their intricate little compartments with feathery tentacles periodically emerging and retracting, you'll quickly agree that they belong in the animal kingdom. But just where in the animal kingdom may be even more confusing.

The beginner is apt to confuse bryozoans with sponges, hydroids, compound ascidians and seaweeds because their texture and form vary from gelatinous to membranous, to chitinous and calcareous depending upon the species. Identification to genus and species is an arduous task even for experts because the original descriptions of some of the commonest species are often incomplete, too general and do not include really distinguishing key characteristics.

Bryozoans should be studied alive so their brushlike tentacles can be observed. These lophophorate organs are most difficult to preserve fully expanded, and if the animals are kept in plenty of cool sea water, they will live long enough to be taken back to the laboratory for study. Soon the entire feeding process can be viewed with great fascination; the tentacles extend out and look like thousands of tiny feather-duster worms emerging from an apartment-house colony, then individuals whip back in with a jack-in-the-box movement.

Bugula neritina
Brown Moss Animal

Chances are that if you see a piling or boat bottom covered with a tufted, brown sea moss, you are looking at the bryozoan *Bugula neritina*, which is not a plant. More often than not it is confused with hydroids.

Bugula grows heavily on pilings and rocks throughout the eastern United States. It comes into its own, however, when it reaches the Gulf because during the winter months, every boat bottom, every wharf piling and every clump of sea squirt is covered with it. The colonies grow into luxurious clusters often over a foot high. They spring up from shell bottom, on grass, and when a shrimp net passes through an area packed with *Bugula* it can get so loaded that it will be unable to move and will get bogged down.

But this is seasonal. *Bugula neritina* becomes prevalent in the Apalachee Bay region starting in October, blooms heavily into June but almost totally disappears during July, August and September. At such times hydroids and algae take its place on the pilings, but usually if you look hard enough, in particularly shaded, cool areas away from direct sunlight there may be a few hidden, tufted colonies.

They are much used as laboratory specimens to demonstrate polymorphism, since they contain a number of complex structures each performing a different function. Thousands of feeding ciliated tentacles warily expand, and when the slightest vibration touches them they whip down into the protective sheaths, only to come creeping out again a moment or two later.

Bugula has peculiar organs called avicularia, which grow amidst the zooids in the branching stems. Each avicularium is shaped like a bird's head and has a pair of jaws that snap shut on any small organism that chances to cross its path. The purpose of this unique organ is supposedly not to add nourishment to the colony, but to keep larvae of other small animals from colonizing. Perhaps in areas of good strong current, plenty of clear water and tidal flush it does a good job, but *Bugula* in enclosed bays and estuaries where there is little water movement becomes heavily overgrown with algae, infested with copepods and even coated with sponge and ascidians.

Membranipora tenuis
Sea Mats

The encrusting, lacy sea mats that you find on shells everywhere up and down the Atlantic coast probably lie in the genus *Membranipora*. In the Gulf and southeast coast of Florida, it is hardly possible to walk up and down the beach on any sort of tide and not find specimens of shell encrusted with whitish or yellow *M. tenuis*.

Only under the dissecting scope will you see the little tentacled zooids that live within a network of calcareous compartments, telling you that this fancy bit of encrusted lacework is really a colony of living animals.

Bryozoans are generally hardy in a large aquarium with plenty of sea water. If they are placed in a petri dish and observed, the hungry little individual animals inside the compartments will start their jack-in-the-box movements. However, when the water stagnates after a few hours they will die, completely retracted, in their compartments.

Membranipora prefers clear oceanic waters, with a minimum of silt and suspension material. However, now and then a few colonies will be found on shells along the mudflats.

Schizoporella unicornis
"Staghorn" Bryozoan

The amateur collector who happens upon a pink, orange or yellow branching cluster of this moss animal will be certain that he has found himself a handsome piece of coral. The chance of finding a piece or two of *Schizoporella unicornis* almost anywhere along the Atlantic and European coasts is good, since it occurs from the low-water mark to 600 feet.

However, when found in the Atlantic waters, *Schizoporella unicornis* is likely to be encrusting on shell, stones or algae holdfasts. In certain relatively protected areas it grows into branchlets, like *Schizoporella* from St. Marks, Shell Point Reef and even Alligator Harbor. But in St. George Sound off Carrabelle, Florida, we find it growing in branching profusion, forming an entire reef as a substratum for encrusting ascidians, algae and corals.

The fishermen refer to it as "sand coral" and curse it greatly when they strike the reef at night and ball their gill nets up on it. At times when the bryozoan is abundant, a net can get loaded down, causing many hours of suffering as they beat the tangled threads out.

One fast way to distinguish *Schizoporella* from a milleporean or a coral is to break it; you will find the pieces are hollow.

Amathia convoluta
Sheeps Wool

Great piles of brown, rough seaweedlike *Amathia convoluta* often pile up on the outer beaches of the Gulf coast. This species grows in plantlike bushes much the way *Bugula neritina* grows, but it is more of a bottom-dweller and does not colonize pilings.

The majority of *Amathia convoluta* is seen during the fall, from October through December, and when the white shrimp season is on, it balls up into the shrimp net in certain areas, often distending and gorging the net so further fishing is impossible.

When you sit upon the deck of a trawler and look at the mounds of *Amathia*, the hundreds of pounds of it, then you wonder if someone couldn't find any use for it. There is no published account of its being used for any pharmaceutical testing, nor is there any record of its being used as a commercial fertilizer, although certainly this is one organism that would lend itself to that.

Amathia is seasonal and sporadic. The same area that is packed with it one month will be clean and barren a few weeks later. Whether it breaks off from its holdfasts, and washes shoreward, or goes out to sea is unknown. The colonies are often found luxuriously blossoming up from living shells of the large ark, *Noeta ponderosa*, on Alligator Point. Although it does appear intertidally, the majority of the colonies live below the low-water mark.

Thalamoporella gothica floridana
Lettuce Bryozoan

Thalamoporella gothica floridana, a frilled, calcareous and crunchy bryozoan is a hardy dweller of the intertidal zone, having great preference for growing on the tubes of the plumed worm (*Diopatra cuprea*). They occur in warmer waters, especially in the Gulf where they are tremendously abundant during certain years and

223

make up half of the refuse that is cast up on the beaches from June through September. When you walk along the grass-covered beaches you can feel it crunching noisily and unpleasantly under your feet.

What is so impressive about this colony of animals is its frilled, oblong shape, with its intricate convolutions that appear so handsomely put together, yet it is so fragile that a light squeeze will disintegrate it into finely crushed shell. The zooids appear to be hardy in this species and very tolerant of mudflat, silty conditions.

We never paid much attention to *Thalamoporella gothica floridana*. It is not a well-known species and it does nothing exciting. However, a few years ago we sent a sample of it to the National Cancer Institute, where it was tested for its drug activity.

The results were quite exciting and *Thalamoporella gothica floridana* was one of a number of organisms that demonstrated a strong antineoplastic activity and extended the survival time of mice injected with a leukemia strain. Details on the testing procedure are discussed in the tunicate chapter.

However, when we were asked later to collect a large amount of the *Thalamoporella* sample for the drug-screening and testing program, we learned there were some headaches involved. For example, it takes over 100 colonies of dried *Thalamoporella gothica floridana* to make a pound, and no amount of dredging or trawling can produce the volume of *Thalamoporella* that one good tropical storm can by hurling it up on the beach.

We are still working on gathering up two or three hundred pounds of this bryozoan. The method of gathering it is slow, but not unpleasant. It involves long treks over sandy beaches in the late evenings. We walk along following the sunset, next to the waves lapping on the beach, stopping now and then to pick up a colony amidst the piles of cast-up seaweeds, and going onto the next cluster of *Thalamoporella gothica floridana*, thankful for the opportunity to partake of the relaxed profession of beachcombing.

Preservation of Bryozoans

Bryozoans are one of the more difficult groups to expand, if natural-looking alcohol specimens are desired. Such forms as *Bugula* are particularly interesting and desirable when the zooids and avicularia are distended and look natural.

This is done by first anesthetizing the animal in a 1 percent solution of chloral hydrate, or an isotonic solution of magnesium chloride. Unless the volume of water is at least 10 times that of the animal, the animals will not expand. A binocular dissecting scope mounted on an arm is almost essential for observing the avicularia during preservation.

No drug of any sort should be added to the water until the tentacles are fully and naturally distended. Then and only then should the preserving process begin, because contracted specimens do not expand when they are even slightly irritated. The preserving process should not begin until the specimens have sat in their dishes of cool sea water for several hours.

When the polyps no longer respond to a glass probe they may be killed with a flood of Formalin. They too have the ability to contract at the last minute, but once the tentacles are immobile from the anesthetic, they will generally die before they have a chance to draw in. These should be stored in 70 percent alcohol and that solution changed once or twice, because most forms leach out their color into solution after a few days. Color notes are important.

Phylum Phoronida

Phoronida is an extremely small phylum limited to two genera and approximately 15 species of wormlike animals that live either buried in the sand or attached to rocks, shells or other objects in shallow water. They are all encased in a chitinous tube and all have the brushlike tentacles (lophorate organs) that relate them to bryozoans and brachiopods.

Phoronids are not common in many parts of the world, and many coasts are completely without them. Much confusion exists as to where phoronids belong in the animal kingdom; some have placed them in the hemichordate group and considered them as a class by themselves. However in modern taxonomy phoronids are regarded as a separate phylum. They have a U-shaped digestive system, are generally hermaphroditic and have a conspicuous blood system where their red blood cells can be readily observed moving through their blood vessels.

Only one species of phoronid exists along the Atlantic coast and that is *Phoronis architecta*.

Phoronis architecta

Phoronis architecta can sometimes reach a huge abundance in the Gulf of Mexico. On low tide when you shovel down into any given area and tear up the turf, you'll notice that rigid, but slightly bent sticks come out that may resemble worm tubes. But no worm tube is that rigid. *Owenia fusiformis*, the tubed polychaete, has a more or less rigid, gray tube that looks something like a phoronid, but a simple touch will tell the difference and the two will not be confused.

When the sand and mud are broken apart in longitudinal layers, 3 to 10 phoronids on the average will appear. Then the rest of the earth is broken away from them. It appears that their seasonal abundance peak is reached about the same time the brachiopod *Glottidia pyramidata* reaches its seasonal peak.

The entire circulatory system and the movement of giant single red blood cells can be viewed through the body wall after a few cemented grains of sand are removed from the tube. We have had them survive for several weeks in a simple aerated aquarium, but eventually, after a month or so, the captive specimen dies.

Phoronids are best placed directly into 70 percent ethyl alcohol or 5 percent Formalin.

Brachiopoda

Brachiopods are perhaps the oldest living creatures to be found on this earth. They date back to the Ordovician period, and the genus *Lingula*, which survives today along the Hawaiian coast, can be traced back to similar species over 400 million years old.

Fundamentally there are two types of brachiopods surviving

today, ones that live attached to rocks, looking like little clams hooked on by a peg, and the other lingatulid brachiopods that burrow in the sand.

Glottidia pyramidata

On the East coast the lingatulid brachiopod is represented by a single species, *Glottidia pyramidata*, that is found from Cape Hatteras to Texas. The range sounds impressive, but actually, if you were tediously to hunt the beaches of Carolina and the Georgia coast, the likelihood of coming back with even a dozen specimens on a good day's collecting would be quite slim.

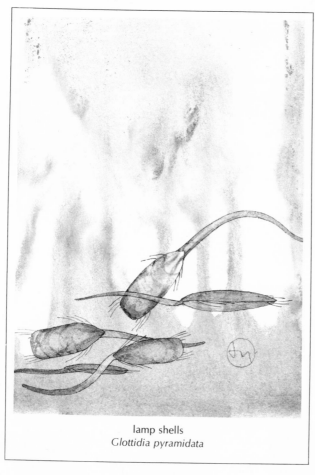

lamp shells
Glottidia pyramidata

Biologists have told me at the Duke University Marine Laboratory that after digging out on the flat for weeks, they finally spotted one small slit that looked as though it were made by a penknife, and there was the brachiopod *Glottidia pyramidata*, small and all alone.

But in the Gulf, from Tampa Bay to Pensacola, *Glottidia* is commonly encountered. When the tide goes way down and all the sandbars are completely exposed and grass beds are everywhere, you begin to find them. They are highly seasonal, shunning the hot weather and growing luxuriously in the cold winter. And when you come to a flat and see small slits everywhere looking as though someone had taken a penknife and stabbed deeply into the sand and grass, then you know you have hit brachiopods. Digging alongside the slit with a shovel you pry up a clump of grass, and if you break the slit along the side, splitting the slit, you will see the brachiopod exposed. It will immediately contract down into its burrow, but it is easy to pull it free.

Sometimes they are easily recognized. Aside from the slits on low tides, the ebbing waters will cause the valves to project from the surface, and when slightly disturbed both *Lingula* and *Glottidia* will squirm down so quickly into the sand, you doubt that you ever saw them to start with. Once in a while you can snatch the valves between your fingers and, keeping a firm but steady pressure on it, pull it from its burrow without breaking the pedicle into two pieces.

Preservation of Lingula and Glottidia

Both *Lingula* and *Glottidia* when dug up from the eelgrass tend to contract and twist, tie and contort their pedicles into knots. They can of course be dropped directly into alcohol in this state and still be easily identified because classification depends largely on the contour and shape of their shell.

But for the sake of preparing neater-looking and more natural specimens, I have found it useful to straighten the pendicles of such forms, making it possible to include measurements.

This is done by gently stretching and pulling down on the foot with wet fingers until it becomes straightened. This will be easier if the specimen is first narcotized by any one of the many narcotizing agents. Weak alcohol, however, makes them most flaccid and seems to produce best results. If a steady pulling pressure is exerted on the foot, it will stretch out, and size can be increased by an extra half inch of pure stretching. This is not an artificial device, because when they are down in the mud they are greatly extended and stretch themselves way up to the surface so they can respire and feed.

After the narcotized brachiopod has been stretched out and straightened into its natural position, then it may be dropped directly into Formalin or alcohol. If it has been sufficiently narcotized, only a little perceptible contraction will occur when it hits the killing fluids.

22.
Phylum Mollusca

Shell-bearing mollusks, the chitons, tusk shells, whelks, conchs and bivalves are by far the most well-known of all marine invertebrates. In almost any part of the United States and many parts of the world there are shell clubs that routinely go on field trips looking for sea shells. And along almost any coast — rocky shores, sandy beaches or mangroves and marches — collectors can be seen meandering along, searching, peering into holes and turning over rocks for their prizes. They scramble over boulders, lift up seaweeds and peer into tidepools.

In fact I have seen serious shell collectors go through the same motions in search of specimens, ranging from a few millimeters in size up to several feet, that a professional biological collector goes through when searching for tunicates or hydroids. Many of these enthusiasts have become highly competent amateur scientists and taxonomists who can key out the seashells they find, right down to species and even subspecies. And many an amateur has collections of identified seashells that have considerable value. Shell clubs have been formed in many communities where individuals get together to compare and trade specimens.

One of the ground rules of these collectors is that shells must be accompanied with locality data to have any merit. And many a collector will record not only the township, but the particular point, the nautical location, water depth and bottom substrate on his data label.

The scientific shell collector or serious hobbyist should at no time be confused with souvenir shell collectors and wholesalers who manufacture toys, trinkets and shell jewelry. These novelty suppliers strip the tropical coral reefs and tide flats of almost every living shell they can get their hands on. They buy them from indigent natives for only a fraction of a penny and barge them to Florida where they are embedded in cheap plastic molds, made into trinkets and sold to the tourist trade. Bushels of cowries, spider shells, murex, tritions and stacks of giant Tridacna clams are killed so they can be turned into ashtrays, lamps or centerpieces. Killing these seashells for novelty items is about as destructive and senseless as using tiger and leopard skins for fur, or alligators and sea turtles for leather handbags and shoes.

I cannot believe that such large numbers of animals being pulled out of the tropical reefs will not drastically upset the balance of nature. Although pesticides and dredging have been blamed, it is believed that one of the causes of the population explosion of *Acanthaster planci*, the crown of thorns starfish which has been eating up coral reefs in the Indo-Pacific, has been due to overcollecting of the giant triton conchs, the starfish's primary predator.

There is nothing wrong with using empty shells for decoration, but there is no reason why living snails should be used. Shell-bearing mollusks are eaten by a great many animals in the sea, and their remains are cast up on the beaches along every coast; perhaps the shells are a bit worn or chipped, but removing them hurts no one. Dead coral can be found along beaches, and this material can be successfully used as souvenirs when bleached and dried, or dyed a multitude of colors.

On a simple beachcombing expedition in west Florida, especially the famed Sanibel Island, a beachcomber can walk along and pick up bushel baskets of empty cockle shells, Florida lucina, ark clams, turkey-wings. There are dead olive shells that wash in on the beaches, moon snails, conchs, pen shells, quahogs, sunray clams and many varieties of other shell-bearing mollusks, in addition to sponges, sea whips and sea fans, crunchy branches of bryozoans that are handsome when dried, and even hordes of dead crabs and already cleaned and odorless crab cast shells. Those who appreciate the intricate and varied life forms in the ocean can fill their buckets with nature's discards and, if they are so inclined, haul bushel baskets or truckloads of dead shell, coral and discarded marine life and not cause any damage to the environment. Good sense and conservation should always be practiced in collecting. Thoughtless schoolchildren and a few thoughtless collectors grabbing up everything in sight, more than they can use, can be a detriment to an area. However, the shell enthusiast should not be considered responsible for denuding the habitats of mollusk, because he takes out only a small sample, and if the area remains unpolluted and unaltered by mankind, then the species will be able to replenish itself because a man with his bucket is just one more predator.

Class Amphineura

Chitons are best known to rocky-shore collectors along Pacific coasts, where some of the great gumboot chitons reach over a foot long. They are one of the most primitive forms of mollusk, having eight plates encircled in a firm, leathery body. During the embryological stages of development the eight shelly plates arise from a single shell gland. A chiton has a foot, a well-developed set of teeth called a radula, and no eyes or tentacles, such as one might expect to find in its snail-like cousins.

Although the casual visitor to the seashore might conclude that a chiton is totally sessile, and does not move about, this is not the case. They can inch along, even if it's just a few millimeters during the night, but do so only if conditions are unfavorable or if they run out of food.

Keeping chitons alive in a simple salt-water aquarium can be interesting. We have collected chitons (*Chaetopleura apiculata*) by dredging them up on scallop and oyster shells on outer grassy reefs where there is a good tidal flush and clear water, and placed them in tanks. Many of them remain on the shells until they eat all the algae off, and then crawl on the side of the glass. When you remove them from their holdfast, they begin to curl into a tight ball. We found this species to be hardy and it survives for long periods of time, since it is content to remain in the aquarium below the water level. The tropical

tropical chitons
Acanthopleura granulata

Atlantic chiton (*Acanthopleura granulata*) that measures three inches is gathered from tidal rocks and boulders of the Florida Keys. When placed in an aquarium, these chitons will immediately seek their intertidal position by crawling up above the waterline in the tanks, and often they crawl out of the tank and cling to the outside glass walls, where they will dehydrate and perish if not pushed back in the water.

Class Scaphopoda

Scaphopods represent a small primitive group of mollusks that are easily recognized because they resemble a long, white tooth or a miniature elephant's tusk, giving them the common name of "tusk shell." There are approximately 1000 species of scaphopods in the world. They are found on every coast ranging from the subtidal down to a depth of 1000 feet.

Nowhere along the Atlantic coast are they common, but using the right equipment they can be collected. About 20 years ago species of *Dentalium* were taken in dredge hauls along the coast of Massachusetts, but lately none has been produced.

Scaphopods are strictly burrowing forms found only in sandy substrates. The narrow pointed end protrudes from the sand, and has an orifice that draws in water and expels it at intervals. The wide, conical foot, which stays down in the sand, has a multitude of ciliated threadlike appendages called captacula which capture single-celled organisms which they crush with their strong radular teeth.

Once in a while, after a severe storm, beachworn shells of *Dentalium pilsbryi* wash ashore along the Florida beaches and can be found when the beach sand is sifted through screens. However, to get good specimens of living animals, a powerboat with a bucket dredge is

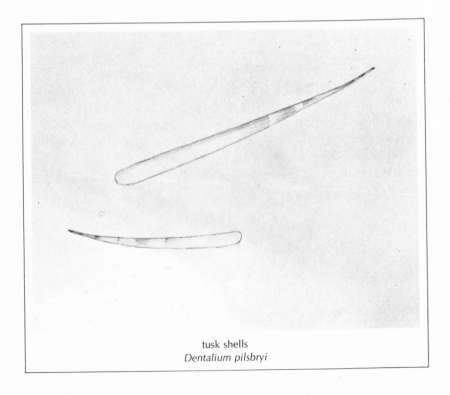

tusk shells
Dentalium pilsbryi

required. The dredge is chucked overboard and bites into the bottom. The engine is speeded up until the dredge takes a good bite into the substrate and then it is brought to the surface. It should be packed with coarse sand, but if there is soft, oozing mud, you might as well dump the sample back overboard because there will not be any scaphopods. When you dredge a good haul which contains crushed shell and coarse sand, you'll probably have a number of tusk shells after the sand is sifted.

Chances are that only a few *Dentalium pilsbryi* are alive, the rest are dead shells or shells occupied by tiny hermit crabs. Since fresh dead shells often bear the same pinkish color as living ones, the only way to tell if you have living specimens is to bring them back to the laboratory and let them sit in a dish of sea water. In a few moments the living specimens will expand their fuzzy white foot and begin to thrust around with funny, erratic jerky motions.

They survive moderately well in the aquarium if three or four inches of the original substrate, from which they were dredged, is placed on the bottom of the tank. Within seconds after they are placed in the aquarium the tusk shells will pull themselves down into the sand and out of sight.

Class Pelecypoda

Bivalves or pelecypods are one of the most abundant forms of life in the ocean, found from the edge of the sea to the greatest depths of the ocean. They are abundant in every habitat in one form or another, some, such as mussels, have threadlike byssuses that anchor them to rocks and they make up an entire habitat or community; others, such as oysters, anchor themselves to shell or rock by calcareous secretions, also making up a habitat. Then there are burrowing clams, and boring pholads that cut into mud or rock. There are clams that live over three feet down in the airless, dark, smelly mud, thrusting their siphons up to the surface to get oxygenated water and food, which they suck in and filter out of the water.

Clams range in size from the monstrous *Tridacna* clams of the

Indo-Pacific to tiny forms only a few millimeters long that are
attached to tunicates or commensals on the gills of mantis shrimps.

Mercenaria campechiensis
Quahog Clam

Along the Atlantic coast, especially in New England, the quahog
clam (*Mercenaria mercenaria*) has a tremendous economic impact.
They are served in restaurants, bars and clam bars as "cherrystones" or
"little necks" or as "stuffed quahogs," which all mean small, medium
and large sizes. Working the mudflats off Long Island, I have helped
gather them by the bushel basket and have spent many pleasant hours
opening them and eating them with hot sauce.

There is a southern species of quahog (*Mercenaria campechiensis*)
that has a slightly thicker shell and grows larger than its northern
form. It does not survive nearly as long in captivity as *M. mercenaria*,
which can live for weeks in a cool burlap sack and can be shipped
successfully to any part of the country. "Mail-order" clams are a
reality.

But unfortunately our southern subspecies doesn't taste nearly as
good, doesn't survive as long, and is not found inshore in abundance.
The population along the beaches of Panacea and Alligator Point
remains relatively stable from year to year; there are hardly enough
specimens to collect for laboratories and research programs, and
certainly not enough to eat. At the end of a collecting day, after
walking miles of tidal flats exposed to northerly winter winds you'll be
lucky if you get half a bushel. Always they can be seen on the flats by
their broad keyholelike slits, which are characteristic of other clams,
but their digging powers are somewhat limited and the clam always
lies an inch or two beneath the sand.

Mercenaria campechiensis was not always scarce in north Florida.
Great mounds of opened shells have been found in Indian settlements
along Panacea that date back over 5000 years. This clam at one time
was their staple diet. The entire river basin of the Ochlockonee River
is almost paved with *Mercenaria campechiensis*, and after a hurricane
the shores are littered with their fossilized shells. They are not found
offshore; clam boats dredging off Port St. Joe to the west of Panacea
find only a handful of specimens.

Quahogs are abundant in Mississippi and Louisiana where they

are commercially fished, and along the Central Gulf coast of Florida
Mercenaria is abundant in grass beds.

Are they gone as a dominant population in west Florida forever?
Or will they come back in multitudes in another 5000 years if the
ocean isn't too polluted to support life by that time? When I walk over
these 20-foot mounds of quahog shells I can't help asking myself,
"What happened?" Were they killed off by some disease, or could the
few Apalachicolee Indians that lived by the shore have overfished the
population to the point of near extinction? Perhaps the water
temperature has changed, the beds eroded away or the salinity
changed. But they are gone nevertheless.

We cannot blame the demise on industrial or domestic pollution,
nor can we say pesticides took their toll, or even dredging and filling.
There are still plenty of clams in Boca Ciega Bay, according to local
residents, where massive dredging has destroyed much of the
ecosystem and rendered the bay bottom uninhabitable for many forms
of life. But the clams are still there in places and people still go out and
harvest them.

Macrocallista nimbosa
Sunray Clam

Only in recent years has the sunray venus clam assumed any
commercial importance. Until the Quality Seafood Company in
Apalachicola, Florida, purchased a Nantucket clam dredge, converted
a shrimp boat and went to Port St. Joe Bay and tried dredging for them,
Macrocallista nimbosa, the sunray venus was considered just another
pretty shell found on the beach.

Shrimpers reported that when they went aground on the St. Joe
Shoals and spun their propellers to wash themselves off, they blew up
hundreds of these clams. Some clams were brought back to
Apalachicola, opened, tasted and pronounced edible. Not tasty enough
to eat on the half-shell, however, and also they contain gristle, so the
verdict was they were to be turned into soup. Two boats were rigged
up, an oyster house converted into a clam-shucking factory with
conveyer belts and the business of fishing for clams bloomed.

How stable the beds are, and how abundant the clams are no one
knows. Exploratory fishing so far has revealed that only in St. Joe
are the clams abundant enough to fish for. But they occur in

substantial numbers in Alligator Harbor and Alligator Point, and after a storm large numbers are often tossed up on the beaches. When collecting them for specimens, a good low tide is the best time.

The sunray venus is a typical clam and demonstrates its appearance on the sand flats in the most typical manner. It has the usual keyholelike slit that the siphons of clams leave in the mud after they retract, and usually a foot or two away is a little pattern of splash depressions on the substrate where the clam spurted water out of its siphon. When left exposed by the tides and somewhat subject to desiccation, the clam pumps water out of its body cavity and forces up a spurt by rapid closure of its valves. Then you scoop the sand away with your hands or dig with a shovel and up comes the beautiful polished shell of *Macrocallista nimbosa*, which is delicately tinged with pinks and yellows. The clam will probably continue to squirt, drawing in its foot, siphons and mantle.

These splash depressions invariably give the clam's presence away to the collector. You may not be able to see the hole, but if you see a whole series of splash imprints, then you can keep looking until the keyhole becomes evident, and the clam is all yours. Be sure the splash marks are not from a wet, dripping dog or water coming off someone's boots. That can be deceptive.

On high tide, if you swim over the tidal flats with a mask, you can often see the white siphons with dark tips erecting from the sand. Often they expand completely into a feeding, respirating and moving position when the tide has covered them, but when the tide falls they contract down into the mud and their burrows can be covered by sand and completely hidden. Then you can walk the flats and not find a single specimen.

When the tide starts to seep in, the siphons may start to rise, and the collector may ask himself, "Did I miss seeing all these burrows? Could I have been that unobservant not to see these siphons sticking up out of the mud?" he wonders, looking at a big siphon next to his footprint. Then he'll realize that they emerged after he had left.

Sunray clams are not easily kept. Some clams, like the quahog, can be kept in aquariums for long periods of time, but the sunray will soon perish if water conditions and temperature are not kept optimum. They are very susceptible to siltation, and die quickly when there is low oxygen from bacterial pollution. Suprisingly enough, however, they will remain alive if kept dry and cold in a refrigerator for several days.

We have purchased them by the bushel from the fish house in Apalachicola where they have been stored for a week or more in a cooler. Then we placed them in our tanks where the water temperature was identical to the ocean and in three days we lost 150 clams out of 200. And nothing fouls up the water faster than dead sunray clams. It seems that the younger and smaller the specimen is, the better are its chances of survival. Specimens dug by hand out on the flats remain in much better condition and live longer than those taken by hydraulic dredging.

Recently we have developed some technology in keeping *Macrocallista*. Since it is a burrowing form it must have pressure against the shell to alleviate the strain of the adductor muscle, so clams packed in a tank with gravel around them survive well. That is, if the temperature stays under 70 degrees; when it reaches 80 degrees a high rate of mortality occurs.

Crytopleura (Barnea) costata
Angel-wing Clam

Few shells have the fragile, sculptured beauty of the angel-wing. When you find them on the beach, they are usually white, clean and a fine addition to anyone's collection, whether it is the serious malacologist or just someone wishing to bring back some beautiful seashells for a display.

But few people ever get to see the living animals because they live buried two feet and more deep down in the sand on the low-tide zone at the edge of the sea. They are only occasionally found in New England, in a peat bog or a clay bank once or twice a year. Just as some northern animals are scarce and changed in size when they are found in Florida waters, the angel-wing changes and comes into its own from Virginia and North Carolina into the Gulf where it can become so abundant that the entire bottom can be covered with their large pink siphons erecting from the sand.

Cyrtopleura costata is thought to live a sessile existence, burrowing into the sand, clay or peat with the same rotating, chiseling movements used by the date mussel and the false angel-wing. Unless they can retract their siphons deeply into the mud, let the hole cover up and pack in and stay out of shovel's range entirely, I question this sessile existence. Angel-wings move. How they move is a mystery to me. We frequently check a particular sandbar and find that during any given period, be it summer or winter, the population will suddenly flourish and siphons will be all over the flats, or it will completely diminish in a few weeks time and no amount of searching or digging will produce a single animal. Even in sandy depressions that form into tide pools which are fixed localities off Alligator Point, it is impossible to locate specimens that were seen a week before.

Of all the clams I know, angel-wings present the greatest challenge in collecting. The novice collector will see these large, fleshy pink organs projecting from the sand and will pounce upon one. Immediately, with strong muscular force, it contracts down into the sand, but your grip is firm and it comes free. There it is, about a foot long or less when contracted, fleshy pink and hollow, with two holes at the top. Chances are you'll think you've caught some new and indescribable monster, and chances are you'll think that's the end of it, take it to some learned scientist or, worse still, try to key it out in an invertebrate zoology book, and sooner or later someone will tell you it's the siphon of some clam.

Then it's back to the flats. There is the siphon thrusting up, and you attack the ground around it with a shovel. There is a spurt of water, the clam retracts down into the mud. Your hole is over a foot deep, and the muddy pink siphon is down at the bottom. If you reach your hand down and dig by hand, you'll soon feel the tips of the valves. If you use the shovel, chances are you'll chop the animal in half, or crush the shell because the animal is so firmly rooted into the mud. If you dig two feet or more away from its burrow and come in at the angel-wing on a 45° angle you stand a better chance of not exerting pressure against its fragile shell.

When the siphon is completely retracted and tips of the shell are exposed, your hand reaches down the burrow, grasps the shell from the underside and tries to bring it to the surface. The angel-wing has a great mass of slimy mud around it, and the shell is very fragile and very sharp; many will be broken in the process, and if anyone is serious about getting any number of angel-wings to the surface, he must realize that his fingers will be slashed brutally and bleed copiously. The shells are sharp as razor blades. But at long last, there is a tremendous feeling of triumph when an angel-wing is brought to the surface unharmed.

Donax variabilis
Coquina Clams

Everywhere on southern, wave-swept sandy beaches dwells the coquina (*Donax variabilis*) with its multitudes of pastel green, red, yellow, orange and blue tones. They live just at the edge of the sea, burrowing rapidly through the sand as the rolling waves wash up.

With each wash of surf they are exposed, and when the wave recedes and the water and sand are pulled off the beach they rapidly thrust their hatchet-shaped foot into the sand and pull themselves down with jerky movements until they are out of sight. And they all do this in unison, so the collector will see thousands of the colorful little clams all lurching down into the shifting sands.

A species of the genus of tufted brown hydroid, *Lovenella* sp., lives attached to the beak of a few of these clams. In the sand of Alligator Point approximately one out of 500 is infected with this hydroid, but on the sandy beaches of St. George Island the number must be well over 50 percent. The relationship with the hydroid must be interesting, probably benefiting only the hydroid, which gets free transportation through the sand in order to seek food. But on a low tide the tufts of *Lovenella* stick out everywhere along the flats indicating the presence of coquinas below. The hydroid may draw much of its nourishment from the plankton in the shifting sea water.

Although coquinas are overwhelmingly abundant, they are not always easy to collect. They follow the level of the tide to a great degree. On high tide they are found on the upper limits of the sand beach where the waves are washing up. On neap tide they follow the surf-line down, thrusting their siphons out, sucking in the diatoms and detritus that are so plentiful in areas where the sand is constantly astir. But when the tide drops the coquina digs deep into the sand and all traces of it vanish.

In the late fall, around November when the temperature drops way down and they are stranded, they appear as little pockmarks all over the dry upper zone, and can be hand-picked one by one and put into a bucket. Low temperatures make them sluggish and they are not actively burrowing. In January not a coquina is to be found anywhere. Only after we dug down two feet at the edge of the sea were we able to uncover any specimens at all, and then only a dozen.

It is hard to believe that an animal so abundant along the flats in the summer can become so scarce with a few months of cold weather. In the warm seasons you can step out on the beach with another collector, scoop a big pile of sand containing coquinas into a screen, and shaking the screen back and forth, separate the sand from the animals. And there will be bucketfuls of the beautiful little clams. Collecting them can be not only gastronomically and aesthetically rewarding, but a challenge and excitement as well.

Class Gastropoda

Gastropod mollusks, the whelks and conchs and snails are by far the most well-known and well-collected form of all the marine invertebrates. The large predatory conchs and whelks are the most conspicuous, easy-to-find creatures living on a sandflat, and these are the most easily destroyed from overcollecting. So it is best to take only a few specimens.

The horse conch (*Pleuroploca gigantea*) slides over the uncovered sea grass beds and devours left-handed whelks, crown conchs and tulip shells. These are predators that expand their meaty foot, smother and devour bivalves such as quahog clams, cockles, lucinas, arks and sunray clams and keep their numbers substantially reduced on the tide flats. However, the horse conchs will not eat bivalves at all, just the predators of bivalves, so if they are removed in large numbers (even though they have attractive shells) the predators can multiply and the clam population can be destroyed.

Gastropod mollusks are interesting to keep in a tank, and make good carnivores. However, there is a constant battle to keep them from eating each other, and they should certainly not be placed in tanks with clams. They in turn should not be placed in tanks with stone crabs or box crabs that have a penchant for ripping their shells apart and devouring them. When you operate a salt-water aquarium you get

242

the impression that it is one mad orgy of everything devouring everything else, but that is precisely how it is in nature.

Gastropods live in a variety of habitats. They are divided into two groups, the carnivores, the big whelk that feed on decaying flesh or predatory clams, and the herbivores, mesogastropods that scrape rocks and shell for algae. These are small forms, the filter-feeding slipper limpets that live attached to rocks and horseshoe crab shells and the littorinid snails that are found by the millions on the rocks.

Polinices duplicatus
Moon Snails

No matter how barren and desolate a sand flat appears, and there are many days when it does, you can almost always find a lone moon snail (*Polinices duplicatus*), also called cat eye, plowing a narrow furrow beneath the sand. It doesn't have to be an especially low tide either; almost the low point of any low tide will do, because the little round *Polinices* shell is always on the move, sliding along with its massive gray foot expanded.

With its great, meaty, gray foot expanded to twice the size of the little gray shell, it looks something like a fried egg with the yellow yoke in the middle. It makes one wonder how the moon snail can draw all this massive flesh into its shell and seal itself completely with its operculum. But it can do so quite rapidly, particularly if you grab hold of the soft parts, trying to pull it from the shell. Generally it expels a good bit of water in the process. It also rapidly pumps this water into its vascular system in order to be able to expand so completely.

If you are a regular collector of moon snails, and go exploring on the sand flats digging up the furrowed trails, then you'll probably find one engulfing a lucina clam, or a small surf clam, *Spisula*. The great meaty foot expands about the clam, the proboscis rasps the clam's tough shell probably the way a dentist's drill works on your teeth and the snail works into the soft parts. The clam is killed, the shell gapes and the moon snail feasts and then moves on. Some clams can draw down into the substrate and get on a deeper level which saves them from the moon snail. The great, deep-burrowing pholad clams like *Cyrtopleura* and *Petricola* are seldom bothered by moon snails; neither are the cockles or the scallops that can move around.

On the sand flats moon-snail marks are often confused with the winding trails of young horseshoe crabs, but if you look closely you'll find the furrow is much deeper and narrower. When you come to the end of this furrowed trail, dig down a few inches and you'll produce the snail.

To maintain them successfully in the aquarium use fine gravel or coarse sand with good aeration, since they are exclusively burrowing and tend to remain hidden and therefore they would not be chosen as the ideal aquarium snail. They will feed actively, especially if you have any living clams in the tanks, but *Polinices* is also good at devouring carrion.

Sinum perspectivum
Ear Shell
_____

The ear shell (*Sinum perspectivum*) has similar feeding habits to the moon snail's, only because of its unsightly external appearance it seems to be even worse. The amateur shell collector might walk right on past this prize and never give it a second thought when he sees this thick blob of mucousy, white porklike flesh oozing along in the sand.

Even when you dig this creature out of its broad, semicircular furrow and examine it on the palm of your hand, you may never realize that it has a beautiful shell tucked away in its mantle. The shell is a delightful, fragile thing of beauty. But who would know that from the sluglike flesh that surrounds it so completely comprising ¾ of its body size? Only the very tip of the shell may protrude through the mantle, if you let it crawl about your hand for a moment — never mind all that oozing mucus.

I shall digress on the subject of its mucus for a moment. A professional biological collector who often works with formaldehyde or alcohol always has wrinkled, dried and discolored hands because these reagents work on his fingers the way they do on the tissues of the animals. Regardless of the use of rubber gloves, sooner or later your fingers get pickled. *Sinum* should be used by the hand-lotion people, because nothing softens skin like a good slimy mucousy ear shell, or just as good, the massive, slimy annelid, *Lysarete brasiliensis*. I firmly believe it speeds up the healing process and offers a great deal of relief.

The shell collector can quickly remove this shell by dropping the *Sinum* into a jar of alcohol. It will instantly and violently contract, the slime will be fixed and the tip of the shell exposed. *Sinum* is unable to draw its voluminous foot into its shell. Taking a razor blade and slitting it around the mantle, you will reveal the shell in all its beauty. The inside of the shell does look like a partially completed ear with a spiraling lobe, giving it the name ear shell. The outside of the shell resembles a moon snail's shell, only flattened. The two snails are fairly closely related.

Sinum is a most efficient burrower. On low tides they often burrow up to the surface and leave themselves stranded high and dry, but they can also dig down quite deeply and slide along with relatively great speed for a snail. When their foot touches the tip of a clam the attack begins, and then the gaping valves are left behind, and the snail slides on.

Busycon contrarium
Left-handed Whelk

The genus *Busycon*, or fulgur whelks, has existed along the eastern American coast for over 60 million years. There are at least four species of *Busycon* ranging from Nova Scotia to Texas. The Atlantic Kiener's whelk (*Busycon carica*) is considered by some as a subspecies of the Gulf of Mexico perverse whelk, *Busycon contrarium*. There are six well-known species of fulgur whelks living in American waters today.

All of them are used in both teaching and research. Few people have survived an invertebrate zoology course without having looked at these animals, either embalmed in their shells, or removed from their shells, or preserved with red latex injected into their heart and spread throughout the circulatory system. They are large, with well-developed, easy-to-see organs, especially the radula, the long ribbon of teeth which can be pulled out from the proboscis with a razor blade and a pair of forceps.

Along certain Florida beaches, particularly near oyster bars, you can soon have buckets filled to the top with these large gastropods. Usually they are found with only their shells protruding, their large, expanded black foot dug down into the sand. Be careful as you wrench them out because the anterior tip of the shell is often sharp and can leave you with a bleeding cut. They come out with a sucking sound as their vacuum hold on the substrate is broken, and they squirt out a long, erratic stream of water and will continue to do so as they draw into their shell while in your collecting bucket. After a while you'll have five or six inches of water and more suddenly produced from a collection of whelks, so to lighten the load you can pour it off. They are generally tough creatures and can withstand limited dehydration and carrying without any damage.

We have maintained *Busycon contrarium* for periods of six months and possibly longer with good success. They are murderous on any clam that happens to be in the tank, and overnight a number of sunray venus and quahog clams that may have taken weeks to collect can be reduced to a rubble of empty shell. Their survival in captivity is certainly much longer than six months, but since we distribute them so regularly it is an effort to keep up with the stock demands.

Busycon contrarium has successfully bred in our closed-system sea-water tanks. During the late spring and early summer months they can frequently be seen on the tidal flats ejecting a horny necklace of shining round discs and each disc is packed with minute active eggs. These egg necklaces are sometimes a yard long. And many a novice beachcomber walking the flats for the first time has picked up this accordionlike egg case, examined it, and carried it off wondering what sort of creature it was or where it had come from.

We have had them lay great strings of eggs and watched the growth and development of the young conchs in each horny segment. After two months the young conchs hatched, and soon they emerged from the horny casing into the rest of the tank, where most of them were subsequently and unceremoniously eaten by batfish which have a fondness for young snails.

Fasciolaria hunteria
Banded Tulip Snail
___

The banded tulip (*Fasciolaria hunteria*) is easy to find on the beach, for it is one of the most conspicuous gastropods of all and at certain times of the year, the most dominant. It is a beautiful snail with marble, mottled vertical shadings of grayish brown, cream rose and greenish tans. Distinct black bands spiral around the shell from its sharp apex to the base; they spiral as intriguingly as the whorls around a barbershop pole.

We have found them in a variety of habitats including rock, shell, mud and grass. But if one were in search of a large number of *Fasciolaria*, he would have to go to the grass flats of St. Teresa Beach, or Turkey Point, where they are not hard to spot. When cold weather arrives, *Fasciolaria* digs down into the sand, but it is not a very efficient burrower and the top of the brightly colored shell sticks up conspicuously.

In the shallows they move along quickly in search of prey, their foot extended just sliding over the sand, their siphon expanded and tentacles out. When they find a smaller snail they attack. *Chione cancellata*, the sculptured venus clam, is their favorite food.

Fasciolaria hunteria seeks out shell or rock to lay its trumpet-shaped eggs upon. We have had them lay eggs in our laboratory and have even hatched out the eggs over a period of three months.

Oliva sayana
Lettered Olive Snail

The olives have the most pretty, glossy, polished shell of any mollusk that I know of along the west Florida coast. And *Oliva sayana*, the lettered olive, is no exception. It is an elongated shell, that spreads out with a mottled, yellowish foot that matches the shell, and plows a small, sharp furrow in the sand.

Oliva sayana has become one of my favorite snails because it feeds so voraciously. If you ever want a conversation piece, then set up a salt-water aquarium with three inches of sand on the bottom and place two or more olive snails in it. They will immediately burrow out of sight, and generally will not leave any trail or hole telling of their presence; all you'll see is a nice empty tank full of sand. For dramatic effect, don't put fish or other invertebrates in the tank; just leave it with its stark nakedness.

Then drop in a piece of shrimp. At first nothing happens. Then suddenly a long brownish-gray siphon pops up from the sand, almost like the periscope of a submarine. Then across the tank another siphon springs up. Suddenly the sand begins to heave, it shakes and quivers. Then the miniature monster emerges in a cloud of sand and with great rapidity converges on the piece of food like a convoy tank. It glides rapidly across the sand, erected from the bottom by its meaty foot. It's

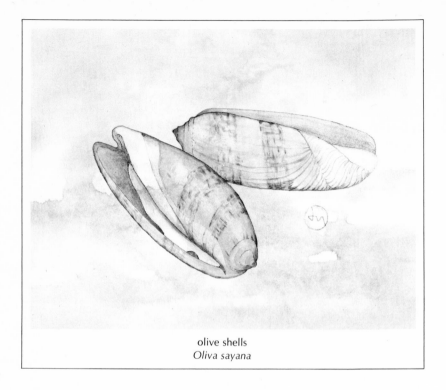

olive shells
Oliva sayana

shining polished shell glistens, as it attacks the food. The snail then drags it down into the sand and out of sight so it can devour the food in peace away from the other snail which is stirring and searching in vain for the shrimp.

All this will take place before the astonished eyes of visitors in less than two minutes, if the snails are sufficiently hungry. The trouble is, there are so many repeat performances demanded that they become overfed and sluggish.

Littorina irrorata
Periwinkle Snail

All along the miles upon miles of tidal marsh grass along the South Atlantic and Gulf coasts dwell the small brownish-gray periwinkle snails (*Littorina irrorata*) crawling up the blades of the marsh grasses, busily lapping up diatoms and microscopic encrusting algae with their radular teeth. On low tides you can pick the snails off the grass blades much the way one picks berries off a bush, and this is all right if one wants only a few dozen individuals. We found a way of harvesting collections of littorinid snails on *Spartina* grass by waiting until the tide gets high when they rise to the top of the grass. Then, taking a flat, small-meshed minnow dip net and pushing it over the grass blades, the snails are wiped off and fall into the net. They can be harvested by the bucket. But unless there is a definite use for such a volume of animals, collecting them in this manner would be a waste of life.

At one time they were so abundant in the Panacea marshes that if crews of men working round the clock with scoop nets attacked a 200-acre marsh, I seriously doubt if they could have decimated the littorinid snail population.

But as civilization moved into the Gulf, houses were built, people began to complain about the mosquitoes that lived in the marsh. So the local and state governments set out to eradicate the pesky mosquito and their fog trucks drove up and down the roads alongside the marsh belching out clouds of pesticides. The little periwinkles may have lapped up the oil-coated poisons as they crawled up the grass, or they may have died of diseases. But in any case the ground was covered with dead periwinkles, and for mile after mile the marsh was filled with rotting snails.

And the arthropod control unit said, "So what—they're not good to anyone, anyway." This is of course not so; thousands of bushels of littorinid are shipped into the New York fish markets every day; and they are an important food for thousands of birds, raccoons and other wildlife.

Littorinids are believed to be in the evolutionary process of changing from a marine snail to a terrestrial form. They live above most mean high tides and are wetted infrequently, although they can stand being submerged for weeks at a time. By the same token, some species can be without water for periods up to two weeks and still survive. They withdraw into their shells and seal themselves up with their chitinous operculum. *Littorina irrorata* can withstand considerable flux in salinities, and even the specimen coated with oil from a recent oil spill managed to survive, digesting the oil coating the grass blades. *Littorina irrorata* ranges from New Jersey to Texas and grows on *Spartina* grass or other marsh grasses.

Subclass Opisthobranchia

The opisthobranchs are sea hares and sea slugs, soft-bodied, snail-like mollusks that either have a vestigal shell or no shell at all. Their taxonomy is difficult, their position in the phylum Mollusca is hardly agreed upon by experts, but they are so beautiful and interesting that a seashore naturalist finds them hard to resist. Along many coasts they are commonly seen waving their fluted skirts or gently undulating their wings. The novice sees them as little flowering blobs and may lump them into a category of flatworms or confuse them with sea anemones.

Nudibranchs, the true sea slugs, have no shell whatsoever contained in their fleshy mantles. They are by far the most colorful of soft-bodied snails and come in a great variety of colors, shapes and sizes. Along the Pacific coast of North America nudibranchs become the dominant conspicuous organism and mass on the intertidal rocks in every imaginable description. A good many brilliant color

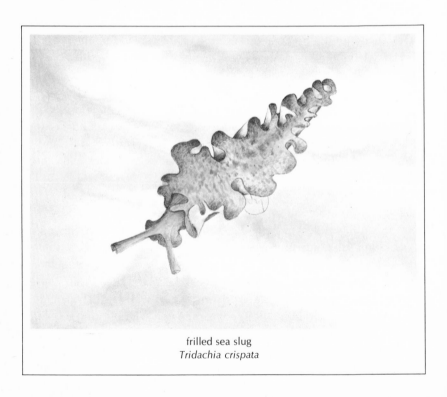

frilled sea slug
Tridachia crispata

sea hare
Aplysia dactylomela

photographs of eolid and dorrid forms can be found in the revised edition of *Between Pacific Tides.*

Large conspicuous sea slugs are most uncommon along the Atlantic coast. Occasionally a few large specimens of *Dorris* are encountered on the rock piles of New England, but to adequately view most of them requires a strong hand lens. Almost always the little dragonlike eolid nudibranchs are found in association with *Tubularia* hydroids or on sea anemones, or feeding on barnacles. With these species, a nudibranch over a half inch in length is a giant, but when you look at one under a dissecting scope you will astounded at what a complex and beautiful creature it is with its extended red or blue projections called cerata.

However, no matter how small or large an opisthobranch is, it is a seasonal beast at best. Many forms known from Woods Hole are found exclusively during the summer months if they are found at all. But a collector who waits for the "right season" may be sadly disappointed to find that there are no sea slugs when they should be in season, and when he least expects to find them, they'll be all over the place.

In collecting sea slugs or sea hares, one must adapt the attitude that they are a gift from the sea, to be taken when offered, but not to be expected. Invariably, if one goes down to a reef on the Florida Keys and finds hundreds upon hundreds of the speckled, greenish-white nudibranch *Tridachia crispata* crawling over the car bodies in the marine garbage dump, the next time he goes back that is the first place he'll head, but chances of finding them again are very slim.

Aplysia willcoxi
Sea Hare
———————

Throughout the winter in Alligator Harbor, during certain years, not a single specimen of the sea hare *Aplysia willcoxi* can be found anywhere. You can dredge for them, trawl for them or go beach-collecting day or night, but still not one single specimen will be found anywhere within 100 miles. Then suddenly, without apparent rhyme or reason, the beaches and tidal flats are invaded and covered by hordes of *Aplysia*.

They flock inshore and pile up on the beaches, sometimes by the thousands and stain the sands with their purple ink. When the tide suddenly recedes they are exposed and trapped and the burning sun may dehydrate and parch them by the time the tide comes gently lapping in, covering a number of corpses. The sea hares that are trapped in the sandy tide pools or in small depressions on the beach where a boat has gone aground and washed out a hole will survive. We have noticed others that squeeze, slide and manage to bore a hole down into the sand by mucus secretion and muscular action and protect themselves from the sun's burning rays.

When the tide comes back, these wiggle out and start swimming again, back to the grass flats to lay their eggs. Whenever *Aplysia willcoxi* comes shoreward in these mass movements it is associated with spawning activities. They lay greenish-yellow eggs in great twisting strings over the sea grass, on pilings and on shell on the bottom. Often after you gather sea hares up and place them in an aquarium, they plaster the glass walls with strings of egg masses. I once delivered some to the New York Aquarium and within a day after they arrived, they proceeded to lay eggs which finally hatched in

252

captivity. *Aplysia* is hermaphroditic and we have seen them mating in captivity with a number of males and females connected. They are vegetarians and sit on the sea bottoms grazing on algae like contented cows, but in the aquarium they will crawl up and down the side of the tank like a large snail, scraping off the encrusting algae from the glass. Upon rough handling *Aplysia willcoxi* emits a large amount of dark purplish fluid from specialized glands. Presumably this thwarts potential predators.

Once in a while, when the *Aplysia willcoxi* are invading the shallow sea grass flats and washing to shore, they are accompanied by a very few jet black *Aplysia morio*. These handsome creatures are few and far between, but nonetheless they stand out conspicuously among the other sea hares lying on the beach. We have seen them swimming on occasion while standing on a pier at St. Teresa Beach in North Florida, but have collected most of them by beachcombing.

Although we often see a sea hare winging its way over the surface of the water when we are cruising in a boat, we have not found this to be the most practical way of gathering them. By the time you slow the boat down, turn around in a wide, sweeping circle and speed back to the general area—if you can find it, there are no landmarks—the sea hare is gone. Only with the greatest of luck will you be able to locate it again.

Sea hares are a gift of the tide. They are best collected after they have been washed ashore by high tide and picked up in the course of pursuing that ancient and venerable art and science of beachcombing.

Bursatella leachi
Frilled Sea Hare

The sporadic nature of opisthobranch mollusks is also exemplified by the frilled sea hare, *Bursatella leachi*. In November of 1960 they were so thick at Lanark Beach in Franklin County, Florida, that if one were to wield dip nets energetically, in a few hours' time he could load a boat until it would sink from pure weight, and never even begin to dent the population. They massed to shore along miles of coastline: every beach, inlet and grass flat was jammed with them. There they lay, their little oval gills rhythmically opening and closing, opening and closing.

When *Bursatella leachi* invaded the shore that year shrimpers were complaining they couldn't get their nets on board because of the sheer weight of these animals. Their nets burst at the choke lines every time they tried winching them up. Seine fishermen striking their nets off Dog Island were unable to land fish because *Bursatella* was so common. They had to quit and go home.

Then suddenly *Bursatella* was gone, and I did not see anymore until the following summer. The literature on *Bursatella* is slim at best, they are known from the tropics and appear and disappear sporadically. I thought they were a winter-time animal, but we have found them commonly in July and August and in the spring and fall, but never have they come back like the winter of 1960.

Bursatella leachi also exudes ink when handled. You have to give them a fairly good squeeze to get them to really exude, but sometimes when walking along the flats if you nudge one with your foot you'll get a trickle of blackish-blue ink.

On the tidal flats they appear as little, mottled metallic gray puffs with hundreds of waving orange-tinted hairlike projections resembling the cerata of nudibranchs.

In the aquarium frilled sea hares climb the walls of the tank and feed avidly on algae. Most of them will live for several months or longer if well fed and kept in well-aerated, filtered sea water. They are extremely sensitive to changes in pH and curl up, and even ink when the water becomes fouled.

Class Cephalopoda

Lolliguncula brevis
Dwarf Squid

The problems modern zoologists are faced with in the study of cephalopods, the squids and octopuses, are not how to collect and preserve them, but rather, how to collect them in a manner in which they can be kept alive, and how to maintain them under laboratory conditions so that they may be studied for behavior and physiology.

Along the Southeastern coasts the octopus is generally more accessible to the beachcomber than the squid, although sometimes at night squid dart into the shallows and can be trapped in a small seine net, or taken with a hook-and-line off the end of a pier. But to collect squid one must have a regular otter trawl. The problems of keeping squid alive in open- or closed-system aquariums have never been solved. They are extremely nervous and, unless very carefully treated, die of shock before they reach the tanks.

If they are transferred immediately into bags of sea water and charged with oxygen there is a good chance they will be brought back to the base alive. These bags are put in large containers, kept cool and dark, well covered.

Squid boats of the supply department in Woods Hole have large vats aboard ship, which rapidly pump water into the containers and let it run back into the ocean. Even under those ideal conditions many specimens do not reach the laboratory alive. Squid have a giant axon and a number of neurophysiologists have used this animal for electrophysiological recordings. Therefore, special attention has been given to the techniques of rearing them in captivity. Their eggs have been hatched in the laboratory, and the young have survived for periods of two months and longer, but invariably, in the end the squid die.

The small Gulf form, *Lolliguncula brevis*, will often live for a week when freshly captured and maintained in an aquarium. But it invariably happens, you come in one morning and find the specimen that you had the most hope for lying forlornly on the bottom of the tank—dead.

Watching them feed is a thrill in itself. Sometimes you can get small squid, once we even got the large *Loligo plei*, to feed, dropping numbers of small *Fundulus* minnows into the tank. Turning red with rage, swimming like little jewels with flashing colors, they swim up to the minnow. In a split second they whip out their elongated arms, and next minnows are removed from their formation and are being chewed up by the squids' strong little beaks. Even with this hopeful sign of eating, the squids end up dead.

Octopus vulgaris
Common Octopus

Almost every public aquarium can tell stories about their octopuses that became pets and even recognized their curators. Extensive behavioral studies have been conducted on them, and their intelligence is thought to exceed that of fish. Many of them have strong personalities.

I had one once that became a pet for the month he stayed with us. We caught him quite inadvertently. One day our net hung a cement block and in it was this large octopus with a two-foot spread. This one lived very well in our tank, adjusted to our conditions and from time to time came out of the rocks we left for it, fed on crabs and did very well. He even learned to eat from our hands.

At night it would emerge from the rocks and search the bottom for food. We kept it in the same tanks that we kept blue crabs in, and it managed to keep the crabs pretty well terrorized. The octopus crept out of the filter and would lightly slide over the bottom. The crabs retreated, their claws outstretched. Several of them would group together and try an attack on the octopus, and this was effective; the octopus retreated. Then it would swoop out again and sooner or later narrow the chase down to one hapless blue crab, and with a puff of ink the crab was captured, wrapped up in a slimy mass of sucker-disc-covered legs and dragged into the clay pipe. A few minutes later the cleaned shell was tossed out. Unfortunately business demands and pressing bills made us sell our pet to a school that kept him in the aquarium for some months before he expired.

Octopuses in the Gulf are more common offshore in deeper water and are collected by special octopus traps which are nothing more than two-foot lengths of sewer pipe on a 60-foot rope with a cork. A large, open boat is needed for extensive trapping.

Shore-collecting in areas where octopuses occur such as the Pacific coast and the Florida Keys is often a more feasible way of collecting them. However, while it may be a more feasible way it is far from an easy way. Finding an octopus on a boulder-strewn flat at low, low tide is about as easy as finding a flea on a hairy bear.

All about are puddles and pools of water, with seaweed growing out into them, full of greens and browns, and reds of algae, sea anemones and hydroids, boulders, small rocks, crevices, tunnels and burrows. Where is the octopus? Once in a while you'll see a little burrow with a number of crab and mollusk shells spewed out and piled up messily around the entrance. This is where the octopus lives and he's hiding down at the bottom with perhaps just his eye peering up.

Sometimes if you turn over a boulder you'll see one slither about and race for a crevice and if you are very fast you'll be able to catch it. I have come to the conclusion that some people are better at finding octopuses in these situations than others. I pride myself on being a good collector, but I am not a good octopus-finder.

In Nossi-Be, an island off Madagascar, I used to hunt the boulder-strewn flats for specimens, keeping a particularly wary eye out for an octopus, which I needed badly for my collection. The Sakalavas also used to hunt the same flats with long spears, looking for octopus. My eyes would peer long and hard among all the greens and browns, look into every tide pool and down into each crevice, but not an octopus.

A few feet away from me, just where I had been a moment ago, a Sakalava would stop, look down into the water, make a mighty thrust with his spear and lift out a writhing, squirming octopus. Then he would dash it against the rocks until its legs hung limp, remove it from his spear and put it in his sack.

This happened time and time again, and eventually I almost developed a neurosis about going out with them. I could find more flatworms than they, more nudibranchs, but never octopus.

In aquariums, octopuses should always be kept in a tank with a very secure cover weighted down, because they will often slip out, fall onto the floor and die of suffocation. An octopus can hold some water in its gills, but it won't live very long out of water.

Octopus vulgaris generally is too large to keep in an aquarium. *Octopus joubini*, the dwarf octopus that is dredged from shell bottoms along the southeastern coast of the United States, is much smaller, only a couple of inches long, but it is very shy, nocturnal in nature and stays hidden behind rocks most of the time. It will feed actively on small crabs at night, and several specimens can be maintained for months in a 20-gallon salt-water aquarium and may even lay eggs.

Preservation

Class Amphineura. Chitons may be adequately preserved for study by simply immersing them in 70 percent alcohol until they are well preserved, then removing them from solution and letting them dry. This treatment will cause them to curl up like a pill bug, so some specialists place them between two glass plates, tie them securely so they can't curl up before preserving. It is advisable to allow them to attach naturally to the glass first. They are often displayed in museum collections in a small pasteboard box with their name and locality.

For anatomical studies they should be preserved in 70 percent alcohol.

Class Scaphopoda. Generally scaphopods are dropped directly in 70 percent ethyl alcohol, and are later dried. Scaphopods in alcohol are generally rare in most museum collections, and well-expanded materials are rarer still. We have produced some beautiful specimens by letting them lie in a dish of propylene phenoxetol until they were completely expanded, and then putting the dish into the freezer. The ice thawed in alcohol and specimens resulted that were so naturally expanded they looked as though they were about to shoot down into the sand.

Class Pelecypoda. The collector who is interested in a wide and varied shell collection has little or no problem in preserving just the shell. Bivalves such as clams, oysters, scallops, and mussels may be left in stagnant or alcoholized sea water until their valves gape, or they may be left out in the sun until dead. The shell is then pried apart and the meat scooped out. The shells are encrusted with fouling organisms such as serpulid worms, boring sponges, and other mollusks; they may be cleaned by soaking them in a solution of weak bleach and picking off the encrusting organisms with a needle and forceps.

Care should be taken not to injure the ligament hinge of bivalves. It may be softened in water after the shell has been dried to facilitate closing the valves. The paired shells are then bound together with transparent thread. This is very important; unpaired bivalve shells have little value. The shells themselves have a fine membrane which should not be scratched or damaged, or etched. Formalin and isopropyl alcohol should therefore be avoided when cleaning them.

Most pelecypod mollusks are not difficult to preserve in an expanded condition. Many will relax in an 8 percent solution of magnesium chloride or in a saturated solution of magnesium sulfate.

Chloral hydrate has also been used with great success, but few narcotizing agents are better than propylene phenoxetol.

When the siphons are fully extended, and the foot is protruding from the valves, the mollusks may be killed by pouring in strong alcohol. With highly contractile forms, it is helpful to place them in the freezer until all responses are dulled and then preserve them in alcohol.

Class Gastropoda. To prepare dried shells of snails and whelks for a museum collection it is necessary to remove all the soft parts. Although many tough-shelled forms like *Busycon* and *Pleuroploca* may be killed by plunging the shell into hot water and boiling them until the tissues are loosened, this treatment can destroy the luster of polished shells. Gastropod mollusks are therefore best killed by letting them soak in a saturated solution of magnesium chloride or tap water until they die and begin to rot. A pressure hose can then be used to blow out the soft parts that remain in the whorls. They may be soaked in ethyl alcohol for a while to cure any tissues that remain inside.

Some collectors hang the snails in the air, suspending them from ropes or wires and allowing the soft parts to rot out. I again mention that nothing smells more putrid than rotting mollusks, so it pays to cure them in alcohol and dry them whenever possible.

With gastropods it is essential that you save the operculum, the horny tissue that the snail uses to seal the entrance to its shell. Always wrap the operculum in newspaper along with the shell from which it was removed because it is necessary in aiding identification.

When storing or shipping bivalve and gastropod mollusk shells, wrap them firmly in newspaper or cotton wool. Small shells which can easily be lost should be stored in vials or small pasteboard jewelry boxes.

Although prosobranch mollusks are all classified by their hard, clean shells, there is a growing interest in the anatomy of the soft parts, therefore well-expanded specimens protruding from the shell are desirable.

Although various preservation manuals recommend a number of chemicals, including chlorotone, propylene phenoxetol and magnesium chloride, we have found that simply lowering the temperature produces superior results.

The animals are allowed to expand in paper cups filled with sea water. A little magnesium chloride or sulfate can be added to bring them out of their shell and dull their responses, but this is not always necessary. The cups are placed directly in the freezing compartment of a refrigerator or directly in a deep-freeze. Generally the snails will become frozen in three or four hours, depending upon size and, in the majority of preparations, the snail will be fully distended with siphon, tentacles and foot protruding from the shell.

The paper cup may be peeled away from the ice, and if the preparation is large and bulky the majority of ice may be chipped off or washed away under a running faucet. Do not wash the snail out of the ice or allow the snail to thaw for an instant because many specimens can be solidly frozen and still be alive and can remain alive for several days. As soon as they thaw they will contract back into the shell. To prevent this, place the ice in prechilled alcohol which should be at least 32°F if not lower.

Room temperature alcohol will quickly thaw the animal out and possibly permit last-minute death contractions, but chilled alcohol will penetrate the tissues while the animal is still frozen and unable to contract. Using this freezing method we have been able to produce beautifully extended moon snails, periwinkles, coquina clams and a variety of other mollusks in less than three hours after putting them in paper cups of sea water. This technique might be explored with a whole variety of other organisms.

Formalin should not be used as a final preservative for pelecypods or gastropods because it toughens the tissues as well as etches and whitens the shells. And no matter how much the snails are soaked in water, they will not harden up. The best results are achieved if the specimens are run slowly through an alcohol series.

Opisthobranch Mollusks. Sea hares and sea slugs are one group of animals that cannot be merely placed in alcohol or Formalin and later identified. They not only contract but distort, and few experts are able to classify a contracted specimen. Such specimens can be used for radular studies and for certain details of their internal anatomy, but they should be most carefully relaxed before preservation if they are to be useful.

Nudibranchs are best identified by their form, color and structure from living specimens. And a serious student of nudibranchs will be quick to tell you that the next best thing to a living specimen is a color photograph, and after that one should have a well-expanded specimen and a good listing of color notes.

The sea hares such as *Aplysia* and *Bursatella* may be identified from well-preserved specimens. The cephalic tentacles, wings and foot must be extended, and this requires a certain amount of workmanship. We have produced such specimens by slowly warming the sea water in which the animals were contained, at the same time adding very small amounts of magnesium sulfate. Almost any anesthetic that is administered in even slightly high concentrations will cause sea hares to contract severely. Eolid nudibranchs may shed all their cirrata, the little hairlike projections on their backs.

It seems that our best results have been obtained by placing the animals in dishes of sea water and freezing them, and later thawing them in alcohol. The opisthobranch mollusks can be preserved in 10 percent Formalin or may be run through a lengthy alcohol series to avoid shrinkage of their tissues. *Aplysia* even after death continually inks up the Formalin or alcohol, but if a drop or two of bleach is added to the solution, it soon clears up entirely.

Class Cephalopoda. The cephalopods present little or no problem in preserving. They do not have to be anesthetized or relaxed in any way before they are preserved, but may be thrown into a killing solution. Squids will generally be dead by the time they are ready to preserve anyhow. But nothing looks as lifelike as a squid taken live, squirming and spitting ink out of a net and tossed directly into a bucket of Formalin.

Its legs stiffen, its chromatophores tighten; then they must relax and all its pigment is shown and a beautiful specimen results. But a few rules in the preservation of all cephalopods are important for systematic studies. Octopus should be killed in chloroform or some other solution so their legs won't knot up and distort.

The freshly dead animal should be stretched out and the arms straightened out so that their relative length can be measured in proportion to the mantle and body lengths. Large octopus and squid should be thoroughly injected with preservative to prevent deterioration of their internal organs.

If the octopus is to be used for display, you can pin its legs to a board and let it soak, board and all, in 10 percent Formalin for a week or so until it is hardened, and then remove it.

The preservative is perhaps the most critical part of preserving cephalopods. Use buffered Formalin for systematic study because cephalopods have slightly calcareous rings on the inside of their suckers. These are removed and matched against keys for proper identification by specialists. Octopods, and decapods, as squid are called, are extremely difficult to classify even under the most ideal conditions.

Ideally, a freshly dead specimen should be soaked in 30 percent ethyl alcohol for 24 hours, then transferred to 50 percent and finally 70 percent. Do not place them directly into 70 percent alcohol because they quickly dehydrate and deflate; the tissues collapse and become hardened.

23.
Limulus polyphemus
The Horseshoe Crab

If I had to choose a single representative of the American Atlantic Coast for its most distinctive animal, I would have to say it is the horseshoe crab (*Limulus polyphemus*). No other single animal in the sea has been as extensively studied for its eyes, blood, nervous responses and movements.

Horseshoe crabs belong to the phylum Arthropoda, the jointed-legged animals with a chitinous exoskeleton. While this phylum includes insects and crustaceans, only the horseshoe crab comprises the subclass Xiphosura. *Limulus* is one of the oldest living creatures upon this earth; its fossils go back over 200 million years without any significant change. They were once found in many parts of the world, and in the Late Pleistocene era when they first appeared on earth, they were fresh-water forms, and even today they are more abundant in brackish waters than in the open ocean.

Limulus is found from Maine to Mexico, but it does not occur on the American Pacific coast. There were attempts to introduce them there some years ago, but they would not breed in the cold waters. Another species, much more spiny and unpleasant than ours, occurs in the mangrove swamps of Southeast Asia.

The closest relatives of these living fossils are the terrestrial scorpions and spiders, but unlike certain of their close relatives, they are absolutely harmless. Even though they appear as armored tanks lurching along the beach with the rounded shield of a shell, they have mouths that cannot bite, and claws that have tiny ineffectual pincers. They only use their grinding claws to shred food. Most formidable looking is its long, pointed tail (telson) that looks like a dagger or some sort of stinger, but this is merely a levering device. When they swim shoreward, the surf flings many of them on their backs, and using their telson they flip over with agility and lumber back into the sea. The margin of their abdominal, flexing segment is armed with little spikes which leave a serrated trail in the sand. People who see a horseshoe crab for the first time think it has quite a frightening look, and appears dangerous. Even a few biologists coming from the West Coast or inland and meeting the creature on the beach for the first time, confess they are hesitant to handle such a formidable-looking creature even though they have dissected preserved specimens in classrooms; although in recent years living horseshoe crabs in class are becoming popular.

Everything about *Limulus* anatomy is purely functional. For one thing, its ominous appearance, heavy shield and sharp telson seem to ward off predators or make it appear unappetizing and too difficult to grasp. They are seldom, if ever, found in the abdomens of fish in their adult form, although I heard one fisherman tell of cutting open a mako shark and finding a specimen in the stomach.

Limulus along the entire Atlantic and Gulf coasts are strictly a seasonal animal. They seem to prefer water about 70°F in Florida, and lower in New England. Their habits have been studied extensively in Woods Hole. They move out into deeper water in the fall and burrow up in the mud, and are only occasionally taken by heavy dredges from their hibernating beds.

In Florida they do much the same, and even burrow when the water gets about 50°F but when it warms up to 60°F, they stay offshore prowling around the bottom, and come shoreward when the water temperature increases to 70°F.

When they hit the shore, they come up in multitudes and the beaches are literally covered by them. Sometimes they appear in such numbers that frightened bathers flee from them. In the South, they are often confused with sting rays that cause severe injury to bathers.

I always regard the coming of *Limulus* as the official harbinger of spring and the leaving of cold weather. I recall one afternoon on Panacea's Mashes Point when the sky was cloudy, the water was rough and the tide very high. The surf sloshed far up over the white sandy beaches, which seldom got wet. Sloshing and bobbing in the rough surf, the horseshoe crabs came in mating pairs, to conglomerate all up and down the shoreline.

It seemed that the rougher the water, the higher the tide, the more they came shoreward as if they were getting away from the rough sea. Actually they come to shore to lay their eggs, and small lumps of rubbery greenish-blue balls are deposited in the sand by the female. These can be found by lifting a heavy female out, digging a few inches below her and finding the eggs.

All through the spring, summer and fall the *Limulus* are in copulating positions. The male, being small, rides piggy-back on the female, holding onto her by his small limbs provided with special, hooked nippers. Only the males are equipped with these nippers, and these appendages are very strong and grasping. Once you see them, you can instantly sex the specimens, if there is a need for young females or males. The male grasps the female's tail and abdomen, so when you grab the smaller male by his telson and lift it from the water, both he and his mate come up with their legs kicking frantically and impotently. If the female is too heavy, his grasp will break loose and she will get away.

After they have been on shore for a while, a strange thing happens. When the tide begins to fall, suddenly they all turn about and head out to sea, and in the space of an hour, those same beaches that appeared to be paved with copulating pairs just a short time ago are suddenly empty and not a single crab remains.

The smaller horseshoe crabs that measure anywhere from a half inch to four inches across must be collected on low tide. Out on the low, low tide in sandy flats — not sea grass, just sand — a great maze of flat trails wind in a labyrinth that seems to be devoid of rhyme or reason.

And these trails are apt to befuddle the novice with their endless complexities of turning, twisting, coming back on each other. The logical person who prides himself on reason and order may say, "Here I have a trail that goes on and on, twists and winds, so I will follow this trail with my eye and foot and will come either to the beginning where the crab was or the end where the crab is."

But with *Limulus* hunting, this approach is a pure delusion and a deception. Dozens of trails criss-cross each other, all identical and if unwound would probably stretch out for several hundred feet.

But if you are patient, you will be rewarded by seeing a little mound of sand and mud lurching forward somewhere in the labyrinth of plowed-up furrows, and then you have your crab. Temperature may be the cause of not seeing crabs in the midst of their mazes on certain days. If it is cold they are sluggish and stay down in the sand without moving. Then some evenings, just as the sun is setting all at once you see little horseshoe crabs emerge from the sand and start chugging along like so many miniature bulldozers. Moving animals are the easiest to spot, they are seen only by their jagged abdomen and a bit of their tail bulging out from the sand.

But when it is too cold, or the tide has just fallen, too much sunlight or too little, or perhaps some other condition that we don't know about, they burrow down an inch or two and all disappear. The waves wash in and cover the trails in the sand and you'll never know they are there. You can search the beach, but it's wasting time. You might as well pack up your buckets and go home.

Limulus polyphemus is a very important research animal and is used in a wide variety of teaching and research programs. Their hard, clear eyes and adjoining optic nerves are utilized in electrophysiological research, and their blood contains copper-based hemocyanin, which is used in biochemical studies. Recently experiments at Harvard Medical School have shown that the blood of the horseshoe crab is tremendously sensitive to endotoxins, or dead bacteria. Almost any minute trace of endotoxins will cause the horseshoe crab's blood to clot, and it may therefore someday be used as an indicator of endotoxins in glassware and instead of a pest will be regarded as a valuable medical tool.

It is difficult to say how well *Limulus* will continue to survive on this planet. Since they are sensitive to bacteria, they avoid areas where there are sewer outfalls, and these are becoming more common as population centers grow. In 1956 *Limulus* died by the hundreds and washed ashore at Woods Hole, and their blood was found to be clotted. We have found that when they die in captivity they must be removed immediately, or they might start a death chain-reaction with the other crabs in the tank.

The horseshoe crab populations are under a lot of pressure from the clamming industry in New England. In Massachusetts a bounty of five cents is paid for each crab's telson, and schoolchildren go out and kill them by the hundreds. However, the enthusiasm for killing them is low and fortunately even children find that it is not profitable. *Limulus* move through the newly planted beds and consume young clams as they go. However, their damage is certainly minimal compared with offshore hydraulic clam dredging that stirs up the bottom, suffocating all marine life. In Maine a fertilizer plant tried to utilize them, but soon found it was impractical and gave up.

Man, by cleaning fish and dumping wastes into the sea, has provided food for birds, and herons and gulls have increased prodigiously in some areas. They feed upon the young horseshoe crabs, and may cause their populations to diminish.

Finally, the unfortunate horseshoe crab is one creature that is most vulnerable to vandalism and senseless slaughter. I have seen them come shoreward en masse, and have seen people meet them on the beach with rocks, sticks and stones and kill them as they hit the shore. Many people think of them as monsters with their jointed legs, spines and "stingers." I have seen children shoot them with .22 rifles, throw them up into the high grass or crush them with heavy boulders.

The poor horseshoe crab needs a friend. He needs someone to tell people that he's harmless, that he hasn't hurt anybody and doesn't intend to and maybe he'll go on living another 200 million years.

Preservation

The preservation of arthropods will be treated alike for the most part in this book, because the differences in preparing an isopod, crab, shrimp or barnacle are not that great. But there is one problem with *Limulus:* they tend to bloat in preserving fluid even when injected. Be sure they are kept in a very large, ample volume of Formalin or alcohol. They will soften and discolor in Formalin after a year or so, but if they are used for dissection in classrooms, Formalin is a good general preservative.

24.
Phylum Arthropoda
The Crustaceans

Class Crustacea

The class Crustacea is made up of numerous subclasses, orders and suborders. Most of the lower crustacea are very small, measuring from two to five millimeters. Copepods, ostracods and the multitudes of small amphipods and isopods do not lend themselves to extensive discussion in this book. They are groups that indeed need study because they are an essential part of the food chain, and they are abundant in waters throughout the world, living as planktonic forms making up much of the zooplankton, or as interstitial forms dwelling in sand and mud.

The primitive, minute crustaceans can be found everywhere, as commensals and as parasites on oysters, in sponges, and hydroid masses, crawling like little bugs over algae clumps, in oceanic, brackish and fresh water. A washing from a hydroid colony might contain as many as 3000 copepods, hundreds of caprellid amphipods and ostracods, and a few isopods.

Unless one is willing to devote a great amount of time to these minor groups, the best one can hope to do is to sort these creatures into subclasses; so if one is collecting amphipods, he can at least distinguish them from copepods, branchiopods and ostracods.

There are a number of techniques used for collecting interstitial forms. One is to dig a big hole in the sand and wait until it fills up with water. Swimming around like mad little water bugs are amphipods and cumaceans, sometimes by the thousands.

There is a commensal form of burrowing copepod that inhabits burrows of annelids and larger crustaceans, and these are collected by inserting a small hand-pump into the burrow and pumping the water out and passing it through a fine screen.

We have collected multitudes of copepods and other crustaceans by washing hydroids in weak alcohol, or getting old, floating wood that is infested with shipworms from the ocean and letting it sit in stagnated water, then adding alcohol. The sand and mud under rocks are prolific with minute crustaceans; rocks on a low tide can be good places to look.

The copepods that are commensal or parasitic on other invertebrates are legion. You have merely to dip a sea anemone in Epsom salts and add alcohol, then examine the slime under a dissecting scope and you will probably find a rich source of copepods. Echinoderms have copepods, so do tunicates. They are the fleas of the sea. Fish are most notably infected with copepods, and one such parasitic copepod will be discussed in detail.

The first time I became acquainted with the parasitic copepod *Tucca impressus* was on a seining trip off Alligator Point in north Florida. I had been working closely with a barnacle specialist who was interested in commensal and parasitic forms and I was on the lookout. The net was dragged in with hundreds of frothing, beating and splashing fish, large sting rays, skates, small sharks, gars and an abundance of pinfish, grunts and pigfish. But only the puffers and spiny boxfish came bobbing to the surface like seine corks after they had inflated themselves with air and water until they were rigid balloons, floating upside-down, exposing their top-heavy bloated abdomens.

The puffers (*Spheroids nephelus*) were obviously clean of parasites, but the spiny boxfish or striped burrfish (*Chilomycterus schoepfi*) had small yellow lantern-shaped appendages growing out from their fins. Upon closer examination each of these bore a trunk which was attached deep into the fin, and since each fish had them in a different place on the fin, and many fishes did not have them at all, I presumed they were not part of the fish but instead a parasite, and wanting to see barnacles very much at the time, I presumed they were barnacles and I promptly sent them to a barnacle specialist.

The specialist identified them as copepods and turned them over to a parasitic copepod specialist at Boston University who placed the

269

name *Tucca impressus* on them and later declared them to be a new, undescribed subspecies of the species known from the Caribbean.

These turned out to be immature specimens — later we collected others that had strings of egg cases which hang off the animal like a "V." Once you know what to look for when collecting parasites, finding them is not very difficult. You could handle thousands of fishes and never see the first copepod, no matter how large, unless you were aware of what to look for.

There are many species and families of parasitic fish copepods. Some of them are host specific and live on a particular fish, like pandarid shark copepods that are found on elasmobranch fish. There are others that live only on teleost fish, particularly on anchovies, and there are some that live in the mouth of remoras. To really check for copepods you scrutinize the fins, the body, the eyes, the gills, the mouth and even the anus of a fish.

Collecting copepods requires that you be a competent icthyologist, capable of putting an accurate identification on the fish. The amateur's best choice is to preserve the fish with parasite attached; then there's no doubt about the host, and often the host record is just as important as that of the copepod.

A great deal has been done in the way of systematics on parasitic copepods, and many thousands of species have been described in minute detail by dedicated zoologists. However, relatively little work has been done on the growth rate and natural history of the majority of species of parasitic copepods.

Tucca impressus is no exception. Yet if one places a spiny boxfish in a small aquarium and feeds it regularly, there is an excellent chance that the copepods will bloom on the fins and hang on like stringers. These will soon multiply, and chances are your boxfish will be covered with copepods. The copepods disappear just as suddenly as they appear.

Temperature has a lot to do with their life-cycle. We have found that when the water temperature reaches 75°F copepods undergo a tremendous bloom. We've had mullet in our tanks for months and no parasites until the temperature rose; then they became heavily infected. The same is true for sharks. When the water temperature reaches 80°F and higher, the copepods tend to die off. Although much of this observation is conjecture, one who maintains a small aquarium can contribute much to science and its knowledge of parasites.

If you ever haul a large shark aboard your boat, or spear a sting ray and can stop long enough to look at this frantic struggling animal closely, chances are you'll see little flattened bugs scuttling over the surface of the skin. These are *Argulus*, the fish lice, and they are so abundant at times that the fish is crawling with them.

They not only occur on elasmobranch fish but on the bony teleost fish as well, and there are many. Even after the host has died, hunting *Argulus* down is a problem. Many species will fall right off the host when the going gets rough and the fish is hauled aboard the boat; whether they are beaten off in the panic or slide off in the dripping water is unknown.

But if you're going to collect *Argulus*, you'll have to act quickly. Get someone to hold the shark or ray down, while you take the forceps and start picking bugs. It's as simple as that. But *Argulus* lives well in the aquarium if it has a host, so if you can keep a large host you should get a sufficient quantity of lice along with it.

Fish isopods are common in many parts of the world, and of all the parasites in the sea, their appearance is far less attractive than any creature I know. They appear as a white leech with their jaws embedded firmly into the flesh of their host. Pinfish often have large white *Cymothoa excisa* and *Lironeca ovalis* hanging to their gills sucking their blood. *Olencira praegustator* crawl into the mouth of threadfin herring and hang on with greatly exaggerated hooks and mouth parts.

If you try removing them from the host they will rip the flesh apart. The aquarist has simply to catch the fish, determine that it is infected and bring it back alive, place it in an aquarium and study it. Are the habits of infected fish different from those that are not infected? How long does the fish live? How weakened is it? How long will the isopod live isolated from the host? These are questions that can be answered by the graduate student doing behavioral studies, or the private aquarist who has a fish infected with an isopod.

Isopods also attack invertebrates, and once in a great while you'll find a hermit crab or a mud shrimp with its gills swollen from an isopod infection. We have found isopods living in sponges, and one of them, *Exocorallana*, is a newly discovered species that will someday be described.

Free-living isopods are much more common than their parasitic relatives. A walk down to any wharf piling will send dozens, hundreds and sometimes thousands of sea roaches *Ligia exotica* scurrying off in all directions, running upside down beneath dock planking. With their grayish-black, segmented bodies; long, waving antennae; hairy legs; and rapid movement they remind one of an invasion of cockroaches and are enough to make even the strongest stomachs turn. However, it takes a warm day and plenty of sunshine to bring them out in numbers. If a cold snap sets in, not a sea roach is anywhere to be seen, and they must be hunted among cracks in the wharfs or under rocks on the high beach. Although *Ligia* is an amphibious amphipod, it is reluctant to dash into the water and usually stays just above the water line.

The pill bugs, or Oniscoidea, are well represented at the edge of the sea, either crawling in seaweed or living in rotten tree stumps on eroding beaches. Upon touching one of these little creatures, it promptly rolls into a small ball; hence it is given the name "pill bug."

There are numerous pelagic isopods that can be collected at night with a gasoline lantern and a dipnet, and tiny, blue isopods that live high up in the tidal marsh along with numerous ostracods, copepods and amphipods.

At one time beach-hoppers, rather large amphipods that live on the high-beach area, were so thick that fishermen walking along the edge of the beach in search of flounders were bothered by them pelting their feet. They can also deliver a rather unpleasant bite, and I remember nights when their numbers were so thick that I had to abandon collecting, or had to wear thick pants.

Orchestia and *Talorchestia* have been on the decline in the past decade. At one time every clump of seaweed exploded with them on a marshy shore; now they are difficult to find. They were the chief food of ghost crabs that patrolled the beaches in search of these little bugs, but in the past few years ghost crabs have become scarce also. I firmly believe that pesticides are causing their decline, perhaps something else is, because slowly and surely beach-hoppers and many other small crustaceans are disappearing from our coast.

The scientific mind may well ask, "How can you come to that conclusion, what data do you have?" The answer is not easy to give. I can only say that eight years ago we collected a one-gallon jar full of beach-hoppers in less than an hour's collecting; today it would take a week to gather that number.

There is a small burrowing amphipod belonging to the family Ampeliscidae which lives below the tides. Fish, crabs, birds and many other creatures feed upon them, and many depend on them exclusively for their diet. We have no way of knowing whether they are declining in north Florida, because we have never looked for them. It is frightening to think that thousands of species of minute organisms may be disappearing like the beach-hopper, and since they are small and inconspicuous their passage may go completely unnoticed.

Amphipod crustaceans are particularly sensitive to all forms of pollution. On healthy bottoms they are common, even abundant, but on dredged bottoms they become scarce. When the big oil spill occurred at Woods Hole, the ampeliscid amphipods died by the multitudes, as mentioned earlier. Their complete absence in an area indicates there is something wrong with the environment.

But barnacles, which are another crustacean form, proved to be resistant and survived the spill. In fact, after the Santa Barbara spill, barnacles were observed feeding actively even with their feathery feeding appendages coated with crude oil. Barnacles grow happily in powerplant cooling canals where hot water is continuously discharged, and they are even seen growing around some sewer outfalls. They grow abundantly and happily in dredged-out areas as long as there is something for them to attach to. It may be that some day barnacles will be one of the few creatures left in the sea to exist with mankind.

Most novices who visit the seashore and see barnacles growing on the rocks confuse them with mollusks because of their hard shells. Many never know the barnacles are alive, but once you have seen them in an aquarium or even in a glass jar, then you will never question whether they are alive or what type of animal they are.

Suddenly the barnacle opens, feathery legs jump out and pop back in, and the whole colony of barnacles displays a rhythmical, rapid, beating action. In this manner they respire and retrieve their food from the sea. When the tide goes down, they withdraw into their shells and wait until conditions are favorable for them to come out and feed again.

The barnacle is one specimen that anyone can collect, no matter how short his visit to the seashore. What is more, most specimens will keep for long periods of time in the aquarium. Perhaps the most difficult barnacles to collect are the ones attached to rocks: cosmopolitan species such as *Balanus balanoides* and *Chthamalus tetraclita* which have only a membranous base and cannot be removed from rocks without breaking the shell or tearing the gonads.

Their larvae attach to the rock and they bond with it and in a sense become part of the rock. Therefore, the best approach is to chip off a piece of rock with barnacles growing on it, using a geology hammer, or find the same species of barnacle on a more reasonable substrate such as wood, shell or sandstone where the substrate may be undermined from beneath the animal with a flat-bladed knife.

Finding clean barnacles, free of fouling growths, may at times be a problem. While collecting along wharf pilings, bridge bottoms or any area where arboreal fouling organisms cluster, it is often desirable to seek out individual barnacles. When barnacles are wanted specifically for display purposes or perhaps for certain neurophysiological research programs, only the largest specimens should be chosen. This of course is not for a series collection where a great variety of sizes is required, but only when an animal is to be on display.

Providing they are species that do not have membranous bases, they may be broken directly off the wharf without damaging the specimen or tearing the gonads. The large barnacles will often be overgrown with encrusting, slimy green algae, tiny sea anemones and growths of encrusting hydroids. If you want a clean, shiny, white barnacle for display then it will be necessary first to scrub the outer test with a strong wire brush.

In Florida and along much of the southeastern Atlantic coast, the ivory barnacle (*Balanus eberneus*) grows on wharf pilings. We have been able to "culture" these successfully on our floating dock, the bottom of our boats, specimen-holding pens, on wood, metal, rubber or anything else that sits or floats in the waters of Panacea Bay. They grow rapidly. Within a month after setting wooden planks or plastic sheets attached to boards off our dock, they will become overgrown with barnacles. Another species that dominates pilings and even grows vigorously on marsh grasses and rocks far up to the high tide mark is the tiny brown *Chthamalus fragilis*.

This species can withstand days, perhaps a week, of exposure. We have shipped them in damp seaweed and even moist paper towels across the country and invariably they have arrived alive, ready to start popping in and out of their little shells when placed in sea water.

Barnacles lay down a gluelike secretion when they attach to a piling or hard surface in their larval stages. The dental industry has been giving barnacles a long, serious look to see if their secretions could not be used in teeth fillings and for other dental work. In fact, we know a dentist who grows barnacles on dead teeth by embedding the teeth in Styrofoam and floating it off our dock in Panacea. Later, he removes the barnacle-encrusted teeth and studies them in detail.

In our never-ending work to grind up marine invertebrates and test them for antineoplastic activity in leukemic mice, we once attempted to grind up 10 pounds of *Balanus eberneus*. Hundreds of different species have gone through our powerful electric grinder, some with difficulty, some with great ease, but only with the ivory barnacle did the grinder begin to smoke and suddenly the grinder head cracked down the middle. We replaced the head at considerable expense, suffered two weeks of shut-down time, and for all that the barnacle extract did nothing to prolong the life of mice infected with a leukemia virus strain.

However, whatever form of calcium carbonate they are made of is tough material, and perhaps we may some day be wearing it in our mouths as teeth fillings or bridge work.

Even many biologists tend to think of barnacles only as the sharp, white-shelled creatures that adhere to rocks and wharfs, but this is far from true. There are peculiar barnacles that live embedded in sponges and gorgonians, barnacles that are attached to fish and to the hides of whales. There are *Octolasmis* barnacles that dwell on the gills of crabs inside their carapace and quickly shed their eggs when the crab molts. Despite their form and numbers, barnacles are one of the more poorly collected groups of marine animals and special attention should be given to getting tiny barnacles that drill into oyster shells looking very much like boring sponges. The only clue that they exist are the thin, elongated burrows they make. If a dredge haul is made in deep water, the sea urchins should be examined carefully because they may contain barnacles that live only on echinoids.

The genus *Chelonibia* is basically a turtle barnacle, and a number of species live exclusively on ocean-going sea turtles, but *Chelonibia patula* is also epizootic on crabs.

In fact, of all the diamond-back terrapins examined at the Harvard collection, only specimens that we shipped up from Alligator Harbor and Lanark Reef were infected with these barnacles growing on their carapace and plastron. Diamond-backs from Texas, North Carolina, Virginia and Maryland were all barnacle-free, but most of these species do not penetrate high-salinity waters the way our *Malaclemys* turtles do.

Old blue crabs (*Callinectes sapidus*) and stone crabs (*Menippe mercenaria*) that are slow to molt and cast off their shells frequently have one or more of these barnacles. Sacculinid crabs, ones that do not molt because of an infection of a degenerate barnacle, are prone to heavy infections of *Chelonibia patula*.

If the host, be it crab or turtle, is kept in plenty of clean sea water and not allowed much exposure, the barnacle lives well in captivity. They are able to sustain a goodly amount of heat and exposure, because the diamond-back terrapins in particular are very fond of sunning, and often you can find dozens of specimens during the summer perched on a sandbar with dried shells, baking in the sun like tourists on Miami Beach. Still, they are often covered with barnacles, and when we need a quantity of *Chelonibia patula* we find diamond-back terrapins the natural habitat for them.

Unlike the balanoid barnacles, *Chelonibia* has a lazy, leisurely movement of the cirripeds, only occasionally opening its plates wide, slowly ejecting its feathery legs that take a lazy sweep of the ambient waters for plankton. They are submerged for long periods, and carried from place to place and there is no great competition for survival or environment.

But it must be a precarious and short life for one attached to a shell that will molt on a crab, or a carapace that will peel on a turtle. And what *Chelonibia* does in the wintertime when the terrapin digs down into the sand a foot or so to hide from the cold, I haven't the faintest idea, yet in the spring when they emerge on the first warm days, many specimens are covered with barnacles.

Chelonibia testudinaria is a true sea-turtle barnacle; to my knowledge it has not been reported living on crabs or any other marine animal, so if one is in search of *Chelonibia testudinaria*, he should hunt a sea turtle. However, this species does not appear to discriminate between hosts and carriers, as we have collected them on loggerheads, Atlantic Ridley's and leatherbacks.

Sea turtles are big, living habitats within themselves. *Chelonibia testudinaria* lives on the carapace and plastron; there is some other species of *Chelonibia* that lives on the skin of the sea turtle, and barnacles (*Stomatalepas preagustulator*) that actually live in the turtle's mouth and gullet. In the Galapagos there is an amphipod that lives under the sea-turtle's tongue, and we have found millions of caprellid amphipods on the carapace of sea turtles, although unfortunately we neglected to save them for identification.

Since you have to collect sea turtles in order to collect *Chelonibia testudinaria*, this is a good place to comment on these large, lumbering reptiles of the ocean. In our large concrete tanks we have kept loggerheads weighing up to 300 pounds, and young Ridley's that weighed less than 10 pounds. They all made good pets, especially the Ridley's that learned to feed from our hands.

During this time we've had an opportunity to observe the barnacles on their back, and found that they too survive well if there is enough suspended plankton material in the sea water. Like *Chelonibia patula* they have a slow, almost feeble movement of their cirripeds. But unlike the latter species they grow to massive size, almost as big as an oyster and we have commonly collected specimens with a three-inch base, a most handsome specimen of a barnacle.

They will live for a time when removed from the host, but their gonads are torn when pried off their shell, since their attachment is through a membranous secretion. On some big loggerheads it is commonplace to chip off over 200 specimens; their entire backs and plastrons can be covered with them. If you ever try riding a turtle, they can be quite cutting. In fact when they surface, from a distance they may appear as a floating reef containing many barnacles.

There are pelagic species of barnacles that live out in the open ocean, and the ardent beachcomber is likely to come across one of several species of *Lepas* that are cast up on the American shoreline.

Goose-neck barnacles live attached to floating logs and in some tropical areas tend to cluster around floating mangrove seeds. They float about in the oceans, following the currents and winds, stretching out their feathery cirripeds, slowly and gently sweeping in the plankton. Sooner or later many of the clusters will end up on the beaches, particularly if there has been a steady blow of offshore winds.

Not even in rapid-exchanging, open-system aquariums have I seen *Lepas* survive for any length of time. We once kept them for a week but usually they expire after a day or two. Therefore, it is best to preserve the specimens you come in contact with, and since they are studied in most school systems, such labor is well worth the effort.

It is possible that if taken at sea, when one is miles offshore and finds them drifting about, *Lepas* can be recovered and maintained in better condition. In general barnacles are difficult to culture in well-filtered closed-system aquariums because all the particulate matter is removed from the sea water and they starve to death. They grow handsomely inside of tanks that are fed by open systems, water being pumped continuously from the ocean, and eventually clog up the sea-water pipes. They can be grown in a closed-system aquarium if diatoms and finely suspended detritus are dripped into the water each day.

Decapod Crustaceans

The decapod crustaceans are probably the most important of all the invertebrates in the sea, as far as man is immediately concerned, because they are the most highly prized as food. No seafood dinner is complete without heaping plates of boiled shrimp, bright red broiled lobsters and steamed blue crabs.

Fish also love decapod crustaceans. If you examine the stomach contents of a grouper, red snapper or rock bass, chances are you'll find some grass shrimp or small xanthid crabs or even larger blue crabs. If these were absent from the food chain, it is doubtful that we would have large fish populations, even though many of the smaller fish feed heavily upon mysids, amphipods and other smaller crustaceans.

The classification of the class Crustacea is confusing at best, and even the decapods have major breakdowns and divisions within divisions. The decapod crustaceans are divided into two major suborders: Natantia (which means "swimming") containing true shrimp; and Reptantia (meaning "crawling"), which contains lobsters and crayfish (Macrura), hermit crabs, mole shrimp, mud shrimp, and porcelain crabs which all belong to a rather untidy classification Anomura—which is believed to be an evolutionary transitional phase between macruran and natantian stocks. Finally there are the true crabs, or Brachyura. They all have one thing in common and that is five pairs of legs, which give them the name Decapoda. The exact differences between the groups can be looked up in any good zoology text.

The decapod crustaceans range widely up and down the Atlantic coast, from Maine to Florida. Commercial shrimp often get up to the Virginia coast, slipper lobsters can be dredged off the Carolinas, fiddler crabs are found from Maine to Texas but the flame-streaked boxcrab (*Calappa flammea*) ends its northern range in the Carolinas.

Of all the decapods, none have the economic importance of shrimp, and shrimping operations are spreading throughout the world. Shrimping, I have found, is a dangerous disease; it has caused many a man to leave his family and head for the free and easy existence on a trawler away at sea, into familiar ports with pockets loaded with fast green money. No other profession gives you such a good feeling of independence, that is, except when there's no shrimp.

The trouble with shrimping is that it can become addictive, and no matter how much of a financial beating a shrimper takes, he always thinks that if he gets a bigger boat, hits the right season, that he will make a killing. And sometimes he will.

Penaeus setiferus
White Shrimp

September finally arrives, there is just a touch of autumn in the air, just a bit of cool breeze coming down from the north, and the calm Gulf waters of Alligator Point seem to be saying something: the shrimp are coming. The fishermen stand on the beach of Mud Cove looking out to sea and waiting. In another month or two fall will really be here, and with it comes the runs of mullet and the migrations of the white shrimp, *Penaeus setiferus*.

This is the big sleek fall shrimp that swims and feeds by day and goes into the mud bottom at night. It is a big shrimp, and sometimes it comes in such numbers that a short strike will load down a net with a most welcome catch.

Penaeid shrimp spawn in depths ranging from 20 to 50 fathoms almost at the edge of the continental shelf. Each female releases over a quarter of a million eggs, which sink down to the depths and within a few days hatch out larvae that look nothing like the adult. The larvae begin a slow migration toward the estuaries, carried by tides and current, but they are capable of some independent movement.

By the time they reach the nursery grounds, the productive marshlands where there is plenty of vegetable and animal matter to feed upon, they have grown to seven millimeters and abandon their planktonic way of life to become part of the benthic communities. They grow rapidly in the nursery grounds, hiding up the creeks away from predators, burrowing in the soft rich mud. Within a few months they grow to maturity and are ready to leave the protection of the marsh and move out into the bays where the shrimp nets and hordes of other predators are waiting for them.

There are bumper seasons for all forms of marine life, and shrimp are no exception. Some fisheries biologists have noted that when there were a great many intense southerly winds blowing the offshore waters toward the beach during the summer when the shrimp are hatching, the following season will produce extra-good yields. But there are just too many variables to predict what the yields will be.

Even though the shrimp have successfully arrived at the estuary, if the water temperature is too cold or the salinity too high or low, the the crop isn't going to be very large. If the larval shrimp encounter hordes of jellyfish or some other predators as they move shoreward their numbers will be diminished. And if they happen to be moving into an estuary at the same time that fresh water run offs are carrying chlorinated hydrocarbons from tobacco and cotton fields, chances are the populations will be wiped out entirely.

An uninformed conservationist seeing hundreds of shrimp boats working side by side catching shrimp by the hundreds of thousands of pounds, might be inclined to think they are decimating the population, particularly if the next year's shrimping isn't good. But the reduced stock may have nothing whatsoever to do with the fishing activities; it may stem from a dozen causes.

When Chevron had its oil spill in Louisiana, one wonders what effect it had on the larval, sensitive shrimp that had to pass under it and through it on their way to the marshes. What happens to the larval shrimp when they enter an estuary that is thermally polluted from hot water discharged from a nuclear power plant?

But shrimping is still good along much of the United States. Pascagoula, Mississippi, enjoys a good shrimping season, and so does Empire, Louisiana, where white shrimp reaches its peak abundance. And all along the west Florida coast in the late summer and the fall, you can see little white shrimp crowding into the tidal creeks that wind in and out of the marshlands.

When the spring rains come, the growing shrimp are washed out of the rivers and creeks by the flooding waters and move into the bay. Strong northerly winds and extreme low tides cause them to leave the creeks and concentrate in great numbers along the shorelines. Gulls scream, diving down and grabbing shrimp, all they can hold. Fish

suddenly appear from offshore to gobble them, followed by hungry
sharks. When the white shrimp come in, all sorts of good collecting
can happen if you have an otter trawl. Electric rays and skates
converge on the area, so do cutlass fish, flounder and croakers.

When the nets are hauled aboard, and dumped on deck they are
massed with hopping, kicking and jackknifing shrimp. Amidst them are
the large predators, and they are gorged with shrimp. Speckled trout
flop around, with dozens of shrimp antennae protruding from their
mouths. Eels slither over the deck. Sharks are drowned with their
mouths packed with shrimp and fish which they gobbled up at random.
The net has interrupted a feeding frenzy of large hungry predators,
skates, rays, sea robins, flounders all with bulging stomachs.

The shrimpers work feverishly—there is gold on deck. They
eagerly grab up handfuls of shrimp and fling them into wire baskets,
and cull the trash overboard. Gulls scream with delight and dive down
and grab up the scores of floating dead fish. More trash is whisked
over the side, and another basket of shrimp is filled, and another. Then
it's down into the fish hold to ice the catch, and that must be done in
a hurry because the net is ready to come up with another load.

The shrimpers work long and hard when the white shrimp
migrations come in. A little boat can haul a thousand pounds or more
aboard and make good money. They shrimp hard until the shrimp
move on and then follow them around the coast, until cold weather
comes and the shrimp disappear entirely. Some boats fish for white
shrimp by day, and seek pink shrimp by night.

Penaeus duorarum and Penaeus aztecus
Pink Shrimp and Brown Shrimp

Just as the sun sets over the Florida coast in the springtime and
dusk appears, the pink shrimp (*Penaeus duorarum*) stirs from its long
daytime rest, and kicks the mud out from under it with its swimmerets
and pops up on the surface of the sea bottom. First a few come out,
then more, and soon the whole bottom is covered by the shrimp,
waving their long inquisitive antennae, their dark brown eyes mounted
on stalks peering through the darkness.

Then a great rattling, thundering noise comes from the distance.
Great otter boards jostle above them, the clatter of chain, then the
lashing of tickler chain that beats up the bottom into a stormy cloud of

281

mud. The shrimp leap up and start to swim, but a long, wide funnel net comes along next and in they go, the water pressure forces them to the back of the net, up the shoot and into the bag, where they are stopped by the tightly tied rope. The net drags them on, more and more shrimp are swooped up, so are the sharks, the eels, the pinfish and perhaps even a sea turtle that were feeding upon them.

The shrimp are agitated; they are jumping and leaping, frantic with the noise and the activity. Fish spot the movement, the water is agitated, the predators come in from all over, frenzied by the kicking, crackling noise of the shrimp, the clatter of the net. The net drags past the majority of the bottom life, which is everywhere. Porpoises swim in, snapping up fish here and there, big sand sharks cruise in and swoop, and a mackerel is gone.

Those in the net are compressed, shaken and exhausted. Catfish struggle with their fins embedded in sting rays, and still other catfish are stabbed with other catfish like an hors d'oeuvre on a toothpick. Suddenly the net stops, the otter doors sink down and close the net off as the great trawler above slows.

The winch turns, and the net is lifted from the bottom. Up, up and up it comes through the surface slowly, steadily. The captives in the net press against the webbing, try to wriggle through, but everywhere the wall of net is too small, there are no openings and no way of escape unless the net should have a hole in it or get snagged on a rock or a piece of wreckage.

The doors break the surface with a splash and the net, over 45 feet in length, hangs from the davit. Then the death-run begins. The boat speeds up and tows the net, running wide open. A frothy white wake breaks behind the boat as the shrimpers pull the net to wash everything down the chute, down into the very bottom of the bag where they are packed together closer than sardines in a can. There sharks are mashed up against shrimp; soles, pigfish and grunts are squashed partway through the webbing; some anchovies are pushed through. Death is everywhere from the pressure, squid blanche and die; some shrimp are killed, and so are many of the smaller creatures that are pressed up against the webbed wall.

The net slows and the lazy line is pulled in from the cathead; it is fastened two-thirds of the way down toward the bag, cutting off the escape to the mouth of the net from the choke line. The net is pulled up alongside the trawler and it is hoisted up from the sea. Sea robins, pinfish and pigfish grunt in frightened chorus. Sea pansies glow with a shimmering bioluminescence, and everywhere the glowing orange eyes of pink shrimp flash. With a jerk of the bag rope, the net is opened, and its contents cascade out onto the gleaming white decks. Shrimp, pink-gold, go wild, scuffling, scampering, and jackknifing over the deck.

So many, and so much on the deck at one time. Everything is a delight to the enthusiast who is interested in getting a variety of organisms. But we are concerned with pink shrimp on this expedition, as are the shrimpers who grab them up in handfuls and throw them into wire baskets. In a few minutes its all over, the shrimp kick less and less as they are starved of oxygen in this hostile environment. Soon they are dead, and their pink bodies lay piled up in the wire buckets.

But the 200 pounds of shrimp hauled aboard are only a minute fraction of the shrimp population below that the net missed. The net drags on, harvesting more shrimp until the first rays of dawn strike. It is time to rest again, and the wild dance of the night before is over. The last strike is brought up, it has less shrimp in it, as the orange sun is rising over the horizon and the silhouette of treetops on St. George Island stands out darkly in the sea. The vividly pinkish-red shrimp fade in color. Night is gone.

Sleepily the remaining shrimp settle down to the bottom. Their swimmerets on their underside begin fanning the sand and they settle into their holes. Their bodies are covered; only their red eyes show for a moment, then the bottom is covered with antennae projecting, acres of waving hair, then nothing, no sign that there ever were shrimp as they dig out of sight to wait the night.

Many environmental factors will cause shrimp to move in and out of the bays, to burrow into the mud or even to get up and swim on the surface of the water in mass migrations. Not all of them are understood. Seasonal currents, temperatures and salinities are well-known factors, but I have seen thunder and lightning have their effects on the populations as well.

I was shrimping in Pascagoula, Mississippi, at the start of shrimping season. We were doing great, and our little shrimp trawler, which we named *Penaeus*, was straining under the great loads of brown shrimp we were pulling aboard two and three barrels per tow.

Then the wind picked up, and in the darkness lightning split the sky, revealing great black clouds. Thunder roared frighteningly over the bay, and the lightning flashed and lit the buoys and shoreline as clearly as if it were daylight. For 15 minutes thunder rolled and sheering light penetrated down into the depths of the bay.

We hauled up our net and found almost no shrimp. Every boat we spoke to on the radio reported the sudden disappearance of shrimp, and few had more than 30 pounds aboard. Whether the shrimp responded to the rumbling vibrations of thunder or the glaring illumination of their dark world, I do not know. Perhaps it was the shift in the wind, but by the time the rains began pouring down on us, the shrimp were gone.

At night when the shrimp are swimming cheerfully in our sea-water tables, we have learned to dim the lights in our wet lab gradually. The sudden glaring fluorescent lights caused them to go into a panic, leap and jackknife onto the floor, where they lie kicking helplessly.

Spring lasts from March to May in north Florida before the shrimp leave. They come up the Gulf coast in an east-to-west movement, hitting first at Cedar Keys, then Alligator Point, Apalachicola and later Panama City, Pensacola, Mobile and Mississippi. Where they come from, no one is quite sure. There is a population of *Penaeus duorarum* that stays in the shallows throughout the year, and another much larger population that the fishermen call "running shrimp" that comes up from the south. They come to Alligator Point and Duers Channel, stay for a bit and then swim on.

Then as summer progresses another shrimp comes out of the rivers and shallow bays where it has been growing. They grow very rapidly, within a few months they grow from two inches to six inches or more. These are the brown shrimp (*Penaeus aztecus*) that live in the Apalachicola River and other rivers along the Gulf Coast. They are distinguished from the pink shrimp because they are lighter in color, and do not have a large purple or dark red spot on the second-from-last abdominal segment. They too swarm into the bays in a good year, and the nets harvest them.

Sometimes "brownies" are out in the daytime, particularly in murky waters. The same may be true of *Penaeus duorarum*; we have collected them during the day, but not in vast numbers.

Shrimp may be kept alive by placing them in a container with an aerator and keeping clean water in their tank aboard the boat. There are regular bait rigs that have small nets that scoop the shrimp up and dump them into tanks that are fed by pumps; they are taken back and transported to base. Since live bait shrimp are frequently abundant, they can be purchased from bait dealers; it is easier and cheaper than capturing them yourself. Putting them in a plastic bag with oxygen and sea water is not secure, because they can become frantic and puncture the bag with their sharp rostrum.

Sicyonia typica
Rock Shrimp

Only when the trawler goes far out into the Gulf, out of sight of land as a rule, will it come to the populations of the delicious little rock shrimp, *Sicyonia typica*. This shrimp delights the palate, and is an inspiration to the entrepreneur who is looking for something new to utilize from the sea.

It has a hard shell, which is discouraging to the fainthearted, but they can be peeled easily after they are boiled. They are a small shrimp, seldom measuring over four inches total length, purple-and-white in color, almost zebra-striped and highly attractive; their legs are a vivid purple. Like certain penaeid shrimp, they are nocturnal and seem to disappear during daylight hours, although we have collected a few in our dredge while working offshore. Much investigation needs to be done on the movements and concentrations of rock shrimp. I have seen as much as one-third of the catch made up of rock shrimp.

They taste as sweet as Maine lobster or, even more, like stone-crab claws. We have kept them alive in tanks with gravel and shell on the bottom, and if they are given ample sand, not mud, to burrow in they will live for months. You almost never see one walking about in the daytime, but at night they are all over the bottom of the tanks along with the penaeid shrimp.

Like penaeid shrimp *Sicyonia typica* also has a nasty habit of jumping out of the tanks at night and should be kept covered. When viewed from the top, they do not appear attractive. The dorsal side of the shell is a muddy brown or gray, the rostrum (the spearlike point on the top of the head) is heavily jagged, and for a moment, when you see them in the tanks, they look like insects.

The Florida Board of Conservation and the Bureau of Commercial Fisheries have studied their movements. This may well be the gourmet shrimp of the future.

Alpheus heterochaelis
Pistol Shrimp

Alpheus (Crangon) *heterochaelis* is the largest pistol shrimp found along the southeast Atlantic coasts. It is an attractive creature, with blue and sometimes a pinkish tinge in its body. It is a secretive creature that crawls in the mud and sand, living in tin cans, and burrowing under logs and rocks.

They are collected in dredge hauls occasionally, but are more accessible to the collector who turns over objects at low tide. Sometimes you can hear them from a distance when their large claw gives off a startling, loud "pop," which they may use to scare off predators or perhaps to attract each other during mating.

It can be quite startling to be picking through a pile of mud, intent on collecting some other organism like sea spiders or polychaete worms, and hear loud popping sounds disturbing this world of silence.

Providing there are no predators, snapping shrimp can be raised successfully in the aquarium. We have found dozens of them living in the filters of our sand tanks, both *Alpheus heterochaelis* and *A. packardi*, which may be proof that they can be raised in captive conditions.

This latter species, a smaller, brownish form, is quite abundant in *Molgula* and *Styela* clusters which are hauled up by the ton in Alligator Harbor, and when the specimens are brought into our tanks the snapping shrimp, which hide between the tunicates, using the spaces as tunnels, probably leave the clusters and go into the filters.

One of the most successful ways we have maintained them was in laboratory floats, screen supported by Styrofoam kept in large concrete vats. They have lived for three months in this manner, forgotten until rediscovered.

Hippolsymata wurdmanii
Red Cleaning Shrimp

Although a number of caridean shrimp appear in ascidians, algae or sponges, you should not make the mistake of thinking they are abundant. The terms "common," "abundant," "rare," and "uncommon" are all relative until you look for a fixed number of specimens. When you seek a dozen *Hippolsymata wurdmanii*, that small bright red shrimp covered with longitudinal stripes, you may find there is more of a problem than anticipated.

For example, in a dredge haul of tunicates only nine might be found after the entire boat load had been culled, and the tunicates broken apart. If it were not for flatworms, nereids, small crabs, snapping shrimp and minute sea cucumbers that were taken in the culling process, the work would be pure drudgery.

However, when you aren't particularly looking for *Hippolsymata wurdmanii*, then your chances of finding them in multitudes are great in some obscure place like a yellow crumb of bread sponge. They are a good-sized caridean shrimp, one of the largest species to be found in Florida, sometimes running over three centimers.

For some time there has been considerable debate among crustacean specialists as to whether *Hippolsymata wurdmanii* is a true cleaning shrimp. In many instances the fish try to feed on them as soon as they are placed in the tank, and since they have not been observed actively cleaning fish underwater in their natural habitat, it cannot be said for certain that cleaning is their natural way of life.

But we have observed them cleaning a scorpion fish in our tanks. I have come to the conclusion that when fish line up for a cleaning session, as described by several divers, that it is not a pleasant affair. Getting "cleaned" is something that fish must do, rather like visiting one's dentist.

If you put your hand in a tank that has a dozen *Hippolsymata* or so, they will immediately converge on your fingers and start the swaying, back-and-forth motion of cleaning. Then you will feel a series of sharp little pinpricks as they search for particles among your fingernails and over the surface of your skin. Should they find a slight abrasion they really have a ball, and begin digging away at the soft wounded tissues. It is a very perplexing experience to have your hand manicured by a series of cleaners.

We have also observed *Palaemon floridanus* living in a tank with *Hippolsymata* to start actively cleaning our fingers, so this action must not be limited to a particular species.

Palaemon floridanus
Zebra Shrimp

Palaemon floridanus was the first described from specimens obtained at Captiva Island, Florida, in 1942. They are large, spotted shrimp that inhabit wharf pilings, often perched upon *Styela* clusters. These are easily collected by taking wire- or plastic-screen net, bringing it under them and suddenly pulling it up to the surface.

The result is a net covered with frantically jumping *Palaemon floridanus*. They may be gravid throughout the year, because whenever we have taken them there were always females with egg sacks attached.

This shrimp appears to occupy a restricted habitat of wharf piling, and can be called one of the true dwellers of the fouling habitat, although on occasion they are found in small numbers in sea grass hauls.

This is one species that we have successfully "farmed" by building floating docks made of Styrofoam and wood bracing. The

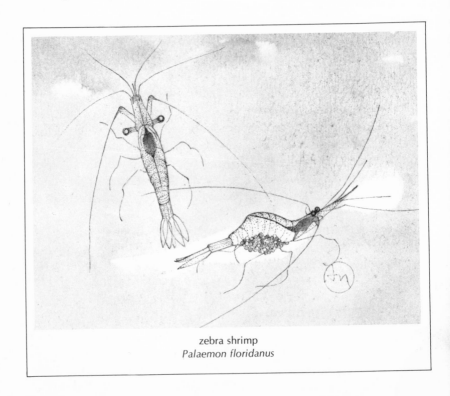

zebra shrimp
Palaemon floridanus

dock, in the period of one year, became massed with sponges, profuse branching clusters of hydroids, barnacles and tunicates, and hundreds of *Palaemon floridanus* have bred among the protective coverings of fouling organisms, And since mariculture has become popular and many large corporations are working with techniques of raising shrimp in captivity to sell, I feel we·have the jump on them, since we are already growing and marketing these shrimp. When an institution wants some of the handsome, zebra-striped shrimp with red spots at every joint of their legs, we simply walk out on our dock with a dip net, scoop up some hydroids and pick out the shrimp and put them in a plastic bag for shipment.

Palaemonetes pugio
Grass Shrimp

The great salt marshes that stretch over the Gulf coast and up the Atlantic coast are home to the little grass shrimp (*Palaemonetes pugio*). If they were any size larger than a half-inch, they would be one of the most abundant commercial shrimp in the world. Throughout the extensive network of brackish tidal streams and drainage ditches that range through the marshes of the coastal United States, millions upon millions are swarming in the shallows feasting upon diatoms and micro-organisms in the rich black bottom muds.

Palaemonetes vulgaris, Palaemonetes intermedius and *Crangon septemspinosus* are all found in marshes and shallow tidal flats of the New England coast as well as in the south. Using a flat scoop net with small mesh or a small minnow seine a collector can strike a drainage ditch and bring up a handsome catch of small shrimp mixed in with killifish and other species of fish and crabs. On very high tides, larger fish move into the marshes and gorge themselves on grass shrimp. We once dressed a hundred pounds of spotted sea trout and found all their stomachs jammed with *Palaemonetes vulgaris*.

Many commercial and sports fishermen confuse these grass shrimp with commercial species, and consider them juvenile white shrimp, and are deeply concerned over their survival when dredging operations start. Even though their taxonomy is far from perfect, their heart is in the right place in preserving the habitat and their livlihood or favorite pastime. In all probability, a very large percentage of adult eating fish feed largely upon *Palaemonetes* and *Crangon*.

289

Grass shrimp tend to be seasonal in their appearances and disappearances. When winter sets in, they go down into the mud and are difficult to find. But if there are a few warm days they come out in mass. And a quick strike with a minnow net will get enough to fill a one gallon jar to the brim.

We have found that *Palaemonetes pugio* and *P. vulgaris* make good pets, but they must be kept isolated in the aquarium. Fish love them and gobble them up, but they in turn will gobble up anything else in the water with them. They will pick clams clean of their shells, will attack bristleworms and will even bite hunks out of amphioxus. When there is nothing else they will eat each other. As soon as one molts and becomes soft and weakened and there is no vegetation for it to hide in, all the other *Palaemonetes* pounce on it and soon there is nothing.

We have used them as natural food, because they occur in such large numbers. The shrimp are simply captured and distributed among a large number of aquariums and holding tanks, and the fish eat them when they are able to catch them, just as they do in their natural environment.

The grass shrimp also make excellent chum if properly utilized. We found in trout and redfish fishing that if you take a bucket of grass shrimp and dump them into the water, fish are drawn from all around and are in a much better disposition to take your hook. Live shrimp darting off in all directions simply seem to throw fish into a feeding frenzy.

Palaemonetes is also a very valuable experimental animal used in research laboratories throughout the United States. Quite a number of physiologists study their color pigments, and hormone regulation that makes their chromatophores expand and contract. This enables the animals to blend in with their background.

A common experiment, using *Palaemonetes*, demonstrates neurosecretory control over crustacean chromatophore changes. When the eye stalks which contain sinus glands are removed the shrimp turns dark from a redistribution of the red and yellow body pigments. If these eyestalkless shrimp are then injected with a sinus gland extract made from pulverized eyestalks, the white pigment disperses rapidly over the body and the shrimp blanches.

Just the opposite thing happens in fiddler crabs. If you cut their eyestalks off they lighten, and when the extract is injected, they soon darken. Even if grass shrimp sinus extract is injected into the crab the results are unaltered.

I know biologists who have spent over 15 years working on hormone regulation in grass shrimp and fiddler crabs. They all remember when it was no trouble to go down to the eel pond behind the laboratory in Woods Hole and catch thousands of grass shrimp in a few minutes' time, and now there are almost no grass shrimp in the eel pond. They go elsewhere for their supply. Perhaps *Palaemonetes* are declining from DDT, perhaps from all the gasoline and oil continually spilled from outboard motors, or from the sewage build-up and increase of nitrates, or perhaps it is all of these things. But the tiny amount that the laboratory collects each year could not have had any substantial effect upon the vast populations.

Scyllarides nodifer
Slipper Lobster

The slipper lobster, *Scyllarides nodifer* is one of the monstrous-looking creatures in the sea. It has an exoskeletonous shell with the texture of brick, with orange, yellow and purple coloration,

slipper lobster
Scyllarides nodifer

but its appearance is most unlike a lobster. It has short, insectlike, pointed legs and no big claws. But its tail—which reminds one of roofing tile in texture—can jackknife vigorously, and when one is brought aboard it flounces about and kicks wildly, making even the most bold collector stop and consider whether he should pick it up or scoop it into a plastic bag with a shovel.

Scyllarid lobsters have intrigued Gulf fishermen for years. Many have tried trapping them, but few of these lobsters ever enter traps. They are caught, sometimes abundantly, in shrimp nets in deep water where there is hard, sandy, shelly bottom and plenty of sponge, particularly in areas where there are basket sponges. *Scyllarides* uses them as protection. Their legs are too short to permit them to enter lobster traps, so to harvest *Scyllarides* a new type of trap would probably have to be invented.

The fishermen call them "bulldozers," probably because they look like one with their big chitinous flaps projecting over their eyes, and prize them as a great food delicacy. I have eaten slipper lobsters and found them to be even superior to the Florida lobster (*Panulirus argus*) and almost as good as the Maine lobster (*Homarus americanus*).

Both the slipper lobster, *Scyllarides nodifier*, and the Florida spiny lobster, *Panulirus argus*, may occur in substantial numbers out in the Gulf of Mexico. The slipper lobster is routinely taken in 60 to 80 feet of water when shrimpers are trawling over sand bottom. The Florida lobster, or "crawfish," seldom enters when shrimpers are trawling on sand bottom. I know one shrimper who accidentally dragged his nets across a big rock in 90 feet of water. The boat lurched, the cables shook, and when he ran back to slow the boat down and hauled up the nets, he found his trawls torn to shreds. However, tangled up in the torn, shredded black webbing were four spiny lobsters.

This may be some indication that if sufficient money and effort were devoted to locating lobsters in the northern Gulf, a new industry might be possible. The amount of lobsters that presently come from North Florida is too small to measure. Much more needs to be learned about scyllarid lobsters. A few investigators at the University of Miami have studied their developmental stages and can now define scyllarids in their larval stages, but what it eats, where it lives and how long needs more study.

We have had some success in keeping slipper lobsters alive in our aquariums, but most of the time they are dead when brought back to the laboratory by commercial fishermen. The specimens that fishermen pack on ice arrive alive, but die shortly afterward when placed in sea water, even with very gradual acclimation to higher temperatures.

There is a very small slipper lobster (*Scyllarus americanus*) that measures about three inches. These have always done well when kept in sand-and-gravel tanks and have fed actively and even grown in captivity. The Florida crawfish (*Panulirus argus*) is excellent for the aquarium, makes an active and interesting pet and generally is very hardy and can survive for years. I know some people in the Florida Keys who have maintained them in their living-room aquarium and grew as fond of them as any house pet.

Clibanarius vittatus
Striped Hermit Crab

Now and then one comes upon a marine animal that is really hardy. It can be kept in captivity and requires no babying, no worry about whether it will feed and, even before that, whether it will withstand shipment across the continent. Many marine creatures do not meet all these requirements, but *Clibanarius vittatus*, the striped hermit crab certainly does. A good clue to its hardiness is that it spends almost as much time out of water as it does crawling around in the shallows. When our open-system tanks overflow, *Clibanarius vittatus* can crawl over the side, plop on the floor and crawl away. A day, perhaps a week later, it can be found scuffling its way, perhaps even having worked its way out of the building, and be dragging its shell over the hot sands.

We have seen over 1500 conglomerate during the summer time on a small portion of Shell Point Reef. Most of them were living in shells of *Melongena corona*; the rest were in *Busycon* shells and an occasional *Strombus alatus*. In Italy hermit crabs are considered a delicacy, and hungry Italians would do well in such places and probably not even dent the population.

I have actually seen a striped hermit crab attack a *Busycon spiratum*, kill it and eject it from its shell and devour the animal. The specimen of *Clibanarius vittatus* that I observed eating a fig whelk in August of 1963 moved into the new shell, squirmed about in it for a while, then dragged its new shell over to the old one, and in a jiffy

293

jumped back comfortably into the old, familiar home covered with barnacles and slipper limpets. But you can be certain that the fig whelk shell went to some other dissatisfied hermit crab looking for a new home. However, since this activity is so seldom witnessed, they most probably occupy shells where the conch died from old age or some other cause. But there is a great trade going on among hermit crabs, trying on one shell, discarding it and moving into another. They are looking for the best shell, the one with the most perfect fit; they go at it with the same intensity as women trying on hat after hat.

Petrochirus diogenes
Red Hermit Crab

When you find a large *Busycon* conch shell or a Scotch bonnet shell (*Phalium granulatum*) that is occupied by what appears to be a large, bright red lobster after it was boiled, then you have found *Petrochirus diogenes*, the largest and most distinctive hermit crab in the western Atlantic. It is a subtropical form that occurs in the Carolinas and on both sides of Florida and into the tropics.

Although it is primarily an offshore form in northwest Florida; it also comes to the beach during the fall, and is occasionally found in winter. Of all the hermit crabs, this species is most heavily overgrown with slipper limpets, barnacles, sometimes tunicates, and almost always it is a bonanza habitat for the cloak anemone (*Calliactis tricolor*), and the pretty red and white porcellanid crab (*Porcellana sayana*) which shares the same shells.

They survive extremely well, and are the pride of a great many public aquariums. They walk along, dragging their heavy shells almost on tiptoes with their antennae stretched out; probably that is why they are called *diogenes*, because they always appear to be in search of something.

Their large, red chelipeds are covered with tubercles, and these big claws are very impressive—they easily rake a mullet apart. The hermit crabs can readily be removed from their shell by tugging on them.

Pagurus pollicaris
Flat-clawed Hermit Crab

The flat-clawed hermit crab, *Pagurus pollicaris* is common along the shallow grass-flat estuaries of the southeastern Atlantic and Gulf coasts. It is predominantly found occupying moon-snail shells and its flattened claw can close up the entrance of the shell much the way the original inhabitant's operculum did.

We have collected gravid females in the fall and sporadically throughout the winter. The eggs are a bright purple and are massed on the ventral side of the abdomen. Although *Pagurus pollicaris* can always be found in a day's collecting they appear to have certain seasons of marked abundance—certain years when their numbers increase and decrease, although we have not yet determined their seasonal variations.

This is one hermit crab that will bite, and the large claw has a scissorlike snipping action that can hurt almost as much as any blue-crab pinch. It is most likely to catch the eye when the tide rises up to the edge of the shore, because suddenly you may see a crown conch, fig whelk or tulip shell get up and scuttle rapidly over the sand. *Pagurus pollicaris* is most likely to be wearing commensal *Calliactis tricolor* anemones or *Hydractinia echinata* hydroids or both.

The crab makes a very amusing aquarium pet, and watching their antics, which have earned them the title "clown of the tide pool," can be fascinating—so much so, that you may never get any work done. The enemy of all hermit crabs is *Calappa flammea*, the flame-streaked box crabs that can peel hermits out of their shells, and naturally the two varieties should never be kept in the same aquarium.

Pagurus pollicaris is a difficult animal to keep, because it will eat nearly anything in the aquarium unless it is kept well fed. I have even seen them devour sea anemones and climb onto sea horses. They can be kept with many fish that don't settle on the bottom, but they cannot be kept with spiny boxfish or puffers, which are fond of nipping their chelae off.

Pagurus longicarpus
Dwarf Hermit Crab

At the edge of the marsh grass in the brackish estuaries, you stand a good chance of finding a few hundred, or a few thousand, small, brownish-white hermit crabs (*Pagurus longicarpus*). They inhabit periwinkle snails, *Nassarius* shells and almost any other small gastropod they can find, and conglomerate in large numbers where they scuttle actively around in the shallows. And it is quite a sight to see the little piles of beach-worn shells with long-legged little crabs extended out as far as they can go, fighting with each other, dodging and mating.

So active are these, that numerous biologists use them for behavioral studies. Even when you pick them up, many will not withdraw into their shells, but will try to struggle and scuttle out of your grasp. When you persist, they will hang out of the shell and some will even leave their shells, exposing their soft, naked parts, and try to make a run for it.

In the home aquarium they are a delight to watch and they make excellent scavengers that will pounce upon any dead fish or other form of marine life, devour it and cut down the chances of biological pollution in your closed system. However, they should not be overfed, and routine cleaning should be left to the aquarists, not to the crab.

Petrolisthes armatus
Porcelain Crab

Pick up a clump of oysters or tear up a cluster of solitary tunicates, and you'll undoubtedly see a multitude of little flattened crabs with long flattened chelae scuttle madly into the crevices and burrows of this little disturbed world. These peculiar, flattened creatures are *Petrolisthes*.

Some of them are quite attractive, having bluish and red spots on their drab brown bodies. I have watched them living among tunicate colonies, looking down from a floating dock, and could not help but be amused how they wave their long flattened mouth parts in a sweeping rhythmic fashion, much the way a barnacle beats the water with its webbed cirri. Then some individuals begin a frantic scratching display, almost like a kitten scrabbling at a hanging ball of wool.

When you try to catch one of these small crabs you've got a chase on your hands. They can dart quickly down into the crevices, and keep eluding your big clumsy fingers. No matter how small the clump of oysters is, they are reluctant to leave it, but when they do, they'll jump onto the dock or boat platform and scuttle out of sight. Their reluctance to leave the sinking ship has advantages; a clump of oyster or tunicate or sponge can be collected, placed in a bucket, and all the associated *Petrolisthes* come along with the catch. Then they can be picked out of the crannies and crevices at your convenience back at the laboratory or holding station.

In isolating them for preservation you'll find that they quickly autotomize, but the diligent collector, manipulating them with forceps gently holding them by the carapace, can avoid having them throw off their legs. However, if they are to be kept alive, collect them on an oyster clump (not tunicates, which may die after a few days) and place them in a standard aquarium where they will survive quite nicely.

Petrolisthes armatus has a wide distribution in tropical American seas, and even in the Indo-Pacific. There are occasional records of it in Massachusetts and it probably ranges from the Carolinas to the Caribbean, although it has not been reported in the Carolinas. It is a relatively rare species elsewhere north of Miami, but it is heavily concentrated in Alligator Harbor.

Uca pugilator
Common Fiddler Crab

While the fiddler crab may not replace the laboratory frog as an experimental animal, it may someday run it a close second. Their numbers have taken a considerable beating from dredge-and-fill operations, and spraying of DDT on the east coast of the United States has wiped them out by the millions, but they are still one of the most abundant animals along the Gulf shore. And because they demonstrate a variety of highly dependable responses such as neurosecretory hormone control of chromatophore changes, they may be used in every classroom in the country.

In addition to chromatophore experiments they can be used in comparative physiology courses to demonstrate stenohaline uptake. This simply means that if they are placed in fresh water they will not absorb the water into their body and can therefore tolerate brackish and even fresh water conditions. However, if a spider crab is placed in the same water it will absorb water quickly and will perish, so it is called a strict stenohaline osmoconformer.

Fiddlers have been used to study mating behavior, community grouping and coordination experiments. They dig burrows deep down into the sand along the edge of the marsh, and collecting them at the right time of year is no problem. Fiddler crabs come out in great hordes at night, and when the tide is low, they come out in the day when the sun is shining. Again, like other crabs, light, temperature and tidal rhythms affect their movements.

Because they have been used extensively in a variety of research programs, *U. pugilator's* movements have necessarily been studied. During the summer when the tide is too high during the daytime, they will swarm out on the beaches at night. If conditions are not entirely right, they will come hesitantly out of their burrows, stay next to them, and dart back in if anyone or anything approaches.

But when conditions are right, they leave their burrows en masse and participate in a gigantic congregation near the low-tide mark.

Several collectors, working together, can make the herd stay together and pile them up by walking around them in a circle. Sometimes bait catchers dig a hole and place a bucket in it and put two long boards leading into it at a 45° angle. The crabs are herded into the boards and march down into the bucket where they pile up.

When counting and sorting them, you can always expect a few to latch onto your fingers. Many then autotomize and leave their claw attached to your hand; prying the claw off is a painful process. However, a good fiddler-crab picker doesn't mind the pain at all; he hardly notices it after the first dozen pinches or so.

Keeping *U. pugilator* in numbers has been something of a problem. A few dozen at a time can be maintained very successfully in a sand terrarium, and they thrive on bread or, better still, on dogfood. But 50,000 fiddlers require a lot of room, and if they are crowded they begin to die and stink, and soon you loose the entire population. They must be kept shaded, away from the sun, because they are sensitive to intense heat. We found that three feet of oyster shell for drainage and continuous spraying of sea water helps considerably in keeping them for long periods.

It is necessary that fiddlers be stocked while the getting is good, because after the first couple of frosts they go into the ground and stay there until the ground heats up, which may not happen for six months.

And since they are a volume-consumed specimen, and many experiments utilize a thousand at a time, a life-support system must be developed for maintaining them.

The fiddler crab is an important food for beach birds and many terrestrial mammals. They are quite frequently found in the feces of raccoons and foxes. I have seen spiny boxfish and redfish devour them when they go for a small swim during high tides. They generally fear the water, and when pursued they herd toward the marsh grass, where catching them is virtually impossible.

At one time *U. pugilator* was tremendously abundant at Woods Hole and could be captured there by scientists who went out and herded them. But as the years passed they either stopped herding or they started diminishing, because the collectors there must dig for every one they catch. The differences between the North Atlantic fiddler and the Gulf are striking; the northern one is rather drab brown and much smaller, yet both are *U. pugilator*.

Our specimens have been checked by systematic zoologists time and again, and they are the same species. I once delivered a lecture at the Woods Hole Oceanographic Institution, and showed color slides of our southern fiddler crabs. One of the scientists asked, "What's the matter with them? Are they sick?"

Fiddler crabs along the Gulf appear to be alive and well, but they aren't what they used to be. When I first moved to Florida in 1957 I was astonished at the vast number of crabs that dwelt along the beaches. I recall stepping out of the motel on the beach near Carrabelle, Florida, and standing there transfixed by the sight of 5 solid acres of beach covered with fiddlers, bubbling audibly, and when I walked into their midst they sounded like a windstorm blowing parched dried leaves about as they raced for their burrows in the high marsh.

Great hordes of fiddler crabs have disappeared from the sandy beaches along the borders of marsh lands, and at one time the sandflats hissed and bubbled with their vast multitudes on almost every single beach along the Atlantic and Gulf coasts. All along the eastern seaboard of the United States fiddler crabs have been steadily diminishing. W. E. Odum, et al., in *Science* magazine described an experiment where fiddler crabs were fed detritus taken from the Carmans River marsh in Brookhaven, New York, that had been continually sprayed with DDT for the past 15 years. The experimental crabs soon developed high concentrations of DDT in their tissues and their behavior became greatly modified: they lost all coordination, stumbled and fell when a hand approached. The control fiddlers which were fed detritus from a nonsprayed area retained their quick responses. This may explain why all the fiddler crabs disappeared from the Carmans River marsh over a decade ago.

Dredging has taken its toll of fiddlers. When the marsh is covered over, their homes are destroyed. Before 1965, if I wanted fiddler crabs in the winter, there was a beach along Mashes Sands in Panacea, Florida that for some reason or other had colonies of fiddlers that were less susceptible to the cold. On chilly mornings when other fiddlers on all the outer beaches were down in their holes, a few thousand rugged individuals that dwelt along the ditches of Mashes Sands were out taking advantage of the morning sun, moving stiffly and feeding on detritus from the marsh. Hungry birds also knew of this population and clapper rails hovered above them, dashing in for a quick crab.

When a development company moved in, advertising that they were selling Florida's last frontier, they purchased the marsh and started digging it up and cutting in roads and canals. Drainage was reduced and soon great expanses of the marsh turned brown, dehydrated and died off. The next winter no more fiddler crabs herded there. Their numbers were reduced until there were only a few straggly individuals running in and out of the grass.

At Shell Point in north Florida when Mobile Homes Industries created "Paradise Village" by filling in several hundred acres of marsh, I saw herds of fiddler crabs crossing the paved highway. They were dispossessed, and seeking new homes. It was sad, like a bunch of refugees driven off their land to seek homes elsewhere. The raccoons ate well; so did the foxes and birds. Cars squashed them flat as they raced down the highway.

At our laboratory in Panacea we have cultivated some fiddlers. The sea water splashes out of the tanks and seeps into the sand on our highland property. The area stays perpetually wet, and it is now colonized with fiddler crab holes. When we bring them back in batches for shipment to laboratories, many escape and they have all taken up residence on the grounds. We don't hunt these to fill orders; they are transplanted, and it is their home. At night they come out, but not as herds, only as individuals.

Uca pugnax
Black Fiddler Crab

You have merely to walk along the upper reaches of a marsh flat or tidal creek to find a multitude of black fiddler crabs (*Uca pugnax*) scampering into their holes. They are odd-looking for a fiddler, the front half of the shell being whitish-blue during their mating seasons, and the very large claw bearing a double, serrated ridge. It is this double, serrated ridge that helps the beginner separate this species from its more abundant cousin, *Uca pugilator*. Locally *U. pugnax* is called the "ditch fiddler" because it frequents brackish water ditches and even gets up into fresh water, usually quite a distance away from the *U. pugilator* populations although there is on occasion an overlap of the two species, and you can pick out a *U. pugnax* from a herd of *U. pugilator*.

The ditch fiddler is almost always found in thick black mud of almost claylike consistency, making it a full-time job to pry them up with a shovel. They do not herd the way *U. pugilator* does, and consequently they must be captured individually, much the same way you gather *Sesarma reticulatum*, which, incidentally, often lives in the same habitat with *U. pugnax*.

What impresses me most about this species is its ability to melt into its hole when a collector is in its midst. If you sneak up on a population in a tidal creek or drainage ditch, you can sometimes see a thousand animals walking. Suddenly you drop into the middle of them, bucket in hand, and start grabbing at crabs left and right. Within seconds, not a crab is to be seen anywhere, just a multitude of holes and perhaps part of the big claws of the males waving out.

If the weather has been warm the crab might not dig its way too far into its burrow and you can cut off its retreat with the shovel blade or even a stick thrust into the ground diagonally just below the fiddler; then pry it out. When you've got your required quota, you'll feel you've done more than one honest day's work.

If someone should find that *U. pugnax* when put through a grinder and an alcohol extract could cure cancer or some other disease, then someone would probably overcome the collecting problem by farming them. Although it is not an important commercial species, we have raised *U. pugnax* in captivity from egg to adulthood. We discovered a population of nearly 100 specimens growing in June in our floating vats that were placed nearly 300 feet from shore. Apparently their pelagic larvae colonized on the floats and thrived on the sea squirts, barnacles and green algae that grew there.

The International Oceanographic Corporation also raised a good crop of *U. pugnax* in their open-system pompano tanks in Cedar Keys, Florida, and achieved mature specimens in less than one year, only they never knew it. In the process of combining running water, oxygen, water space and no predators other than a few pompano, they raised barnacles, oysters, sea anemones, grass shrimp and a whole variety of other creatures.

U. pugnax takes on a beautiful blue mating color during the summer, on the front half of its shell. Gravid females with black sponge masses are not uncommon, particularly if they are submerged in water for a long period of time during high tides.

During the oil spill at Woods Hole, when the barge *Florida* gushed fuel oil into the marshes, many fiddlers died. The polluted *U. pugnax* exhibited its sky-blue colors during the month of September, and normally it does this only during July. There are still fiddlers around; even in the polluted Hudson River one finds this species in the marshes of Tappan, New York. I have seen them making burrows amid the piles of garbage at the Boston dump.

Callinectes sapidus
Blue Crab

Now we come to the most important crab of all, *Callinectes sapidus*, the common blue crab. A whole fishing industry, community and special breed of crab fisherman have developed around this creature that is caught by the hundreds of thousands of pounds and ends up in cooking pots, boiled to a bright orange. It has a delicious flavor and is prized by anyone who appreciates seafood. Although *Callinectes sapidus* was a western Atlantic species, it has spread throughout the world in the last 20 years. It now occurs in the Red Sea, on the Pacific coast and even in the Indian Ocean, and many other countries are harvesting it.

But nowhere is the crab more appreciated than in Maryland, where they are caught by the tons, dumped into boiling vats and flavored and then delivered to restaurants and bars where they are consumed with beer. When the blue crab catch declined in Maryland and Virginia a Congressional hearing was called to determine why they disappeared. Biologists in the area have put considerable time and effort into learning something about their habits.

But the blue crab in Panacea, Florida, has its own history, and that is worth relating. Years ago crabs were fished in Panacea with a long line, a coarse hair rope that was baited with salted bull-noses. It was a stinking, unpleasant mess, but the fishermen put out the thousands of yards of hair rope and bait along the marshes and up the Ochlockonee River working from skiffs. Flies buzzed noisily overhead, and when a summer breeze came along, the fishermen were pleased to get relief from the odorous bait.

The mile-long lines were set and buoyed with an inner tube, one at each end. The salted bull-nose was cut into long thin strips and looped every two feet over the coarse hair rope, and it worked very well. Great big sleek male blue crabs came out of the marshes and up from the muddy bottom, perched on the line and shredded the tough bait with their large claws. The "jimmies," as the big males were called, were prized because of their large size; often they were more than seven inches across the carapace. The fishermen usually worked lines at night with lighted gasoline lanterns. They eased along with their boats, lifting the line and shaking the crabs into weather-beaten fish boxes. The catches at night were better than in the day because the crabs were stunned by the blazing light while they were devouring the bait, and clung to the lines. Nonetheless, all that lifting and shaking was hard work. The catches were lucrative, and a crew of men was able to bring in as many as 40,000 pounds of crabs in a single night.

At the end of the fishing trip when they finished running the lines, they had to coil the rope into a big tin washbasin and sprinkle salt on it to keep the bait from rotting. By the time they reached the dock, unloaded and often helped boil the crabs at the crab house, they were exhausted.

One day a man came down from Virginia and started crabbing. He didn't use a set line, but brought rolls of chicken wire, and began shaping them into wire crab traps, which the residents had never seen. He told them there was no need to fish all night; they could stay home and "make love to the baby's mama." The people of Panacea were skeptical, but he started off into the sunrise one morning with his traps and a box of threadfin herring. The traps worked, they caught crabs while he stayed on the shore: they did all the work for him.

The fishermen immediately began buying rolls of chicken wire and building traps. The population of Panacea soared as it never had before because the men now stayed home at night. Fishermen were bringing in crabs by the ton — the crab traps enabled them to fish in foul weather; they were making more money with less effort, so to make even more money they built bigger boats and bought more powerful outboard motors. Of course their expenses soared and they had to work all the harder to pay for expensive gear.

Suddenly crab houses like weeds began to spring up all over Panacea. A crab house opened in Apalachicola and East Point, and down in Perry, Florida. Everybody started crabbing, even college students had traps set and made extra money. As the industry prospered, the crab houses installed giant steel steamers, erected bigger buildings with more tables where more women could pick more crab meat. One man, with technology from the industry in Maryland, put in a gigantic freezer plant so meat could be stockpiled.

In the middle 1950s and mid-1960s the crabbing industry boomed. The crabs seemed to be unlimited out in the bay, and it was nothing for a man to come back with 3000 or 4000 pounds of crab in a single day's catch. One man and his two sons broke the record and brought in 6500 pounds of crab, working 350 traps in a single afternoon.

Trap after trap would be snatched up, emptied of its contents and rebaited. Fisherman worked night and day striking schools of menhaden and selling them to the crab houses which sold them back to the crabbers at double price for bait. The men worked seven days a week, twelve hours a day and got while the getting was good. The wire traps were set in shallow estuaries around the marshes to catch the male crabs, as well as offshore where the females congregated. The traps have a bait cage with two or more funnels that lead into it. The crab, smelling the decaying fish within, crawls about the sides of the wire-meshed trap until it finds the opening to the funnel and crawls in. As many as forty pounds of blue crabs can end up in a single trap, although the average catch is much less.

The crabbers worked year round, in calm seas and stormy surfs; the ambitious one pulled their traps in freezing pouring rain, wearing yellow-and-black slicker suits. It didn't matter whether they caught males or females, small or big there were no closed seasons, no size limit and no conservation laws. Gravid females carrying sponge-egg masses were pulled out by tens of thousands of pounds. The crab houses cut the price on gravid females by two cents on the pound because the sponge, which was thrown out at the fish house, jacked up the weight, but the crabbers went right on pulling their traps. Periodically the fish houses drastically cut the price of the crabs. The fishermen griped but kept working. The fish houses bought new equipment, the owners built bigger and better houses, bought tractor-trailer trucks to haul crabmeat and fish up north, and still the price kept falling.

The landing where the crabbers went out in their skiffs looked like a crowded parking lot. The water was jammed with boats, littered with rotting bait, conchs and spider crabs discarded from the traps, and the oyster-shell ramp above the boat landing was covered with rusted-out pick-up trucks and old cars that busily roared up and down the rutted sand roads with noisy mufflers at all hours of the morning.

When the prices were high the crews would return to the dock exhausted but happy. They helped each other unload their weighted skiffs, piling the crabs into the old trucks, which sagged on their axles. They backed their trucks up to the loading ramps of the crab houses. Stone crabs were culled out, their claws broken off, and they were cooked and sold as epicurean delights.

Into the small hours of the morning the great cookers steamed and hissed as tons upon tons of blue crabs were killed and cooked, and dumped out on tables. Even with steadily declining prices the fishermen's economy boomed, their wives and children picked the meats, and refrigerated trucks roared out of Panacea, hauling the meat to New York, Maryland and Philadelphia markets.

When the price dropped below four cents a pound, the fishermen grumbled and told the fish-house owners they couldn't make a living. They had to catch an even greater quantity of crabs to pay their bills. After a few years the traps produced less and less from overfishing, and the checks at the end of the week were leaner and leaner. Where the rock-landing boat dock was once jammed with boats and cars, only a few remained, because the crabbers started going to Pensacola and even to Louisiana and Virginia, where the crabbing was better and the prices were high. But nonetheless, the existing crab stocks seemed to drop to nothing in a very few short years.

The packing houses laid off the women; only the fastest pickers stayed on. Eventually the industry disappeared almost entirely, and for many years it was difficult to find any quantity of crabs at all in the bays. It is not a bad thing to exploit a stock of marine organisms if proper conservation measures are practiced. A female blue crab produces 100,000 eggs—and under good conditions, lots of marshes, proper salinity, temperature and pH conditions, low pesticide levels, the crabs will multiply and thrive. But Wakulla and Franklin counties in north Florida have always resisted conservation efforts. Attempts to place closed seasons in Florida and prohibit the taking of sponge females were stopped cold by vote-hungry politicians. In these two beautiful but backward areas, there are few nursery ground areas closed to shrimping and no size limits are placed on speckled trout.

The state of Florida set up a state aquatic preserve system that would prohibit the use of state-owned submerged lands for land-fill and development, and prohibit shell mining and oil rigs. More than 20 aquatic preserves around the state had been proposed and accepted by the communities, but the Ochlockonee River Aquatic Preserve was killed by opposition from the county commissioners, politicians, and developers and fishermen who feared it would close these areas to fishing sometime in the distant future. At a local public hearing the conservationists were outnumbered three to one.

I cannot help but be depressed by the area's future. Panacea is not a Hudson River community where people have seen progress, factories and buildings until they want to vomit, and are now gallantly fighting to save what precious little bit of life is left in the overburdened waters. In Panacea the conservationists are a pitiful minority, voices crying in the wilderness.

I stand on my dock looking out at the green marshes of Fiddler's Point across the bay, one of the areas that so many want to turn into a gleaming white sandy beach, motels, neon lights and high-rise apartments. The marshes are worth fighting to save, and so are the crabs. There are still a few crabs that crawl up on the pilings of my dock, and children come down to fish for them with a string and a fish head, just as I did years ago when I first moved to Florida.

There is a difference though, it takes them all day to get a Styrofoam picnic chest full. Little more than a decade ago, when I was just a boy with time on my hands, it took only an exciting hour to snatch up a heaping bushel of blue crabs. Fishing for blue crabs is a poor man's sport because it takes only a little bait and string. The crab chews on the bait, gets all engrossed in its meal, and is too greedy to let go or is too engrossed in its meal to feel itself being lifted from the water and then rudely dumped into a bucket. And then it's dumped into scalding hot water. The blue crab with its frantic greed and big appetite readily enters traps, as the people who once caught them for a living soon will enter their own particular traps in their pursuit of the developer's fast buck.

There is only one hope for the estuaries in north Florida, and that is a federal coastal zoning law that will protect productive marshes from future development. There is talk of such a bill in Washington, but if something is not done soon it will be too late for north Florida.

If the environment is not substantially altered and conservation measures are placed on gravid females, the bumper crops of blue crabs may come back again the way I remember them almost 15 years ago when I first moved to Florida.

There are still a few crabbers who go out every morning and make a modest living at it. Even though the community has changed there are still a few houses that have crab traps piled up in their front yard. Fishermen keep tunnelboats and crabbing skiffs at the city dock. There should be crab fisherman because the blue crab is delicious and wonderful to eat and there should be plenty of them for everyone.

Blue crabs (*Callinectes sapidus*) make wonderful research material because they are alert and responsive animals. Scientists study their eyes, their nervous systems and their reproduction, and in past years we have shipped them out by the hundreds. They make excellent scavengers for large aquariums and will eat anything that lies dead on the bottom.

It is perhaps the most vicious and alert crab to be found anywhere, no sooner does your hand approach one than it stretches its long, pinching claws up at you, pincers extended and ready to latch onto your fingers. Crabbers use a special set of crab tongs that is most efficient at picking them up; only they latch on the tongs and the pincers must be undone or the chelae will break. When they are particularly disturbed or the chelae is damaged, the crab autotomizes and the leg stiffens and breaks off. They will regenerate a new one after a time.

They use their chelae for shredding their food, which they ravenously stuff into their mouths and in almost no time a blue crab can tear a fish to pieces, enthusiastically gobbling it down. If there is no fish to eat, they eat each other, and in a collection of crabs it is a constant struggle for survival of the fittest. If one is damaged, immediately they all converge upon it and rip it apart.

They have the right to be so defensive because I know of few marine animals with the exception of shrimp and lobsters that are so eagerly sought for food. Aside from man doing his usual job of gathering something tasty by the ton, sharks, sea turtles and any large fish eat adult blue crabs. The young are hungrily swallowed by smaller fish, rays and birds.

The young tend to live in shallow water, amidst the seagrass meadows, up creek beds and at the head of the bay where they can burrow into shallow mud. They are in the process of molting generally, particularly during the summer months, and are eagerly sought after by another grade of commercial fishermen. The soft-shell-crab fishing industry gathers the peelers by the thousands, keeps them in vats of running or recirculating sea water, and just as they molt out of their shell, they are removed and frozen. The soft-shell crab can be fried in its entirety, shell and all, and makes a tasty meal.

One of the primary difficulties in raising soft-shell blue crabs is keeping the hard crabs from tearing the soft crabs to pieces and devouring them. A man in the crab business must be constantly on the watch, removing the soft crabs as quickly as they molt.

When a number of crabs are taken by traps or by net and tossed into a bucket, you can expect the biggest mess of tangled, pinching crabs imaginable. Each crab has latched onto the leg or body of the adjoining crab, and if you lift one crab out there may be a chain of a dozen other individuals attached.

When collecting crabs for specimens where all limbs must be intact, it is necessary to keep them isolated from each other. They readily tear off appendages and pinch themselves to pieces. This is particularly true during transport when crabs are being shipped across country. A good technique, we found, is to wrap them individually in wet paper towels, covering up their eyes. Blocking their sight is most important, for once they are blind they lie still. If they are in a shallow tank and you walk anywhere near, immediately they raise their claws defensively and snap at you. And should you venture too close to the tank and forget about them, you might receive a savage pinch.

Menippe mercenaria
Stone Crab

The stone crab (*Menippe mercenaria*) reminds me of the great Old Man of the Mountain. There the crab sits in his burrow with his great massive claws folded up in front of him daring anyone to come close.

The stone crab in the south is prized as a great delicacy.

stone crab
Menippe mercenaria

Fishermen collect them, break the claws off and throw the crab back. If they survive that long in a defenseless condition, they will regenerate new massive claws over a period of a year. Farming stone crabs has been the interest of numerous entrepreneurs because the claws fetch close to two dollars a pound, but the rate of growth in the crab, according to investigations at the University of Miami, has proved too slow and cumbersome for commercial use.

So they are captured in crab traps along with blue crabs. In certain localities a wooden slat trap that resembles a lobster pot is used. In either case, if the trap is set on a bottom of flat lime rock or oyster reef, chances are it will get quite a few stone crabs. They dwell in crevices and small caves with only their massive brown claws tipped with black sticking out.

When you approach one it quickly draws back into its burrow. A good collector, wearing canvas gloves, can reach into the burrow and snatch the stone crab out. But you've got to watch those claws. Some of them are a full eight inches in length and so strong that the crab uses them to crush oysters, grinding the shell to bits with one claw, scooping out the meat and putting it into its mouth with the other.

Actually, no one has lost a finger from a stone crab to my knowledge. I know several crabbers who have received some vicious pinches from them, severe black-and-blue marks, but have not lost a finger. At one point I was digging around in our gravel-filled tanks for some specimen or other, and my finger found its way into the clutches of a monster stone crab and nearly got mangled.

A word at this point—when any big crab latches onto your finger, the worst thing you can do is snap the claw off. Even though you're in pain, the pain will be worse if you do so, because the claw gives a spasmodic tightening when suddenly broken off. The best thing to do is place crab, hand (or toe) and all, into a bucket of water and let it relax and it lets go of its own accord. Or you can take careful aim with a hammer and crush the claw at the base of the first joint where the muscle attaches. But if you miss you may be worse off than before. I remember one captain on a shrimp boat who had a big *Portunus* grab onto his toe. Shouting, he ordered the crew to bring him a bucket of water, and gently edged the crab into the bucket. Presently the crab tired of holding on and let go. The captain, in a rage, kicked the bucket over and stamped the crab to pieces.

Blue crabs, other portunid crabs and sluggish bottom-dwelling crabs can be the predominant part of a shrimp-boat catch. Therefore, it is very important that a fisherman protect his hands and other parts while culling through the catch. In the Gulf, I knew one deckhand who encountered a great deal of distress, all of it his own doing.

He had leaky pants, and parts of him were hanging out. And as he squatted over the catch taking out handfuls of shrimp, a blue crab reached up and grabbed a claw-full and hung on. The shrimper jumped and leaped and howled and hopped up and down the deck, supporting the crab with his hand but not daring to pull it off. Presently the rest of the crew, holding their sides with laughter, fetched him a bucket of water and the crab and the attached parts were placed in it. After what was described as a very long time the crab let go.

Sesarma reticulatum
Black Marsh Crab

The homely little black crabs that scuttle rapidly on wharf, dock and rock pile along the eastern coast of the United States are likely to be *Sesarma reticulatum*, the marsh-flat crab. These are grapsid crabs, akin to the rock crabs and land crabs that inhabit tropical areas, crabs that splash into the sea to forage for food or protection and then scramble back to the land where they live. All of them can stay submerged for long periods of time.

These crabs show a great preference for dwelling under logs, boards and rags strewn along the marshy, protected beaches. Turn the debris over, and it explodes with multitudes of little black *Sesarma*. Snatching them up takes some doing, because crabs run everywhere, by the hundreds at times, and you succeed in getting only one or two. In marshy areas where there is no civilization, and man has not succeeded in turning the littoral zone into a garbage dump, *Sesarma reticulatum* is content to dig holes into the mud just like the black fiddler crab, *Uca pugnax*.

Marsh crabs are not really seasonal, but you find many more of them in the summertime. I have seen them just cover the pilings and decking on our dock in July, yet in December only one or two can be found above ground. They will survive in the aquarium made of moist beach sand, and will eat any sort of carrion.

Ocypode quadrata
Ghost Crab

On the gleaming white, sandy beaches of the southeastern U.S. and Caribbean coasts, ghost crabs, (*Ocypode quadrata*) race down the beach like the wind, scuttling along on their tiptoes. Suddenly they stop still and blend perfectly into the sand — and you wonder if you ever saw them at all. They dig long burrows that go down as much as four feet, and waste no time in finding their way to the safety of their burrows.

We have at last discovered part of the secret of collecting *Ocypode*. Their burrows tunnel off at a 45° angle for a foot or two, then level off and descend again at another angle. By digging a little ways and finding where the burrow goes, you can head the tunnel off and dig directly down on top of the final burrow. Then using your hands, dig out until you feel the crab's pincers.

Ghost crabs can give you a mean, nasty pinch, and fingers meeting with a cornered crab can have a bad time of it. In fact, since it is a land animal and one must catch it on land, there is a good chance of your fingers being pinched faster than when handling an aquatic crab.

But there are easier ways to catch *Ocypode quadrata*. They are chiefly nocturnal, coming out after the sun has set, dancing over the sands in the darkness on their tiptoes, dashing into the sea when you approach, or ducking into their burrows. But when a blinding gasoline lantern comes within their range of sight, they freeze, and if you hold the light in front of you and make no sudden movement, you can get a net over the crab long before it has a chance to go anywhere.

Use a small-meshed dip net for collecting them; they can get so tangled up in larger meshes that untangling them can take half the night and there is a good chance of breaking their limbs. When released into the plastic bucket they will make a terrible clatter and scuffle as they continuously try to scale the sides, but they cannot get their pointed legs gripped onto the smooth plastic. At first they pinch each other, and several will die after they've lost their pincers.

When fishermen drag their seines on the shore and cull out the mullet, speckled trout, redfish and flounder from the anchovies, small croakers, pinfish and sting rays, which are regarded as trash, the ghost crab emerges from its burrow to feast on the spoils. That is if you're not too close, but watch from a considerable distance. It tears at the flesh with its scissorlike claws and devours the dead and dying fish. In some areas where there is much seaweed on a deposition beach, there are beach-hoppers and they bounce out of the decaying sea grass to feast upon the carrion.

If you happen upon a ghost crab in the midst of feeding and you cut it off from its burrow, the crab will dash wildly into the water and disappear into the waves only to emerge a few yards down the beach and run for the safety of its burrow. When the coast is clear and you've gone, it comes back to the food. You could say that the ghost crab is the sanitary engineer of the upper beaches, and helps eliminate a number of rotting fish.

In 1952 Marvin Wass, a marine biologist, at Florida State University wrote an account of *Ocypode* in his unpublished Master's thesis: "Individuals were frequently seen feeding on *Emerita* (mole crabs). The beach amphipod, *Talorchestia longicornis*, often extremely abundant and somewhat annoying at night because of its biting habits, is probably a major source of food to *Ocypode*. A collecting trip along the beach near the roadside picnic area on Alligator Point, September 8, 1952, in which three people participated, resulted in a catch of 50 ghost crabs."

It is interesting to see how that has changed. *Ocypode* is no longer vastly abundant on the beaches of Alligator Point; it would take quite a long while to get up 50 crabs, and almost all of them would be very small scrawny specimens. The *Talorchestia longicornis* beach-hoppers that were so annoying are not annoying anymore because there aren't any. *Emerita talpoida* (the mole crab) is hard to find, and perhaps much of this is due to the fact that the very beach which Marvin Wass had written about has eroded away. The wayside tables of the State Park are now bulkheaded with a sea wall, and if one wants to find any of these specimens in abundance, he must travel to such north Florida offshore islands as St. George, Dog Island and Cape San Blass.

We no longer collect ghost crabs from Alligator Point. There are still a number of them, and when I go for walks in the evening, I see them poised in front of their holes ready to dash back at any minute. A few meander down to the littoral and survey the cast-up seaweed, and join the sandpipers that search for food.

We have seen them on the harbor side of Alligator Point, where Wass said they never ventured. The beach washes away with each storm, and when it goes, the ghost crabs may too.

Shipping *Ocypode quadrata* was once an insurmountable problem. In order for a dozen to reach their destination, two dozen had to be sent. However, we found that if each crab was isolated in its own plastic bag with a little sand, they survived nicely and came through with flying colors after three days of transport.

Another trick in gathering *Ocypode* when there is no net, is to sneak up on one, grab a handful of beach sand and slap sand, hand and all, on top of the crab, giving a nice buffer between you and the scissorlike chelae.

Ocypode must be kept isolated in captivity. They are amphibious but not marine crabs, so a tankful of beach sand will keep them alive. The sand should be at least six inches deep, and there should be no more than two crabs per square foot; one crab per square foot is even better for keeping them alive.

Metaporhaphis calcarata
Arrow Crab

Among the Gulf weed or sargasso, small, delicate, brown arrow crabs dwell, looking so thin and spidery that any amateur collector who discovers one cannot help but call it a sea spider. They move slowly but very delicately, and are so well camouflaged that there can be a dozen in a cluster of sargasso or other seaweed and you'll never notice them.

But almost every dredge haul in Alligator Harbor produces one, and among the grass you can see the thin, spidery legs flexing. It is a widespread species occurring from North Carolina to the equator.

Almost every large aquarium has arrow crabs; often they are in small tanks by themselves because they are such striking animals. We have found them to survive well under aquarium conditions, and have enjoyed watching them almost float across the bottom when they move.

When preserving this species you must be careful of their autotomizing. They can throw off their legs faster than almost any crab that I know of.

Libinia emarginata
Spider Crab

The drab brown, monstrously ugly spider crab lies on the sandy bottom, half-buried in the sand. At first, early in the season, only a few are found here and there on the flats. None is found in September, or October, and they only begin to appear in November. But from then on, *Libinia emarginata* becomes the most familiar sight of the seashore, particularly to one who is involved in commercial fishing.

Gradually more and more appear in the shrimp nets. At first it's one or two, and you hardly notice them, then 15 or 20, and when the season is on at full pitch, you are not surprised when a third or more of the catch is made up of *Libinia*. They enter crab traps along with the blue crabs, and from December through March they reach their peak, and 100-pound boxes are loaded up with them.

At first crabbers threw them away, but now they find they can be ground up for chicken feed or fed to hogs. Although the meat in the claws is tasty enough, the exoskeleton is so tough that picking this crab is almost impossible, and there isn't that much meat, anyway. However, even with such low-priced markets as feed and pig food, the biomass is so cheap that few fishermen are seriously bothering with them and they are often dumped overboard as quickly as they are hauled up and the traps are emptied.

Looking at crab boats piled high with boxes, you begin to wonder if anything can be done with spider crabs. They occur around the Atlantic coast and reach seasons of peak abundance. Some of the crabs have a two-foot spread and resemble in superficial appearance the Alaskan King Crab.

The sexes of *Libinia emarginata* can be readily spotted. Chelipeds of male *Libinia* crabs are much larger than those of the females. The traditional way of telling by looking at the apron works just as well: males have a narrow, pointed apron, females have a broad-based one.

The scientific community has made use of *Libinia* on a limited scale. It has been used in embryology and as an example of a strict stenohaline osmoconformer, meaning that if the sea water is diluted with fresh water, *Libinia* will absorb the fresh water proportionately. Consequently, a heavy rain will cause them to bloat and can kill off a large population of spider crabs.

But once salinity is stable, they will thrive in a simple marine aquarium. They prefer a salinity of 28°/oo although they can go higher or lower, providing the salinity remains constant. We have kept some for 18 months and they are fine specimens and very hardy, highly recommended for those who want the beast as well as the beauty.

Calappa flammea
Flame-streaked Box Crabs

Calappa flammea, the flame-streaked box crab, has many common names. It has been called the shamefaced crab, miser crab, and queen crab. The first two names are given because it holds its chelae pressed tightly in front of its mouth, like a miser greedily counting his gold, or someone hiding his eyes.

Whenever the local populace gives a name to a marine invertebrate it is because it is good to eat, spectacularly colorful or harmful and can inflict pain and suffering, and *Calappa* is all three.

It is shaped something like a box, very square and striking in appearance with orange and white stripes, and it covers its face with large, flat chelae which are capable of delivering one of the most excruciatingly painful pinches to be found anywhere in the sea. The flattened claws have a scissors action, and when it catches a piece of thumb the victim is lucky if he doesn't faint from the pain. The little meat that is found in its claws has a succulent lobsterlike taste.

Aside from pinching people that are trying to catch it, the crab uses its flattened powerful chelae like a can opener to open snail shells occupied by hermit crabs and remove the inhabitant inside. This is one of the few instances where the hermit crab becomes vulnerable to predation.

What is so amazing about *Calappa* in addition to its opening shells like a can opener is its pumping ability. It draws water in through its gills and pumps it out through an opening above its mouth. And when you hold the crab an inch below the water so the pump can catch its prime, a steady stream of water comes up through the top of the crab, almost reminding one of a whale spout. The flamed-streaked box crab continues to blow a water spout until you lift it far out of water and it loses its prime.

Hepatus epheliticus
Calico Crab

The calico crab (*Hepatus epheliticus*) represents one of the most attractive, colorful crabs to be found along the southeastern coast of the United States. It is small, round and compact, and covered with large reddish-brown splotches on a whitish tan background, making it very striking. Its coloration is similar to *Calappa*, and an aquarium with both specimens is going to have eye-catching appeal. Because of its exceptional beauty it often appears embedded in blocks of plastic placed in a beachlike setting.

Like *Calappa*, the calico crab burrows into the ground, coming out only at night. To watch them squat over a patch of sand, kick their legs and settle down with only the top part of their head and eyes protruding is a delight. It seems a pity that so much color must be hidden in the sand.

Hepatus has powerful chelae which they use to rip fish and even snails apart. To get pinched by one is a memorable experience, but not as bad as the box crab's pinch. But just drop a dead fish in a tank with one and you'll see what an efficient job it does tearing the fish to pieces.

Since it doesn't move around a great deal it has a low oxygen demand and lives very well in aquariums. They can tolerate moderate to low salinity, since they frequent estuaries at certain times of the year.

We have found calico crabs to be highly abundant, and have

gathered over 100 specimens from an individual crab fishermen's discards. They reach a seasonal peak in the springtime, when gravid females are quite common. In periods of extreme heat or extreme cold they migrate offshore. *Hepatus* ranges from North Carolina to Texas, occurring on sandy rock bottoms.

Portunus gibbesi
Iridescent Swimming Crab

The bright glare of a gasoline lantern shone upon the water brings many strange night-faring creatures to the surface. Attracted and blinded by the light, shrimp appear; various swimming polychaete worms rise, doing a gyrating dance; needle fish and minnows dart and splash in the darkness away from the light. And almost always the ghostly forms of the swimming crab (*Portunus gibbesi*) and blue crabs paddle along the surface across the lighted water and then disappear into darkness.

Portunus gibbesi has modified swimming legs that look like paddles, enabling it to swim efficiently. Blue crabs (*Callinectes sapidus*) swim as well, but not as lightly and gracefully as *Portunus*. These little crabs have a lavender-purple color, and are easily distinguished from the blue crab by their long, slender chelae. They seldom reach the size of *Callinectes* and therefore do not have a commercial importance.

But I do not know of any crab that reaches their peak of abundance. We have taken as many as 500 pounds in a one-hour tow in the shrimp net, and they composed more than 70 percent of the catch. Since they are agile swimmers they can move inshore overnight and suddenly take over a whole bottom community, and almost as suddenly move away.

They reach their population peak during the winter months. In west Florida, the greatest volume was taken November through January, and after January they go offshore into deeper water.

Portunus does not make a very good specimen for the aquarium because it is active and its oxygen requirement is high. Even when specimens are individually bagged with oxygen and isolated, there is a good chance that more than half the specimens will be dead when you arrive back at the laboratory, and half again die the following day. Once the initial mortality is over, the remaining specimens are reasonably hardy in a well-oxygenated volume of water.

When *Portunus* is not swimming, it burrows into sand bottom. They too are fond of carrion, but I have seen them feast upon worms and small soft clams. A certain species, *Portunus sayi*, dwells in floating sargasso weed, and on one expedition to Bermuda on the Woods Hole oceanographic research vessel *Atlantis II* we collected numerous individuals in a small amount of the floating Gulf weed hundreds of miles out at sea. These have assumed a completely pelagic existence as the sea bottom beneath the weed was over 14,000 feet down, where they do not live.

Squilla empusa
Mantis Shrimp
___

The beachcomber may spend years digging along the flats and never encounter the mantis shrimp (*Squilla empusa*), although just below the tidal zone they may occur by the thousands, coming out from their sandy burrows at night to swim along the bottom with the penaeid shrimp and other night creatures. A shrimp net pulled over a sandy, muddy bottom will produce quite a number, depending on the location and time of year.

Although there are several stomatopods (eight-legged shrimplike crustaceans) the most common one to be found in the Gulf is *Squilla empusa*. And *Squilla* is a strange-looking little dragon with chelae bent like a praying mantis, a flattened body with stalked, green opalescent eyes and cutting, jagged uropods on the tail. Their chelae or striking legs are used in neurophysiological experiments for high-speed muscle, and with good reason; in a flash they can strike out with their fine claws and gash one's fingers.

They are one of the many reasons why commercial fishermen wear heavy, rubber-coated gloves when culling the catch, and it would be wise for a collector who handles them to do the same. There are some good ways of picking them up by hand, one is to simply fold them in half so that head touches tail. This stops them from flexing and twisting and makes them easy to handle.

It seems that *Squilla* makes good bait, although one might wonder what would want to eat it. Swallowing a mantis shrimp must be similar to swallowing a razor blade, but nonetheless I have found them in the stomach contents of tuna in the Indian Ocean, and in the stomachs of several sharks. Black sea bass readily gobbled them down. Using this deductive reasoning, we carried a few pounds of them taken on the shrimp boat to the snapper banks and practically loaded the boat down with a small grouper and sea bass.

Off Pensacola they could be harvested in commercial quantities. I once saw the deck of a shrimp trawl knee deep with them, and a sight it was too, with their bending, flexing and clawing bodies beating their gills frantically back and forth. They had to be shoveled off the deck.

Squilla empusa lives well in a salt-water aquarium. We found they survived best when placed in a sand aquarium that had gravel on the bottom and six inches of coarse sand above it. The mantis shrimp immediately dug a deep burrow with an entrance and an exit, and for a while we thought it had disappeared. However, one day I dug it out of its burrow and found it was a female distended with eggs. Unfortunately the eggs did not hatch in captivity, so we couldn't determine whether or not "Squilla farming" would be profitable.

Gonodadylus oerstedi
Rock Mantis Shrimp

When the rock dredge is hauled aboard in the deeper waters of the northern Gulf, it is filled with uncountable treasures: large limestone rocks overgrown with bright scarlet sponges, rough brick-red bryozoans shaped like a cup and hordes of glistening tunicates. There are lion's-paw scallops and sunray clams, and rocks covered with turkey-wings. Little octopuses wriggle out from the crevices, and almost invariably there will be a number of jade green or maroon-color rock mantis shrimp (*Gonodadylus oerstedi*) that seldom exceed two inches in length.

At first you will be delighted with this bouncing, bobbing creature that scuttles over the deck, but when you pick it up, almost invariably you'll receive a painful slash of its uropods, which causes profuse bleeding.

In the aquarium *Gonodadylus oerstedi* is a killer, and before you know it, even the fish in the tank are found with gashes in their sides. All your cleaning shrimp will be devoured. The little rock mantis shrimp does all this subversive damage at night however, and remains hidden in its limestone burrow during the daylight hours. Nevertheless, despite its aggressive qualities, many salt-water aquarists prize them as fine specimens because of their color and form and add them to their collections whenever possible.

Preservation

The preservation of marine arthropods is not difficult except that many forms have the ability to autotomize—throw off limbs when severely irritated. The amphipods, copepods, isopods, ostracods, mysids and any other little water-flea can be preserved in the same manner. It matters not whether they are bobbing skeleton shrimp on seaweed of hydroid colonies, tiny copepods living in marsh muds, amphipods dredged up from the sea bottom, or scuttling isopods—all may be dropped directly into alcohol.

The fragile pycnogonid sea spiders may contract violently and throw off their legs, pistol shrimp will shed their large chela and small xanthid and porcelain crabs break off all their legs unless insensitized prior to fixing them. Although chloral hydrate, menthol and other anesthetics have been used, I have found nothing is superior to alcoholized sea water for insensitizing crustaceans.

Generally amphipods, copepods and ostracods may be treated alike and dropped directly into 70 percent alcohol. In sorting dredge-haul collections these smaller forms may be initially preserved in 5 percent Formalin, which more or less preserves their color. Alcohol causes many to turn red instantly.

Commensal and parasitic crustaceans such as parasitic copepods, isopods and barnacles are either surgically removed from host animals or removed by soaking the host in 10 percent alcohol for two hours and then screening the alcoholized sea water through a fine-meshed net. The sediment is then placed in 70 percent ethyl alcohol and later examined for parasites.

Barnacles, like many other minor crustaceans, may be preserved by simply dropping them into 70 percent alcohol and changing the solution once or twice, depending on how much discoloration occurs. Many specialists who work with them prefer the cirripeds contracted within the shell, and this happens when the animals are preserved without prior anesthetization. The barnacles are studied by dissecting the specimens, the mouth plates are opened and removed with forceps and the cirripods are gently pulled out along with their muscles and gonads.

To prepare barnacles for demonstration requires more work. As they are jumping in and out of their shells, a little alcohol is dripped in, and the jumping is slowed down. A few minutes later a little more is poured in, and still more, and eventually they become stupefied.

When the animal no longer moves, the cirri appendages should be barely extended from the mouth, and these should be gently pulled out and fluffed up with forceps and preserved in 70 percent alcohol.

The only obstacle you face in preserving large decapod crustaceans is the animal's ability to autotomize—throw off limbs when frightened or uncomfortable. This same defense mechanism is used when a fish or crab seizes its leg or pincer and it snaps it off at the joint and runs leaving the predator with only a portion of a meal.

Often shrimp, lobsters and crabs arrive at the laboratory dead, having died of suffocation or overheating in the field. And since their taxonomic characteristics are not damaged, they may be plunged directly into preservative with excellent results. Their classification depends upon the contour of their shells, the shape of their legs, the number of marginal hairs, the number of segments, whether they overlap, and so on. None of these characteristics is lost during preservation.

Even if a species has autotomized, and arrives in a specialist's laboratory as nothing but a carapace and ten legs or so broken apart in a jar of alcohol, the specimen can still be identified. But it is best to keep them from autotomizing, because a complete specimen looks much better, and the process of keeping them intact is not difficult.

Many forms may be immersed directly in alcohol and killed without their contracting and throwing off their legs, but this appears to be an individual response. Spider crabs are a good example, out of 25 specimens preserved in this fashion, 20 may die and retain all their appendages, but five will shed from two to five limbs apiece.

Some biologists kill their crabs by slowly adding fresh water to the sea water, or dripping in weak alcohol. Magnesium sulfate works slowly to anesthetize crabs before killing them.

We have found an excellent way of killing large crabs quickly and efficiently. Simply inject them in the heart with concentrated Formalin, inserting the needle at the rear of the carapace in the soft tissue at the base of a leg. In a few moments the animals stiffen and die; however, a word of caution should be applied here: do not allow the crab to pinch or even touch anything during the death spasms because it will immediately break off its chela. Large lobsters may also be killed in this fashion without shedding legs or antennae.

Hermit crabs will often draw into their shells and remain completely contracted and out of sight if immersed directly into preservative. They may be killed protruding from their shells by adding alcohol slowly to the sea water. When making a series of hermit crabs, a number of them should be preserved after completely removing them from the shell. No matter what treatment is used, some individuals will hang onto the whorls of the snail shell, making their removal most difficult or impossible without tearing the crab's soft abdomen. These are best removed by crushing the snail shell in a vise or gently cracking it with a hammer and then removing the hermit crab.

There is much argument among specialists about the best preservative that should be used on larger crustaceans. Some say only 10 percent buffered Formalin, others insist on 70 percent alcohol because, they say, Formalin renders the specimens too brittle. If large crustaceans are to be preserved in alcohol, make sure there is plenty of alcohol available to penetrate the tissues inside their chitinous shell and prevent them from mascerating. Two or more complete alcohol changes will be required.

Many crabs, hermit crabs, shrimp and lobsters can be dried and will serve as museum specimens which can be used for identification and mounted for display. This is done by injecting them with preservative if they are large, letting them soak in Formalin or alcohol for a few days, and then drying them in the shade. The legs and chelae can be positioned into a feeding or walking form.

Store or display dried crabs and lobsters in small boxes so their legs will not be damaged or broken. On specimens used for display or ones that are frequently handled by students, they can be dipped in fiberglass or plastic resin to give the limbs resilience.

25.
Phylum Echinodermata
Starfish, Sea Urchins, Brittlestars and Sea Cucumbers

The echinoderms are made up of five major classes of spiny-skinned organisms. Not a single echinoderm occurs anywhere in fresh water; they are all marine animals, which makes the phylum unique in the animal kingdom. Perhaps this is why starfish have become the symbol of the sea. The most characteristic feature of the group is the minute calcareous spicules of skeletal ossicles which form an external skeleton. These ossicles can be embedded in the skin, as in the case of sea cucumbers (class Holothuroidea), or they can be fused together to form a common shell called a test in the Echinoidea — sea urchins and sand dollars. The brittlestars (class Ophiuroidea) and the starfish (class Asteroidea) have articulated ossicles enabling them to move about with a great deal of flexibility.

There is one other class, Crinoidea, that will not be given any attention in this book. The sea lilies are found when one is dredging down 200 or 300 feet, out in the Gulf and along many areas of the tropical Atlantic. One bottom area about 100 miles off Tampa, Florida, must be paved with crinoids. I have seen them in shallow water of the tropics, but they do not occur within the range of the beachcomber using this book.

It seems difficult to believe that starfish and the wormlike sea cucumber all belong to the same phylum. Add the brittlestars with their furiously lashing legs, and the spiny sea urchins, and you have a most confused group. The best clue to the echinoderm's relationship to other phyla is their larval forms, which resemble the larvae of certain lower chordates which are related to man.

Class Asteroidea

Starfish, the Asteroidea, are the symbol of marine life. Every seashore has them, they live attached to rocks, or they crawl on the sand. They live up in the intertidal zone or out in the depth of the ocean.

And anyone who has been to the seashore will want to return with one as a trophy, either in alcohol or dried. Along the northern coasts the most common form, *Asterias forbesi*, lives attached to rocks, feeding on mussels and oysters. In fact they are one of the largest pests in New England and in recent years have seriously threatened the oyster industry.

It takes virtually no time for the starfish to creep over an oyster bed, pulling itself along by its multitude of little, tubed feet armed with sucker discs. And when it finds an oyster it wants to eat, bends over it and begins a long, steady pressure of prying the valves apart. Eventually the oyster weakens, it can't stand the antagonistic strain against it, and slowly, surely it begins to open. Then the big starfish drops its stomach into the oyster and digests its soft parts and soon the shell lies open, empty, and the starfish slides onto the next victim.

In no time at all a thousand or so starfish can converge upon an oyster bar and almost overnight completely wipe it out, leaving it strewn with empty shells.

But to some the starfish has a commercial importance. It is used in nearly every zoology class in the country, and commercial supply houses collect them by the thousands and embalm them in drums. They charter large fishing boats with a dredge to go out to deep water and drag over the bottom and heap their decks with starfish. After they are embalmed in Formalin they are culled for size.

Souvenir shops also seek starfish, and gather them in dredges and dry them by the thousands on wire racks after soaking them in Formalin. But most of the time the effort is not to save starfish for any purpose, but is concentrated on how to destroy them. At one time oyster fishermen used to hack them to pieces savagely and throw them over the side. If the center disc portion of the starfish wasn't damaged, new starfish would be regenerated from those pieces and there would be an even bigger enemy force.

Astropecten articulatus
Pointed Sand Star

When the ribbed sand is exposed by wind-blown tides, you will find the sand star *(Astropecten articulatus)*. But chances are against finding one everytime you go out, because they are generally rare, even on southern beaches. Usually they are seen completely buried, only a thin layer of sand over them. Only the sandy form of a perfect star depicts their presence.

Astropecten is adapted for the sandy shore habitat, and its slightly pointed tubed feet help it glide rapidly over the sand. It feeds primarily on minute gastropods that live in the sand. It slides on, finds a snail, hovers above it and then drops its entire stomach out, engulfs and devours the little creature, and continues sliding along looking for another. Their tubed feet are not flattened or modified for clinging to rocky surfaces, nor are they suited for surviving in rough, pounding weather. Their tubed feet are pointed and without suckers. They glide over the sand almost on tiptoes, moving along at a fairly rapid rate, covering 10 yards or so in an hour's time. And on the seashore, this can be long enough to move out of the shallows, where they can be picked up, into deep water, out of the way of your dredge or net.

Astropecten will not break off its arms like the sand star *Luidia*. They generally survive for months in a good aquarium with a sand or gravel filter, and will eat bits of shrimp. We have noticed that when the gravel turns black from accumulated hydrogen sulfide, the end of *Astropecten* is not far off, so the closed-system aquarium should be watched closely.

At certain times of the year, *Astropecten articulatus* becomes abundant. The exposed, outer beaches of St. Joe and Panama City are sometimes covered with them, and we have seen *Astropecten*

325

articulatus make up a large percentage of a dredge haul when pulled over sandy bottom. The clam boats operating in St. Joe often drag them in by the bushel and cull through the catch.

The pointed sand star is a rather beautiful starfish, not very typical, because its pointed arms are completely symmetrical. Its colors range from orange to purple on its dorsal surface. It looks like the perfect star, and makes an attractive addition to a dried collection or even when hung on a fish net along with dried seashells, sea whips, sea horses, etc. Since it is rather soft-tissued, a good day's soaking in alcohol will cure it thoroughly before drying.

The *Astropectinidae* have no anus; their mouth serves a dual purpose. They are more primitive than other stars because they lack cribriform organs.

Echinaster spinulosus
Spiny Orange Starfish

Echinaster spinulosus is a bright orange to grayish-orange species, covered with minute short spines, and it is restricted to west Florida and the deeper waters off Alabama in its distribution. A related species, *Echinaster sentus*, ranges further up the Atlantic coast into the Carolinas and down into the Florida Keys. *E. spinulosus* is truly an animal we can claim as belonging to the elite group of creatures that live no place other than the Gulf of Mexico.

However, despite its obscure distribution, the spiny orange starfish is well known in the souvenir business. Almost all the little packages of souvenirs from Florida containing dried sea horses, shells, gorgonians, etc., have a number of *Echinaster spinulosus* in them. Apparently it is much easier to find them in their desirable juvenile stages than the common Atlantic species, *Asterias forbesi*, that is abundant enough to be used for this purpose.

Echinaster spinulosus can be considered a denizen of the sea grass communities, although it is often found on sandy-shore habitats. However, on such sandy shores, patches of sea grass are not far away. And often, when swimming along, you can see the grass peppered with juveniles about the size of a quarter. These are highly desirable specimens for the aquarium because of their size. Of all the starfish I have worked with, on all coasts, *Echinaster* is best suited to the aquarium and survives beautifully at room temperature in a wide range

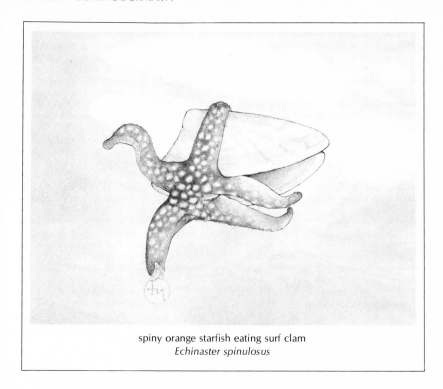

spiny orange starfish eating surf clam
Echinaster spinulosus

of salinities and pH variations. When a tank is allowed to go to pot, and one by one the inhabitants die off, it will almost invariably be the spiny orange starfish that is surviving in eutrophication, high salinity from evaporation and a low pH. The only specimens that do not survive well are *Echinaster* that are highly gravid and about to spill out eggs. These often expire even with the best care, but these may be old animals close to death anyway.

Echinaster is like all other starfish, sporadic in nature. They can move onto a limestone rock shelf and cover the bottom everywhere, and a few days later they are gone. Then, when you are least expecting it, they appear in a grass flat creeping over the bottom devouring snails. Sometimes they are so thick that a diver swimming along can fill a sack with them. Working hard, a man with a sack can gather 200 in an hour or less. As with so many other marine invertebrates, there isn't much exciting about collecting starfish. If it's there, it's moving along very, very slowly, and you stoop down, pick it up. The excitement comes in finding them when you're looking for them.

Echinaster sometimes occurs intertidally, but more frequently it is found in abundance beyond the mark of mean low water; or it dwells in shallow tide pools, browsing among algae or bryozoans.

Luidia clathrata
Gray Sand Star

Luidia clathrata is a grayish, sometimes slightly pink, sand star with five rather long, rough arms. Although occasionally found in mud, this species prefers coarse, firmly packed sugar sands and sometimes occurs so abundantly in the Gulf of Mexico that shrimpers find themselves culling hundreds of pounds of Luidia clathrata overboard with their shrimp catches. The Luididae have no intestines, no intestinal caeca or anus, and waste material is regurgitated through its mouth. The tubed feet are without suckers, and they are adapted for moving swiftly along the sands.

If you wish to keep Luidia clathrata unbroken and intact,

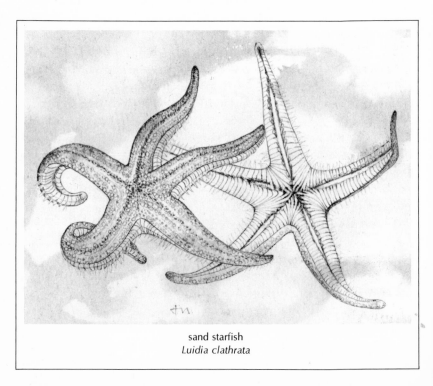

sand starfish
Luidia clathrata

considerable attention must be given to not disturbing it after collection. They are quick to autotomize—throw off their arms. First they writhe and twist up, and then suddenly one or more arms break off quite near the center disc of the sand star. They don't necessarily do this when disturbed by man or animal; I have seen some stranded on low tide that manage to autotomize in the process of digging down into the sand to keep damp and cool.

One nice feature about *Luidia clathrata* is its great mobility, and the flexibility of its arms. In a sea-water table you can flip them over on their back and watch them hunch up, writhe and twist until they turn over. Their whitish, elongated tubed feet are very powerful, and the sand stars manage to propel themselves over the bottom with great rapidity. The struggling, waving and flexing of hundreds of tubed feet on an inverted *Luidia clathrata* is something worth watching.

Along the sea floor, *Luidia clathrata* prefers to burrow down several inches in the coarse sand, and pass water from underneath its body with a ciliary action, passing it out through pores along its dorsal surface. They devour snails and perhaps small clams, and after a severe storm *Luidia clathrata* may be lying as far as the eye can see along the shoreline. Generally they make good aquarium animals if an adequate bed of sand is provided. However, the specimens that are freshly collected, even though they may appear very much alive, and wriggling their big oarlike tubed feet, if burned by the sun, or dehydrated by the chilling winds, will expire in the aquarium within a short while.

The reaction of most people upon seeing a starfish for the first time is to ask whether it is alive. At first they appear motionless, and even when you pick them up, they are slow to react and move their ambulatory tubed feet. But if a starfish is whole, has its color and a firm texture, generally it is alive. When they turn mushy in the tanks, their color fades, and no movement is detected in their tubed feet then you know they have expired.

Luidia alternata
Mottled Sand Star

Luidia alternata is a very distinct starfish in its adult form. It has very large arms covered with pronounced spines, and its color is mottled or splotched with dark brown against a yellowish background.

In its younger stages *Luidia alternata* appears as a brownish color. But regardless of its age, this species has the most amazing ability of breaking its arms off of any starfish in the sea.

Even when you take great pains to keep them alive, you might find at the end of a collecting day that they have broken each arm into at least two pieces. Of course the water temperature in the bucket has much to do with it; on warm days when the oxygen in the water is quickly consumed, *Luidia alternata* autotomizes very quickly.

Luidia alternata is a very large starfish, often attaining a diameter of 16 inches. Dried and mounted, it makes a fine addition to a display collection of organisms.

It seems about as hardy as *Luidia clathrata* in an aquarium, which may not be saying a great deal. We have had younger specimens live for months, the older animals appear to do less well, but if given special attention in a tank, they should do nicely.

We have cut open the disc of *Luidia* and have found them to engulf very large snails, including *Fasciolaria hunteria* and young *Pleuroploca gigantea*. The starfish slide over the sand, moving their arms in an almost serpentine fashion, and upon touching burrowing gastropods, converge upon them. They lower their voluminous stomachs and engulf the snails. Soon their entire discs are gorged with their prey, making it quite apparent that they have eaten.

On Port St. Joe beaches where *Luidia alternata* is frequently found on the low-tide mark, we have cut a number of them open and found a variety of small gastropods, and on occasion a surf clam. As many as 40 pigmy whelks *(Nassarius vibex)* were taken from the stomach of a single *Luidia alternata*.

Their pointed, tubed feet are very sensitive to touch and may aid the starfish in seeking its prey. While they are not adapted to clinging to surfaces or surviving intense waves pounding on their backs, the tubed feet help them glide over the sand and assist them in kicking the sand particles out of the way so they can burrow down out of sight, or brush the sand away from their burrowing prey.

When such a starfish is turned on its back, it gives a very exciting display of frantic wriggling of its tubed feet, and twisting and writhing of its arms. I have seen a great, beautiful mottled *Luidia alternata*, freshly dredged up, twist and contort and finally autotomize, all within 15 seconds after it was dumped from the net.

Aboard the boat when they have been dredged up, this self-destruction can be prevented. If they are immediately placed in a bucket of sea water that is packed in ice, or bags of frozen water placed directly in the sea water with the starfish, excitability can be slowed down greatly and they will not break up.

If sand stars are to be preserved for drying, they can be plunged directly into 90 percent isopropyl or ethyl alcohol and will be killed so quickly they won't have time to autotomize. I knew one fishermen in the Gulf who liked to save starfish and take them home to dry. He learned a technique for getting them to dry out without throwing off their legs: he would take his heavy fist and pound the starfish as soon as it came up, killing it brutally, but stopping it from breaking to pieces.

Starfish and brittlestars have to move their legs first to throw them off. This is not the same autotomizing mechanism that crabs have. In a general respect it is similar to nemerteans and polychaetes that have to twist themselves into knots or violently contract before breaking, and if not given that opportunity they will die in an undamaged condition.

Class Echinoidea

The sea urchins, along with sand dollars, comprise the class Echinoidea. In general sea urchins can be compared to pin cushions; they appear as a round ball with spines bristling out in every direction. Some, like *Diadema*, the spiny urchin from tropical waters, have very long, sharp, projecting spines that have a poisonous protein in them, and when you step on one, or touch it while diving, you'll suffer a painful sting reminiscent of a wasp's. They are quite responsive, and as you swim at them, they turn their spines in your direction, similar to antiaircraft guns following the path of a plane.

Most beachcombers find sea-urchin tests cast upon the beach, and these round balls, with rough, slightly knobby surfaces, are devoid of spines, and often the novice finds it difficult to relate the round ball and the spiny pincushion as being the same animal.

Sea urchins are an important animal for biological research. They are used as classical demonstration and dissection animals in schools, but even more important they are classical material in embryology.

Among cell physiologists, all the large, conspicuous species of both the Atlantic and Pacific coasts are well known, and their breeding cycles are closely followed because research programs are usually built around the sexual maturity of sea urchins. For example, one investigator may get *Arbacia punctulata* from Woods Hole in the summer months, when they are producing their maximum number of eggs, which divide readily after insemination, and then go to Carolina coast specimens in the fall, Florida specimens in the winter, and do without material during the late spring because they are not fertile enough for precise experimentation.

Some investigators work with different species from all over the coast, using *Strongylocentrotus* from the Pacific coast during the winter, and *Lytechinus pictus* throughout the summer.

Not only are sea urchins sought by biological collectors, many nationalities prize their gonads as an epicurian delight. I have heard biologists complain that hordes of Italians, Chinese and Greeks converge on the tidal rocks of the Pacific coasts, carrying wicker baskets, and clean the rocks of sea urchins, leaving the biologist to hunt new areas to exploit urchins for a more noble purpose. And in Boston Harbor, I have been aboard commercial fishing vessels where fishermen pick *Echinarius* from their trawls and crack the edible gonads — and I found the urchins to be highly tasty as well.

But, it seems that the most expert collectors of sea urchins are the gulls, far better, in fact, than any collector I have known. When the tide drops there may be a running competition between collector and gull as to who gets the urchin first. The gulls wrench them off the rocks or pick them up from the exposed grass beds with their talons, carry them high in the air and let them come crashing down and, like the epicurean Italians and Chinese, they feast on the gonads.

Sea urchins are best handled with tongs because many species have long, needly spines that readily penetrate fingers and break off. When the spines break off in your fingers they are often impossible to remove completely, and gradually your skin heals around the embedded spine and works it toward the surface. If you handle any quantity of sea urchins, thick leather gloves should be used, because a handful of spines can make further collecting a miserable experience. Although *Arbacia* spines are slightly venomous, they are not as painful as *Diadema*, but those wounds fester and become infected more readily than those from any other sea urchin that I know of. It may take several weeks or even months before all the spines work out.

It is interesting to note that while biologists at Woods Hole have complained about collectors diminishing stocks of sea urchins, on the west coast of the United States, the kelp industries and a number of biologists work avidly to exterminate sea urchins. In the last few years they have undergone a massive population explosion because the sea otters have been hunted to near extinction for their fur, and sea otters were the sea urchins' chief predator. Furthermore, sea urchins are nourished by sewage discharges and their numbers have continued to multiply. Like a horde of locusts they converge on kelp beds, devouring the young shoots and causing the plants to break off and wash up on the beaches.

When the kelp is destroyed so is the ecological balance of the region because the tall plants are a jungle that provide food and shelter for countless thousands of marine invertebrates and fish. Kelp is used in 300 products including cellophane, paper and glues and it has a great economic importance.

The kelp companies employ divers to smash the urchins with hammers and have dumped quick-lime on the urchins, but this treatment can kill other soft-bodied bottom-dwelling invertebrates. Like removing the starfish that have undergone a population explosion in the Indo-Pacific, it is a slow and tedious process.

However, sea urchins do have a value, and are consumed by the hundreds of thousands in the teaching and research industry, so perhaps there is a possibility of overlap between the two industries.

Arbacia punctulata
Purple Sea Urchin

The purple sea urchin (*Arbacia punctulata*) has become a classical animal for embryology, and has been eagerly sought by scientists and collectors alike. Since it ranges along the entire eastern seaboard into Texas, it has achieved popularity in the laboratory. In fact, at one time there was considerable fear that the species had been radically diminished in Woods Hole by researchers who gathered them from the rock piles. The Supply Department dredged them by the thousands and as soon as they were brought into the laboratory they were consumed. In the early 1950s hardly a purple sea urchin was to be found anywhere, and the Supply Department's vessels began to harvest them from Long Island Sound.

But *Arbacia punctulata* began coming back to Woods Hole in the 1960s and has remained abundant ever since. From my observations of their seasonal migrations in north Florida, it is possible that their diminishing numbers may not be due to overcollecting, but may be seasonal population variations. For example, in 1964 thousands of *Arbacia punctulata* frequented Alligator Harbor, the following year they were fewer, and finally disappeared. Then in 1968 they began to appear in large numbers again, and finally they climaxed their migrations along Shell Point when we collected many *Arbacia* from the intertidal reef in one morning.

There are stable populations that more or less remain on rocky jetties, and then there are hosts of them that slowly rove over grass beds and sandy, shelly bottoms. Along the rocks, when the tide goes out and the green algae are exposed, *Arbacia* spines can be seen sticking out of the tide-pool waters. They adhere to the rocks with their minute sucker discs and scrape off the algae with their Aristotle's lantern. Often a colony of *Arbacia* can clean the algae growths completely from a rocky-shore community and can become a detriment.

The mechanics of collecting large numbers of *Arbacia punctulata* are relatively simple. They can be easily dredged when they are abundant on the sandy, shelly bottom, but damage to the animals and breakage of their spines may result, and can cause shedding of their eggs and sperm. Therefore, picking them off rocks and jetties is more desirable. Wear heavy leather or canvas gloves while picking them up because their spines are very sharp.

Generally *Arbacia* stays hidden from the battering surf, far down in the rocks and away from currents. Some even chew holes into calcareous algae patches and make a type of rocky burrow. *Arbacia* with its extended needly spines is not easily dislodged. You can pull them off with your hands, or push them sideways to break the grasp of their tubed feet.

Arbacia have several advantages typical of many other sea urchins. They are rather tough animals and are easily maintained in the aquarium; and if treated properly in the field, most will survive. The basic field rules are never to crowd them extensively in the collecting bucket, or their spines will penetrate into each other's bodies. Keep the buckets full of water and change the water often, or they will become disturbed from the low oxygen and begin to discharge their gametes.

Although the *Arbacia* have been shown to have some preliminary antitumor activity in drugs from the sea-testing programs, and they have been used in some behaviorial experiments, their primary use is in embryology. It is easy to sex *Arbacia*, a pair of electrodes is inserted on the top of the animal and a charge ranging from eight to 24 volts may be administered. Immediately the spines spring up and begin to gyrate when the current passes through its body, and then within a few seconds white sperm or red ova are discharged. If the animals are then segregated into separate tanks, they recover quickly, and the sexed animals may be used for shedding measured amounts of sperm and eggs. *Arbacia punctulata* is the only species along the eastern United States that can be sexed by the electric-shock method; others such as *Lytechinus* and *Echinarius* require injections of potassium chloride to discharge the gonads.

The male and female sea urchins are placed in an inverted, spines-down position over two beakers of sea water. The vessels must be completely filled, so that the spines and the shell of the sea urchins are submerged. This is very important, or the gonads will not properly discharge.

A 5.5 molar solution of potassium chloride made up with fresh or distilled water (not sea water) is then injected into the soft parts of the urchin. Some embryologists use sharp scissors to cut out the Artistotle's lantern and viscera, leaving a gaping hole, and then fill the cavity with potassium chloride.

This causes the gonads to discharge, and if the urchins are ripe and in season, soon streams of red eggs and white sperm will trickle down in ribbons and pile up at the bottom of the beaker. The eggs emerge rather flakey, and the sperm pours from the male urchins like so much liquid.

The eggs are sucked up with an eyedropper and squirted into a dish of sea water, and then the sperm is sucked up in another dropper and inseminated into the dish of eggs. Within half an hour, at 60°F, a fertilization membrane forms around the eggs, and cell division begins shortly thereafter. The rate of cleavage is a function of temperature, and to some degree, pressure. The dividing eggs become a very useful scientific tool, determining the effects of radiation, chemicals and pressures on cell division and growth. For this reason sea-urchin eggs have been shot into outer space in the NASA program.

Arbacia has been raised to a second generation by Dr. Ralph Hinegardner of the University of California. By carefully changing water on the pluteus larvae, and following their growth and development stages, keeping his specimens in strict isolation and monitoring the pH, he was able to grow a number of small *Arbacia*. These produced eggs, and he has been trying for a third generation.

A good way to get them into an advanced state of development is to fertilize the eggs and keep them in a jar with a silk-screen cover; this cage is then immersed in the sea-water table. Soon the jar is teeming with larvae, and these can be used to feed other organisms in the tank. If plenty of urchins are available, it makes an easier and more economical food than brine shrimp.

Lytechinus variegatus
Short-spined Sea Urchin

Lytechinus variegatus is a large, short-spined southern sea urchin that ranges from Cape Hatteras to the Caribbean. Its colors range from pink to white and dark red, and it primarily lives in sea grass communities beyond the lowest tides. In north Florida, *Lytechinus* can become so thick on certain grass flats and sandbars, that it is impossible to walk without stepping on them. On rare occasions, while you are collecting *Arbacia* on rocky jetties in Panama City, you will find a misplaced *Lytechinus* hanging onto a rocky perch, although this is not its normal habitat.

We have learned a great deal about the habits of *Lytechinus* because it is a valuable sea urchin for embryology studies. For instance, its fertility season lasts from May to October, and during that time it produces large, clear eggs that make it particularly easy to demonstrate mitotic spindles during cell division. When the water gets cold around late October, the large gonads on *Lytechinus* shrink and they no longer produce eggs. However, embryologists in north Florida and other places who use sea urchins, switch to *Arbacia punctulata*, which are fertile from October to June, and sometimes July and August.

Lytechinus has a peculiar habit ot taking mussel and scallop shells and pulling them up against their short spines and holding them firmly with their pedicels, or little tubed feet. What purpose this armor of shells serves no one really knows; perhaps it is some sort of protection: it looks like a pile of discarded shells and perhaps a predator will ignore it. Or—speaking anthropomorphically—perhaps it just likes to collect pretty bits of shell.

Lytechinus is not quite as hardy as *Arbacia*. They cannot stand exposure to the air for more than a few hours, and must be kept very cool, so we ship them in plastic bags of filtered sea water charged with oxygen, and from the moment they are placed in the bags they begin to foul their water, spitting out little pellets that are reminiscent of the little pellets that rabbits emit all over the place. However, once *Lytechinus* arrives and is placed in a clean aquarium, it generally survives nicely.

But if the water becomes fouled, either from bacteria, siltation, a drop in pH or a sudden change in salinity, *Lytechinus* begins to die. Their spines collapse, and upon death they instantly mascerate and their rotten viscera oozes out of their mouth parts. We found that *Lytechinus* is a good indicator of a disturbed habitat. If the filter beds are disturbed in our sea-water system, *Lytechinus* are the first to die off.

The extensive dredging at Shell Point by Mobile Homes Industries resulted in dead *Lytechinus* everywhere. For years we went to Shell Point to dredge for sea urchins and scallops and were always rewarded with a rich, large catch, but in March of 1970, when Mobile Homes Industries created "Paradise Village" and turned the marshes and tide flats into a nightmare of siltation, the bottom was littered with dead and rotten sea urchins. So putrid were they that when our collectors hauled the scallop dredge aboard, the smell was so vile that they had a hard time keeping their breakfast down, and had to scrub the culling platform to get rid of the stench.

When *Lytechinus* dies it exudes lots of rotten ooze and creates more bacteria in the water system. Whether the scallops of the area perished from the siltation, or the general putrid conditions of dead *Lytechinus*, remains to be seen. And whether the *Lytechinus* died from dredging or from the rains and low salinity, as some claim, also remains conjecture, but we know that this sea urchin is an excellent indicator of unhealthy conditions.

When they start to die, quickly remove them from the system or the bacterial blooms will kill off everything else. Check the pH, the salinity and the temperature. When the water is in good condition and well aerated, *Lytechinus variegatus* will survive.

In using them for embryological studies, always remove the mouth parts before injecting them with potassium chloride (KCL). We have had limited success in sexing the animals by giving them minute injections of KCL because most batches start shedding and cannot stop until all their eggs are expelled, and they die when returned to the aquarium.

To the epicurean collector who seeks not only to delight his mind, but his palate as well, there is no finer eating than *Lytechinus variegatus* caviar. Often aboard our boat, when we dredge up *Lytechinus* in far greater numbers than we could hold in our largest tanks, we feast upon their tasty eggs. The urchin is broken open much the way one cracks an egg, the viscera removed, and the yellowish, orange gonads are scraped out. The females taste just a bit sweeter than the males.

Finding *Lytechinus* with distended gonads, ready to shed sperm and eggs, has been something of a problem toward the end of their shedding season. Around October and November, virtually all the specimens from inshore waters have shed their eggs. However, we found that large *Lytechinus variegatus* living on rocky, shelly bottoms offshore, in high-salinity waters, in depths ranging from 45 to 75 feet, are gravid until late in the winter when the water temperature drops below 60°F. Some investigators working with *Lytechinus* have kept them fertile by increasing the water temperature to 80°F and feeding them lettuce in inland, closed-system aquariums.

As time goes on, and sea urchins become as important as the laboratory frog, much more will be known about their habits both in the wild and in captivity. And *Lytechinus variegatus* will be among the better-known species.

Mellita quinquiesperforata
Sand Dollar

Sand dollars are one of the most faithful symbols of the seashore, and a few dried specimens are almost always found in the vacationer's booty. Almost always they live below the low-tide mark on sandy beaches, plowing furrows in the sand in a short, semicircular trail ending in a mound of sand. *Mellita quinquiesperforata*, known as the keyhole urchin, or five-hole sand dollar, is by far the most common species in the southeast.

These fascinating, fragile, flat discs are beautifully designed with

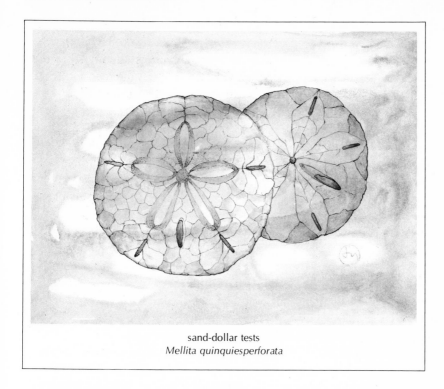

sand-dollar tests
Mellita quinquiesperforata

their five keyhole slots near the margin of their shells; their Aristotle's lantern (chewing organ), highly developed, is raised to form a perfect star in the middle of the test. When picked up, you can see uncountable thousands of tiny spines move and flex like multitudes of short, wriggling hairs, making it somewhat unpleasant to handle. Dead *Mellita* will be on the flats also, but it's easy to tell the living from the dead because the dead do not have the tiny spines that are very efficient at moving sand grains.

Mellita quinquiesperforata have a strange dye which they emit if you hold them, staining your fingers and clothing a purple color. But this dye emission is not limited to *Mellita* alone. Far below the tides, in depths ranging from 50 to 100 feet, live several other species of sand-dollar type urchins. One of these is *Encope michelini*, a very large, heavy rich-purple sand dollar that has five indentations in its test. These also emit a deep purple dye. Another species that lives in deep water with *Encope* is the cake urchin, *Clypeaster subdepressus*, which can get to be a foot across and weigh approximately a pound.

Mellita sometimes gets out to these deep sandy bottoms, but it is most commonly dredged in shallow estuarine sand flats. On low tides, *Mellita* can be so abundant that the entire flat is covered with them and it is difficult to walk without feeling them crunch and break under your boots. Their journey through the sand is short: they make a short hop in a semicircle and end up with the sand plowed up on top of them, sometimes with half their bodies showing, or no part at all, just a raised lump of sand. They can completely bury themselves in less than four minutes, rotating their anterior edge and slicing through the sand. Sometimes there is no trail, just the raised lump of sand with five holes appearing, and when you see that, you know a sand dollar lies buried.

Sand dollars are not exceptionally well suited for the aquarium. They require a deep sand filter, plenty of clean water and a low bacteria content in the system, which can be difficult to control in sandy substrates. We have been successful in maintaining them when they are not extensively crowded; roughly, one sand dollar per square foot of sandy surface in an aquarium is ideal. Then, if allowed to burrow out of sight and not disturbed, they will thrive.

Periodically a tiny, flattened, white brachyuran crab, (*Dissodactylus mellitae*) will occur on the ventral surface of keyhole sand dollars. Their appearance and disappearance is sporadic, but the association is interesting. Other species of *Dissodactylus* are found on cake urchins and deep-sea sand dollars.

All these sand-dollar crabs appear to be host specific — living on one species of organism only, and not changing. We have kept all three species alive in our tanks, and they remain in good condition if the host stays alive, and if there are no fish predators in the tank to do the host a favor by removing its "guest."

Moira atropos
Heart Urchin

This is one species that I do not recommend to the aquarist wishing to keep it in captivity. *Moira atropos* is a sporadically appearing, burrowing form taken in bucket dredges from deep in the sand. When they become extremely abundant, epibenthic dredges will skim them from the surface of the sand, especially when the chains are set so the dredge will fish heavy. Occasionally they enter shrimp nets, or commercial clam dredgers scoop them up, and refer to them as "goose eggs" because of their elliptical shape. They are covered with brown to yellow fuzz, and are very egglike in appearance. Unfortunately, many collectors will never know this because unless the dredge is set perfectly, or they are caught just right, they invariably reach the surface broken to pieces.

During certain years, *Moira atropos* undergoes a population explosion, and you would think that the sea floor is entirely paved with *Moiria atropos* from one end of the Gulf to the other. At such times, embryologists stationed at a marine laboratory can use the exceedingly large, clear eggs, which are few in number but excellent for demonstrating mitotic spindles. But because of the burrowing, tunneling nature of these deep-sand-dwelling forms, they are best shed of their eggs and utilized immediately upon collection, for they die within a few hours. In a rapidly running sea-water system, we have succeeded in maintaining *Moira atropos* for a few days at most. Soon their short hairlike spines flatten and they begin to stink. Their empty test makes an attractive souvenir of the seashore and, when found intact on the beach, is a handsome addition to the beachcomber's collection.

Moria atropos has an offshore cousin, *Plagiobrissus grandis*, found at 30 feet, and deeper at certain times of the year. It is an exceedingly large, ugly, burrowing sea urchin, with longer spines, tan in color; and like *Moira atropos*, it often comes up broken to pieces. We know nothing of *Plagobrissus'* habits, except that our collecting records show it as appearing only occasionally in our dredges, but north Florida may be the northernmost limit of its range. It appears commonly in other museum collections.

Moira atropos is known to make an intricate network of burrows as much as two feet down in the sand. On occasion, it enters the intertidal zone, and when a collector energetically follows a mysterious burrow deep down into the hard-packed sand, and has excavated a goodly pile of sand, he may be pleasantly surprised by finding a lone specimen of *Moira atropos*. But in intertidal collecting, if you should plan on going out with your shovel to dig up a few *Moira atropos*, chances of finding them especially when you want them are slim.

Class **Ophiuroidea**

Brittlestars bear some resemblance to starfish; they have a small disc and long, lashing arms, as active as a tiny octopus. They have an unpleasant habit of snaking along, humping themselves up and slithering out of rocky crevices, which is why they are often referred to as "serpent stars."

Night is the best time to collect them; they slip out from under rocks, or crawl out from beneath seaweed and slide and slip along the bottom, sometimes aggregating by the thousands, literally carpeting the sandy floors of shallow bays and estuaries.

If you scoop up a handful of *Gracillaria* or other algae on the bottom, you can generally find them.

If you can't find them there, when you need brittlestars, then you have to resort to looking in sponges and on ascidian clumps. Small hairy forms, like *Ophiothrix angulata*, live in sponges and also in hydroid colonies, although they are quite small and drab-appearing in those situations.

Brittlestars that live in the temperate zones of the world are generally small animals, but they come into their own when they reach the tropics. A New Englander's visit to the Florida Keys, for example, will be quite an experience when he walks along a tidal flat at low tide and turns over a limestone rock and sees a great, hairy serpentstar come writhing out. They are very sensitive to light, and will always head for the nearest cover. At night the entire flat may be carpeted by brittlestars, and divers who go down to the coral reefs at night are amazed at the vast number of brittlestars that had come out.

The tropical brittlestars are often six or eight inches in diameter, with their disc a full inch or longer. But like many brittlestar species, they quickly autotomize upon being picked up, and if you're not careful, you're left with a handful of broken, writhing arms. The temperate species will break apart if you handle them roughly, but the tropical ophiuroids are far worse. Just a nudge can cause an appendage to come off. For taxonomic purposes, it really makes little difference if the brittlestar has broken limbs, as long as all the parts are kept together.

All ophiuroids are fascinating to watch when alive, and they generally survive well in a salt-water aquarium with a good subsand filter. When an uninformed person spots one, he's sure he has seen a baby octopus. And when walking on a reef and you suddenly see their arms pull in under a rock, you may for an instant think you've seen an octopus. Often I see children playing with brittlestars on the tide flats, and because the arms writhe and twist, they are convinced they have an octopus of some sort. For the elementary teacher, this represents an opportunity to tell them about the differences between the two, one being a soft-bodied mollusk, the other an echinoderm having calcareous plates.

Most of the time, all that is seen of a brittlestar is just the tips of their arms waving out from rocks or sponge. When this habitat is broken up, the brittlestar is exposed.

Ophiothrix angulata
Hairy Brittlestar

Ophiothrix angulata is a rather small, insignificant-looking hairy serpentstar that is often found living in sponges, on seaweed and sometimes in rocks. Although it is not much of an eye-catcher, it has earned a sizable reputation among biologists who work with the physiology of brittlestars because it is so easy to maintain in captivity.

The easiest place to collect them is in sponges pulled aboard in dredge hauls, especially the big orange *Halichondria* sponges that are soft and have lots of canals and convolutions for the *Ophiothrix* to hide in. Then one simply tears the sponge apart and isolates the brittlestars in a plastic bag. Even though the weather may be hot and the oxygen limited in the bag, chances are that *Ophiothrix* will survive in a fine, undamaged condition, and will live for months, perhaps years, in a simple aquarium.

If the sponge can be kept alive in a good system of running sea water, so much the better. Then you can observe the sponge with the hordes of the brittlestar's little hairy arms projecting all over, the only real indication that *Ophiothrix* dwells within. They are by no means host specific; we found them in *Microciona, Halichondria, Axinella* and several other species of sponges.

Very often they are found in the red beard sponge (*Microciona prolifera*) and will take on a protective coloration, turning bright scarlet themselves. This makes them a delightful, eye-catching attraction. Normally *Ophiothrix angulata* is about two inches in spread, slate gray with rows of brownish dots on each arm, and extremely shaggy or "hairy." They are perhaps the most abundant of all West Indian

343

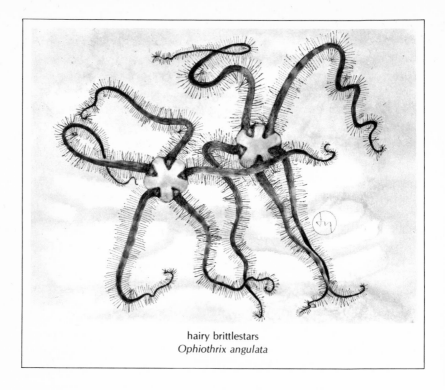

hairy brittlestars
Ophiothrix angulata

brittlestars, and their range extends from Beaufort, North Carolina, to southern Brazil. Because of the wide range and varied colors, no less than six varieties of *Ophiothrix angulata* have been named.

As laboratory specimens they can be used in a wide variety of physiological research programs. This little, hairy brittlestar has a lot of possibilities. *Ophiothrix* is dimly luminescent, and when stimulated in the dark by probing or immersion in weak alcohol, its hairy arms light up, and so does the central disc. They keep well, are very active and usually stay alive long after other invertebrates die in a marine aquarium.

In *Ophiothrix angulata*, feeding can be observed easily, since the central disc area is soft and shows peristaltic movements. They will eat bits of sponge and tunicate, but since they normally stay hidden in crevices, with only one or two hairy arms extended into the water currents, there is some suspicion that they are filter-feeders.

Unfortunately this doesn't make them the very best aquarium specimen for ready viewing, especially the brilliant scarlet or yellow specimens that have taken on the color of the sponge. However, after a few weeks their color turns dull and fades in captivity. They are best studied by isolating them from the sponge mass and placing them in fingerbowls where their feeding and luminescence can be easily observed.

Hemipholis elongata
Long-leg Brittlestars

Sometimes when you trudge way out on a mudflat you may encounter a strange brittlestar named *Hemipholis elongata*, although chances are you'll never even suspect you're seeing brittlestars. Probably you'll think you're in some sort of vegetated mudflat with thousands of hairy, little, stringlike plants erecting from the sand. Should you dig down into the midst of these "plants" and pry your shovel up, you'll be surprised to find you're in the midst of a gigantic pile of brittlestars.

Hemipholis elongata lives buried about six inches, perhaps deeper, in muddy sand with only its extremely long arms extended out into the water. What is so surprising about these creatures is the tiny size of their disc compared to the extremely long tangle of their arms. *Hemipholis elongata* is just that, elongated. They also have blood-red pigment that gives them their generic name. This brittlestar aggregates by the thousands, and when dug up, their arms twist together into such a tangled network that untangling them is sometimes next to impossible.

As part of a drugs-from-the sea program, we once gathered five pounds of *Hemipholis elongata* and became very adept at collecting them. When the tide covers them, their long arms begin rhythmically moving in the currents. Then we dug quite a hole in their midst, and by fanning our hands back and forth created a current which washed them out of the sand.

Records of this species are few and far between. They occur along the South Carolina coast down to Florida, Puerto Rico, Trinidad and Brazil. We have taken them over a wide range of bottom communities in the Gulf in bucket dredges. At times, when the sand was sifted out, the whole screen was matted with *Hemipholis*. Other mud stars found in the same dredge hauls were *Micropholis atra* and *Amphioplus abditus*.

Not much is known about the feeding habits of *Hemipholis*

elongata, but undoubtedly they are detritus feeders. They do not survive for any length of time in the aquarium, probably because they need plenty of sand mud to burrow into. When we have found them on a particular tidal flat, entire communities have remained stable and in the same place for periods of up to three months. We have taken them in the summer, fall and winter off Alligator Point. But they appear sporadically and are not predictable in their movements.

Their red pigment may actually be a form of blood hemoglobin, or it may be a carotine pigment. Only further investigation into this species will tell more. We have gathered these creatures by the pound, 10-pound and even 50-pound lots. That's quite a number of brittlestars, thousands of them, and I have carefully watched the population to see if we have denuded it. But in four years' observation of this species in one locality, I saw no real sign that its numbers have been reduced from one year to the next. When they disappear, the entire population goes at once, due to some seasonal variation. Whether they die off and grow back the following year, or whether they edge their way slowly out beyond the intertidal zone remains to be discovered.

Predictably they occur on one particular flat off Alligator Point, starting in June, and stay there through November. When the cold weather sets in, they leave; but the next summer I can count on seeing the tips of their six- to eight-inch-long wiry arms erecting above the mud, like sea grass swaying in the currents.

Ophioderma brevispinum
War-legs Brittlestar

This is the brittlestar that the crab fishermen in north Florida refer to as "old war-legs," perhaps because they are such a writhing, squirming mass of arms when they are hauled up in the crab traps and dumped out into the fish boxes of crabs. *Ophioderma brevispinum* is by far the most common of ophiuroids in north Florida. Although it dwells on muddy, sandy bottoms, it can be considered a denizen of the sea grass community. It is one of the largest and most distinct brittlestars, having a large disc and rather thick arms; *Ophioderma brevispinum* averages four inches across the arms.

I have found them more dense when diving along a muddy bottom covered with patches of red *Gracillaria* algae. If the sky is heavily overcast and the waters are dark, *Ophioderma* may be spread out all over the sea bottom, but if it is a bright sunny day, none are in evidence. The large brittlestars shun light and hide under the algae or under sponges or anything else on the bottom, and when you lift clumps of the algae, mud rises like a big cloud and diffuses through the water, but you can see the whipping and writhing arms of *Ophioderma brevispinum* in the confusion. Their ventral sides are white, and quite striking, and their dorsal surfaces are gray, although some are banded with a dull red matching the algae in color.

An easy way to collect them is to stuff algae, brittlestars and all into your diving sack and sort them out later. They can get terribly tangled in a fibrous, branching algae and be a major, time-consuming project to pick out under water.

However, an even easier method of collecting them in far greater numbers is to use a scallop or epibenthic dredge. A 10-minute tow pulled over an algae bed or, sometimes, over just a mud bottom will produce thousands of these brittlestars. They can be trapped because they are attracted to the bait in crab traps, and often so many of them are brought up that the entire bottom of the crab skiff can be several inches deep in *Ophioderma brevispinum*. At one time they caused confrontation between local fishermen and the crab houses because there were so many brittlestars mixed in with the crabs that the crab-house owners threatened to lower the price of the crabs. The crabbers argued that it was impossible to pick brittlestars out from a box of tangled, pinching crabs. However, they moved their traps away from certain areas where *Ophioderma* conglomerated, and the problem was more or less solved.

In this particular area, by the second channel-marker going out of the Panacea channel, the *Ophioderma* is so thick that if one drops a baited hook down and lets it settle on the bottom, shortly after it will be covered with the large, greenish-brown brittlestars, and consequently not even the voracious sea catfish will touch the brittlestar-covered bait.

For this reason, *Ophioderma brevispinum* is a good laboratory animal to demonstrate both feeding and locomotion. In an aquarium students watch the serpentlike, lashing movement of their long arms with fascination as they rapidly slide and snake along the floor of the aquarium after a piece of shrimp, madly lashing their snaky arms. And when they get on top of it, they wrap themselves about it and devour it through their mouth, which is on the ventral side of the disc. Dozens of them converge, and struggle and fight each other. It's quite exciting. Each one tries to snatch the bait away from the other.

Because of the abundance of *Ophioderma* we have experimented with new ways of shipping them and learned some interesting bits of information. To begin with, they survive nicely without oxygen in the bag. We have kept as many as six specimens in a four- by six-inch bag for as long as 10 days and have shipped them across the country as fourth-class mail and still they survived.

Class Holothuroidea

The novice collector discovering his first sea cucumber will never associate this fat wormlike creature as a distant relative of a starfish or sea urchin. Even if he is assured it is, if he finds a synaptid, wormlike holothurian, he will be convinced that he has come up with some sort of annelid or nemertean.

But sea cucumbers are echinoderms; they have calcareous plates, a water-vascular system, tubed feet and a number of other characteristics that give them membership. Their diversity in sizes and shapes is confusing even to the student of seashore life. They range in size from a few millimeters to a meter, and weigh up to 10 pounds. They may have the consistency and general appearance of a sponge or the softness and flabbiness of a sea anemone or a tunicate. There are colorful wormlike synaptids and great unsightly lumps of Dendrocrota. They differ from the rigid forms of starfish and sea urchins in their tough muscular body and their ability to change shape by varying degrees of contraction. In the North Atlantic and Gulf areas, most sea cucumbers are easy to handle and do not present any special difficulties. But a note on tropical holothurians should be included.

Such forms as the sticky-guts sea cucumber (*Stycopus*) are not hard to find, but their disagreeable nature makes them unpleasant to handle. You wait for low tide, and walk out among the rocks or on turtle grass beds, and there they lie, like great lumps of feces. But some are really quite pretty, having a speckled design on their skins, others have brightly colored, tubed-feet extensions.

As soon as you touch one, it contracts and if handled, it eviscerates and shoots out long strings of its intestines and guts out at you. These smell oily and have the consistency of chewing gum and marshmallow melted in a big pot and dumped all over your fingers. If you persist further, they rupture their body wall and dump everything on you.

When a fish bothers them they throw out their viscera, and presumably this satisfies the attacker and he retreats. Under the right condition the holothurian grows back its viscera.

Along the Atlantic coastline is another sea cucumber (*Thyone briareus*), which is perhaps the model sea cucumber, because it is used in classrooms and laboratories everywhere. To a certain degree *Thyone* will throw out its guts. Unlike the tropical *Stycopus* that cannot be brought back to the laboratory intact, *Thyone* will not eviscerate if gently handled. There is nothing more bothersome and frustrating than to dip up a bucket of sea cucumbers and find that after all that work they have eviscerated, thrown their floriated crowns off and spilled their guts out.

The most important thing to remember with sea cucumbers is not to jostle the jar, avoid overcrowding even more so than with other specimens, and above all, keep them cool. Change the water every 10 or 15 minutes, since stale water low in oxygen causes them to show their irritation by the rash action of committing hara-kiri. The eviscerated specimens in the bucket cause further irritation to the ones that have not yet eviscerated, and a chain reaction may result.

It is most desirable that sea cucumbers be preserved with their tentacles expanded and in good condition, and this is not always easy because they are prone to retracting them. All dendrochirote holothurians have tentacles which they use to filter-feed. They sweep the water with their sticky, highly branched, feathery tentacles to catch whatever plankton falls in their direction. Each of the eight tentacles is coated with mucus, and when they are well expanded and branched out like a web, minute animals, plant cells and detritus stick to them, and the cucumber stuffs the tentacles into its mouth, a small round hole in the midst of the tentacle-crown, and wipes them clean with two smaller tentacles, something like a child licking his sticky fingers after eating candy.

Not all holothurians have tentacles. The Apoda do not; they sit on the bottom like earthworms, and as they creep about the ocean floor with their muscular bodies, they pass mud through their bodies. Many sea cucumbers swallow sand and mud and digest the organic material, and serve the same function as earthworms in turning over and fertilizing the soils. Movement is accomplished by a multitude of hydraulically powered tubed feet bearing suckers on the ends.

Only in certain parts of the Indo-Pacific do sea cucumbers achieve any commercial importance. They are gathered by the ton and when dried, are known as "trepang," or *bêche-de-mer*, which is used in China for making soup. They are considered a great delicacy and sell for a high price. I know of no one who has tried eating the American varieties, however.

Theelothuria princeps
Speckled Sea Cucumber

Along the outer, oceanic beaches of west Florida, from Tampa Bay to Pensacola, lives a large, fat speckled sea cucumber called *Theelothuria princeps*. Walking along the outer exposed beaches where waters of high salinity lap against the shore, you are likely to find a number of *Theelothuria* washed up by prevailing winds and high tides.

This species also has that unpleasant habit of disgorging its entire viscera when handled or the least bit disturbed. We have tried keeping it in aquariums without much success; the tissues keep breaking down after the animal eviscerates. These sea cucumbers are quite abundant over sandy bottoms in St. Joe Bay and Panama City, Florida, in depths ranging from six to 30 feet. The shrimpers often catch them by the bushel. In the midst of jumping fish, thrashing shrimp and all the confusion are these sea cucumbers, each bursting its body wall and covering everything with an unpleasant marshmallow stickiness and its oily smells.

In the cloaca of almost every *Theelothuria princeps* lives a small commensal crab, *Pinnaxodes floridensis*, which was first described by Harry and Mary Wells, formerly of Florida State University. Surveys aboard clam boats at Port St. Joe revealed that only during certain times of the year are *Theelothuria* heavily infected with these small crabs, handsomely cream-colored with red spots. The crabs are filter-feeders and derive their nutrients from the food being pumped through the sea cucumbers.

At times the clam boats of Apalachicola, Florida, dredge up so many *Theelothuria*, that a full third of the clammers' time is spent culling them overboard. They are referred to as "sea pricks" because they are elongated, grow hard when touched, and have been the object of many an obscene conversation when a dredge is hauled aboard full of them.

However, another name given them by shrimpers is "chicken guts" because of their long, stringlike intestines that keep breaking and spewing out of the animal when it is dredged up. *Theelothuria* has no tentacles, and depends entirely on pumping minute particles out of the water. Other cucumbers use their tentacles to pick diatoms and bits of plankton selectively from the sea.

Leptosynapta crassipatina
Worm Sea Cucumber

The student of invertebrate zoology who has just come to the seashore for the first time might say to his instructor, "You must think I'm out of my mind, if you think I'm going to believe *that's* a sea cucumber. It's a worm!" And well might he say this, for *Leptosynapta crassipatina* is vermiform in shape, pinkish white, very flexible and lives six inches or more down in the mud. Its ten branching tentacles are the only immediate giveaway that this "worm" is really a holothurian. Like other synaptid sea cucumbers, *Leptosynapta* is capable of tremendous contraction, and when pried out of the ground, it may be well over six inches long and can pull itself down to less than two inches.

You can't get away from comparing *Leptosynapta* to a clear, elongated worm. However, if you look closely, you'll see a crown of pink tentacles that readily erect when the specimen is placed in a bowl of water. They come up from your digging as deflated strings, but in sea water they soon swell up and even look like sea cucumbers after a while.

But chances are that in the process of its tremendous contractions, the worm sea cucumber (*Leptosynapta crassipatina*) will break in two, three or four pieces, or if really disturbed, into a lot more pieces. Getting a specimen completely intact is a major job in itself. They autotomize like starfish, and are capable of regeneration of the body if the pieces aren't too small and are proximal to the head.

This is a sporadic sea cucumber, appearing along the Gulf and

351

Atlantic shores throughout the year, sometimes with only a few individuals on a flat, other times the entire flat is covered with them. Areas that were once good, such as Lanark Beach near Carrabelle, might not produce a single specimen, and other areas where they were never seen suddenly become thickly colonized with them. They have their own cycles and seasonal abundances. For example, in 1963 the entire flats were peppered with them along Panacea, and not a single specimen was taken there the following year. In 1970 the same flats were beginning to fill with *Leptosynapta*.

They frequently live in mudflats and sand on the upper tidal zone, which is routinely covered and uncovered by the daily tides. This makes the worm sea cucumber *Leptosynapta* one of the few echinoderms to live so close to land under such rigorous conditions. It is a frail creature, yet it can withstand exposures that its hardy relatives avoid.

Leptosynapta burrows are as perplexing as the animal itself. On a tidal flat where they occur with as many as nine animals to the square foot, their burrows appear as pock marks. Commonly they spew out little mounds of digested sand. When you pry them up with a shovel, invariably a number of them are bound to break in the process as they stretch like so many rubberbands. Here the splashing technique will be helpful. Holding a steady pull on the animal's either extremity, you splash water away from it until the substrate is washed off and then put it in a bucket of sea water, with just enough to cover it. Digging out among the roots of sea grass at low tide, one is also apt to encounter a number of *Leptosynapta crassipatina*, but they make no visible burrows there, and you'll never know you've captured one until the ground is spaded up.

Leptosynapta, like the other synaptids, have a very sticky nature, their tubed feet are well adapted to grasping and you virtually have to pry them from your fingers. In both the Indian Ocean and the Caribbean, I have seen specimens that measure up to four feet, but these synaptids live under rocks. And when you pick them up, the rather unpleasant feeling of this round, hollow wormlike creature clinging to you will make you think twice about picking up another one.

Leptosynapta crassipatina is different from all holothurians and even other synaptid holothurians in that it has the ability to swim. Yet these swimming excursions are poorly known. Very often on moonlit nights in the spring, I have seen graceful wormlike creatures undulating along the surface in a ghostly manner, rapidly expanding and contracting under the glare of lantern or boat-dock lights. Upon swooping these creatures up with a fine-meshed dip net, you'll be surprised to find a thin, empty-looking, pinkish-white sticky skin, and when you place it in the water, the tell-tale 10 circular tentacles will pop out, and the "worm" will inflate into a sea cucumber. Although many larval sea cucumbers have a swimming stage, *Leptosynapta* is perhaps the only adult form that swims.

Fishes probably eat them when they are doing their moonlight dance, but we have never observed fishes when they are around. But who knows, perhaps the fishes don't like the taste of this sticky and surprising animal.

We have had good success in keeping *Leptosynapta* alive in our tanks, giving them a subsand filter with lots of aeration. Periodically they bloat themselves to a much larger size when they are captured, and may break apart in the process. The less they are disturbed, touched and bothered, the longer they will last. Their transparent body walls make watching their digestive and circulation processes an easy and fascinating experience.

Leptosynapta crassipatina has a small, reddish commensal crab called *Pinnixa leptosynaptae* that lives on the external surface. The crab was discovered over a decade ago, but has only recently been described by Dr. Marvin Wass at the Virginia Institute of Marine Sciences.

Thyonella gemmata
Striped Sea Cucumber

Thyonella gemmata, a rather drab, greenish-brown sea cucumber, is the laboratory animal of the future. When they are rooted out by storm tides, hurled on the shore, and beat against the abrasive beach for a week on end, and still survive beautifully in the aquarium, then you know you've got a tough animal. And in our experiences in shipping them, seldom in 10 years have we had any specimens die in transit no matter how woefully the transportation companies neglected, froze, overheated, damaged or delayed them.

This species has become the object of considerable scientific debate. Holothurians are classified by the shape, arrangement, size, and structure of the minute calcareous spicules and rings which are embedded in their skin. A physiologist, Clyde Manwell, working in

353

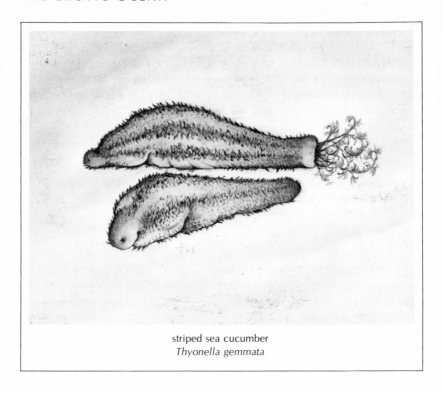

striped sea cucumber
Thyonella gemmata

Alligator Harbor in 1962 found that what appeared to be the same
Thyonella gemmata had two distinct electrophoric hemoglobin patterns.
The sea cucumbers, which contain bright red blood, are bled and the
molecular pattern of the hemoglobin is mapped out in a starch gel.

Very consistently Manwell found different patterns in "stouts" (sea
cucumbers that had bushy tentacles, were fatter and covered with
numerous tubed feet) and in "thins" (which were thinner, had fewer
tentacles and fewer tubed feet). He declared that they were sibling
species. Both kinds were collected from the same tide flat on the tip of
Alligator Point, or along the Wayside Tables of Leonard's Landing in
Alligator Harbor.

Manwell sent samples to Dr. Elisabeth Deichmann in Harvard, a
renowned taxonomist. She identified all the samples sent to her as
Thyonella gemmata and found no taxonomic differences between the
"stouts" and the "thins"; she suggested that the difference in
electrophoritic patterns of the blood may be due to either age or
dietary difference.

The results are there for anyone to follow. Tests have been

repeated time and again, and there are indeed two separate groups of "stouts" and "thins." However, one individual was found by Susan Gentleman, a graduate student at Duke University, to be "hybrid" having both the "stout" and the "thin" patterns in the same animal. Perhaps a great deal of work needs to be done on *Thyonella gemmata*, testing them every two weeks or so until one determines whether the blood chemistry differences are due to a difference in speciation or age.

Thyonella gemmata is supposed to range from the Gulf of Mexico to the Carolinas, but we have not been able to find any specimens along the Atlantic coast or even other parts of the Gulf, other than Alligator Harbor. A few were taken at Shell Point, and once I dug up a handful of specimens near Carrabelle, but both areas are less than 20 miles from Alligator Harbor. Perhaps they occur abundantly along some inlet on the Mississippi coast, or even in Tampa Bay, but only time and ardent collectors will tell. Such specimens are needed to determine if the "stout-thin" relationships still exist. It is interesting to note that Minor's *Seashore Life* doesn't even list *Thyonella*.

Thyonella gemmata lives both in mudflats and among the roots of sea grass. In the daytime, their round holes are clearly seen in the sand, always two together spaced from one to three inches apart. The animal burrows in a U-shape, so the anterior portion and the posterior portion are above ground. They pump water through their bodies.

Under the glaring gasoline lantern or strobe light operated from a boat, the flats appear to be peppered with their floriated crowns of tentacles thrusting up from the sand and mud. At first we dug them up with shovels to harvest specimens for the aquarium, but soon we found that the shovels caused the sand to be stirred up. A good method of gathering them was to reach down and strangle the sea cucumber behind its tentacles, and with a continuous, steady pull, yank it from its burrow. Only occasionally did we tear the crown off in the process; the majority of the specimens did very well.

Scylodactus (Thyone) briareus
Laboratory Sea Cucumber

Thyone briareus is probably the most well known of all American sea cucumbers. If anyone has taken even freshman zoology in college, they probably have been involved in carving up and studying the anatomy of this round, grayish blob with the branching tentacles erecting from its head. There is good reason for *Thyone briareus* being so well known; it ranges along the entire Atlantic and Gulf coasts, but it is far more abundant in the cold north.

Entire mudflats and sandbars are riddled with them off Woods Hole, and routinely the Supply Department goes out and digs them up by the hundreds, and the stock of the little fat, grayish, black balls never appears to diminish. Consequently, the growth, muscular movements, biochemistry and reproduction of *Thyone briareus* have been more extensively studied than those of any other holothurian.

And as a further consequence, the demand for these animals in the scientific and educational community has caused us to pay special attention to their habits in our part of the Gulf of Mexico. When I had first started collecting, I rarely encountered *Thyone briareus*. On occasion when digging up *Thyonella gemmata*, we would unearth these as well, to our surprise.

Thyonella gemmata frequented the inside, protected waters of Alligator Harbor, while *Thyone briareus* generally was found on the outer, exposed beaches of Alligator Point. They live below the tides, and

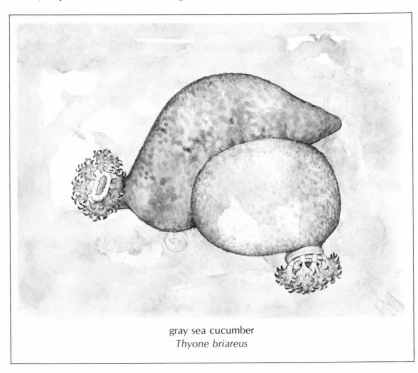

gray sea cucumber
Thyone briareus

when there is a severe storm or hurricane, you can be certain that the beaches will be piled ankle-deep with them as far as the eye can see.

But after such a hurricane, when the populations of *Thyone briareus* are hurled up on shore and subsequently destroyed by the pounding waves, they are scarce for several years to come. Then in a matter of two to four years, their numbers are built up until another disaster strikes. Along Alligator Point, *Thyone briareus* appears abundantly in shrimp nets and has earned the name "sea ball" because that is exactly what it looks like when swollen.

Often they distend themselves until they stretch to three or four times their normal size and resemble a fragile balloon, greatly distended with water and about to burst. They do this only when they are not adjusted to their surroundings, such as when they are in a collecting bucket or net; then some of them may actually rupture their body walls and expel their liquid.

We have had success in maintaining these animals in our filter-bed tanks with plenty of sand and gravel, so they can burrow out of sight. They are reluctant to expand their tentacles after they have been placed in the tanks, but becoming acclimated, they finally blossom out.

We have had variable results in maintaining in captivity specimens we picked up after a hurricane. A large number of them throw off their crowns and disgorge their viscera. Even in this condition they remain alive for months and do reasonably well, indicating that they are probably deriving some of their nourishment by pumping water through their bodies. If the sea cucumbers have been even partially burnt in the sun after lying on the beach, then they are generally doomed. They may live for a few days, but sooner or later will expire.

Of course even *Thyonella gemmata* will expire if it has been dried out for a long period of time, but this species is still much tougher than *T. briareus* and in years to come, if the supply holds out, will probably replace the common *Thyone* in the laboratory. It is interesting to note that the name *Thyone* has been changed by taxonomists to *Scylodactus briareus*, but since the old name is used in so many hundreds of books and references, the old name *Thyone* will probably be around for a long time.

Pentacta pygmaea
Red-footed Sea Cucumber

Now we come to one of my favorite sea cucumbers, *Pentacta pygmaea*. It's not a very large animal, generally measuring less than two inches. Occasionally we have taken some very large adults in deep water that measure a full four inches. Its color makes it rather interesting: it is chocolate brown and has four very large, modified rows of pinkish-red tubed feet. With this species the tubed feet take on a particular importance: they are used for climbing and clinging.

When high tide occurs, they climb to the top of the sea grass and cling there, taking their nourishment from the tides and currents, and often look like the tunicates and sponges that are growing on the upper portions of the grass. The red-footed sea cucumber is just as likely to be clinging to rocks and shell, and occasionally they are found in the mud, but not very often.

They are prone to be parasitized by the small eulimid gastropods *Balcis eberneus*, and are a strange and colorful sight when bristling with the small pearl-white snails protruding from their pink-tubed feet.

What makes *Pentacta* one of my favorite animals is its ability to survive in the most unpleasant aquarium conditions, making it the sort of creature that anyone can keep, no matter how they neglect it. The salinity can increase to 60 parts per 1000 from evaporation, and still *Pentacta* will not die. They can be totally starved and will show their abuse by shrinking a bit, but still they survive. Although I have never run any close checks I am sure they are every bit as tough as, if not tougher than, *Thyonella gemmata*. There is only one small problem with *Pentacta* as an aquarium animal. It does nothing but add color.

Once *Pentacta* has feebly crawled into position on the glass walls of an aquarium, it may sit there for three months and never move an inch. Only once in a great while are you rewarded by seeing them spread out their branching network of tentacles and sweep the water. For a long time I doubted if they even had tentacles.

In Alligator Harbor, *Pentacta* occurs quite abundantly at times on Bay Mouth Bar. We have taken them in dredge hauls and have filled a 10-quart water bucket with them in half a day's collecting time. However, unlike *Thyonella*, they are not restricted to Alligator Harbor, and we have taken them abundantly in Panama City. Their original distribution was known from the West Indies, and they are believed to be largely a Caribbean form, although intensive collecting along the

Atlantic coast might reveal a few specimens. Surprisingly enough, they do not appear in the Florida Keys; at least no collector I have met has reported them.

Thyone mexicana
Mexican Sea Cucumber

When we are out on the tidal flats of Alligator Point in northwest Florida furiously digging for *Bunodactis stelloides* anemones, we sometimes encounter this elongated, thin-skinned gray sea cucumber. In fact, it often so closely resembles the burrow and characteristics of *Bunodactis* that we dig them up and to our surprise see a long stream of water come squirting out from the ground.

Of course, when there are two distinct holes, spread a few inches apart in the ribbed sand, we can generally guess that it is a sea cucumber, and if it is on an outer shore, chances are it might be *Thyone mexicana*. But *Thyone mexicana* also lives right in with *Thyone briareus* on Alligator Point, and the two can be mistaken before the shovel breaks ground and reveals which one you've got.

The difference between the two is quite striking. While *Thyone mexicana* is quite thin and elongated, *T. briareus* is fat and round, as previously described. The Mexican *Thyone* is more reluctant to expand its tentacles in captivity, and generally does not survive as long or do as well as *Thyone briareus* or *Thyonella gemmata*.

Preservation

Class Asteroidea. No special preparation is required to preserve most starfish. Simply drop them into alcohol. One genus, *Luidia*, may contort and break off an arm if roughly handled, but if quickly placed in strong alcohol, such action will be arrested.

Laboratory starfish such as the Atlantic *Asterias* or *Piaster* of the West coast are easy to preserve. They are placed in shallow pans of sea water, well spread out so that their arms can arrange themselves in an extended position. Starfish twist and hold onto things, and when a number of them are placed in a collecting container, they have only each other to twist around and cling to, and end up as one big snarled mess. So after they are separated they should be given a few hours to spread out.

Although it is not necessary for identification, you may wish to extend their tube feet for demonstration. This is done by placing the animal on its back in a small receptacle of sea water with just enough water to cover it, and slowly adding alcohol. The tube feet will stir, and then stretch out and gently, cumbersomely wave through the water until more alcohol is added. After they are sufficiently expanded, siphon off the water and flood in Formalin or alcohol.

They may be preserved in a 10 percent buffered Formalin solution if used for dissection, or stored in 70 percent ethyl alcohol if intended for a reference collection.

Class Echinoidea. Sea urchins and sand dollars may be preserved by immersing them directly into alcohol. In fact, if there is much delay after they are removed from the sea water, their spines will tend to collapse and fall. The stronger the alcohol the faster the arrest, and the less chance that the spines will move. What is more, the alcohol will penetrate quickly through the body, fixing the internal organs.

To ensure complete penetration, an injection of alcohol should be made through the body wall on the ventral surface near the mouth.

Very weak alcohol may be a solution to extending a sea urchin with its fine, waving, tube feet expanded. They of course shrink and contract instantly when placed in alcohol. But of all the methods I have tried, I have never seen one that really gives good results and produces extended feet. The tube feet are so sensitive and active, and independent of movement, that preserving them is like preserving another animal.

Sea urchins and sand dollars are often preferred as dried specimens since they are easy to store and can be readily classified. They should be soaked in 5 percent Formalin or in absolute alcohol for a few hours and then placed on wire racks to dry. A small opening should be made on the soft ventral portion of sea urchins to drain the body fluids and speed up the process of dehydration.

Dried sea-urchin and sand-dollar tests make attractive display specimens and are frequently used in identification, particularly when comparing them with fossil remains. In nature when sea urchins die and soak in sea water for a time, all their spines fall off and the rounded test is frequently cast up on the beach. The test is very fragile and may be dipped in fiber-glass resin or varnish to keep it from crumbling.

Sand dollars may be dropped in a bucket of concentrated bleach and will immediately turn white, and all the minute spines will fall off. Treated in this fashion, they can be used for decoration and display. They too are fragile and should be dipped in some sort of varnish or fiber-glass or plastic resin to give the minute calcareous plates some adhesive body.

Class Ophiuroidea. Brittlestars should be placed in a flat pan or shallow tray to anesthetize them. If they are suddenly dropped in alcohol they will whip their arms, writhe like an angry octopus and snap off all their arms in the death struggle. Although ophiuroids can be identified from broken pieces, it is more of a strain on the taxonomist, who must keep track of all the arms, disc, etc.

The recommended technique for preserving brittlestars for taxonomic purposes is to arrange the flaccid arms of a freshly killed specimen in the form of a comet. The disc is jutted forward, the arms pulled back, almost as though it were jetting itself through the water. This is a more desirable position than arranging the arms in a neat, "natural-looking" circular form.

There are a number of ways to kill brittlestars without having them autotomize. Some people add fresh water to the sea water, and the brittlestars become stupefied, writhe a bit, slip around the pan as more water is dropped in, and slowly they become sleepy, immobilized. Then alcohol is added. They die peacefully and without violence.

But this operation must be done very carefully, with a great deal of attention focused on the animal. If they begin to get too aroused, you must pour in new sea water so they can settle down again.

One ophiuroid taxonomist I know uses 10 percent alcoholized sea water, placing his specimens in the solution until they hang limp, then replacing that solution with alcohol. Formalin should be avoided at all costs, because some delicate forms will crumble and become cheesy after a few days.

Like starfish, brittlestars may be dried. Many museums, such as the Museum of Comparative Zoology, Cambridge, Massachusetts, have them dried in small boxes. This makes them easier to store, and they can be easily identified by the arrangment of their calcareous plates.

Class Holothuroidea. Sea cucumbers that are to be used for laboratory dissection should be preserved with their tentacles fully expanded. If they are encountered on a tidal flat or they are kept in an aquarium, a sweeping network of branching tentacles will be seen erecting from the anterior portion of their bodies. Sneak up on them, taking great care not to stir the water or make any vibration that will cause them to draw their floriated crowns into their bodies in an instant. Then rapidly grasp the animal just beneath its tentacles and strangle it between thumb and forefinger. The powerful muscle bands attached to the floriated crown cannot draw back into the body and the tentacles are forced to remain out and distended. Still holding it securely, plunge the animal into alcohol solution and inject it with a steady stream of alcohol to keep the body distended.

The collector who wishes to produce fine specimens that look distended, with tentacles well expanded and natural, may be discouraged from taking all that effort when he learns that a holothurian specialist takes the same animal, simply drops it into ethyl alcohol, allows it to contract and harden into a rounded glob. The specialist merely cuts a piece of skin off the cucumber, soaks it in bleach to bring out the spicules and studies them under a dissecting scope. The arrangement of these spicules, no matter how bushy the heads, no matter what the size of the animal, its thickness or thinness, determines what species it is.

The big fear that specialists have is that the collector will preserve the sea cucumber in Formalin. Dr. Elisabeth Deichmann of Harvard's Museum of Comparative Zoology says they are not to touch Formalin even for an instant, as the spicules begin immediate deterioration. The acid in Formalin destroys the spicules and makes the whole animal slimy and cheesy and certain species will break to pieces when handled after they have been hardened.

Many sea cucumbers have come back from expeditions and soaked for a year or two in Formalin, and then proved totally useless. If space is limited, cut a section of the skin away and preserve it in alcohol, and cross-reference it with the entire animal in Formalin. If laboratory alcohol is not available, isopropyl may be used, but that also has a cheesy effect on the spicules. Wine and even beer have been used with good results. Otherwise, don't bother to bring sea cucumbers back.

For best results to prevent shrinkage, preserve the sea cucumber in 50 percent ethyl alcohol for 48 hours and then transfer to 70 percent. The animal should be injected because it preserves out in a deflated condition, looking like a balloon that has lost all its air. Again, this is satisfactory for taxonomists, but not for laboratory or demonstration specimens. Even after the specimens have been preserved for a long time, a good squirt of preservative into the anal aperture will cause the tentacles to fluff out more.

26.
Phylum Hemichordata
Acorn Worms

Class Enteropneusta

Ptychodera bahamensis
Southern Acorn Worm

If you ever stood on a sandflat or a mudflat, looking casually at the ground and suddenly saw a long string of mud spewing out of a little hole and piling up like rope into a mound, chances are good that an acorn worm was lurking a foot or so below the substratum. And if you shoveled vigorously after it, you might succeed in bringing one of these elusive and puzzling creatures to the surface.

The acorn worm is not a true worm; it has a rather perplexing position in evolution and its true grouping has been a matter of confusion among zoologists for some years now. They range in length from three inches to almost a yard, and have a cylindrical and flaccid body when not distended with sand. The acorn worm has an anterior proboscis which it uses to thrust itself down into the sand, and a dorsal tube extending into the proboscis from the digestive tract and called a "notochord"; this accounts for the placement of acorn worms among the chordates.

The chordates are the most highly evolved of all phyla, having a notochord and a dorsal nervous system. However, acorn worms cannot legitimately belong to the vertebrate club because the pseudo-notochord or buccal diverticulum, has been shown histologically to be nothing more than a pre-oral extension of the gut and certainly not a notochord. So after many years, its rating has finally dropped.

However, the Atlantic hemichordate, *Saccoglossus kowalevskii* (formerly classed as *Balanoglossus*) has achieved much fame in comparative anatomy classes and is still much in demand and hunted avidly by collectors. It is extensively studied in institutions, and some biology books still class it with the chordates, so knowing how to collect it can be quite useful.

Along the Atlantic and Gulf shores, two genera of hemichordates are commonly found, *Saccoglossus* in the north, and *Ptychodera* along the southeast coasts and the Gulf shores. They all have one thing in common: they are one of the most difficult creatures to capture because they are fragile and exude copious slime as they tunnel down. Their powers of locomotion are limited and they are rather sluggish, but they can slide through the mud easily and can elude a shovel with ease.

Acorn worms make a characteristic broad U-shaped burrow; the posterior opening is used as a dumping ground for wastes spewed out of the animal, the anterior opening has a rather funnel-like shape. The natural approach to digging them is to spade up the spewed-out pile, which sometimes even has a piece of the acorn worm's posterior end sticking up. If this doesn't work, the worm is generally broken in the process.

The technique of having two collectors, one at each end of the burrow, dig toward each other is often successful. They must dig rapidly until they are a foot or more down, and then slow their pace or they may chop the worm in two during the process. The presence of the worm is easily detected because the sand is sticky with mucus, and there is a very sharp, acrid odor coming from the mud, which is characteristic of acorn worms, particularly *Ptychodera bahamensis*.

As the acorn worm has more and more of its protective covering of earth removed, it begins to fill the hole with more mucus and water. Finally a pale white, soft and rather slimy body is exposed and the collectors begin digging with their hands, keeping a gentle grip on the animal. The odor coming from the hole is almost stifling, but still they dig. The scent remains on the hands of the digger for several days and will not wash out. Most gently the animal is pulled out by one collector; the other washes the sand away with a gentle splashing action, and then, bit by bit, a giant 22-inch acorn worm is excavated from the soil.

What remains is a big hole in the sand, often as much as four feet across. The problems of getting such an animal out are legion; the sand keeps caving in as you dig. More often than not the collector ends up with only acorn-worm fragments.

We saw smaller acorn worms colonize a tide flat on Alligator Harbor several years ago, and these were lying quite near to the surface and were easily dug out without half as much trouble as excavating the larger *Ptychodera*. In digging out the smaller animals, the washing technique is quite useful, but with larger ones it can be a disaster, especially when a chunk of sand falls away under water presssure, pulling the worm into two parts during the process.

An extremely handy tool for removing creatures from a shovel is a bulb syringe or squirt bottle filled with sea water. As soon as the animal is dug out, you gently squirt the sand away from its body, freeing two or three inches of body at a time.

When *Ptychodera* was abundant we had good opportunity to observe its habits. They were everywhere spewing out little piles of sand that resembled spaghetti, but were themselves very much out of sight, especially if the tide had been out for four or five hours. When the tide seeped back in and covered the flat, almost half the specimens on the flat oozed out of their holes and exposed their soft bodies to the waves, shifting sands and numerous predators, which I thought was rather unusual behavior.

We have noticed that there is a complete absence of acorn worms in a dredged-up area where the ground has been disturbed. I was interested to note Joel Hedgepeth's remarks about them in the fourth edition of *Between Pacific Tides*: "Thirty years ago it (*Saccoglossus pusillus*) was abundant in San Diego Bay and in what is now Los Angeles harbor, but suction dredging and industrial wastes have very materially changed the shorelines where it was once found. W. E. Ritter (a biologist working the Pacific northwest coast in 1900), when working up the embryology of the animal, wrote of taking more than a hundred on one tide, but now even the most proficient collector must be locally knowledgeable if he is to procure any in the southern region. There was once a fine bed of them in front of the laboratory at Charleston, Oregon; but that sand flat is now a large parking lot, and the laboratory no longer has a waterfront."

Of course many other organisms disappeared in the process of such dredging and filling. Keeping track of acorn worms is not an easy job because they are subject to more seasonal variations than many other stable populations. One year the flats may be peppered with them, and then for five years more, the flats are almost devoid of hemichordates.

I have seen large populations of acorn worms on the flats of

Honduras, and once when in Madagascar I noticed a number of them on tidal flats. They always prefer clean, unpolluted waters which are decently removed from a thriving human population. I have never seen any evidence of them near a paper mill, sewer outfall or garbage dump. Therefore, it would be a good idea to take a sample of these animals when they are abundant.

Hemichordates do not live very well when kept in captivity, although we have not really given them much of a try. They exude copious slime and their tissues begin to deteriorate even while they are alive. If given a large mudflat tank several feet deep, well aerated and filtered, perhaps they would do well. Most of our effort has gone into preserving them.

Preservation

When collecting in a new area where species of hemichordates are likely to be undescribed, even fragments of the animal are worth saving and preserving. Ideally the head with proboscis, collar, etc., should be taken because these are critical appendages for making positive identifications. The whole worm is even more ideal, but there is a good chance that the tail will still be left in the ground.

Collectors at Woods Hole have developed a workable technique of anesthetizing acorn worms. They place it in a large pan of fresh sea water, and begin to trickle in alcohol. When the worm spasmodically draws up, they quit and let it recover, and when it relaxes they add a little more. Complete extension of the worm may take a full 24 hours, but finally it no longer responds to probing or increased concentrations of alcohol and is ready for fixation. This is a creature that cannot be dropped into Formalin and an identification easily made; the relaxing process is very important. Magnesium chloride can be tried, but this stimulates that animal's slime-exuding tendencies and if there is a bowlful of mucus, fixative will not penetrate easily and the acorn worm may undergo contraction before it dies.

Since identification is primarily made through histological sectioning and examination of the gonads and internal muscle bands, the acorn worms should be flooded with Bouin's fluid. This is done by draining all the water off the animal, or leaving just enough to cover it, and pouring in the strong-smelling yellow acid fixative.

After it hardens for 24 hours in Bouin's it is essential that it be removed from solution and the Bouin's washed out in 30 percent solution of alcohol. When the yellow color is more or less leached out, the specimen can be transferred to a 50 percent and finally a 70 percent alcohol solution. This may be somewhat tedious, but if you've gone to all the trouble of digging it up, isolating it in a bucket and taking care of it until you get back to your base of operations, the extra time in preparing it for a museum collection is well spent.

27.
Phylum Chordata/
Subphylum Urochordata
Sea Squirts

Class Ascidiacea

The tunicates. Who would believe that these large, fleshy blobs resembling a sponge for all practical appearances, are one of the most highly evolved of all marine invertebrates? In their adult form they are little more than a water pump, pumping water in through their vascular system, extracting nutrients and pumping the water out, but it is in their larval stage that the tunicates display the characteristics which make them part of the same chordate phylum to which all fish, birds, reptiles and mammals belong.

The tadpole larvae develop from union of sperm and egg, and they swim about freely as part of the great mass of planktonic life. They are strange-looking creatures, having a notochord, the rudiments of a backbone running the length of the body. Eventually the tunicate larvae get heavier and start to settle down. Some attach to wharf-pilings, others grow on shell, almost any hard surface. Then like a child prodigy that starts out doing something great and ends up driving a streetcar, the tadpole larva slowly absorbs its notochord much the way a tadpole absorbs its tail, only instead of growing limbs, it turns into a blob and takes on a very unexciting spongelike existence.

In some instances it is very difficult to tell the difference between a sponge and a tunicate, particularly when the sponge mimics the tunicate in appearance. There is a slippery, whitish-gray sponge called *Chondrosia* that encrusts rocks and only the experienced eye could tell that it is not another form of colonial ascidian or sea pork. Then another grayish-white sponge, *Chrondrilla nucula*, that grows on sea grass the way so many colonial ascidians do, looks and feels very much like some of the slippery, soft colonial ascidians. And until you become very familiar with both the tunicates and the sponges it will be most difficult to tell them apart.

There are tunicates that most closely resemble sponges, even in texture, and Steinbeck and Ricketts wrote about some in *The Sea of Cortez:* "There were great colonies of tunicates, clusters of tiny individuals joined by a common tunic and looking so like the sponges that even a trained worker must await the specialist's determination to know whether his find is sponge or tunicate. This is annoying, for the sponge being one step above the protozoa, at the bottom of the evolutionary ladder, and the tunicate near the top, bordering the vertebrates, your trained worker is likely to feel that a dirty trick has been played upon him by an entirely too democratic Providence."

Like sponges in general, tunicates take on many intricate colors and shapes from round, muddy potato-lump clusters such as the solitary forms like *Molgula* and *Styela* to the great, glistening chunks of sea pork, *Amaroucium* or *Ascidia. Halocynthia pyriformis*, which is found on the Atlantic coast north of Cape Cod, greatly resembles a peach in size, shape and coloration and is commonly called "sea peach." *Perophora viridis* that grows on piling and sea grasses like little berries is given the common name "sea grapes." The fishermen have other names for some tunicates when they get a deck loaded with them, but these names are not suitable for publication.

Tunicates are found on every coast, highly abundant in some areas and so dominant that they may make up three-quarters of the biomass in a dredge haul. In other areas where there is hard sandy bottom, they may be scarce, but a wrecked ship will be luxuriously overgrown with tunicates in every imaginable shape and color. They grow in every habitat, on rock, grass, shell, mud and sand, and frequently the same species will traverse all habitats and grow on everything. The size, shape and even color of the ascidian will vary with its change in habitat, but the same species might occur on a piling or at the end of a blade of sea grass.

Although there are pelagic tunicates, *Salpa*, that are clear and float about the ocean in chains and sometimes wash ashore and pile up on the beaches, the great majority of tunicates are taken in dredge hauls from bottom communities. One form, *Ciona intestidunalis*, has a completely clear body wall and its entire digestive, circulatory and reproductive systems can be easily viewed. Zoologists work with these animals in the Cape Cod region, and their distribution may go as far south as Virginia. But in Florida and throughout the Caribbean, another clear-walled form, *Ecteinascidia turbinata*, is common, although the individual animals are much smaller than *Ciona* and occur in massive bunched clusters.

Ecteinascidia, Ascidia, Molgula, Styela and *Clavelina* are just a few of the tunicates that have attracted the eye of the biochemist and the researcher in pharmaceuticals. Many of the tunicates have exhibited antitumor abilities, have inhibited leukemia strains in rats, and have even shown antibiotic abilities. Certain species concentrate vanadium in their tissues, a chemical used in dyes that occurs only one part per billion in sea water but is heavily concentrated in the blood of the tunicates. From being "blobs" on the beach confused with lowly sponges, the ascidians may someday be very valuable to medicine and research.

Amaroucium stellatum
Sea Pork

Along many parts of the Atlantic and Gulf coasts beachcombers sooner or later see chunks of glistening, rubbery protoplasm cast up on the beach. They range in size from a few inches to a yard in length and can weigh over 40 pounds. This is sea pork, probably *Amaroucium stellatum*, and it comes in a variety of forms ranging from smooth round blobs with numerous convolutions like a brain to a perfect round ball. These great masses of flesh come in a multitude of colors and have a spectrum ranging from warm pinks to slate blues and dull grays. It is no wonder that uneducated visitors call them everything from ambergris to jellyfish.

They frequently wash into the beaches near our laboratory, and at least once a week during the tourist season someone brings us a lump, wanting to know what it is. And explaining it to someone without a background in zoology, who does not know the position the urochordates have in evolution, can be a chore at best; and even when you do your best, the answer is not terribly clear. It is very hard to imagine that this lump may be our remote ancestor.

These colonial animals grow in massive forms on rocky outcrops along the Gulf bottoms, and when they reach a large size and have probably spawned, a rough sea comes along, causing them to break

sea pork
Amaroucium stellatum

off and come tossing and spinning shoreward to be moved around by the surf until they pile up on the beaches.

This pile-up of dead and dying sea pork appears to be seasonal. Late fall, after spawning, the beaches are littered with them, and if you walk along with a bucket, you can soon gather several hundred chunks. But it is important that the animals be collected alive, whether you are going to try to keep them alive or preserve them. If the flesh is beginning to slough off or the zooids are hanging out like small, white threads, you can believe the piece is dead, and if you pick it up and get a whiff of it, you'll know its dead. *Amaroucium* decomposes almost immediately after it dies, although it is quite possible to have a colony with portions dead and rotten, and other portions alive and healthy.

Amaroucium stellatum is one animal that should be studied alive by taking it out of the sea, working with it for a few hours and then preserving it. We used to think that they could not be kept alive in an aquarium, but lately with the expansion of running-sea-water systems we have been having better results. They certainly cannot be crowded or their tissues will soon begin to slough, and they begin to stink.

Nothing will destroy an aquarium quicker than putting a chunk of sea pork in it that is dying. Like many sponges that die in an aquarium, dying tunicates can reduce a beautiful tank to a revolting mess, killing both fish and fragile invertebrates overnight. Yet the temptation to gather a little colony of striking purple or red sea pork to brighten your aquarium is great; it should be avoided unless you plan to scrutinize the colony very closely and are prepared to remove it if it starts to turn bad.

Didemnum candidum
White Sea Pork

As your boat glides over thriving sea grass communities, you may get an occasional glimpse of something white growing down among the bright green grasses. Chances are that such striking white patches are the encrusting colonial tunicate *Didemnum candidum*, and when you turn around, and drift over the grass and finally shut the motor off and get out, you'll be rewarded by finding a piece or two. But sometimes the colonies become so massive that not much hunting will be necessary, and whole sections of grass are completely engulfed in it.

What has always surprised me was that the grass blades are always alive and healthy when the tunicate has been peeled away. Perhaps after a few months or so the grass dies off. *Didemnum* must grow quite rapidly. It is usually crawling with *Ophiothrix angulata* brittlestars, has a number of amphipods and isopods crawling and the tissues may be riddled with pink nereid worms.

We have seen small encrusting colonies of *Didemnum candidum* encrusting larger solitary tunicates and have seen it growing at the base of pilings as a small white patch. There are numerous species of *Didemnum* in north Florida, but *Didemnum candidum* is the most plentiful and regularly collected species.

When the sea water is warm, the color of the colony may change from white to gray or yellow. The entire test becomes filled with fecal pellets which can influence the appearance of the whole colony. Perhaps because these fecal pellets are so constantly spewed out, brittlestars and other animals are commonly found in a commensal arrangement.

Didemnum candidum becomes particularly dense from November to April and covers large patches of grass in Alligator Harbor. We have gathered it and kept it alive in our tanks, and when kept in strict isolation it does rather well. It appears to be one of the tougher colonial ascidians because it survives without attention.

Botryllus schlosseri
Golden Star Tunicate

Botryllus schlosseri, the golden star tunicate, is one of the most attractive tunicates, and for that matter one of the prettiest creatures in the sea. The star-shaped zooids are embedded in a jewel-like tunic, and colors range from blue, blue-green, to yellow and red. The zooids are usually dark purple and brown, and the colony is so striking that once seen it will not be readily forgotten.

W. G. Van Name, who was an authority on tunicates, wrote that they were the most handsome and conspicuous compound ascidian found on the eastern coast of the United States: "Its soft, velvety appearance and striking and varied colors (which fade, with death or even with any removal from its natural environment) attract the notice of even casual observers"

Because of its beauty and its large zooids, considerable attention has been devoted to rearing this animal in the laboratory. As Van Name said, the animal begins to change immediately after it has been removed from its natural environment. Within a day or two three-quarters of the colony dies off.

Investigators at the University of Iowa have kept *Botryllus schlosseri* in artificial sea water, and upon keeping it scrupulously filtered at 70°F the colonies that died back began to regenerate. In this manner a number of invertebrate zoologists have colonies growing in their temperature-controlled, filtered life-support units. However, it is indeed an accomplishment if one can show you a colony they have been growing for some months. One biologist maintained *Botryllus schlosseri* for over 18 months in captivity.

Shipping these animals is a substantial problem, and a number of techniques have been worked out by Dr. Roger Milkman at the University of Iowa using specimens from Woods Hole. A colony is cut into tiny pieces and these are put into jars contained in an open sea-water system. At least two-thirds of the colony sample are expected to die off in a day or two. Each colony should have about 15 settled zooids and no more. The pieces are best cut about one centimeter square and shipped in individuals plastic bags.

374

Even with all these precautions we have had 50 percent mortality, and have had to repeat shipments over and over again. The temperature in the shipping container is important; if too much ice is added and the water temperature plunges to 60°F or below, the zooids will regress. If the water temperature is allowed to get much over 70°F then the colony starts to disintegrate.

Botryllus schlosseri seems to be more abundant in the spring and fall months when the water temperature is 70°F. It is often found growing on other tunicates, making a beautiful, encrusting coating. We find it on grass blades, and during one November we found several massive colonies that were enough to fill a water bucket and weighed over five pounds.

Botryllus schlosseri, like many other forms of ascidians, disappears in the summer months along much of the west Florida coast. Van Name reports that this species was probably brought here on the bottoms of ships. It is widely distributed in European waters, and reported from southwest Australia and New Zealand. This makes one reflect on the distribution of ascidians in general. They are markedly affected by hydrographic conditions and most species live where salinity is high and constant. High rainfull can kill off large ascidian populations.

Joe Branham while working on a Master's thesis at Florida State University in 1953 pointed out that in Alligator Harbor, "it is significant that the species that thrive during the winter and spring when the water is cold, have a wide geographic range and the species that were abundant only in the spring, summer and early fall were of more tropical distribution."

He notes that the tropical genera such as *Clavelina*, *Ecteinascida* and *Trididemnum* may occur in the winter months, but only as small, hard-to-find individuals. In the summer when the water warms up, they come into their own and appear as large, luxurious colonies.

Ecteinascidia turbinata
Glass Tunicate

Ecteinascidia turbinata is a very beautiful tunicate, orange, purple or perfectly clear in color. It is a colonial form consisting of dense clusters of elongated zooids, each in its own tunic. And in past years the pharmaceutical industry has been turning a keen eye to this species because of its potent action on leukemia strains in rats.

Touch alone will distinguish *Ecteinascidia* from all other species, because it is soft and very watery to the touch. They are often found massively encrusting wharf pilings below the *Styela* and *Amaroucium* levels, but may also be found in dense clusters clinging to turtle grass or chunks of shell.

We have never had much success in bringing colonies in from the field and maintaining them in captivity. They excrete constantly, and are always spewing out debris into the sea water. Their beating heart can be viewed readily through their body wall, but their mortality rate makes them anything but a desirable specimen for shipment to inland stations.

We have had the most success in raising *Ecteinascidia turbinata* by bringing in colonies attached to rocks and letting them die back. As soon as the animals die and turn opaque white and become moldy, we remove them so they will not foul the sea water. Then, in a matter of a week or less, the zooids begin to grow again and soon the rock is covered with the clear little *Ecteinascidia* erecting above the rocks. The transparent tests are often tinged with red, giving the zooids a rubylike appearance, or they may be emerald in color. The siphons on the top of the zooids are ringed with red, and an aquarist who has successfully cultured them has a specimen that he can be proud of.

On a few occasions I have collected *Ecteinascidia* and placed them in large, flat well-aerated tanks with gravel-bed filters and have succeeded in keeping them alive for many weeks. These specimens were collected in the early part of the spring when the colonies were just beginning to appear, so it is possible that the cool water did not cause any appreciable shock which might have started the colonies deteriorating.

It is conceivable that someday techniques will be developed for farming *Ecteinascidia turbinata* and fishermen will be employed for harvesting it from docks and wharfs everywhere. Dr. Michael Siegel at the University of Miami has demonstrated that it has a strong antineoplastic activity. As part of his screening and testing for drugs from the sea, Dr. Siegel gave a series of laboratory mice daily intraperitoneal injections of 10^6 P-388 (lymphocytic leukemia) and innoculations of crude extracts from *Ecteinascidia turbinata*. A control set of mice also infected with lymphocytic leukemia were given daily injections of sterile saline, but the tunicate-injected animals survived for 30 days and were "cured" while the controls died after 10 or 12 days. The term "cure" was based on an observation period of 30 days when the experiment was terminated and the animals destroyed. Further testing is in progress to see how long leukemia-infected mice will survive with refined extracts of *Ecteinascidia turbinata*.

The National Cancer Institute found that *Ecteinascidia turbinata* extracts resulted in a 200 percent life extension of infected mice. Other species of tunicates such as *Molgula occidentalis* increased the survival time of the mice to 175 percent. Many marine invertebrates, especially tunicates and bryozoans, have demonstrated possibilities of antineoplastic agents. From the preliminary results of assaying hundreds of marine invertebrates, fish and algae, many of the "sea pests" have shown promising results in testing, and in the years ahead, these specimens may be regarded as quite valuable.

Styela plicata
Leathery Tunicate

Styela plicata is by far the most abundant and dominant ascidian in north Florida, although it is common throughout the Atlantic and Gulf coasts. Its close relative, *Styela partica* of the Cape Cod region, also reaches peaks of abundance, but I know of nowhere in the United States that *Styela* reaches such a dominance as Franklin and Wakulla counties in Florida. Every dock, wharf and boat that is allowed to sit in one spot for a period of time will soon be overgrown with them.

We have cultured *Styela plicata* on oyster strings and found that within six months they became so overgrown that it would require a winch, block and tackle to lift them. Both *Styela plicata* and *Molgula occidentalis*, the other major solitary sea squirt, grow in such an abundance in Alligator Harbor that most shrimpers avoid the area completely because their nets become so gorged with these little round potatolike organisms that their boats can sink under the weight.

The thick leathery test comprises the greatest part of their bulk, and this test material has a high concentration of cellulose in its tissues. So abundant is this form that we have ground it up and sent samples to paper companies to see if the cellulose could be used for anything, but no results were ever given. *Styela plicata* has been observed to produce viable eggs and sperm year round and tadpole larvae have been raised in captivity by a number of investigators.

This species is an excellent laboratory animal because it is hardy

377

leathery sea squirts
Styela plicata

and will live in a simple aquarium for months at a time. In nature it can tolerate a variety of unpleasant conditions ranging from extreme heat to freezing cold, and when everything else dies from unsuitable temperature conditions, *Styela plicata* remains. They seem to prefer boat basins and marinas, where they attach to floating docks and boat bottoms, sometimes growing in such abundance that two-thirds of an inboard outboard's speed will be diminished. Since they can grow very rapidly, a boat must be hauled out at least every four months, particularly in the summer, to rid the bottom, wheel and shaft of these pests.

Their larvae must be more persistent in taking over a place of attachment than oysters, mussels hydroids or bryozoans, because these are always secondary growths. You cannot help wondering about the pros and cons of a *Styela plicata* community. Their ability to clear surrounding waters of particulate matter including diatoms, larval oysters, fish eggs and other plankton can lead you to consider them a detriment. However, hundreds of small nereid worms, *Petrolisthes* crabs, amphipods, isopods, and even sea anemones grow on and

378

between the clumps of *Styela*. The large solitary tunicates are constantly filtering sea water, but at the same time expelling a huge amount of fecal material in the form of detritus. And when you walk around the marina docks, invariably you will see hundreds, if not hundreds of thousands, of minute croakers, anchovies and at times even young mullet nosing around the tunicates nipping at small organisms or actively feeding off the detritus that is expelled from the colonies of *Styela*.

In these marinas man has altered the environment. He has come in with his dragline and dredges and destroyed a piece of marshland or in the case of the Shell Point marina, a marsh pond. The bottom is deepened, the waters are sheltered and protected, and a community of tunicates that were not there previously have a place of attachment and move in and cover floating Styrofoam docks, pilings and boat bottoms, affording shelter and food for fish. How much more or less productive is this area than the original salt marsh would have been?

The conservationist is tempted to approach the marina buildings with a closed mind. Nature has been destroyed for the profit of a few, but it seems in some instances that nature compensates by taking advantage of the newly created environment. Certainly more studies of productivity in newly created and old environments must be conducted before you can be certain.

To a biological collector, a marina can be a blessing, especially when he needs a collection of the leathery sea squirt, *Styela plicata*, or some of the organisms that live on *Styela plicata* and the winds are howling, seas are running six feet and rain is pouring down. Then you go to the marina, squat down out of the weather, and rip off handfuls of the needed tunicates.

The little lumpy, leathery potatolike *Styela plicata* tunicates are easily kept in captivity, as mentioned before. Not only have we been able to keep them, but we have been able to maintain commensals on them at the same time, which is quite a feat. Nudibranchs have even laid eggs, and fresh growths of encrusting sponges and bryozoans are seen when the animals are kept in captivity.

Styela that grows in clean water with a little current is bright tan and shiny, but in certain murky waters where there is a heavy population of larvae settling, it may be overgrown with every encrusting organism imaginable from other colonial ascidians to rich growths of hydroids.

Generally these sea squirts are found in shallow waters less than

12 feet deep. They will attach to dead sand dollars, and have been seen growing on *Pleuroploca* conch shells and even on *Aequipecten irradians* scallops. We have taken *Styela* in dredge hauls off #26 Buoy off Alligator Point, but are not yet sure that this is really *Styela plicata*.

In depths ranging from 45 to 90 feet, another tunicate of the family Styelidae, *Polycarpa circumarata*, replaces *Styela plicata*. In many ways their rough appearance is similar, being potatolike, with two pronounced incurrent and excurrent siphons sticking up from the top of the animal. But *Polycarpa circumarata* is much more handsome, being brick red, larger and having a thicker test. Usually it is overgrown with a mass of hydroids, algae and bryozoan and its real, magnificent color is hard to see. Its inside has a pretty pearl lining. This species has a strict tropical distribution, being limited to the West Indies and Florida. Periodically it is washed up on the beaches after a storm.

Styela plicata ranges throughout the Gulf of Mexico up to the Carolina coasts, but goes no further north. A small sea squirt, *Styela partica* is found above the Carolina coasts up into Maine. We have looked for *Styela plicata* in the Florida Keys down to Marathon and down in Honduras, but have failed to find any specimens; this does not mean that they do not exist, it simply means they are not in such profusion that even the most casual and disinterested observer could not fail to miss them, as they are in north Florida.

Molgula occidentalis
Sandy Sea Squirt

Molgula occidentalis is the species that commercial fishermen refer to as "porpoise turds," and if porpoises didn't defecate in a long, white watery stream, the name would be as good as any. *Molgula occidentalis* is a very large, lumpy tunicate that is round, often the size of a golf ball, and grown over with mud which is woven into its tunic. A colony of individual sea squirts might have as many as 50 animals in it, and can be quite a clump.

When a fisherman strikes his seine around a school of mullet and at the same time ensnares about 300 clumps, each weighing anywhere from one to three pounds, one can understand why he does not hold them in very high regard. Like *Styela plicata* and *Polycarpa circumarata*, they are true sea squirts and when you pick up a clump, generally they do just that—squirt like a bladder that has been distended for just too long a period of time. They really let fly a jet when a slight squeeze is given to the body wall, otherwise on low tide they can be seen spurting out small intermittent streams of water.

We have seen them carpet the entire bottom of Alligator Harbor. They reach their maximum population in the winter months, when certain portions at the head of the harbor are literally infested with them. I was aboard a shrimp boat that made a half-hour tow and was forced to take over 1500 pounds of them on deck. The pile stood as high as my chest and we had to shovel for almost a solid hour before we cleared the decks. Since white shrimp are raised in Alligator Harbor, the shrimpers in Panacea once decided to have a privately financed community project to clean the "porpoise turds" out. Three 45-foot trawlers strained and groaned as they pulled the heavy load of tunicates from the bottom, and then carried them into the shore and dumped them out on the beaches so they would die and the channel be clean of them. The boats worked for three solid days and in the end gave it up as a lost cause because no matter how much they dredged, the supply was just as thick as when they had started.

The majority of the sea squirts were mixtures of *Molgula* and *Styela* growing together in the same cluster. This presents a rather interesting sight: round, very brown, muddy *Molgula* growing next to a shiny, leathery, tan oblong, *Styela plicata*, and usually the clump is well grown over the with bryozoans (*Bugula neritina* and *Amathia convoluta*).

We have gained fame in the area by being the only ones who could ever make a dime out of those "worthless good-for-nothing blobs." But we have found an entire community of animals that live on *Styela* and *Molgula* clusters, ranging from the pretty orange flatworm, *Prostheceraeus floridanus*, to the pistol shrimps, the cleaning shrimp, anomuran crabs, nereid worms, the small commensal mussel, *Musculus lateralis*, that dwells almost exclusively on these blobs. We have taken big flowery eolid nudibranchs from them, and have picked off fat yellow dorid nudibranchs.

All you do is grab a cluster of *Molgula* and *Styela*, break them apart, separating the individual animal colonies from each other, and pick the organisms out from between the spaces. There are amphipods and ostracods, and some of these actually live inside the tunic, but the more conspicuous creatures are found in the spaces. During this picking and collecting process, you really appreciate why *Styela* and

Molgula are called sea squirts. At close range, a colony of 20 individuals all squirting in different directions can manage to hit the bullseye and squirt their foul-tasting water into your mouth or eye. Worse yet, some are in the process of dying, rupture their body walls as you are tearing them apart, you get a face full of rotten ooze. Enough to make anyone want to give up on sea squirts!

There is one more species that is worth mentioning, but not elaborating on and that is *Bostrichobranchus pilularis*, which looks very much like *Molgula*, but is much smaller and has thinner walls. Its siphons erect above the test and look very distinct. This species lives in muddy sand and occurs during the winter, but it is not seen every year.

Preservation

Tunicates are one of the few groups that most specialists insist be anesthetized before preservation because it is often very difficult to observe anatomical features of fresh, unrelaxed ascidians, since they strongly contract when dissected. To prepare specimens for anatomical studies or for identification, relaxed and properly fixed materials should be used.

The colonies are placed in pans of sea water; Epsom salts is either added directly or in a supersaturated solution. After 12 to 24 hours of anesthetization, the specimens are more or less flaccid and should be fixed for at least an hour in 5 percent to 10 percent sea-water Formalin before dissection. This treatment permits easy observation of features nearly impossible to discern in delicate, contractile living zooids or in contracted preserved materials.

Specimens that are to be kept in reference collections should be allowed to soak for 24 hours in fixative, then transferred through two changes of 70 percent alcohol. Large specimens should have slits made in them to facilitate penetration.

Solitary tunicates such as *Molgula*, *Styela* and *Polycarpa* have large orifices which should be preserved in an open, siphoning position. Even after a bath in a saturated solution of magnesium sulfate or a 1 percent solution of chloral hydrate, many individuals are still capable of contracting their orifices. A wooden peg or glass rod inserted in the opening will prevent closing and will permit internal preservation.

In the event that the animals contract in spite of all your efforts to preserve them, it is essential that you inject them with preservative. Too often when the specimens are placed directly into preservative, the internal organs will mascerate completely and specialists complain that when they cut open the specimen to examine the arrangement of the zooids, branchial chamber and reproductive organs (all necessary for identification) a rotten ooze gushes out and the specimens are worthless and consigned to the garbage can.

28.
Subphylum Cephalochordata

Class Amphioxi

Here we come to the end of the invertebrate phyla, we have
trekked across the protozoans and sponges, through the jellyfish and
worms, snails and crabs, starfish and finally the tunicates. At the top of
this wriggling pile of creatures sits this majestic wormlike sliver of flesh
called amphioxus — the lancelet — the most highly evolved of the little
sea creatures that writhe and squirm because it has a true notochord
running down its dorsal side. The notochord is there to stay, it does
not appear in the larval stages and then disappear, as it does in the
tunicates; it is there from conception to death. All courses in vertebrate
anatomy begin with amphioxus so we shall end with it here, in our
review of invertebrates.

Other features also make amphioxus a member of the Chordata,
and a close relative of the vertebrate stock. It has a dorsal tubular
nerve cord, and pharyngeal gill slits that have a filtering action. These
slits are similar to the respiratory organs in fish.

Lancelets are extremely muscular, pointed at both ends and can
swim as quickly through sand as a fish can swim through water. They
are reported to come out and wriggle about in the water at night, but
during the daytime they lie with their mouth protruding from the sand,
filtering out diatoms from the sea water.

When you scoop up a shovelful of sand or examine a dredge haul
containing a great deal of substrate and see a sudden movement, a

madly oscillating slender bit of pink flesh disappear back into the sand, you can be almost sure you have an amphioxus. It happens so quickly that you may doubt that you have seen it, unless you are well acquainted with the nature of the lancelet. You'll recognize that it was a lancelet only by methods of deduction: no worm ever moved that quickly and certainly no eel or other creature actually dives and moves as rapidly through coarse sand.

When you spade up sand that contains lancelets and drop it on a screen and wash the substrate out, the amphioxus wildly gyrates when it touches the screening. It squirms and dances and wriggles to and fro. Grabbing it between your fingers requires skill. Even when you get hold of them, they manage to squirm and wriggle out of your grasp. A circular screen with high sides is a good piece of equipment to use when you are collecting them. This enables you to give the screen a few hard taps and shake the amphioxus out into your collecting buckets.

In the course of collecting specimens, you will more than once manage somehow to turn your bucket over. You may have it filled with a thousand scurrying fiddler crabs or worms, or a multitude of creatures that will start to scurry away when they are freed. But nothing is more tragic than a bucket crammed with amphioxi, a full day's work in screening, shoveling sand, accidentally spilled out on a sand bar.

It is a memorable, and saddening, experience to watch each lancelet instantly burrow down and disappear into the sand. By rapid shoveling you may recover a few, but the majority will be lost by the time you collect your wits. This unfortunate experience was mine on an isolated sandbar off Madagascar, and there was nothing I could do about it. Next time I was more careful and tied them up securely in plastic bags of sea water.

There are several species of amphioxus that occur in Florida waters, and their taxonomy is under revision at present. *Branchiostoma floridae* is found in shallow bays and estuaries. There are amphioxus that can be found in the intertidal regions off sandy beaches, and there are some that occur up in the tidal salt marshes.

We have noticed that they will not live in mud, only in coarse sand hauls. If there is a great deal of fresh-water run-off they will disappear or die. We once followed the Army Corps of Engineers' dredge boat and took samples of the bottom where they had dredged, and we found that all the *Branchiostoma floridae* had diminished.

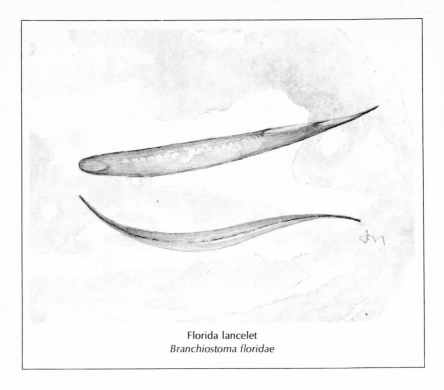

Florida lancelet
Branchiostoma floridae

However, within six months they began reappearing on the dredged bottom.

Because of their important evolutionary position, amphioxus was once collected by the thousands from the tide flats of Boca Ciega Bay in Tampa, Florida. But after the massive dredge and fill operations that took place in the early 1950s, the bottom changed from sand to silt and few if any amphioxus exist there now.

Preservation

Traditionally amphioxi are screened up and dropped directly into a 10 percent Formalin solution. They wriggle frantically for a second, then stiffen and die. After they are hardened they may be transferred to 70 percent alcohol for storage.

Many. people who prefer to examine the notochord by making histological section first fix them in Bouin's fluid before transferring to alcohol. The distinguishing characteristic of lancelets is the fringe of short, stiff tentacles that surround their mouths, and these can be extended if the animals are placed in weak alcohol for a few minutes before fixation.

29.
Phylum Chordata
Marine Fish

This book has been primarily concerned with the collection, preservation and culturing of marine invertebrates. To properly present fish would require another volume. Each ecological habitat has its own population of fish, different species that occur in one area and not in others.

Along the sandflats you'll find flounder, lizard fish, cusk eels and sting rays. Electric rays with their ominous-looking grayish-black spots that resemble ancient Egyptian hieroglyphics like to fan out a little hole for themselves in the sand, and then burrow almost completely out of sight, as do the spotted electric stargazers. Although they emit only a few volts nothing is more startling than stepping on one.

Batfish swim along the bottom with their flipperlike fins, searching for minute snails. They are more often taken in muddy bottoms along sheltered bays. Toadfish inhabit tin cans, get under rocks and dig down into oyster beds. But they also cross muddy bottoms and move into grass beds, along with the spiny boxfish, which frantically gulps air or water upon being handled and inflates itself to twice its size and bristles with sharp spines.

There are hundreds of species of fish in the estuaries of the Gulf alone. The tidal marshes are full of juvenile trout, redfish, mullet and croakers. The rocky shores abound with blennies and gobies. Snapper, grouper and black sea bass are rock dwellers, making their homes in caves and holes.

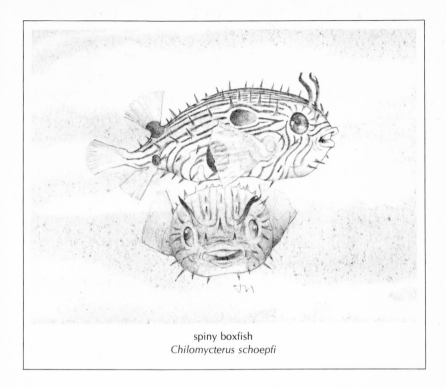

spiny boxfish
Chilomycterus schoepfi

Certainly the most colorful and exotic of all the fishes live in tropical coral reefs, and one can spend hours and days just swimming over the clear waters, fish-watching. In fact I wish there were an underwater handbook, printed in waterproof ink, on waterproof paper, that you could carry along and use for identifying the parrotfish, beaugregories, angels and queen triggers encountered as you swim from coral head to coral head.

There are two approaches to collecting fishes. The first is bringing them back to maintain in an aquarium. Generally, many of the inshore, easy-to-collect species are hardy and will live well in captivity. There are some expensive marine tropicals that require a great deal of time and attention to keep alive and in good condition. There are several good books that can be purchased on the care, feeding and disease-control of marine tropical fish. Not much has been written on maintaining estuarine fish because they are not as colorful, but from my observations and experiences in keeping them for years in the aquarium, the dull-colored small flounders, grunts, sea robins and pigfish are extremely interesting and active. They are also more hardy than most tropical forms.

smooth dogfish sharks
Mustelus norrisi

The next approach to collecting fishes is preserving them for a reference collection, which is discussed at length in this chapter.

The professional ichthyologist is involved with costly fishing gear: tackle and nets, trawls and traps, drags and dredges, spear guns and slurpguns, poisons and drugs. And unfortunately, if one is going to make a thorough sampling of marine fish for an institutional reference collection, then one must use all these techniques.

Yet many amateurs with a simple seine, dip net and a few other bits of equipment including a fishing rod have made substantial contributions to ichthyology, especially when collecting in new areas. It is most difficult to discover a new species of fish, since they have been intensely studied in every area of the world; however, there is much need of good distribution records in new areas.

Although we have added many new distribution records of sharks, rays and assorted teleost fish to north Florida, one of our most important contributions to ichthyology was the discovery of the little ophidioid fish, *Guntherichthys longipenis*. The little peculiar-looking pink fish with small eyes and smooth, slimy skin and an elongated

390

penis was first described by Dr. Charles E. Dawson from the Gulf Coast Research Station in Ocean Springs, Mississippi, in 1966. He found the odd little goby during a collecting trip that immediately followed periods of unusual climatic conditions. The week's torrential rainstorms produced a single specimen in a state of cold shock.

In the early fall of 1969 we discovered our first specimen in the marshy creeks of Fiddler's Point in Panacea. We were trawling for white shrimp with a 15-foot shrimp net pulled from behind a small tunnel boat. For years we shrimped the same area, culled through boatloads of white shrimp that were living in the marshes and never a single red goby did we find. But that year there were weeks upon weeks of intense rains and the salinity dropped down to nine parts per 1000. Fresh-water bass, sunfish and shellcrackers migrated out of the Ochlockonee River and entered the bays and estuaries. In less than one week 14 inches of rain were dumped on north Florida. There was intense flooding everywhere. It was then that we found our strange-looking pink-skinned eel-like creature with its small, pinpointlike eyes. In one week's trawling time, we collected three adult specimens. We brought them back to our laboratory holding tanks and one gave birth to four, tiny live pink fry, providing the only juvenile specimens on record. It also demonstrated that *Guntherichthys longipenis* is a live bearer—something that is very rare in teleost fishes. The mother perished immediately afterward and we preserved the young.

What may be most important about *Guntherichthys longipenis* is that it is a high-stress-environment indicator. Although a few specimens have subsequently been taken by students in Mississippi who were digging deep in the mud for invertebrates, it is normally seen only when there is a disaster.

A collector who is constantly roving the seashore will see numerous natural disasters from time to time. Small fish kills result when fish cannot get out of a tidepool that loses its oxygen because of scorching heat. When the icy winters push down into the tropical Florida Keys, fish perish by the thousands. And walking along, well dressed in heavy clothing during a freeze in the Keys, I have seen fish dying everywhere. Beaugregories, cowfish, queen triggers, moray eels slid out of the rocks and lay gasping and dying on the beaches. For weeks after the hard freeze of 1969 the beaches were littered with rotting, decaying skeletons of fish; in some places they stretched out as far as the eye could see. Fish died that year in the Bahamas and other tropical islands.

If you arrive on the scene in time, you can get freshly killed or dying specimens and preserve them for a reference collection. This will accomplish two objectives: first, to gather a reference collection, and second, to determine and record which species are most susceptible to environmental-stress conditions. During the fish kill, for example, we did not find a single dead shark or ray.

Seasonal migrations and movements of fish are a science in themselves. Various species are affected by changes in salinity, water temperature, currents and habitat.

Along the Atlantic coast fish follow a seasonal pattern, moving offshore into deeper waters or moving south during the winter, and coming inshore during the summer months. Many tropical species follow the Gulf Stream, and records of file fish, triggerfish and sea horses taken off Cape Cod are common during July and August. But these are not natural occurrences, and the chances of swimming off the New Jersey coast and finding a queen triggerfish are slim, even though some ichthyologist came up with one five years before at some particular spot.

Your collecting techniques will depend upon the ultimate uses of the fish. If they are to be gathered for the aquarium then they must be carefully and gently handled, kept in cool well-aerated or oxygenated water during transport. But if they are to be preserved for a reference collection, another set of collecting procedures that produce bigger yields may be employed.

Seining engulfs schools of frantic fish, dragging them up on the beach. Large fish traps baited with dead fish will often bring in crabs as well as a variety of fish. A scoop net run through a tidal stream will bring up a collection of small minnows.

Preservation

Shortly after capture the process of preserving fish should begin. The techniques are the same, whether one is preserving a two-inch minnow or a 200-pound shark; the amount of storage space and volume of preservatives are important.

For most collections it is impractical to bother with very large specimens such as sharks, rays, tuna, etc., as they are kept in formaldehyde or alcohol coffins. If they are to be put in jars, smaller specimens or juveniles are more desirable. One should be very familiar with the characteristics used in keying out fish before attempting any cut-downs.

Cut-downs are used in the field when a fish specimen is too large. In sharks, for example, the jaws are most important, as well as the eyes and head, in determining a species, so the head should be removed and preserved; but also the distance from the dorsal fin to the caudal fin should be measured, and the total length and standard lengths recorded. On large fish, such as groupers, scales are important, so a portion of the skin should be preserved, and since the number of rays in the fins must be counted for a precise determination, all fins should be saved.

A good way to make a cut-down on any fish, shark or ray, is to cut the head and caudal fins, pulling off as much skin and appendages as possible, roll it up into a package and put it into weak formaldehyde.

The smaller fish, ranging from a few inches to two feet should be preserved intact. They are best preserved immediately in the field or within 24 hours after they have been kept on ice. Fish tossed directly into the freezer may be thawed out in formaldehyde and when they are completely softened, they should be injected with formaldehyde to preserve their internal organs.

For well-preserved, lifelike specimens it is preferable to submerge a live fish into Formalin. This is a most unpleasant thing to do if you have any feeling toward life, but a fish killed in reagent will keep the shape of its body and its fins distended. You can often get a lifelike appearance, as though it were ready to swim away or bite something. A fish that has been dead for a day or so looks flaccid, with compressed fins and colors faded—and it will fix that way.

Fishes should be preserved straightened out. To do this you should place them in large shallow pans and straigthen them out with ample preservative. In preparing small minnows, injection of the internal organs is not necessary, as Formalin will penetrate their body cavity through osmosis, anyway. Five percent Formalin is all that is necessary.

Fishes, unlike most of the invertebrates, require more thorough preservation to keep the complicated internal structures from deteriorating. Ten to 15 percent Formalin must be injected into the abdominal cavity until the fish's abdomen distends with hardening fluid. Be sure that preservative, not air, has gone in when using a bulb syringe. This prevents the liver, stomach and intestines from decaying, so if a researcher or student cuts through the abdominal muscles into the digestive system months or years later, he can see what the fish's last dinner was.

If the fishes are not internally preserved and allowed to soak in formaldehyde, they begin to bloat and float upward, as they mascerate internally. Then they begin to smell, and if one wants to salvage his specimen he has to open the mess and remove all the rot. On field trips it is often too much trouble to inject each fish, so the abdominal cavity may be opened with a knife, cutting a straight line from the anus down the belly, just enough of an opening to permit the thorough penetration of preservative.

It is most important to know the exact concentration of preservative to be used on specific fishes. If the concentration is too strong, the fish comes out like leather and is difficult to work with. If too soft, a much worse situation, rot, sets in.

There are certain species like alewife and shad that deteriorate shortly after they die and become mushy because they have such a huge quantity of oil in their tissues. The flesh becomes soft as it breaks down in normal preservative. This type of oily fish is best injected immediately with 15 percent Formalin, and immediately thereafter placed in a large volume of 12 percent Formalin and watched closely to see if it is becoming sufficiently hardened.

Although not fully proved, we have found that fresh-water Formalin seems superior to the traditional salt-water Formalin in preserving fishes in general, and particularly the soft fish. The electric rays, *Narcine* and *Torpedo*, tend to become soft in preservative; their tissues slough off easily. Therefore it is best to preserve them immediately after capture, using a 15 percent Formalin solution, making sure they have been injected two or three times. Their electric organs are extremely soft and mushy, and a hypodermic needle filled with Formalin should be injected directly into the electric tissues. If you wish to make an anatomical preparation, Formalin should be profused into the arteries and veins by an injection into the heart of a living animal.

On a collecting trip where space and preservative are limited, you may embalm your specimens until they are hardened, which takes a day or two; then they may be removed, wrapped in burlap or cloth saturated with concentrated Formalin, and placed in a plastic bag, sealed to keep them moist. They last several weeks, and even months, in this manner; later they can be placed in fresh preserving fluid. Of course they should be soaked in fresh water for a while to fluff out the tissues.

Embalmed specimens may be placed directly into alcohol, after they have been hardened in Formalin, but never place the fish that have not been hardened in Formalin into alcohol. Alcohol instantly fades the colors, makes the eyes opaque and causes the tissues to shrink.

There has been a long-standing debate among ichthyologists about the preservatives to be used on fish. Harvard's Museum of Comparative Zoology prefers the fishes initially preserved in 10 percent Formalin, then transfers them to 50 percent ethyl alcohol and after a few days places them in 70 percent ethyl alcohol.

Other laboratories place them directly into 35 percent isopropyl alcohol, but some argue that isopropyl alcohol will break down the fatty tissues in the fish, causing unnatural shrinkage and deterioration over a period of time. Most authorities do not recommend that a fish be left in formaldehyde for a period of more than two years as this is supposed to cause the tissues to break down. However, other icthyological laboratories keep their fishes permanently in 5 percent formaldehyde and still find them useful.

Ethyl alcohol is by far the best, not only because it is more pleasant to work with, but because it preserves the tissues better. As Formalin specimens are handled all the time, they can irritate you, and isopropyl alcohol is almost as unpleasant as Formalin if used in any large quantities.

Marine Algae

Macroscopic, benthic algae are found only around the margins of the world's oceans where there is adequate light penetration for photosynthesis. This zone is approximately 2 percent of the ocean's total area. Nevertheless, wherever algae grow, they are an essential part of the marine community, providing shelter and (to a limited degree) food for countless millions of large and small marine animals.

It is important to build up a reference collection of marine algae since it will provide a basis for future studies, including coastal inventories, habitat surveys and studies of faunal-floral relationships.

Preservation

Two methods of preserving marine algae are commonly employed. If intact specimens are required for cytological studies, they should be preserved and stored directly in 5 percent sea-water Formalin. Most algae specialists, however, make dry herbarium mounts.

Mounting specimens involves a plant press, which usually consists of two frames of crisscross slats, with canvas or leather straps that are attached to the bottom of the frame. The straps are used to close the press and sandwich the plants together.

For absorption and dry mounting you should have a good supply of blotter paper, corrugated cardboard, and a stack of newspaper, herbarium paper, or other paper that has a high rag content.

Before mounting it is a good idea to soak the algae in Formalin for 24 hours since this prevents them from rotting. The first step in mounting is to float the algae, speading them out in a large pan. Then slide the herbarium paper into the tray underneath the algae sample, and carefully lift it up so that the algae are spread out upon the paper. The algae should then be arranged with a probe or brush so that all the diagnostic features can be clearly viewed.

The algae are sandwiched between paper and cardboard as follows: place the bottom half of the plant-press frame on a large table. Then put on a layer of corrugated cardboard followed by a layer of newspaper and the herbarium mount. Cover the algae with a piece of cheesecloth or wax paper to prevent them from adhering to the second layer of newspaper, which is on top. Then continue the layers of cardboard, newspapers, algae and waxpaper until the press is full.

When you have all your algae samples in the press, cover them with the top frame and close it with the straps. It is important that the press be closed firmly, but not tight enough to crush the plants. The newspaper and blotting paper should be changed every 24 hours until the specimens are thoroughly dry.

Labels bearing the species name (when known), locality, date, and collector's name should be glued onto the herbarium paper as soon as it is thoroughly dry. This is important because collections can get lost or confused.

30.
Collecting Equipment and Ecological Data

A collector must anticipate what type of animal he is going to come across in a particular habitat and select his collecting equipment accordingly. Burrowing creatures are found in sand and mud, and thus require a shovel, while coral-dwelling creatures that move about rapidly will require a net, and under-rock animals necessitate a crowbar. However, if you have to walk over great expanses of mudflats carrying shovels, buckets, trowels, screens and even diving equipment, it can become an unbearable burden. Nothing is more tiring than lugging equipment around all morning, loaded like a pack mule and never using it. Collecting in itself can be exhausting work and it takes considerable effort to go sloshing through shallow water turning over rocks.

Over the years I have made suppositions that may be disputed because they are not rooted in solid facts. If you go out loaded like an African safari with everything you should have, you'll probably come home empty-handed. Often if you go out with nothing more than a shovel and a bucket, there are more specimens than you can manage.

A good way to bring everything along, is of course, to use a skiff and outboard motor as a base of operations. However, even a boat can quickly become overloaded by the time it has two or three sets of diving gear, five or six plastic garbage cans plus smaller buckets, a

398

small otter trawl, a scallop drag, at least two dip nets, a plankton net and bucket dredge. To top it off, such a boat may even have a gill net in it, and before long there is no room to move about. Add three or four collectors and you have a real jam on your hands.

There is no simple answer to the whole problem. If you go unprepared, you may see something out in the bay for which you need the particular piece of equipment you left behind. On the other hand, when you are turning over rocks with a crowbar, you'll be standing on the ledge and may see a number of blue-tinged jellyfish pulsating by and not have a dip net to reach out and swoop them up. However, had you carried the dip net it's possible that you wouldn't have seen a single jellyfish.

Following is a list of some of the more commonly used collecting gear.

Annotated Checklist
of Collecting Equipment

1. **Containers.** Plastic pails are excellent for field work and are generally superior to metal or wooden pails that were once in common use. However, be prepared to buy new pails from time to time, since they become brittle and crack, and the metal handles pull out under a strain.

2. **Floating Containers.** These are very useful when collecting some distance offshore. They can easily be constructed by placing a nylon net or burlap sack inside an inflated inner tube. A bucket may also be inserted directly into the center of the tube and the float may be anchored with a crowbar or geology hammer. If the anchor line is tied to your waist, you can wade through the shallows towing the float and have both hands free for collecting.

3. **Vial and Small-Bottle Holder.** Nothing gets lost faster or more completely than an orange-spotted, rare flatworm placed in a bucket with sea urchins, tunicates and sponges. It is therefore necessary to isolate the small rare animals in vials, which are successfully carried in an ammunition belt. Larger jars can be hauled in a custom-made

399

bottle carrier that looks like a wooden case for holding soft drinks and has handles.

4. **Plastic Bags.** These can be used to replace vials and jars. The animals can be immediately placed in small plastic bags with sea water and tied securely in the field or closed with rubberbands. Plastic bags have a variety of uses including capturing forms that would be frightened away at the approach of a webbed net.

5. **Forceps.** Both large and small forceps are useful in picking up specimens in any type of habitat. They have advantages over fingers in that they are very precise, and in a strange area where you are not familiar with the fauna, they can save fingers from being bitten, pinched, stuck or stung. That small, soft-bodied ominous worm with bristles protruding or that spiny sea urchin may be something that no one would want to pick up with bare hands.

6. **Brushes.** For extremely soft-bodied, fragile invertebrates like turbellarians, a camel's-hair brush is effective. Simply wipe them off a rock with the brush and delicately dip the bristles in a vial until the animal is released.

7. **Eye-dropper.** This handy item has a variety of uses both in the field and in the laboratory. It can be used to suck up frail nudibranchs, flatworms, mites and other creatures in tidepools without damaging them. You can get an eye-dropper into a crevice where your big clumsy fingers don't stand a chance. In the laboratory it can be used to draw up and isolate very small creatures from a watch glass which is viewed under a dissecting scope.

8. **Hand Pump.** To remove water and small organisms from burrows or crevices in rocks, we have found that a small hand pump is very effective. The technique was first developed by Dr. Arthur G. Humes of Boston University for collecting commensal copepods that live down sand burrows that belong to unknown marine animals, which no amount of digging could successfully reveal.

The intake tube is inserted down into the burrow and a small hand pump used for transferring chemicals is pumped rapidly. The effluent water is strained through a plankton net and the crustaceans and other associated organisms are trapped.

9. **Nets.** A stout crab net with approximately one-half-inch webbing is useful for large specimens. Small nets with a circular or rectangular opening and a fine-meshed nylon bag are helpful when gathering small, free-swimming invertebrates. Seines are used for catching small, and large, fishes in shallow water, and various grades

and sizes are available from fishermen- and biological-supply houses.

10. **Screens.** When a substrate sample is dug up from a beach or hauled aboard a boat from a dredge, it can be put through a series of three or four screens with various-sized meshes. If a lot of sand is to be sifted, a deck pump will greatly facilitate washing. In rolling seas, slopping buckets and washing specimens through screens can be a memorable experience.

11. **Standard Equipment.** This includes shovels, trowels, geology hammers, and cold-chisels, which have been referred to throughout the book. These are available at most hardware stores. My advice is to buy the best possible grades, using good steel, because corrosion will take its toll and make the shoddy merchandise break down all the faster.

12. **Fishing Rod and Angler's Equipment.** Believe it or not, this is one of the most effective ways of catching many fishes and crabs. It does not require a lot of expensive gear such as seines, traps or dredges, and when the weather makes collecting impossible, or the boat is broken down you can still fish. Especially when you travel to some remote area, and you are unable to get out and dive for animals because of a pending storm, fishing with a hook and line is great.

Many species can be taken in this manner that would escape a net, or might be too deep to dive for, or you couldn't catch them if you did dive for them. Of course, for preserved specimens, just taking the fishes off the line is easy. If the fish doesn't swallow the hook, it can be kept alive. You just have to be careful in removing the hook from the fish's mouth.

Aquarium shark collectors often set hooks overnight and, if the hooked sharks haven't drowned the next morning, bring them back alive. The hook is seldom damaging and the wound heals quickly. The specimens are often much less damaged than if they were caught in a gill net or otter trawl.

13. **Spears or Gigs.** In shallow water, when walking along at night with a gasoline lantern, many of the flat fishes such as flounder, sole and various rays can be speared and added to a preserved reference collection. Small sharks can also be speared, but this can be a risky business. While diving, the use of a speargun is helpful in getting larger fish.

14. **Speargun.** Moray eels can be pulled from the the rocks with a good shot of a speargun but be cautious, they are vicious and can maul you badly. If you must have a dead moray eel, shoot for the

head. Grouper and jewfish live around reefs, pilings and old boat wrecks and may be collected by spearfishing, While the majority of divers spearfish to eat, the naturalist can employ this successful method for gathering a series of fish specimens for a reference collection. A fish with a hole through the middle of it is not the best specimen, but with a rare or unusual specimen it is better than no specimen.

15. **Slurp Guns.** The principle of a slurp gun is a piston plunger that is spring-released in a tube. When the piston springs forward, a vacuum is created. Water and perhaps a small fish are sucked into a tube and then deposited in a plastic bag. Professional fish collectors tend to stay away from slurp guns and rely on nets. Their range is limited, and there is some evidence that they will damage fishes. However, when diving over a coral head, they are effective in getting small clownfish or neon gobies out of crevices.

16. **Bucket Dredges.** The purpose of a bucket dredge or a Peterson grab is bringing up a sample of the substrate. The bottom may be soft oozing mud, sand mixed with shell, pebbles or pure hard-packed sand. Each type of bottom will support an entirely different community of burrowing organisms often including small tellinid clams, sedentary polychaetes, brittlestars, etc.

The dredge is constructed of heavy metal and is completely closed in. Two protruding blades assure that the dredge will bite into the substratum regardless of the angle.

17. **Biological Dredge.** A biological dredge is one of the most effective methods of gathering marine life. An epibenthic dredge can weigh 1000 pounds and be pulled from a large oceanographic vessel sampling the ocean bottom, or it can be a simple home-built device used from the back of a skiff and pulled with as little as a 5½-horsepower outboard motor. If you look around most fishing villages, you can find ready-built scallop dredges.

The fisherman's variety is built out of steel ⅜" rods in a rectangular frame usually 48" × 18", although there seems to be no set rule. Scallop dredges 36" × 24" are not uncommon. Some have a piece of flattened steel for a cutterblade, some have no cutterblade at all, and rely on the steel rod for pushing down the grass along the bottom. Some have four chains meeting at a single point where the rope is attached to form a bridle, others have rods welded out and angled at a 30° angle to keep the dredge from jumping off the bottom. The force of the water pushes the benthic animals back into the bag.

The bag is usually made of large meshed webbing approximately one inch bar and two-inch stretch. This is excellent for gathering many larger organisms such as scallops, sea urchins, starfish and many fish feeding among the sea grass. It does well with sand dollars, and can get up heart urchins. Small shrimp, hermit crabs, and blennies are often trapped in the mass of dead grass and algae that comes up.

But if you want to be sure you're getting all the smaller fishes and invertebrates, the shrimp, and small brittlestars, you can use a finer mesh. A nylon fine-mesh bag is effective in gathering the minute crustaceans and worms.

18. **Otter Trawl.** This is the same type of net that commercial fishing vessels use to catch flounder, croakers and shrimp. However, small otter trawls measuring 20 feet or less can be pulled behind the average 18-h.p. outboard motor. The more powerful your motor the better the spread of the net. The net is spread apart by two ironclad boards called "otter doors" which weigh it down, and keep the net gliding over the bottom like a gigantic kite.

The size most collectors would use is called a "try trawl" and is available at most fishermen's supply houses. These can be easily handled from a small boat, and will bring in a very large sampling of fishes, crabs, starfish, sea urchins and almost anything else on the bottom that can be easily broken loose. Unlike a dredge it can be snagged on a rock, coral or dead tree and if you don't slow the boat down immediately, back up and pull it in, your net can get torn to pieces.

If you use one often, it pays to learn how to patch webbing, or know good commercial fishermen who can.

Ecological Data

The primary difference between a scientifically valuable collection of marine animals and a jumbled, haphazard assortment of pickled and dried specimens that are of very little use, can be summed up in one small word: Data. When was the specimen collected? Where? How? What were the hydrographic conditions, and what did it look like when it was alive? All of these questions and countless others should be answerable when one picks up a specimen in a museum collection and examines it.

The most contracted, distorted and even half-rotten creature in brown alcohol, if properly labeled, has greater value than a well-preserved, expanded specimen with no label whatsoever. If the investigator doesn't know whether it came from Honduras or the Florida Keys or the Indian Ocean, of what value is the specimen?

In giving locality data, list the latitude and longtitude whenever possible. If the locality is near land, list the nearest township, county, province or anything else that can be found on standard U.S. Coast and Geodetic Survey maps. Be as specific as possible: mention which highway is nearest to the beach; give landmarks like lighthouses and motels; include the location of a jetty, or a tide pool on a particular jetty. Be sure to include any information that can be found on nautical maps.

Give extensive notes on the substrate. A good book on marine geology will be of great assistance. If it is rock, indicate whether it is shale, granite, sandstone or limestone, compact clay or mud. If sand, describe the texture, color and grain size. If the mud smells like rotten eggs, say so in your data records.

All specimens should be documented with data labels that are placed inside the bottle after the collection has been sorted and broken down into smaller units. Use a high-rag-content paper and print with India ink, or the harsh preservatives will soon disintegrate the label. Lead-pencil writing on labels is also good and often holds up for months, sometimes even years in alcohol or Formalin. But at a later date it is a good idea to make permanent labels written in India ink. A typical data label might read:

```
┌─────────────────────────────────────────────────────┐
│                                                       │
│   SPECIES _____ │
│                                                       │
│   PHYLUM _____ DATE _____ │
│                                                       │
│   LOCALITY _____ │
│                                                       │
│           _____ │
│                                                       │
│   COLLECTOR _____ FIELD NUMBER _____ │
│                                                       │
└─────────────────────────────────────────────────────┘
```

Labels will have variations, depending upon use. Some labels have spaces to indicate depth, water temperature or whatever standard information one feels should be supplied with his collections. You can have them printed to suit individual need.

It is very important to keep a field notebook with these collections. Each lot of specimens is assigned a collection number which is recorded in a field notebook. The collection number should always appear on the data label that goes inside the jar with the specimen. Many naturalists use nothing more than the collection number in a bottle of specimens, thus requiring someone working with the collection to make frequent references to the field notebook.

There is no standard rule on when to use a new collection number during field operations. Aboard a ship every dredge haul or otter trawl might be considered a separate collection and so require a new number. But in the field, specimens collected on an all-day walk along a rocky coast would be assigned one number. However, if you left the rocks and went over to a sand flat and started digging for animals you might want to assign the specimens obtained there an entirely new collection number.

The more notes you enter the better. I have never heard of anyone complaining that someone's field notes were too wordy; they complain when they are too skimpy. Any diagnostic traits such as color, texture and form that may be lost during the preservation process are important to note. Very often you will encounter a certain organism and have no idea of its identification; in fact you may not be able to place it into any of the phyla because it appears so different. Assign it a separate number, and proceed with any descriptions or behavioral notes that you care to make. Later, when the identification has been made, you can write in the identification next to the number. An entry might read, "No. A-233-1 was frequently encountered under rocks along the mid-tide region. We succeeded in netting this one with great difficulty in one of the shallow tide pools." Later, after the preserved specimen has been keyed out, *Gonodadylus oerstedi*, a stomatapod crustacean, may be substituted for A-233-1.

If possible make note of hydrographic conditions. This can be done in two ways. The first is a general observation such as whether there was a swift current, the water was turbid, choppy or calm. Second, if instruments are available take note of salinity, turbidity readings, dissolved oxygen and, perhaps most important, water temperature. The last-named is one of the most regulating factors in the movements and migrations of marine animals. There are many other things one might include in his data, such as coloration and color variations, geographic distributions, sex ratios of specimens seen but not collected.

When writing field notes words like "common" and "not uncommon" should be avoided whenever possible. Even a rough estimation of how many snails or worms were found in a given radius of rocks is more helpful than saying the snails were "uncommon." Say approximately how many were seen, or how many were collected over how many hours of collecting time.

Depth is very important and should be accurately measured with a Fathometer, if you are working from a large boat. However, a sounding line, which is simply made by using an anchor with rope tied into knots at foot or meter intervals, lowered to the bottom will give an accurate reading. Even a good estimated depth is better than none at all, but say "estimated depth" in your notes. Note if an animal is collected in a tide pool or is found under rocks or in the substratum beneath rocks.

Good data will help ecologists understand a great deal about regional variations within a species. Even a seashell marked "Florida" or "North Carolina" on the label is not entirely without value because the same mollusk existing in a different geographical range may look and behave in an entirely different way. To further complicate morphological variations within a geographical distributional range, a great many species traverse a variety of ecological habitats ranging from tidal marshes and mangrove swamps to submerged rocks at depths of 200 feet. The same species of tunicate or sponge may be found on intertidal boulders as fine, encrusting fouling layers while at a 100-foot dredge haul, it appears as globular masses weighing 10 pounds or more.

When a collection of assorted marine animals including fishes, algae and even rock and sand samples is unpacked, the long process of sorting and individually labeling them begins. The Smithsonian Oceanographic Sorting Center in Washington, D.C., is responsible for sorting out collections of specimens taken on expeditions throughout the world.

The conglomerate mass of animals must be isolated into groups. First the most obvious divisions are made, such as fishes, invertebrates and algae. Then all crabs are put together, all sea anemones, all shrimp and worms where they can be subsequently identified by experts. This is not difficult with macroscopic organisms, but when looking through dishes of plankton the task becomes more difficult and even tedious.

Although it may take only a few minutes to make a sand collection, or even a plankton tow, the real work comes back at the laboratory when the specimens are carefully sorted and put into tiny vials, the copepods isolated from the ostracods, the phytoplankton sorted from the pelagic fish eggs. The really interesting finds in zoology do not come aboard ship when the dredge is hauled up; they come from the zoologist looking at the catch through his microscope and then probing some strange, unknown, unnamed blob.

Pogonophorians, a phylum closely related to the hemichordates, were first discovered in the 1900s from an Indonesian dredge haul, but only after the specimens had been sorted out. The discovery of a new phylum is something extra special, because by the middle of the nineteenth century nearly all the phyla of animals had been described by zoologists.

One of the biggest dangers in sorting specimens is losing the data label or lot number. The best way to avoid this is to unpack preserved specimens slowly and sort one lot at a time, breaking each group of animals down into vials and jars, each marked with the lot number which corresponds to the notebook entry, the collector's name and the date; whether or not the specimens are going to be classified immediately the complete data label should always be included in the jar.

Several small vials of specimens may be placed in one large jar filled with alcohol along with the lot data label. This is effective, minimizes storage space and keeps the little collections from getting lost.

Whenever working with parasites, whether they are commensal barnacles living in the gills of a crab or tapeworms from a whale, always be sure you include the name of the host as well as all the locality data where the host was found. If you can't identify the host, take it along as a specimen for later identification. If it is too large, take a photograph. But if that is not possible, draw a picture of the host, showing diagnostic features such as distances between fins, shape of teeth or scales.

The observations of a naturalist are very valuable in today's world of rapid change. Only through the notes of a few dedicated zoologists and botanists do we know what life in certain areas was like a few years ago, because these areas have been radically altered by the activities of mankind. I wish I had a good, documented reference collection of the marine organisms that inhabited the tidal salt marshes of Shell Point in Wakulla County, because it is too late now. Whatever was there in the past is now under tons of earth sealed with asphalt and concrete which probably will not be resurrected in our lifetime.

31.
Shipping Specimens: Techniques

There are four standard methods of packing marine animals for shipment: preserved, live, frozen and packed on ice. Each method of packing and shipping has a different purpose, and each will be treated individually.

Building up a well-identified collection of marine invertebrates, fishes and algae is essential to properly evaluate the ecology of a set region. After collections are made, the animals anesthetized, fixed and preserved in bottles with data labels, you may wish to ship them out to a number of specialists at various museums or institutions who, by prior agreement, will furnish an identification. Never send specimens to museums unless you have their express permission. In some instances identification will be provided by specialists for a financial consideration; in other instances they may wish to retain some of the specimens for their own collections.

Regardless of the arrangements, the specimens must be packed in such a way that they will not be jostled and shaken up—otherwise fragile forms will break to pieces. Even though hours were spent in the field, considerable time and expense invested in gathering the material and in preparation, all can be lost if the collections arrive in a broken-up condition.

Proper shipping of specimens has almost as many perplexities as proper collecting and preservation techniques. While it is possible to ship some forms by merely bottling them in some preservative, putting them in a well-padded parcel and sending them on their way, other forms like highly fragile ctenophores, spiny sea urchins and brittlestars must be packed carefully with special consideration given to seeing that they are not allowed to be jostled.

Large bulky collections are best shipped with the animals packed in plastic bags full of preservative and then placed in a shipping drum with more preservative for cushioning. This is firmly sealed with either a ring-bolt sealer or a professional sealing device.

Dry-packed fishes and invertebrates are removed from the embalming fluid, wrapped in alcohol- or formaldehyde-soaked cheese cloth, and then placed in a plastic bag. These may be placed directly into a pasteboard or wooden carton and made ready for shipping.

It is most important that the animals be preserved thoroughly before shipping. This business of dropping a specimen into alcohol when it is freshly dead, then adding a shipping label and putting it into the hands of the freight office leaves much to be desired. I know one shell collector who made an extensive mollusk collection in the Indian Ocean, gathered some of the most beautiful sea slugs, octopuses and squids, but failed to preserve them thoroughly before shipping, or the alcohol he used was too weak. By the time his animals arrived at Harvard six months later, more than half had to be thrown out because they were mascerated and of no use. A good rule is always to use plenty of preservative; even though this additional weight boosts freight rates, it is worth it.

The methods of packing extremely fragile jellyfish are not complex. Use as small a jar or vial as possible; don't cram the animal in, but leave very little room for it to turn about or spin. Then fill the jar to the very top with preserving fluid. Even one tiny air bubble can cause absolute disaster. A good method we use for *Mnemiopsis macrydi*, which is the most delicate of all ctenophores, is first to pack them in plastic bags filled with preservative. A knot is tied down to the water level, squeezing out *all* the air, then the plastic bag containing the ctenophore is placed in a jar, and that jar is also filled with preservative. This way the ctenophore or any other extremely frail creature, like a pycnogonid sea spider, or an ophiuroid, or an arrow crab can only spin around within the bag, and the bag is cushioned in the bottle.

Charles E. Cutress at the University of Puerto Rico outlined some techniques for shipping anemones in a letter to a collector in Australia.

He was kind enough to give me a copy of the letter, and it really applies to all soft-bodied invertebrates:

"Small anemones are best shipped in vials or small bottles filled completely with preservative. Use no packing in the vials as this distorts the specimens. As a precaution against leakage the individual vials and bottles should be sealed with adhesive or plastic tape. Do not use Scotch tape! Whenever a number of vials are to be shipped it is best to pack them in water-tight friction-lid tins. For just a few vials, and specially if they are to be sent by air, it is desirable to tie them up in leakproof plastic bags.

"For large anemones much space and weight can be saved if they are shipped moist. To do this wrap each lot of specimens loosely in several layers of gauze or soft cloth, saturate the bundle with preservative, put in a water-tight plastic bag and tie securely. As an extra precaution against leakage rebag several of the packaged lots in another plastic bag. These bundles of specimens should then be packed in water-tight friction lid tins or something comparable (i.e. paint buckets and biscuit tins).

"When packing specimens in liquid remember that the package will rarely if ever stay right side up, also changes in temperature and air pressure will cause leakage."

When packing it pays to be generous with cushioning material. All jars, bottles and even certain specimens should be thoroughly wrapped with newspaper. Shredded newspaper is excellent for cushioning and, in the event of breakage, will absorb all fluid. Now there is a great variety of packing materials on the market that can be used for shipping bottles filled with liquid. There is a plastic sheeting filled with thousands of tiny air pockets that does well, Styrofoam is a good method, and excelsior sandwiched between paper is also excellent.

In shipping, select good strong pasteboard boxes and use plenty of filamentous tape and string. In this day when things are so often crushed in the mails, extra-careful packing is vital.

In shipping living specimens, many of the same procedures apply. The specimens must be cushioned against jostling, but a whole new set of problems arises in getting specimens to their destination in living, healthy condition. Each situation is different; there are hard and easy animals to deal with. Just as you take a preserved shark, wrap it in cloth and ship it off without further difficulty, you can take certain species of crabs or whelks or clams, throw them into some damp seaweed in a crate and send them on their way with relative ease. But if you want to ship a living squid, octopus, or shark someplace you should go to great pains.

Delicate creatures that are quick to die of oxygen starvation, temperature or light shock require a great deal of special handling. If you observe them in their natural environment sometimes this will give you a clue to how well they will ship. Oysters, mussels and certain gastropods that are adjusted to long periods of exposure, will survive if simply kept damp while shipping. Rock crabs (Cancer) which one can often find out of the water do well shipped in damp seaweed.

The rocky-shore collector rightly concludes that the sponges, hydroids and sea urchins that he finds at the base of rocks, perhaps briefly exposed for a few hours every month or two, should be shipped in an adequate volume of sea water. Any sudden drop or increase in temperature may be lethal to such forms, so you should try to make the conditions in the shipping box as stable as possible.

The technique that commercial tropical fish suppliers use is standard. The best and healthiest fish are selected, placed in a plastic bag with an ample volume of sea water to cover them and then charged with oxygen. Make sure that all the air is first collapsed out of the bag before blowing it up from the oxygen cylinder. The oxygen tube is jerked out of the bag, allowing as little oxygen as possible to escape, and the bag twisted and tied in a knot or tied with rubberbands.

A good, heavy .003 mill bag is good for most fishes; however, if large spiny fish are shipped, at least three bags should be used. Newspaper or other packing material may be used as cushioning between bag layers.

Shipping frozen organisms is not difficult. The specimens are simply packed in Styrofoam or heavy cardboard, and dry ice is placed on top of them. Since cold travels downward it is imperative that the ice be on top of the specimens.

When shipping on wet ice, wrap the specimens in plastic and bury them in the middle of an ice chest full of ice. It is that simple.

32.
Preservatives and Fixatives

Formalin

This is the most inexpensive and most effective fixative and preservative for a large number of specimens. Formalin comes as 37.9 percent formaldehyde gas dissolved in water, the full-strength saturated solution. It is available at most drugstores in pint quantities or it can be purchased from biological supply houses and chemical supply houses in gallon jugs, five-gallon jugs or 50-gallon drums. Each gallon of Formalin makes up 10 gallons of 10 percent stock-preserving solution.

Formalin hardens the tissues by denaturing the proteins and stabilizes them against further chemical change. When making up solutions always work outdoors, in a well-ventilated room or under a vent, so the fumes can be sucked out. It can be exceedingly irritating to the lungs, nose and eyes, and constant indoor exposure can cause serious damage. The gases given off from the solution can mix with the fluid in your lungs and go into a weak solution inside your body, which may cause emphysema. That is why biological supply houses that work with thousands of gallons of Formalin every day have huge vent fans that carry off the fumes.

Always wear rubber gloves when working with Formalin; never handle it directly with your bare hands. It destroys the oil in your fingers; they become discolored and after a while turn black. Use forceps or tongs when handling Formalin-preserved specimens. After

413

prolonged use some people become sensitive to the odor and may develop allergic eruptions on contact. For this reason many museums prefer to fix their specimens in Formalin briefly and transfer them to alcohol for storage as quickly as possible.

A 10 percent Formalin solution is used for hardening large animals such as squids, octopuses and fishes. It can be used on large crabs and shrimp, although many specialists object to its use; yet others prefer their larger crustaceans preserved in Formalin. A 5 percent solution is effective in preserving a great many small animals such as jellyfish, crabs, tunicates, etc. However, regardless of which solution is used, the volume should be at least four times the bulk of the animal to get good penetration and thorough preservation.

Formalin is basically acid and there is considerable objection to it because it breaks down the calcareous spicules, etches shells and damages other lime exoskeleton structures. Therefore, it is a good practice to neutralize the Formalin by adding one pound of hexamethylenetetramine to one gallon of full-strength Formalin and using that as a stock solution. If this is not possible, add one teaspoon of borax to two quarts of 10 percent Formalin solution, but the animals should be removed and transferred to alcohol when convenient because borax is said to have a mascerating effect, and will gum up the specimens in the residue at the bottom of the container. There are several other buffers that may be used, including magnesium carbonate, but in a pinch if marble chips or crushed limerock is added in sufficient quantities, the acid action of the Formalin will be retarded.

Even though the solution is well neutralized, certain specialists will violently object to holothurians, alcyonarians or sponges preserved in Formalin. These experts insist upon alcohol, and when you hope to have these experts identify your specimens, it is wise to preserve them according to the specialists' instructions.

When preserving large fishes such as grouper or sharks, it is necessary to place them in large wooden vats to soak. Finding a bottle for a four-foot hammerhead shark is next to impossible. Therefore, some museums and laboratories have big stainless-steel coffins filled with Formalin to hold 10-foot sharks and even porpoises.

Formalin solution can be made up with either sea water or tap water. When preserving delicate marine invertebrates that have sensitive osmotic balance at best, the Formalin solution should be made up with sea water. However, when preserving fishes or crabs, octopuses, etc., Formalin seems to do better when made up with fresh tap water. To find out the best method, some experimentation on the part of the collector will be necessary.

Gohar's Formalin Poisoning Technique

This has time and again impressed me as being one of the most effective methods of preserving a large number of highly contractile marine invertebrates that proved to be otherwise most difficult. The animals are killed gradually, from insensibility to death, by Formalin. They are placed in a great bulk of sea water: 50 to 500 times its volume or more, and allowed to fully expand. A few drops of dilute Formalin are added (3 drops of 1 percent formaldehyde to 100 cc. sea water) and this is repeated at intervals of about 15 minutes. The amount of Formalin added should be doubled every hour until the animal expires with very little or no contraction.

Gohar mentions that with this technique he preserved two species of *Aeolis* nudibranchs that defied every other method. The cerata fall off at the slightest disturbance, even when simply handled, and all sorts of narcotics had the same effect—but with Formalin they died expanded.

I have found this technique to work well on almost any contractile species. It must be watched constantly or the animals may die and mascerate. When death ensues, strong Formalin should be added.

Boiling Formalin

No fixative is more rapid, penetrating and lethal than boiling Formalin. If it is boiled in a narrow-mouthed flask and stoppered with cotton wool, the harsh effects of the vapors can be inhibited. But if you have a batch of animals that invariably withdraw their tentacles or curl when you've tried every other way, boiling Formalin will invariably kill them expanded. After they are anesthetized to their maximum, pour off as much water as possible. Then flood in boiling Formalin in equal volume to the sea water and chances are all retraction will be arrested. Gohar recommends this technique for many highly contractile coelenterates.

Bouin's Solution

This is one of the most important histological fixatives used for rapidly penetrating and staining tissues, especially when working with plathyhelminthes. The solution is made by adding picric acid crystals to a glass or beaker of water; when the crystals no longer dissolve over a 24-hour period, the aqueous solution has become saturated. It is then ready to be used as the primary ingredient of the Bouin's fixative which is made up as follows:

Picric acid aqueous solution	75 parts
Concentrated Formalin	20 parts
Glacial acetic acid	5 parts

Bouin's is not a stable fixative and should be made up and used in relatively small amounts and kept dark. A large volume is apt to deteriorate in light if kept much over two weeks. Bouin's solution is only a fixative and specimens should never be allowed to remain in it for any length of time or they will become too hardened for histological purposes. The usual procedure is to wash the Bouin's fixed specimen thoroughly in running tap water and transfer it to alcohol.

This fixative is a bright yellow color, and stains fingers very deeply. Forceps or gloves are important when handling animals, or your fingers can end up yellow from Bouin's, green from copper sulfate and black from Formalin. Add some of the other colorful histological stains and you might have fingers that have every color of the rainbow, as some laboratory technicians have had.

Ethyl Alcohol

Denatured ethyl alcohol is widely available at chemical and biological supply houses and makes a good all-around alcohol preservative. A 1 percent benzol solution or some other denaturing agent is added to make it undrinkable but still effective for most systematic work. The difficulties in obtaining pure-grain ethyl alcohol, tax free, are almost insurmountable unless you are working with an accepted scientific and educational institution or a hospital. A federal permit granted through the alcohol and tax division is required. Only in a very few instances is pure ethyl alcohol essential, such as when collecting specimens for drug extraction. The denaturing ingredient may be retained in the tissues, while pure-grain ethyl alcohol will evaporate completely.

As indicated throughout the text, many species are best preserved directly in alcohol because their calcareous structures are likely to disintegrate in harsh fixatives. Denatured ethyl alcohol is more expensive than Formalin, but it is certainly more pleasant to handle. However, it will dehydrate the oils in your fingers with extensive handling, so rubber gloves are again a must.

The standard preserving solution is 70 percent ethyl alcohol or seven parts full strength (99 percent) alcohol to three parts water. Fresh water, not sea water, is advisable in making up alcohol solutions because the latter will cause the solution to become cloudy and remain that way.

Only hard-skinned or shelled animals such as crabs or starfish should be dropped directly into 70 percent alcohol. Many species such as squid, nudibranchs, worms, etc., will dehydrate and wrinkled specimens may result, unless the specimens are gradually run through an alcohol series. The recommended procedure is to drop the animal into 30 percent ethyl alcohol for 24 hours, then transfer it to a 50 percent solution the next day, and 24 hours later it may be immersed in 70 percent alcohol. These changes prevent shrinkage and excessive water-loss into solution. They permit the gradual penetration of alcohol, and the specimens look more natural: the tissues are firmer and they make better material for systematic dissection.

Isopropyl Alcohol

This may be substituted for ethyl alcohol, but bear in mind that it is only a substitute because the results are somewhat unpredictable. We have found that isopropyl alcohol will result in making the appendages of minute crustaceans extremely brittle and break off. It etches the glossy shells of cowries and other mollusks where luster is important in perfect museum specimens, and it makes the skin of sea cucumbers and the calcareous plates of starfish break down and become rather cheesy. However, isopropyl is still better than Formalin on echinoderms.

Its one advantage over ethyl alcohol is in being cheaper and more readily obtainable. In a pinch, common drugstore rubbing alcohol, which is usually 70 percent isopropyl will adequately preserve animals that should not be placed in Formalin. When you happen to be at the seashore and find creatures that you want for your collection, and are not prepared for collecting, then simply run to the corner drugstore in town and get all you need.

Many museums, including the American Museum of Natural History, store their fish in 50 percent isopropyl alcohol after they have been well fixed in Formalin. It should never be used full strength because the tissues will shrink down to a hardened, wrinkled and highly distorted lump resembling petrified wood. Many specialists run both invertebrates and fish through a 35 percent solution of isopropyl alcohol for 24 hours before transferring them to a 50 percent solution.

I have avoided the use of isopropyl alcohol whenever possible, but have a number of collections made with drugstore alcohol that were later transferred to ethyl alcohol. There are all sorts of emergency measures that might be considered in the field.

Elisabeth Deichmann of Harvard's Museum of Comparative Zoology once told me that when collecting in Central America she tried to get some alcohol, and found that it would take an act of Congress to get more than the quart that the laboratory provided. She bought a cask of cheap wine and preserved a large collection of hermit crabs, taking care to get a series of males and females, and when they were brought back to the museum in the United States, the specimens were in good shape and preserved out well when transferred to strong laboratory alcohol.

Glycerine

Glycerine is added to alcohol or Formalin, or both combined, to keep specimens from becoming brittle. It is especially useful in large preserved crustaceans and fragile echinoderms such as brittlestars, echinoids and some starfish. Glycerine is made up in a 10 percent solution by volume mixed with the preservative. It tends to extract tannic acid and pigments from corks on bottles, so glass-stoppered or plastic-capped bottles should be used exclusively. Another advantage of glycerine when mixed with 70 percent alcohol is that it retards evaporation, and in the event that a bottle is not completely sealed, the specimens will not be completely desiccated.

Anesthetics and Narcotizing Agents

Magnesium sulfate, or common Epsom salts, is one of the best anesthetics to be found anywhere. Actually if you went on an expedition and carried 25 pounds of Epsom salts, some formaldehyde and alcohol, you would be able to handle almost any situation and come back with well-preserved, expanded specimens.

Magnesium sulfate is extremely soluble in water and is used in a saturated solution. To avoid disturbing the animals, the Epsom salts should be tied up in a piece of porous cloth and just the corner of the bag allowed to touch the water. Diffusion will take place so slowly that the animals will not be agitated while becoming insensitive.

For anesthetizing marine animals, beginning with coelenterates and ending with tunicates, magnesium sulfate is one of the superior chemicals that can be found. Other chemicals will be described, but their results are no better than magnesium sulfate if proper care and handling is given to the specimens during the process of anesthetization.

Magnesium chloride is strongly recommended by many zoologists who work with very delicate, sensitive and highly contractile marine invertebrates. Dissolve 75 grams of crystalline magnesium chloride in one liter of tap water. Such a solution is practically isotonic with sea water, and if carefully applied will not cause the hyperextended or abnormally relaxed specimens that may on occasion result with magnesium sulfate when used in a supersaturated solution. An isotonic solution of magnesium chloride works fast, from one-half hour to four hours and the specimens are ready for fixation.

Using both magnesium salts, some specimens may be examined in an expanded condition, probed and, if they have not been in solution for more than 12 hours, they may be returned to normal sea water and will revive and become responsive again. This method is good when photographing or drawing an animal that is difficult to handle or moves around the aquarium excessively.

Menthol crystals are practically insoluble in water and take a long time to dissolve. Use a very few crystals per dish to avoid waste. Menthol is, however, completely soluble in ethyl alcohol, and a teaspoon dissolved in alcohol and added to sea water, a drop at a time, is very effective. However, as soon as the specimens are completely anesthetized and no longer respond to probing with a glass rod, they should be fixed. If allowed to stand for even two hours they will die and quickly deteriorate.

Chloretone (acetone chloroform) is treated in much the same way as menthol crystals. This is recommended as a 1 percent solution for small polyzoans, added very slowly. However, chloretone has the disadvantage that if the animals are not narcotized as desired, they cannot be returned to sea water because they will probably die. It has the advantage of being stable in a saturated solution, is not bulky and is easily stored.

Chloral hydrate is a good, all-purpose anesthetic that has been effective on numerous polychaetes, mollusks, and tunicates. The crystals may be dropped directly into the water or it may be made up in a 5 to 10 percent solution and introduced very gradually over several hours. It has been used for killing animals in rock crevices or growing in encrusting algae. The animals should remain in the solution from four to six hours.

Alcohol poisoning is a good technique and works with a great many creatures, especially polychaete worms. Drop by drop the alcohol is added to the sea water until the organisms become insensitive. It works beautifully with hydroids, but should be avoided on watery invertebrates because even slight shrinkage of the tissues will cause them to contract in a distorted position. A 10 percent alcohol solution is effective in narcotizing many brittlestars, crustaceans, and even echinoderms.

Propylene phenoxetol comes as a viscous liquid in one-pound quantities. Propylene phenoxetol has been widely used in preserving soft-bodied mollusks, and we have found it effective in anesthetizing other invertebrates. Ruth Turner, a renowned mollusk specialist at Harvard, reports in "Some Techniques for Anatomical Work" (a museum publication) that it is particularly useful if one wishes to relax marine or fresh-water mollusks for study purposes without killing them. The specimen will revive if placed in fresh, well-oxygenated water. It is good with clams but many prosobranch gastropods that can withdraw themselves completely into their shells and tightly close their operculum are more resistant to propylene phenoxetol.

Propylene phenoxetol has proved effective in narcotizing many polychaete worms, crabs and some tunicates. It has given poor results with coelenterates and echinoderms. It is important that the narcotic have access to the soft parts; in the case of tightly closing bivalves this can be facilitated by pegging the valves. When the animal is siphoning actively you ease up and shove in a wooden peg.

Two approaches are used in administering propylene phenoxetol; the first is to shake 5 ml. of it in a 15-to 20-ml. beaker until a fine emulsion is produced. This is added to a small quantity of sea water and within a half-hour or so the animals should be completely relaxed and may be fixed in this condition without causing noticeable contraction.

Another method is to take an eyedropper and insert a single drop of propylene phenoxetol in the bottom of the dish. Let it sit for a few hours until the specimen no longer responds to touch. Propylene phenoxetol may be explored on a whole variety of marine invertebrates. We have found it caused major distention of coral polyps, but did not inhibit their ability to contract when fixative was added.

Propylene phenoxetol can be used as a preserving agent, but it is not a fixative. All specimens must be previously fixed in Formalin or alcohol. It has the advantages of keeping tissues soft, and retarding color changes, especially in soft-bodied mollusks. Propylene phenoxetol is made up as follows:

Water	86 parts
Glycerol	10 parts
Propylene Phenoxetol	1 part
95% alcohol	3 parts

Propylene phenoxetol is manufactured by Nipa Laboratories, Ltd., in Wales. It comes in one-pound quantities and this makes about 20 liters or 25 quarts of preservative.

The Sevin and Rapid Freezing Technique for the full anesthetization and killing of muricid and naticid gastropods was developed by Melbourne Carricker at the Marine Biological Laboratory at Woods Hole, Massachusetts. A stock solution of Sevin (1-naphthyl N-methyl carbamate, available from Union Carbide Chemical Co.) is made up and stored in tightly capped glass jars and placed in a refrigerator. Add 0.1 g. Sevin crystals to 15 ml. (11.6 g.) acetone to prepare a solution of 10 ppm. Add 1.16 ml. of stock solution of Sevin to one liter of sea water and thoroughly mix. This must be prepared daily when it is to be used, as it does not keep.

Place the animals in the Sevin solution at room temperature for one hour. The depth of the solution should be at least three times the height of the animals. It is best if the specimens are preserved in individual containers. After one hour, transfer the animals to a fresh solution of Sevin and leave them in it for three hours. Carricker suggests that slightly better narcotization is sometimes obtained if the second change of Sevin is held in 1 atmosphere of CO_2, and if a salinity 30 percent lower than the environment is employed.

To kill the specimens, he removes them from the Sevin solution and places the soft extended parts on a block of dry ice, adding chipped dry ice around the specimen. Freshly thawed, relaxed and unpreserved snails are excellent for detailed anatomical study since the organs retain lifelike texture, pliability and color. Living tissues take aqueous stains readily.

The techniques of freezing specimens with Sevin and the techniques of freezing them without Sevin (see Chapter 22) should be explored on a great number of other invertebrates. It is certainly a more natural process of anesthetization, commonly found in nature where frozen, dead creatures lying on a tidal flat are found extended, and therefore it may be the best technique of all.

The specimens of moon snails that I have seen prepared by Dr. Carricker have certainly been well expanded; the big fleshy mollusk looked as if it had just been plucked from its meandering furrowed trail along the sandy beach.

Chromic acid is made up in an aqueous solution used for killing and hardening soft, gelatinous forms. Specimens become fragile, shrink and become deeply tinged if left in the solution longer than necessary. Furthermore, the chromic acid solution does not keep very long and should be made up fresh before each major usage. When it turns green, the solution is no longer useful.

The standard procedure after using chromic acid is to wash the. specimens through three or more changes of alcohol to remove all the color and acid from the tissues.

Glacial acetic acid is a widely used fixative that kills contractile specimens by instantly permeating and hardening tissues. Tissues remain relatively clear during the fixation process, but they can soften if left in the solution too long. Chromic acid is often combined with glacial acetic acid to make a strong, killing solution for noncontractile as well as highly contractile invertebrates.

Osmic acid is expensive and hard to get, and unless the preparation is to be used specifically for electron microscopic preparations or some special histological use, it should be avoided. When used it hardens gelatinous forms and preserves transparency. It is used as an ingredient in other preserving solutions such as chromic-osmic mixture, potassium bichromate-osmic acid and Flemming's solution. Osmic acid is extremely damaging to the lungs and should be worked with outdoors.

Recommended Preservative Solutions
(General Purposes)

1. **Sea Water and Formalin**
   10% solution
Sea water	9 parts
Formalin (37.9% solution)	1 part

   5 Percent Formalin Solution
Sea water	19 parts
Formalin	1 part

2. **FAAG or Tapeworm Fixative**
95% ethyl alcohol	24 parts
Formalin	15 parts
Glacial acetic acid	5 parts
Glycerine	10 parts
Tap water	46 parts

3. **Bouin's Fluid**
Picric acid saturated aqueous	75 parts
Formalin (commercial)	25 parts
Glacial acetic acid	5 parts

4. **Zenker's Fluid**
Potassium dichromate	2.5 g.
Mercuric chloride	5.8 g.
Distilled water	100 cc.
Glacial acetic acid	5 cc.

5. **Kleinenberg's Solution**
Saturated picric acid	100 cc.
Concentrated sulfuric acid	2 cc.

   (Filter and add to 3 times the volume of distilled water)

6. **Flemming's Fluid**
1% chromic acid	25 cc.
1% osmic acid	10 cc.
Glacial acetic acid	5 cc.
Distilled water	60 cc.

7. **Perenyi's Solution**
10% nitric acid	40 cc.
0.5% chromic acid	30 cc.
90% ethyl alcohol	30 cc.

8. **Chrom-acetic acid, No. 1**
   1% chromic acid .... 100 cc.
   Concentrated acetic acid .... 5 cc.

   Chrom-acetic acid, No. 2
   1% chromic acid .... 100 cc.
   Concentrated acetic acid .... 10 cc.

9. **Muller's Solution**
   Potassium bichromate .... 2 gr.
   Sodium sulfate .... 1 gr.
   Distilled water .... 100 cc.

Bibliography

General Reading

Abbott, R. Tucker, *American Seashells*. Princeton, N. J.: D. Van Nostrand Company, Inc., 1954.

———, *How to Know the American Marine Shells*. New York: The New American Library, Inc., 1961.

Barnes, Robert D., *Invertebrate Zoology*. Philadelphia: W. B. Saunders Company, 1963.

Bayer, Frederick M., and Owre, Harding B., *The Free-Living Lower Invertebrates*. New York: The Macmillan Company, 1968.

Berrill, N. J., *The Living Tide*. New York: Dodd, Mead and Co. 1951.

Berrill, J., and N. J., *1001 Questions Answered About the Seashore*. Hardback: Dodd, Mead and Co.: Paperback: Grossett and Co. 1957.

Breder, Charles M., Jr., *Field Book of the Marine Fishes of the Atlantic Coast from Labrador to Texas*. New York: G. P. Putnam's Sons, 1948.

Brown, Frank A., Jr., *Selected Invertebrates Types*. New York: John Wiley & Sons, 1950.

Buchsbaum, Ralph, *Animals Without Backbones*. Chicago: The University of Chicago Press, 1948.

Buchsbaum, Ralph, and Milne, J. J., *The Lower Animals: Living Invertebrates of the World*. New York: Doubleday & Co., 1961.

Bullough, W. S., *Practical Invertebrate Anatomy*. New York: St. Martin's (Macmillan), 1954.

Carson, Rachel L., *Under the Sea Wind*. New York: The New American Library, Inc., 1941.

———, *The Sea Around Us*. New York: Oxford University Press, 1951.

———, *The Edge of the Sea*. Boston: Houghton Mifflin Company, 1955.

Crowder, William, *Between the Tides*. New York: Dodd, Mead and Company, 1931.

Ekman, S., *Zoogeography of the Sea*. London: Sidgwick and Jackson, 1953.

Galtsoff, P. F., ed., "Gulf of Mexico: Its Origin, Waters, and Marine Life." *U. S. Fish and Wildlife Service Fishery Bulletin 89*. Washington, D. C.: U. S. Government Printing Office, 1954.

Halstead, Bruce V., *Dangerous Marine Animals*. Cambridge, Maryland: Cornell Maritime Press, 1959.

Hardey, Allister, *The Open Sea: Its Natural History, Including the World of Plankton and Fish and Fisheries*. Boston: Houghton Mifflin Company, 1965.

Harvey, E. Newton, *Bioluminescence*. New York: Academic Press, Inc., 1952.

Hyman, L. H., *Protozoa through Ctenophora. The Invertebrates*, vol. I. New York: McGraw-Hill, Inc., 1940.

_____, *Platyhelminthes and Rhynchocoela. The Invertebrates*, vol. II. New York: McGraw-Hill, Inc., 1951.

_____, *Acanthocephala, Aschelminthes, and Entoprocta. The Invertebrates*, vol. III. New York: McGraw-Hill, Inc., 1951.

_____, *Echinodermata. The Invertebrates*, vol. IV. New York: McGraw-Hill, Inc., 1955.

_____, *Smaller Coelomate Groups. The Invertebrates*, vol. V. New York: McGraw-Hill, Inc., 1959.

_____, *Molluska I. The Invertebrates*, vol. VI. New York: McGraw-Hill, Inc., 1967.

Lane, Frank W., *Kingdom of the Octopus*. New York: Sheridan House, 1960.

Lauff, G. H., ed., *Estuaries*. American Association for the Advancement of Science, Publ. 83, Washington, D. C., 1967.

MacGinitie, G. E. and Nettie, *Natural History of Marine Animals*. New York: McGraw-Hill, Inc., 1949.

Marx, W., *The Frail Ocean*. New York: Ballantine Books, 1967.

Minor, Roy Waldo, *Field Book of Seashore Life*. New York: G. P. Putnam's Sons, 1950.

Moore, H. B., *Marine Ecology*. New York: John Wiley & Sons, 1958.

Needham, J. P., et al., *Culture Methods for Invertebrate Animals*. Ithaca, New York: Comstock, 1937.

Nichol, J. A., *The Biology of Marine Animals*. 2nd. ed., New York: John Wiley & Sons, 1960.

Pratt, Henry I., *A Manual of Common Invertebrate Animals (Exclusive of Insects)*. New York: McGraw-Hill, Inc., 1935.

Pratt, H. S. *Manual of Common Invertebrate Animals*. New York: Blakiston Co., 1951.

Ray, Carleton, and Ciampi, E., *The Underwater Guide to Marine Life*. New York: A. S. Barnes and Co., 1959.

Ray, Dixy Lee, ed., *Marine Boring and Fouling Organisms*. Seattle: University of Washington Press, 1959.

Raymont, J. E. G., *Plankton and Productivity in the Oceans*, New York: Pergamon Press, 1963.

Ricketts, Edward F., and Calvin, Jack, *Between Pacific Tides*. Revised edition edited by Joel Hedgepeth. Stanford, California: Stanford University Press, 1968.

Rudloe, Jack, *The Sea Brings Forth*. New York: Alfred A. Knopf, Inc., 1968.

Smith, F. G. W., *Atlantic Reef Corals*. Coral Gables, Fla.: University of Miami Press, 1948.

Smith, Ralph J., ed., *Keys to Marine Invertebrates of the Woods Hole Region*. Contribution No. 11 Systemics-Ecology Program, Marine Biological Laboratory, Woods Hole, Massachusetts. Boston: Spaulding Co., 1964.

Steinbeck, John, and Ricketts, Edward F., *Sea of Cortez*. New York: Viking Press, 1941.

Teal, John and Mildred, *Life and Death of the Salt Marsh*. Boston: Little, Brown and Company, 1969.

Waterman, J. H., ed., *Metabolism and Growth*, vol. I. *Sense Organs, Integration, and Behavior*, vol. II. *The Physiology of Crustacea*, New York: Academic Press, 1960.

Webb, W. F., *A Handbook for Shell Collectors*. Rochester, New York, and St. Petersburg, Fla.: W. F. Webb, 1935.

Wells, M. M., *The Collection and Preservation of Animal Forms*. Chicago: General
Biological Supply House, 1932.
Youngken, Herbert W., Jr., ed., *Food-Drugs from the Sea*. Washington, D. C.
Proceedings, Marine Technology Society, 1970.

Collection, Culturing and Preservation Techniques

Abbott, R. T., *American Sea Shells*. Princeton, N. J.: D. Van Nostrand Co., Inc., 1954.
American Fisheries Society, *A List of Common and Scientific Names of Fishes from the
United States and Canada*. Washington, D. C.: American Fisheries Society, 1960.
Anderson, R. M., "Methods of Collecting and Preserving Vertebrates." *Bull. Nat. Mus.
Canada*, vol. 69 (1949), p. 162.
Axelrod, H. R., and Vorderwinkler, W., *Salt-Water Aquarium Fish*, revised edition. Jersey
City: T. F. H. Publications, 1963.
Bailey, R. S., and Briggs, Fred C., *Salt Water Aquaria*. Educational Series No. 9,
Gloucester Point: Virginia Institute of Marine Science, revised, 1961.
Baker, J. R., *Principles of Biological Microtechniques*. London: Methuen and Co., 1958.
Bell, Gordon R., *A Guide to the Properties, Characteristics, and Uses of Some General
Anaesthetics for Fish*. Bulletin No. 148, Fisheries Research Board of Canada, 1964.
Bianco, S. L., "The Methods Employed at the Naples Zoological Station for the
Preservation of Marine Animals." *Bull. U. S. Nat. Mus.*, vol. 39, Part M (1899), pp.
1-37.
Bigelow, H. B., and Fartante, I. P., *Fishes of the Western North Atlantic*. Part 1, Sears
Foundation, 1948.
Bigelow, H. B., and Shroeder, W. C., *Fishes of the Western North Atlantic*. Part 2, Sears
Foundation, 1953.
Boyle, Robert H., "Panacea for a Salty Yankee. The Waters Off Florida's Big Bend
Provide Jack Rudloe with Sea Creatures and a Good Life Collecting Them." *Sports
Illustrated*, vol. 32, No. 16 (April 20, 1970).
Breder, C. M., *Field Book of Marine Fishes of the Atlantic Coast*. New York: G. P.
Putnam's Sons, 1948.
Branham, J. M., "An Ecological Survey of the Ascidians of Alligator Harbor, Florida, and
the Adjacent Gulf of Mexico." Unpublished M. S. thesis, Florida State University,
1958.
British Museum of Natural History, *Instructions for Collectors, No. 9A. Invertebrate
Animals Other Than Insects*. London: Adlar & Son, Ltd., 1954.
Burkenroad, M. D., "The Penaeidae of Louisiana, with a Discussion of Their World
Relationships." *Bull. Am. Mus. Nat. Hist.*, vol. 68, No. 2 (1934).
Carlgren, O., and Hedgpeth, J. W., "Actinaria Zoantharia and Ceriantharia from Shallow
Water in the Northwestern Gulf of Mexico." *Pub. Inst. Mar. Sci. Texas*, vol. 2
(1952).
Carpenter, D., "Distribution of Polychaete Annelids in the Alligator Harbor Area,
Franklin County, Florida." *Florida State University Studies*, No. 22 (1956).
Carricker, M. R., and Blake, K. J. W., "A Method for Full Relaxation of Muricids."
Nautilus, vol. 73 (1959), pp. 16−21.
Clark, A. H., "Echinoderms of the Gulf of Mexico." *Fish. Bull.*, vol. 89 (1954).
Coe, W. R., "The Nemertean Fauna of the Gulf of Mexico." *Fish. Bull.*, vol. 89 (1954).

Cooper, G. A., "Brachiopoda Occurring in the Gulf of Mexico." *Fish. Bull.,* vol. 89 (1954).

Costello, D. P., *et al., Methods for Obtaining and Handling Marine Eggs and Embryos.* Woods Hole: Marine Biological Laboratory, 1957.

Curl, H. C., "The Hydrography and Phytoplankton Ecology of the Inshore, Northeastern Gulf of Mexico." Unpublished doctoral thesis.

Davis, C., *The Marine and Fresh Water Plankton.* East Lansing: Michigan State University Press, 1955.

Deevey, E. S., "Hydroids from Louisiana and Texas with Remarks on the Pleistocene Biogeography of the Western Gulf of Mexico." *Ecol.,* vol. 31 (1950).

Deichmann, E., "The Holothurians of the Gulf of Mexico," *Fish. Bull.,* vol. 89 (1954).

deLaubenfels, M. W., "A Discussion of the Sponge Fauna of the Dry Tortugas." *Carnegie Inst. Wash. Pub.* 467 (1936).

Fisher, W. K., "New Genera and Species of Echiuroid and Sipunculoid." *Proc. U. S. Nat. Mus.,* vol. 97 (1947).

Fraser, C. Mcl., *Hydroids of the Atlantic Coast of North America.* Toronto: University of Toronto Press, 1944.

Galtsoff, P., et al., *Culture Methods for Invertebrate Animals.* New York: Dover Publications, 1959.

Gerould, J. H., "The Sipunculoids of the Eastern Coast of North America." *Proc. U. S. Nat. Mus.,* vol. 44 (1913).

Gilbert, M., *Starting a Shell Collection.* Newark: Hammond, 1961.

Gohar, H. A. F., "The Preservation of Contractile Marine Animals in an Expanded Condition." *J. Mar. Biol. Assoc.,* vol. 22, No. 1 (1937), pp. 295 – 299.

Guyer, M. F., "Preparation of Microscopic Material." Appendix D, *Animal Microscopy.* Chicago: University of Chicago Press, 1953.

Hartman, O., "Polychaete Annelids of the Gulf of Mexico." *Fish. Bull.,* vol. 89 (1954).

Harvey, E. B., *The American Arbacia and Other Sea Urchins.* Princeton: Princeton University Press, 1956.

Humm, H. J., "Notes on the Marine Algae of Florida." *Florida State University Studies,* No. 7 (1952).

Humm, H. J., and Taylor, S. E., "Marine Chlorophyta of the Upper West Coast of Florida." *Bull. Mar. Sci. Gulf and Caribb.,* vol. 11, No. 3 (1961).

Hutton, Robert F., *et al.,* "Investigations on the Parasites and Diseases of Saltwater Shrimps (Panaeidae) of Sports and Commercial Importance to Florida." *Tech. Series No. 26,* Tallahassee: Board of Conservation, 1959.

Johnson, Martin W., and Miller, Robert C., "The Seasonal Settlement of Shipworms, Barnacles and Other Wharf-Pile Organisms at Friday Harbor, Washington." *Oceanography,* vol. 2, No. 1 (1955), pp. 1 – 18.

Joseph, E. B., "The Fishes of Alligator Harbor, Florida, with Notes on Their Natural History." *Florida State University Studies,* No. 22 (1956).

Knudsen, Jens W., *Biological Techniques. Collecting, Preserving, and Illustrating Plants and Animals.* New York: Harper & Row, 1966.

Lamb, MacKenzie, "A New Method for the Permanent Preservation of Algal Material for Microscopic Study." *Extrat de la Revue Algologigue,* No. 3 (1959).

Lewis, William M., *Maintaining Fishes for Experimental and Instructional Purposes.* Carbondale: Southern Illinois University, 1963.

Little, F. J., "Sponge Fauna of St. George's Sound, Apalachee Bay and Panama City Regions of the Florida Gulf Coast." *Tulane Stud. Zool.* (1963).

Lo Bianco, Salvatore, "The Methods Employed at the Naples Zoological Station for the Preservation of Marine Animals." Translated from the original Italian by E. O. Hovey, *U. S. Nat. Mus. Bull.,* No. 39, Part M (1899), pp. 3 – 42.

428

BIBLIOGRAPHY

Long, C. D., "A Phornoid from the Gulf of Mexico." *Bull. Mar. Sci. Gulf and Caribbean*, vol. 10 (1960).

Mayer, A. G., "Medusae of the World." *Carnegie Inst. Wash. Publ.*, No. 109 (1910).

Mayr, E., Linsley, E. G., and Usinger, R. R., *Methods and Principles of Systematic Zoology*. New York: McGraw-Hill, Inc., 1953.

McFarland, W. N., "The Use of Anesthetics for the Handling and Transport of Fishes." *California Fish and Game*, vol. 46, No. 4 (1960), pp. 407–431.

Menzel, R. W., ed., *Checklist of the Marine Fauna and Flora of the Apalachee Bay Region—St. George Sound*. Florida State University Department of Oceanography, Contribution No. 61, 1971.

Moore, H. B., *Marine Ecology*. New York: John Wiley & Sons, 1958.

Morgan, Alfred, *Aquarium Book*. New York: Charles Scribner's Sons, 1959.

Morris, P. A., *A Field Guide to the Shells of Atlantic and Gulf Coasts*. Boston: Houghton Mifflin Company, 1951.

Needham, James G., Galtsoff, Paul, Lutz, Frank, and Welch, Paul, *Culture Methods for Invertebrate Animals*. New York: Dover Publications, 1959.

Newman, H. W., *The Phylum Chordata*. New York: The MacMillan Company, 1939.

Osburn, R. C., "Bryozoa of the Tortugas Islands, Florida." *Carnegie Inst. Wash. Publ.*, vol. 182 (1914).

Owen, G., "Use of Propylene Phenoxetol as a Relaxing Agent." *Nature*, vol. 175 (1955), p. 434.

Owen, G., and Steedman, H. G., "Preservation of Animal Tissues, with a Note on Staining Solutions." *Quarterly Journal of Microscopic Science*, vol. 97, Part 3 (1956), pp. 101–103.

———, "Preservation of Molluscs." *Proc. Malacol. Soc., London*, vol. 33 (1958), pp. 101–103.

Randall, J. E., "Methods of Collecting Small Fishes." *Underwater Naturalist*, Bulletin of American Littoral Society, vol 1., No. 1 (1963), pp. 6–11, 32–36.

———, *Caribbean Reef Fishes*. Jersey City: T. F. H. Publications, 1968.

Rosewater, Joseph, "An Effective Anesthetic for Giant Clams and Other Mollusks." *Turtox News*, vol. 41, No. 12 (1963), p. 300.

Rudloe, Jack J., "Science in Action—The Biological Collector." *Natural History Magazine*, vol. 73 (Nov., 1964), pp. 59–62.

———, "On Collecting and Preserving Animals That Live Along the Edge of the Sea." *Scientific American*, vol. 212, No. 3 (March, 1965), pp. 119–126.

———, "Specimens—A Future in the Sea." *Oceans Magazine*, vol. 2, No. 2 (July, 1969).

———, "Northwest Florida: A Last Frontier." *Underwater Naturalist*, Bull. Amer. Littoral Soc., vol. 6, No. 4 (Fall–Winter, 1970), pp. 8–15.

Russell, Henry D., *Notes on Methods for the Narcotization, Killing, and Preservation of Marine Organisms*. Systematics-Ecology Program, Marine Biological Laboratory, Woods Hole, Mass., April, 1963.

Smith, F. G. W., *Atlantic Reef Corals*. Coral Gables: Univ. of Miami Press, 1948.

Smith, J. L. B., "A Neutral Solution of Formaldehyde for Biological Purposes." *Trans. Roy. Soc., S. Africa*, vol. 31 (1947), pp. 279–282.

Smith, Ralph J., ed., *Keys to Marine Invertebrates of the Woods Hole Region*. Contribution No. 11 Systematics-Ecology Program, Marine Biological Laboratory, Woods Hole, Massachusetts. Boston: Spaulding Co., 1964.

Spotte, Stephen H., *Fish and Invertebrate Culture, Water Management in Closed Systems*. New York: John Wiley & Sons, 1970.

Straughan, Robert P., *The Salt-Water Aquarium in the Home*. New York: A. S. Barnes and Co., Inc., 1964.

Taylor, W. R., "The Marine Algae of Florida with Special Reference to the Dry Tortugas."

Washington, D. C.: Carnegie Institute, 1928.
_____, "Marine Algae of the Eastern Tropical and Subtropical Coasts of the Americas." *Univ. Mich. Stud.,* Ser. 21 (1960).
Turner, R. D., "Some Techniques for Anatomical Work." *American Malacological Union Annual Reports for 1959,* Bulletin 26 (1960), pp. 6–8.
Van Name, W. G., "The North and South American Ascidians." *Bull. Am. Mus. Nat. Hist.,* vol. 84 (1945).
Vaughan, T. W., "Reef Corals of the Bahamas and South Florida." *Carnegie Inst. Wash. Yearbook,* vol. 13 (1915).
Verill, A. H., *Shell Collector's Handbook.* New York: G. P. Putnam's Sons, 1950.
Wagstaffee, R., and Fidler, J. H., *The Preservation of Natural History Specimens. Invertebrates,* vol. I. London: H. F. & G. Witherby Ltd., 1955.
Wass, M. L., "The Decapod Crustaceans of Alligator Harbor and Adjacent Inshore Areas of Northwestern Florida." *Jour. Fla. Acad. Sci.,* vol. 18 (1955).
Webb, W. F., *A Handbook for Shell Collectors,* Rochester, N. Y., and St. Petersburg, Fla.: W. F. Webb, 1935.
Wells, Harry W., "Hydroid and Sponge Commensals of *Cantharus cancellarius* with a 'False Shell.'" *Nautilus,* Contribution No. 58, January, 1969.
Wells, M. M., *The Collection and Preservation of Animal Forms,* Chicago: General Biological Supply House, 1932.
Williams, Austin B., "Marine Decapod Crustaceans of the Carolinas." *Fish. Bull.,* vol. 65, No. 1 (1965).

Pollution in the Marine Environment

Arnold, D. L., "Man's Alteration of Estuaries by Dredging and Filling. A Grave Threat to Marine Resources." *Proceedings Southeast Game and Fish Comm.,* Eighteenth Annual Session (1967), pp. 269–273.
Butler, Philip, *A Reaction of Some Estuarine Mollusks to Environmental Factors. Biological Problems in Water Pollution.* Third Seminar, U. S. Health, Education, and Welfare, Health Service Publication No. 999-WP-25, 1962.
Butler, Philip, and Springer, Paul, "Pesticides, A New Factor in Coastal Environment." *Transactions, Twenty-Eighth North American Wildlife and Natural Resources Conference,* 1964.
Coutlas, C. L., "Some Saline Marsh Soils in North Florida." Part 1, *Proceedings Soil and Crop Science of Florida,* vol. 29, 1909.
Gunter, Gordon, "Reef Shell or Mudshell Dredging in Coastal Bays and Its Effect upon the Environment." *Transactions of the Thirty-Fourth North American Wildlife and Natural Resources Conference,* 1969.
Kurtz, H., and Wagner, K., "Marshes of the Gulf and Atlantic Coasts of Northern Florida and Charleston, South Carolina." *Florida State University Studies,* No. 24 (1957).
Lanier, Sidney, Centennial Edition of the Works of Sidney Lanier (vols. I, VI). Baltimore: Johns Hopkins, 1945.
Newsom, John D., ed., *Proceedings of the Marsh and Estuary Management Symposium.* Baton Rouge: Louisiana State University, 1968.
Odum, Eugene P., *The Role of Tidal Marshes in Estuarine Production.* New York State Conservation Department, Division of Conservation, Educational Leaflet, 1961.

BIBLIOGRAPHY

Odum, W. E., Woodell, G. M., and Wurster, C. F., "DDT Residues Absorbed from Organic Detritus by Fiddler Crabs." *Science*, vol. 164, No. 3879 (1969), pp. 576–577.

Ogren, Larry, and Pearce, Jack L., "Oil Pollution, a Threat to Maine Resources and Recreation." *Bulletin of Underwater Naturalist*. American Littoral Society, 1968.

Taylor, John L., and Saloman, Carl H., "Some Effects of Hydraulic Dredging and Coastal Development in Boca Ciega Bay, Florida." *Fish. Bull.*, vol. 67, No. 2 (1968).

Thompson, Seton, "What Is Happening to Our Estuaries?" *Transactions, Twenty-Sixth North American Wildlife and Natural Resources Conference*, 1960.

"Why Wetlands?" *Open Space Action Magazine*, vol. 1, No. 5 (1969).

Woodburn, Kenneth D., *A Discussion and Selected, Annotated References of Subjective or Controversial Marine Matters*. Florida State Board of Conservation Technical Series, 46 (1965).

———, *A Guide to the Conservation of Shorelines, Submerged Bottoms and Saltwaters with Special Reference to Bulkhead Lines, Dredging and Filling*. Educational Bulletin No. 14, Marine Laboratory, Salt Water Fisheries Division, Florida Board of Conservation, St. Petersburg, Florida. FSCMBL No. 63-1.

Zobell, Claude, "The Occurrence, Effects and Fate of Oil Polluting the Sea." *Proceedings, International Congress on Water Pollution Research*. London: Pergamon Press, 1962.

INDEX